STUDIES IN THE PURE THEORY OF INTERNATIONAL TRADE

STUDIES IN THE PURE THEORY OF INTERNATIONAL TRADE

Raveendra N. Batra

St. Martin's Press   New York

AFFILIATED PUBLISHERS: Macmillan Limited, London–
also at Bombay, Calcutta, Madras and Melbourne

TO SHRI ANANDAMURTI JI

Contents

Preface

Writing a textbook, especially on as vast a subject as the theory of international trade, requires a considerable amount of intellectual investment and time. Perhaps for this reason alone, the author should be able to provide justification not only for the prospective reader and reviewer but also for himself. My interest in writing this book, which is meant to be a textbook for graduate and advanced undergraduate students interested in trade theory, stems from the revolutionary strides which the theory of international trade has achieved in the last decade. What we have inherited from the classical economists and the neo-classicists have by now become standard and indispensable tools of analysis. No book can hope to proceed without these tools. However, given the unavoidable lag that characterises the popularisation of most new theories, concepts and developments, general books in trade theory have not as yet accorded comprehensive and systematic treatment to topics such as the implications of factor market imperfections, the theory of imperfect product markets, the concept of effective protection, the repercussions of the introduction of intermediate goods, etc., topics that have by and large attracted the attention of the trade theorist in the last ten years. A large portion of this book is allocated to the development of these topics.

The level of analysis in general is quite simple. Although the analysis gives the impression of being predominantly algebraic, geometry has not been slighted. In fact a very liberal use of diagrams is made to supplement the results derived from the mathematical formulae the derivation of which requires only a knowledge of simple differentiation. Throughout the book I have used the mathematical tools developed and popularised by Jones† in his article in

---

† Jones, R. W., 'The Structure of Simple General Equilibrium Models', *Journal of Political Economy*, LXXIII (Dec 1965) 557–72.

the *Journal of Political Economy* (1965). I sincerely believe that the use of Jones's approach, suggested by activity analysis, considerably simplifies the mathematics and makes the results that much more intelligible. A case in point is the dynamic model of international trade developed in a voluminous article by Oniki and Uzawa.† Their results are discussed in the last chapter of this book. Anyone already familiar with their work and its recent related developments can readily appreciate how simple the model becomes when we utilise the Jones-type approach rather than the one used by Oniki and Uzawa.

This book is not comprehensive, in the sense that the historical as well as the empirical aspects of trade theory have been by and large ignored, mainly because, I think, these subjects belong to another genus of international economics and for that reason constitute the subject-matter of another book.

In dealing with each topic I have deliberately tried to be precise and to the point. Few words are wasted on huge introductions or the history of a subject, except where I thought it was absolutely necessary to do so. The stress all along has been to provide the reader with a fresh look at most of the standard topics and to examine in detail some of the more recent developments.

Most of this book was written while I was at the University of Western Ontario from 1970 to 1972. I wish to express my special gratitude to my friend and former student, Francisco R. Casas, for very helpful discussions, suggestions and extensive reading of the earlier drafts of this book. Some of the material appearing here is a by-product of our joint articles. Thanks are also due to J. R. Melvin, V. S. Rao, J. C. Leith, P. C. Ip and C. Y. Kuo, who during my stay at Western Ontario contributed much to the clarity of my own thinking. I should also like to express my gratitude to Bun Song Lee for careful reading of the penultimate draft. Chapter 6 of this book is a condensed version of my dissertation submitted to Southern Illinois University in 1969. There I received very helpful guidance and criticisms from my adviser, Albert Y. Badre, and from Charles Stalon and Thomas Martinsek.

Finally, I should like to acknowledge my great debt to Jagdish Bhagwati, who as my teacher at the Delhi School of Economics in

---

† Oniki, H., and Uzawa, H., 'Patterns of Trade and Development in a Dynamic Model of International Trade', *Review of Economic Studies*, XXXII (Jan 1965) 15–38.

1965 greatly stimulated my interest in the pure theory of international trade. Last but not least I wish to express my gratitude to my wife Diane, who for several months had to live through the tedium of drawing my diagrams.

July 1972 RAVEENDRA N. BATRA

1 Introduction

Although the pure theory of international trade has much in common
with the micro-economic theory, for obvious reasons trade theory
should be and has been treated as a separate discipline. Nevertheless,
a clear comprehension of the micro-economic concepts is essential
for the exploration of various issues that arise in the field of international trade. Accordingly, the present chapter is devoted to a brief
examination of mathematical concepts, definitions and geometric
tools which have been utilised quite extensively in the literature and
which as an aid to exposition will be used on numerous occasions in
subsequent chapters.

1.1 The Production Function

At the heart of all studies in the theory of international trade lies the
concept of the production function which attempts to describe a
certain technical process, as of a given technology, through which
productive inputs like capital and labour are transformed into
output. A number of restrictions are usually imposed on the function
that provides this information.

To begin with, we assume that the production process can be
represented by a sufficiently smooth function

$$X = F(K,L) \tag{1.1}$$

which shows that the output flow X is obtained from given amounts
of homogeneous factors K (capital) and L (labour). This production
function is assumed to possess the following properties:

(i) Both factors are indispensable in the sense that

$$F(0,L) = F(K,0) = 0.$$

(ii) $F(K,L)$ is homogeneous of degree one, so that

$$\lambda X = F(\lambda K, \lambda L) \quad (\lambda > 0)$$

that is, if both inputs are changed in some proportion λ, the output also changes in the same proportion.

(iii) The first partial derivatives of $F(K,L)$, denoted by F_K and F_L, are positive, but the second derivatives, F_{KK} and F_{LL}, are negative. This implies that all marginal productivities are positive but diminishing:

$$F_K = \frac{\partial F(K,L)}{\partial K} > 0, \qquad F_L = \frac{\partial F(K,L)}{\partial L} > 0,$$

$$F_{KK} = \frac{\partial^2 F(K,L)}{\partial K^2} < 0, \quad \text{and} \quad F_{LL} = \frac{\partial^2 F(K,L)}{\partial L^2} < 0.$$

A production function which satisfies these properties is usually called a *neo-classical production function*.

The second property of the production function enables us to write it in an intensive form. Suppose $\lambda = 1/L$; then (1.1) can be written as

$$X = LF\left(\frac{K}{L}, 1\right) = Lf(k) \tag{1.2}$$

where k equals the capital/labour ratio. When the production function is presented in this form, it can be shown that all marginal products depend on the capital/labour ratio only; that is,

$$F_K = \frac{\partial X}{\partial K} = \frac{\partial(Lf)}{\partial K} = Lf_k \frac{\partial k}{\partial K} = f_k$$

$$F_L = \frac{\partial X}{\partial L} = \frac{\partial(Lf)}{\partial L} = f + Lf_k \frac{\partial k}{\partial L}$$

$$= f - kf_k \quad \left(f \equiv f(k) \quad \text{and} \quad f_k \equiv \frac{\partial f(k)}{\partial k} \right). \tag{1.3}$$

Evidently, both F_K and F_L depend solely on k. Furthermore,

$$F_{KK} = \frac{\partial f_k}{\partial K} = f_{kk} \frac{\partial k}{\partial K} = \frac{f_{kk}}{L}$$

and

$$F_{LL} = \frac{\partial(f - kf_k)}{\partial L} = f_k \frac{\partial k}{\partial L} - kf_{kk} \frac{\partial k}{\partial L} - f_k \frac{\partial k}{\partial L} = \frac{k^2}{L} f_{kk}.$$

The negative signs of F_{KK} and F_{LL} imply that $f_{kk} \equiv \partial f_k/\partial k < 0$, which, in turn, implies that the marginal product of capital declines (rises) as a result of a rise (decline) in the capital/labour ratio. Simultaneously, the rise (decline) in k leads to a rise (decline) in the marginal product of labour. This can be appreciated by differentiating F_L with respect to k to get

$$\frac{dF_L}{dk} = -kf_{kk} > 0.$$

The magnitude of the change in the two marginal products is determined by the elasticity of substitution between capital and labour, which is defined as

$$\sigma = \frac{dk}{d\omega} \cdot \frac{\omega}{k} \tag{1.4}$$

where σ is the elasticity of factor substitution and ω the ratio between the marginal productivities of labour and capital:

$$\omega = \frac{F_L}{F_K} = \frac{f - kf_k}{f_k}$$

so that

$$\frac{d\omega}{dk} = -\frac{ff_{kk}}{f_k^2}$$

and hence

$$\sigma = \frac{-f_k(f - kf_k)}{kff_{kk}}$$

which, in view of $f_{kk} < 0$, is positive. If we assume that the entrepreneur seeks to minimise the unit cost of production in order to maximise his profits, then for a given set of factor prices, w, the wage rate, and r, the rental rate of capital, prevailing in perfect factor markets,†

---

† Let $T = rK + wL$ be the total cost of production, and $\bar{X} = F(K, L)$ the fixed level of output. The problem is to minimise T subject to the constraint imposed by the production function. For this purpose, form a Lagrangian

$$H = (rK + wL) + \alpha_1(\bar{X} - F(K, L))$$

where α_1 is the Lagrangian multiplier. The first-order conditions for the minimisation of T for given w and r are then given by

$$\frac{\partial H}{\partial K} = r - \alpha_1 F_K = \frac{\partial H}{\partial L} = w - \alpha_1 F_L = 0.$$

Solution of these conditions yields

$$\frac{w}{r} = \frac{F_L}{F_K}.$$

Note that this condition, associated with the minimisation of the unit cost, must be valid so long as there is perfect competition in factor markets, irrespective of conditions in the product markets.

$$\omega = \frac{F_L}{F_K} = \frac{w}{r}. \tag{1.5}$$

Thus, so long as there is perfect competition in factor markets, the ratio of the two marginal products equals the wage/rental ratio.

From (1.3) follows another well-known result: namely, the total product is fully exhausted by the contribution by the two factors:

$$LF_L + KF_K = L(f - kf_k) + Kf_k = X.$$

There is yet another way in which the production function can be expressed. With the marginal products of both factors determined exclusively by the factor proportions, the entire information concerning the production surface in the two-dimensional capital and labour space can be summed up in the unit isoquant, representing one unit of the output. Suppose $\lambda = 1/X$. Then (1.1) can be written as

$$1 = F(C_K, C_L)$$

where $C_K = K/X$ and $C_L = L/X$ are the input–output coefficients. From this and (1.5) the definition of the elasticity of substitution given in (1.4) becomes

$$\sigma = \frac{K^* - L^*}{w^* - r^*} = \frac{(K^* - X^*) - (L^* - X^*)}{w^* - r^*} = \frac{C_K^* - C_L^*}{w^* - r^*}$$

where the asterisk indicates the proportionate change, e.g. $K^* = dK/K$.

If, in addition to facing a competitive factor market, the entrepreneur produces his output under conditions of perfect competition, then the commodity price faced by him is fixed. Facing a given price and the neo-classical production function such as (1.1), the producer is assumed to select that combination of factor inputs which maximises his profits (Π):

$$\Pi = pF(K, L) - wL - rK. \tag{1.6}$$

This maximisation is accomplished by setting the derivatives of (1.6) to zero; that is,

$$\frac{\partial \Pi}{\partial L} = pF_L - w = \frac{\partial \Pi}{\partial K} = pF_K - r = 0.$$

Evidently, the competitive producer employs the two factors up to the point where the value of their marginal products equals their given prices:

$$w = pF_L$$

and

$$r = pF_K.$$ (1.7)

Further comprehension of the rudimentary production analysis presented above may be gained from Fig. 1.1, where X_1 is the unit isoquant, which is a locus of the various combinations of K and L

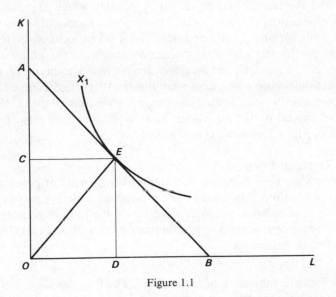

Figure 1.1

necessary to produce one unit of X. Different points on X_1 represent different levels of the capital/labour ratio and hence different marginal productivities for the two factors of production. For example, at point E the capital/labour ratio equals the slope of the ray OE, the marginal product of capital associated with this capital/labour ratio equals $1/OA$, and the marginal product of labour equals $1/OB$, where points A and B are obtained by drawing AB tangential to the unit isoquant at E. The demonstration of these results proceeds as follows. From the product exhaustion theorem stated earlier, $OD.F_L + DE.F_K = X_1 = 1$. Moreover, the slope of X_1 at E is given by

$$\frac{OA}{OB} = \frac{DE}{DB} = \frac{\Delta K}{\Delta L} = \frac{\Delta K/\Delta X}{\Delta L/\Delta X} = \frac{F_L}{F_K}.$$

Substituting, we get

$$F_L(OD+DB) = 1, \quad \text{or} \quad F_L = \frac{1}{OB}.$$

Similarly, it can be shown that $F_K = 1/OA$.

Now suppose that AB also represents the isocost line, so that the slope of AB equals the wage/rental ratio. Point E then furnishes the capital/labour ratio ($k = DE/OD$), the capital/output ratio ($C_K = DE$) and the labour/output ratio ($C_L = OD$), which are uniquely determined, provided the entrepreneur seeks to minimise his unit cost. Thus for any given w/r ratio, and a given technology represented by the neo-classical production function, the equilibrium values of k, C_K and C_L are uniquely determined. Furthermore, with production taking place under conditions of perfect competition, the commodity price from (1.7) can be expressed in terms of the cost of capital or labour alone. That is, $p = w/F_L = r/F_K$, or, in terms of Fig. 1.1, $p = w \cdot OB = r \cdot OA$.

1.2   Technical Progress

Until now we have assumed that the transformation of productive inputs into output expressed by the production function occurs at a given level of technology. What happens if the level of technology itself changes over time? The production function in the general form may then be written as

$$X = F(K,L,t) \tag{1.8}$$

where t denotes the state of technology. The function described by (1.8) is assumed to possess the same properties as those characterising (1.1) for a given state of technical know-how. In addition, $F_t > 0$. We have already seen that, with the neo-classical production function, the marginal factor productivities depend solely on the factor proportions. Since technical progress usually results in a rise in the marginal productivity of one or both factors, the latter is also affected by t. In other words,

$$\omega = \frac{F_L}{F_K} = \omega(k,t). \tag{1.9}$$

Total differentiation of (1.9) yields

$$\omega^* = F_L^* - F_K^* = \frac{1}{\sigma}k^* + \alpha \tag{1.10}$$

where $\alpha = (1/\omega)(\partial\omega/\partial t)\,dt$ exhibits the incidence of technical progress on the two marginal productivities; the partial derivative notation used in obtaining α shows that k is kept constant.

Equation (1.10) enables us to explain what is widely familiar as the Hicks [1] measure of technical progress. According to Hicks, technical progress is neutral if, at the pre-technical change capital/labour ratio, the marginal productivity of both factors rises in the same proportion; technical progress is labour-using (or capital-saving) if the proportionate rise in the marginal productivity of labour exceeds the corresponding rise in the marginal productivity of capital; it is capital-using (or labour-saving) if the greater proportionate rise in the marginal productivity occurs for capital rather than labour. Since the capital/labour ratio has been kept constant in obtaining α, the sign of α determines the nature of the Hicksian technical improvement. Specifically, for the neutral technical change, $\alpha = 0$; for the labour-using type of technical improvement, $\alpha > 0$; and under the capital-using type, $\alpha < 0$. Although technical progress normally leads to a rise in the marginal productivity of both factors, it is at least conceivable that the factor-using type of technical improvement could be compatible with the absolute decline in the marginal productivity of one factor.

In the literature on economic theory, the Hicks technical progress has been defined in still another way. Although Hicks originally emphasised the productivity-raising role of technical innovations, his definitions imply other ways of stating the nature of improvements where this role is not so explicit. Under the assumed condition of cost minimisation, the equilibrium capital/labour ratio has already been shown to be determined solely by the wage/rental ratio which in turn equals the ratio between the marginal productivity of labour and capital. It follows, therefore, that there exists a dual relationship between the marginal factor productivities and the capital/labour ratio; the latter affects the former because of our assumption of constant returns to scale but diminishing returns to factor proportions, whereas the former influences the latter because of our assumption of profit maximisation, or alternatively cost minimisation, on the part of the producer. When technical progress is introduced, the capital/labour ratio is also affected by the nature of the improvement. Thus the dual of (1.9) is written as

$$k = k(\omega, t) \tag{1.11}$$

so that

$$k^* = \sigma\omega^* + \beta \tag{1.12}$$

where $\beta = (1/k)(\partial k/\partial t) \, dt$ represents the effect of technical change on the capital/labour ratio; the partial derivation notation used in writing β implies that the factor–price ratio is kept constant; and it is the sign of β which crucially determines the nature of technical inventions. With the wage/rental ratio kept constant, it is not difficult to see that $\beta = 0$ implies Hicks-neutral improvement, whereas $\beta \gtrless 0$ represent capital-using and labour-using improvements, respectively.

The Hicks definitions of technical inventions can also be illustrated in terms of simple diagrams. Consider Fig. 1.2, where, as before, X_1 is the unit isoquant and AB represents the unit cost associated with the production of one unit of X. Since normally the effect of technical progress is to raise the marginal productivity of one or both factors, the unit isoquant X_1 shifts towards the origin to X_1', thereby showing that smaller quantities of capital and/or labour are now required to produce one unit of X. In order to determine the nature of the improvement, the change in the marginal productivity of the two factors must be evalutated at the original capital/labour ratio given by the slope of OE or OE', where E' lies on the ray OE. Draw GH tangential to X_1' at E'. If GH is parallel to AB, then technical progress must be Hicks-neutral. For the proportionate rise in the marginal productivity of capital equals

$$\frac{\Delta F_K}{F_K} = \frac{(1/OG)-(1/OA)}{(1/OA)} = \frac{AG}{OG}$$

whereas the proportionate rise in the marginal productivity of labour is given by HB/OH, so that with the Hicks-neutral improvement requiring $(AG/OG) = (HB/OH)$, GH must be parallel to AB to ensure this equality. Notice further that GH parallel to AB implies that the wage/rental ratio has remained constant at the old capital/labour ratio. If technical progress is labour-using, then GH will be steeper than AB to show that the proportionate rise in the marginal productivity of labour exceeds the corresponding rise in the marginal productivity of capital at the original capital/labour ratio. This case is depicted in Fig. 1.3, where $HB/OH > AG/OG$. The alternative way of defining the labour-using (or capital-saving) improvement is also clear; at the same wage/rental ratio given by the slope of MN (parallel to AB), we find that the capital/labour ratio has declined to that represented by the slope of OQ.

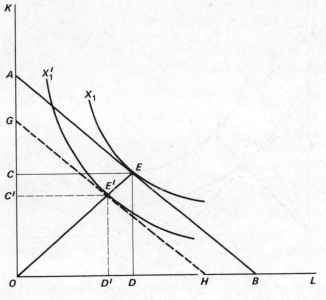

Figure 1.2

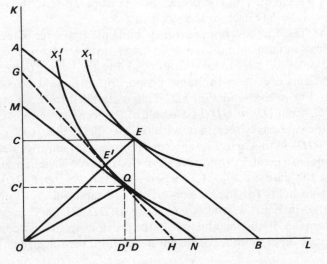

Figure 1.3

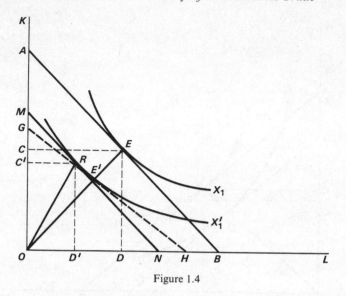

Figure 1.4

The case of capital-using (or labour-saving) technical progress is depicted in Fig. 1.4. Here $HB/OH < AG/OG$, so that at the same capital/labour ratio the marginal productivity of capital has risen in a greater proportion than that of labour, or equivalently, at the same wage/rental ratio reflected by the slope of MN, the capital/labour ratio has risen to the slope of OR.

The stage has now been set for defining the character of technical progress in terms of input–output coefficients. Under neutral technical progress, the capital/output (C_K) and the labour/output (C_L) coefficients decline in the same proportion at the old wage/rental ratio. For instance, in Fig. 1.2, C_K has declined from OC to OC' and C_L from OD to OD' as a result of the technical improvement, and it can be easily seen that, with GH parallel to AB, $(CC'/OC) = (DD'/OD)$. With capital-saving (or labour-using) improvement, C_K declines in a greater proportion than C_L at the old wage/rental ratio, as is the case in Fig. 1.3, where $(CC'/OC) > (DD'/OD)$. The opposite holds for the labour-saving (or capital-using) improvement, as in Fig. 1.4, where $(CC'/OC) < (DD'/OD)$.†

From this discussion and that in the previous section we conclude that each input–output coefficient depends on the wage/rental ratio

---

† With non-neutral improvements, it is, of course, possible that one of the input–output coefficients may rise at the original wage/rental ratio. Figs. 1.3 and 1.4 can be modified to portray this case.

as well as on the character of technical improvements; that is,

$$C_i = C_i(\omega, t). \tag{1.13}$$

This relationship will be extensively used in the anlysis of succeeding chapters.

1.3 The Transformation Curve

One geometric tool of analysis, the use of which in trade theory has probably surpassed the use of every other diagrammatic device, is well known by the name of the production possibility curve or simply the transformation curve. In an economy where all factors of production are always fully employed in the production of two commodities, commodity 1 and commodity 2, the transformation curve simply represents the various combinations of the two outputs or, more specifically, the maximum possible output of one commodity, given the output of the other. In other words, the transformation curve is a locus of efficient production points, production efficiency being defined in the sense of what is well known as the Pareto optimality criterion, namely, that a combination of two outputs is efficient if every other feasible reallocation of inputs diminishes the output of at least one commodity.

The efficiency criterion is readily established geometrically in terms of the Edgeworth–Bowley box diagram for the case where the two commodities, with outputs designated as X_1 and X_2, are produced with the aid of two factors of production, capital (K) and labour (L). The dimensions of the box in Fig. 1.5 represent the total, inelastically supplied quantities of capital and labour, so that any point in the box reflects a certain allocation of inputs between the two commodities, whose outputs are measured by reference to the two origins O_1 and O_2. If we assume that production functions in both commodities are neo-classical, then the level of two outputs can be measured by the distances of their isoquants from the respective origins. Here the diagonal $O_1 O_2$, whose slope with respect to the $O_1 O$ axis equals the overall capital/labour ratio in the economy, plays a useful role. Since each point on an isoquant represents the same level of output, the output of each commodity can be measured by the distance between the respective origin and the point of intersection between its isoquant and the diagonal. For example, the output of the first commodity, X_1, represented by isoquants x_1 and x_1', is given respectively by $O_1 a_1$ and $O_1 a_2$. Similarly, the output of the second commodity, X_2, with isoquants

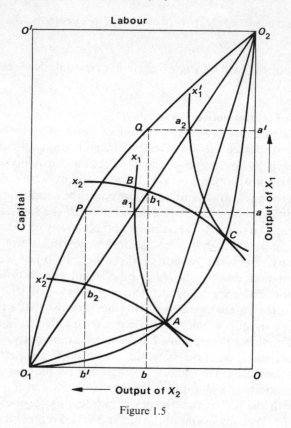

Figure 1.5

x_2 and x_2', equals O_2b_1 and O_2b_2. Clearly, then, a movement away from O_1 towards O_2 is equivalent to a rise in the output of the first commodity and a decline in the output of the second commodity. Conversely, a movement away from O_2 towards O_1 signifies an increase in the output of the second commodity at the expense of the output of the first commodity.

Now according to the Pareto optimality criterion, maximum efficiency in the allocation of resources is attained at points such as A and C, where the isoquants of the two commodities are tangential to each other. The locus of all such points, the curve O_1ACO_2, is called the *contract curve*, or simply the *efficiency locus*. All points on the contract curve represent the maximum attainable output of one commodity, given the output of the other. For example, suppose that the output of X_2 equals O_2b_1. Then the maximum possible

output of X_1, equal to O_1a_2, is obtained at C. At any other point the output of X_1 will be less than that at C. At point B, for instance, X_2 still equals O_2b_1, but X_1, equal to O_1a_1, is less than O_1a_2.†
Hence B is inferior to C.

The location of the contract curve in the box reflects a certain assumption concerning the capital/labour ratio in two commodities. The contract curve in the diagram lies below the diagonal because of our implicit assumption that under all circumstances X_1 is labour-intensive relative to X_2. For example, at point A the capital/labour ratio in X_1, equal to the slope of O_1A with respect to the O_1O axis, is less than the capital/labour ratio in X_2, which is given by the slope of O_2A with respect to the O_2O' axis. If, instead of X_2, X_1 was the capital-intensive commodity, then the contract curve would lie entirely above the diagonal.

We are now in a position to derive the transformation curve from the contract curve. It has already been established that various points on the diagonal represent different levels of output of each commodity. This measuring scale can be easily transformed to the vertical and horizontal scale represented by the origin O. For instance, the output levels of X_1, given by points a_1 and a_2 on the diagonal, can be projected towards the OO_2 axis to points a and a', respectively. Since the production functions are homogeneous of the first degree, the distance O_1a_2 exceeds O_1a_1 in exactly the same proportion as Oa' exceeds Oa. Analogously, the output levels of X_2, given by points b_1 and b_2, can be projected to obtain the respective points b and b' on the horizontal axis OO_1. In this fashion, following the technique developed by Savosnick [2], the OO_2 and OO_1 axes can be used as output scales.

The next step is to derive points in the commodity space, representing the levels of each output along the contract curve. The output of X_1 and X_2 corresponding to point A, for instance, is given respectively by Oa and Ob'. The output combination given by points a and b' is then furnished by point P in the commodity space. In other words, the output combination associated with A, when transformed into output scale, is given by P. Similarly, the output combination at C is represented by Q in the output space. Thus we see that to each point on the contract curve corresponds a unique point in the

---

† Here and elsewhere, X_j is identified with the jth commodity as well as its output. Furthermore, the words 'commodity', 'industry' and 'sector' will be used synonymously.

commodity space. The locus of points such as P and Q is called the transformation curve, which in Fig. 1.5 is given by O_1PQO_2. The transformation curve is thus a mirror-image of the contract curve. One may observe that the curve O_1PQO_2 is wholly concave towards the origin, O.

What is the slope of the transformation curve in equilibrium? To answer this question, we need information about the type of markets in which production takes place. The transformation curve is the locus of efficient points and its curvature depends on market conditions in which the firms operate. The answer turns out to be very simple and elegant, if we assume that all markets are perfect. In the presence of market imperfections, of course, it is possible that the transformation curve, as a locus of efficiency points, may cease to exist, simply because production efficiency cannot be attained under such imperfections. For the time being, however, we gloss over this question, but we shall examine it in detail in the chapters concerning market imperfections.

Under the assumption of perfect competition in all markets, the reward of each factor in equilibrium equals the value of its marginal product and is the same in both commodities. Let MP_{ij} be the marginal productivity of the ith factor in the jth commodity and p_j be the commodity price ($i = K,L; j = 1,2$). Then

$$w = p_1 MP_{L1} = p_2 MP_{L2}$$

and

$$r = p_1 MP_{K1} = p_2 MP_{K2}.$$

From these relations,

$$\frac{p_1}{p_2} = \frac{MP_{L2}}{MP_{L1}} = \frac{MP_{K2}}{MP_{K1}}$$

or

$$\frac{p_1}{p_2} = \frac{\Delta X_2/\Delta L_2}{\Delta X_1/\Delta L_1} = \frac{\Delta X_2/\Delta K_2}{\Delta X_1/\Delta K_1}.$$

Given our assumption that factors are fully employed and inelastically supplied, $\Delta L_2 = -\Delta L_1$, and $\Delta K_2 = -\Delta K_1$. Substituting, we get

$$\frac{\Delta X_2}{\Delta X_1} = -\frac{p_1}{p_2}$$

Now $\Delta X_2/\Delta X_1$ furnishes the slope of the transformation curve, and is usually called the marginal rate of transformation. In other words, in competitive equilibrium the slope of the transformation curve reflects the negative of the commodity-price ratio.

This equilibrium condition is diagrammatically depicted in Fig. 1.6, where TT' is the transformation curve drawn concave to the

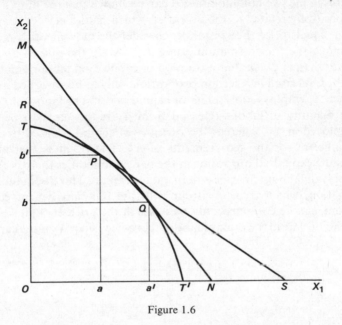

Figure 1.6

origin. Lines such as RS and MN are the budget lines which measure the level of national income in the economy at different production points. The slope of each budget line reflects the relative price of X_1, p_1/p_2. The equilibrium production point is obtained by drawing the given budget line tangential to the transformation curve. Thus, with RS, the production point is given by P, where the slope of TT' equals the relative price of X_1. The concavity of TT' towards the origin implies that a rise in the output of a commodity calls forth a rise in its relative price. This point is illustrated by the fact that the production point associated with MN, showing a higher relative price of X_1, is Q, which shows that the output of X_1 rises from Oa to Oa' and that of X_2 declines from Ob' to Ob.

What is the reasoning behind the concavity of the transformation curve, or, stated differently, what is the economic explanation behind the phenomenon of greater output requiring a greater relative price, even though returns to scale have been assumed to be constant? The reason lies in our assumption, implicit in the construction of the efficiency locus, that the capital/labour ratio in each commodity is different under all circumstances. Because of unequal capital/labour ratios in the two commodities, it can be shown that the output level is positively related to the unit cost, which, under perfect competition, equals price. For instance, consider the movement from Q to P along the transformation curve TT'. At P, the output of X_1 is lower than at Q, so that a fraction of capital and labour employed in X_1 is released in a certain proportion, only to be absorbed by X_2. Since X_2 employs more units of capital per unit of labour than X_1, the quantity of labour released from X_1 is too great to be fully employed in X_2, whereas the quantity of capital released by X_1 is insufficient for the requirements of X_2. The result is that at the existing capital/labour ratios in the two commodities there is excess supply of labour and excess demand for capital. This disequilibrium situation, which is inconsistent with the full-employment equilibrium, can be corrected only by a rise in the price of capital along with a decline in the price of labour. However, since X_2 is the capital-

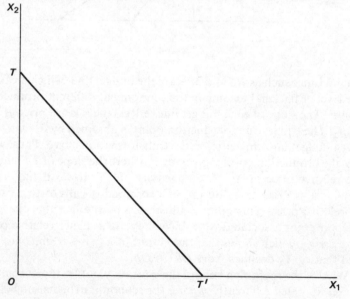

Figure 1.7

intensive commodity, the rise in the price of its intensive factor boosts up its unit cost, whereas for X_1 the decline in the price of labour, its intensive factor, lowers the unit cost. Finally, the full-employment equilibrium is restored through unidirectional changes in the two capital/labour ratios consequent upon the change in factor prices. However, the commodity whose output has risen is the one where the unit cost and hence the price has increased, and conversely.

From this discussion, it follows that if there exists only one factor of production, or if the capital/labour ratio in each commodity is the same, the transformation curve will be a straight line, as shown in Fig. 1.7. The slope of TT' would still reflect the relative price of X_1, but the point of production could lie anywhere on TT' for a given commodity-price ratio, because the unit cost in any commodity would remain constant for all levels of output.

REFERENCES

[1] Hicks, J. R., *The Theory of Wages* (London: Macmillan, 1932).
[2] Savosnick, K. M., 'The Box Diagram and the Production-Possibility Curve', *Ekonomisk Tidskrift*, LX (Sep 1958) 183–97.

2 Structure of Production in Autarky

2.1 Introduction

One of the elemental, though most important, questions in international trade concerns the determination of a country's pattern of trade. Stated differently, why are countries induced to import goods if they can produce them at home? The answer to these questions, however, requires a prior comprehension of the structure of production in a closed economy or autarky. It is this latter question with which the present chapter is concerned. Specifically, we wish to determine the factors which influence commodity prices in the absence of trade.

2.2 Assumptions and the Model

Unless otherwise specified, the following assumptions will be maintained in every chapter:

1. There are two commodities, X_1 and X_2, which in the process of production require two primary factors of production, capital (K) and labour (L).
2. Returns to scale are constant, but returns to factor proportions are diminishing.
3. Factors of production are fully employed but inelastically supplied.
4. Factors are perfectly mobile between sectors, and factor prices perfectly flexible. The latter assumption, of course, ensures the maintenance of full employment at all times.
5. Each commodity utilises a different capital/labour ratio. Furthermore, the inter-commodity capital-intensity relation is non-reversible, or, stated more explicitly, a commodity is intensive in the use of the same factor at all factor prices.
6. There is perfect competition in product as well as factor markets, and factor prices are the same in both industries.

The development of the model proceeds with the specification of the full-employment equations. Let K_j be the amount of capital and L_j the amount of labour employed in the jth commodity. Then with full employment,

$$L_1 + L_2 = L$$

and

$$K_1 + K_2 = K.$$

These equations can be transformed in a manner which, by means of the concept of input–output coefficients, will determine the output level of each commodity. Let C_{ij} be the quantity of the ith factor used in the production of one unit of the jth commodity. For example, $C_{L1} = L_1/X_1$, and $C_{K1} = K_1/X_1$, so that $L_1 = C_{L1}X_1$ and $K_1 = C_{K1}X_1$, and so on. The full-employment equations may then be written as

$$C_{L1}X_1 + C_{L2}X_2 = L \tag{2.1}$$

$$C_{K1}X_1 + C_{K2}X_2 = K. \tag{2.2}$$

The input–output coefficients can also be used to specify equations for the price of each commodity. Under competitive conditions, each commodity price equals the unit cost, which in turn is given by the ratio between total cost and total output. With the first commodity, for example,

$$p_1 = \frac{wL_1 + rK_1}{X_1}$$

where, as before, p_j is the price of the jth commodity, w the wage rate and r the rental of capital. Each commodity price may then be described as

$$wC_{L1} + rC_{K1} = p_1 \tag{2.3}$$

$$wC_{L2} + rC_{K2} = p_2. \tag{2.4}$$

Next, the input–output coefficients must be determined. As established in the previous chapter, each input–output coefficient depends on the wage/rental ratio as well as the character of technical improvements; that is to say,

$$C_{ij} = C_{ij}(\omega, t) \qquad (i = L, K; j = 1, 2). \qquad (2.5)$$

Equation (2.5) contains four independent relations for the four input–output coefficients. Thus there are eight independent relations, four described by (2.1)–(2.4) and four by (2.5), containing eight variables, X_1, X_2, w, r and four C_{ij}'s, in five parameters, L, K, p_1, p_2 and t. In other words, the production side of the model is determinate. To close the system, equations expressing demand for each commodity must be introduced. Let D_j stand for the demand for the jth commodity, p for the commodity-price ratio, p_2/p_1, and Y for national income. Then under autarky

$$D_1 = D_1(p, Y) = X_1 \qquad (2.6)$$

and

$$D_2 = D_2(p, Y) = X_2. \qquad (2.7)$$

Equations (2.6) and (2.7) state that the demand for each commodity depends on the commodity-price ratio and national income, which in turn may be written as

$$Y = p_1 X_1 + p_2 X_2 \qquad (2.8)$$

that is, national income simply equals the total value of the two outputs or the payments made to the factors of production. With this equation, the specification of our two-commodity, two-factor autarky model is complete. We have now added five equations in four more variables, D_1, D_2, p and Y, but from Walras's Law only one of the two equations, $D_j = X_j$, is independent, so that the system continues to be determinate. One may have noticed the differential treatment accorded to p on the demand and the production sides of the model. On the demand side, p is treated as a variable. However, on the production side p is treated as a parameter, because the competitive firm takes the commodity price as given.

The significance of the assumption of differing capital/labour ratios in the two commodities for the unique determination of outputs may now be shown. For a given $t = \bar{t}$, the economy's state of technology is completely defined by the input–output coefficients, which can be collectively expressed by a technology matrix $[C]$, that is,

$$C = \begin{bmatrix} C_{L1} & C_{L2} \\ C_{K1} & C_{K2} \end{bmatrix}.$$

The columns of the C matrix describe the state of technology behind the production function in each commodity, because it is the matrix of the production coefficients associated with X_1 and X_2 in equations (2.1) and (2.2). The determinant of $[C]$ is given by

$$|C| = C_{L1}C_{K2} - C_{K1}C_{L2} = C_{L1}C_{L2}(k_2 - k_1) \qquad (2.9)$$

where k_j is the capital/labour ratio in the jth commodity. Equations (2.1) and (2.2) may be solved with the aid of Cramer's Rule to yield

$$X_1 = \frac{L(k_2 - k)}{C_{L1}(k_2 - k_1)} \qquad (2.10)$$

and

$$X_2 = \frac{L(k - k_1)}{C_{L2}(k_2 - k_1)} \qquad (2.11)$$

where $k = K/L$.

As far as the price equations (2.3) and (2.4) are concerned, the matrix of the input–output coefficients associated with w and r is defined by the rows of the C matrix, or simply by its transpose. However, the sign of the matrix is still given by the sign of $|C|$. The solution of (2.3) and (2.4) gives us

$$\omega = \frac{w}{r} = \frac{k_1[(C_{K2}/C_{K1}) - p]}{[p - (C_{L2}/C_{L1})]}. \qquad (2.12)$$

One glance at (2.10) and (2.11) suggests that if the capital/labour ratio is the same in both commodities, that is, if $k_2 = k_1$, the two outputs are indeterminate. As stated in the previous chapter, the transformation curve in this case becomes a negatively inclined straight line, and any point on the line could be a production point at a given commodity-price ratio. Another important point is that the production of both commodities, or what may be properly called incomplete specialisation, requires that k lie between k_2 and k_1. This is because if the capital/labour ratio in any commodity is equal to the overall capital/labour ratio, the output of the other commodity reduces to zero. For example, in (2.10) if k_2, the capital/labour ratio in the second commodity, equals k, the overall capital/labour ratio, the output of X_1, the first commodity, is zero. Similarly, if $k_1 = k$ in (2.11), the output of X_2 equals zero.

The factors affecting the wage/rental ratio are described in (2.12), which shows that ω is determined by the production coefficients and the commodity-price ratio, p. However, since the production co-efficients themselves are determined by ω, the latter is influenced only by p. Thus there exists a one-to-one relation between p and ω. Here again the condition of incomplete specialisation is relevant. For in the presence of complete specialisation ω is no longer related to p simply because p is then undefined. Consider, for instance, the case where $k_1 = k$, so that only X_1 is produced in the economy. Since X_2 reduces to zero, p is undefined. The wage/rental ratio is then determined simply by the overall capital/labour ratio via the elasticity of substitution in the first industry, σ_1. In other words, ω is no longer related to p in the absence of incomplete specialisation.

2.3 Equations of Change

In order to understand the internal working of the model, it is neces-sary to convert the system of equations presented above into equations of change. In other words, we wish to examine the comparative-statics properties of the model by considering the effects of a change in the parameters on the variables of the system. For this will enable us to see whether or not, and under what conditions, all the variables are uniquely determined.

Let an asterisk indicate the rate of change. Thus $L^* = dL/L$. Differentiating equations (2.1)–(2.4) totally, we obtain

$$\lambda_{L1}X_1^* + \lambda_{L2}X_2^* = L^* - [\lambda_{L1}C_{L1}^* + \lambda_{L2}C_{L2}^*] \qquad (2.13)$$

$$\lambda_{K1}X_1^* + \lambda_{K2}X_2^* = K^* - [\lambda_{K1}C_{K1}^* + \lambda_{K2}C_{K2}^*] \qquad (2.14)$$

$$\theta_{L1}w^* + \theta_{K1}r^* = p_1^* - [\theta_{L1}C_{L1}^* + \theta_{K1}C_{K1}^*] \qquad (2.15)$$

$$\theta_{L2}w^* + \theta_{K2}r^* = p_2^* - [\theta_{L2}C_{L2}^* + \theta_{K2}C_{K2}^*] \qquad (2.16)$$

where λ_{ij} is the proportion of the ith factor employed in the jth commodity and θ_{ij} is the share of the ith factor in the total earnings in the jth commodity ($i = L, K; j = 1, 2$). For example, $\lambda_{L1} = (C_{L1}X_1/L) = L_1/L$ equals the proportion of labour employed in the first commodity, whereas $\theta_{L1} = (wC_{L1}/p_1) = wL_1/p_1X_1$ equals the relative share of labour in the total value of output of the first commodity. By very definition, $\lambda_{i1}+\lambda_{i2} = 1$ and $\theta_{Lj}+\theta_{Kj} = 1$. Let $[\lambda]$ and $[\theta]$ respectively denote the matrices of λ coefficients and θ coefficients in equations (2.13)–(2.16); that is,

$$[\lambda] = \begin{bmatrix} \lambda_{L1} & \lambda_{L2} \\ \lambda_{K1} & \lambda_{K2} \end{bmatrix}, \qquad [\theta] = \begin{bmatrix} \theta_{L1} & \theta_{K1} \\ \theta_{L2} & \theta_{K2} \end{bmatrix}.$$

The signs of the determinants $|\lambda|$ and $|\theta|$ are the same as the sign of the determinant $|C|$, because

$$|\lambda| = \lambda_{L1}\lambda_{K2} - \lambda_{K1}\lambda_{L2} = \frac{L_1 L_2}{LK}(k_2 - k_1)$$

$$|\theta| = \theta_{L1}\theta_{K2} - \theta_{L2}\theta_{K1} = \frac{wrL_1 L_2}{p_1 X_1 p_2 X_2}(k_2 - k_1). \qquad (2.17)$$

Furthermore, since each row in $|\lambda|$ and $|\theta|$ adds to unity, the determinants $|\lambda|$ and $|\theta|$ are also given by

$$|\lambda| = \lambda_{L1} - \lambda_{K1} = \lambda_{K2} - \lambda_{L2}$$
$$|\theta| = \theta_{L1} - \theta_{L2} = \theta_{K2} - \theta_{K1} \qquad (2.17^*)$$

Clearly, the next step in the solution of the system is to obtain expressions for C_{ij}^*. Equation (2.5) can be totally differentiated to obtain

$$C_{ij}^* = A_{ij}^* - B_{ij}^* \qquad (2.18)$$

where $A_{ij}^* = (1/C_{ij})(\partial C_{ij}/\partial\omega)\,d\omega$ is the change in the input–output coefficient that occurs as a result of a change in the wage/rental ratio (the partial derivative notation in writing A_{ij}^* signifies that technology remains unchanged) and $B_{ij}^* = (-1/C_{ij})(\partial C_{ij}/\partial t)\,dt$ is a measure of technical progress that results in a change in C_{ij}; the partial derivative notation in B_{ij}^* shows that the wage/rental ratio is kept constant. Since technical improvements ordinarily involve a reduction in input–output coefficients, B_{ij}^* is defined to be non-negative. Simple expressions for A_{ij}^* can be derived by introducing the definition of the elasticity of factor substitution and taking into account the implications of the unit cost minimisation. Let σ_j be the elasticity of factor substitution in the jth sector. As defined in the previous chapter,

$$\sigma_1 = \frac{\omega}{k_1}\frac{\partial k_1}{\partial\omega} = \frac{A_{K1}^* - A_{L1}^*}{w^* - r^*} \qquad (2.19)$$

$$\sigma_2 = \frac{\omega}{k_2}\frac{\partial k_2}{\partial \omega} = \frac{A_{K2}^* - A_{L2}^*}{w^* - r^*}. \qquad (2.20)$$

The unit cost in the first commodity equals $wC_{L1}+rC_{K1}$. For given factor prices in competitive factor markets, the unit cost in the first commodity is minimised by setting the first derivative $(wC_{L1}A_{L1}^* + rC_{K1}A_{K1}^*)$ equal to zero.† Dividing through by p_1, we get

$$\theta_{L1}A_{L1}^* + \theta_{K1}A_{K1}^* = 0. \qquad (2.21)$$

An analogous procedure can be followed for cost minimisation in the second commodity to derive

$$\theta_{L2}A_{L2}^* + \theta_{K2}A_{K2}^* = 0. \qquad (2.22)$$

Equations (2.21) and (2.22) can be solved in combination with (2.19) and (2.20) to furnish the effect of a change in the wage/rental ratio on the input–output coefficients. For example, from (2.19) and (2.21), and (2.20) and (2.22), we get

$$A_{Lj}^* = -\theta_{Kj}\sigma_j(w^*-r^*) \quad (j = 1,2)$$
$$A_{Kj}^* = \theta_{Lj}\sigma_j(w^*-r^*) \quad (j = 1,2).$$

These relations for the A_{ij}^*'s can then be substituted first into (2.18), and then the resultant solutions for C_{ij}^* can be fed into equations (2.13)–(2.16) to obtain

$$\lambda_{L1}X_1^* + \lambda_{L2}X_2^* = L^* + \Pi_L + \beta_L(w^*-r^*) \qquad (2.23)$$

$$\lambda_{K1}X_1^* + \lambda_{K2}X_2^* = K^* + \Pi_K - \beta_K(w^*-r^*) \qquad (2.24)$$

$$\theta_{L1}w^* + \theta_{K1}r^* = p_1^* + \Pi_1 \qquad (2.25)$$

$$\theta_{L2}w^* + \theta_{K2}r^* = p_2^* + \Pi_2 \qquad (2.26)$$

where

$$\beta_L = \lambda_{L1}\theta_{K1}\sigma_1 + \lambda_{L2}\theta_{K2}\sigma_2$$
$$\beta_K = \lambda_{K1}\theta_{L1}\sigma_1 + \lambda_{K2}\theta_{L2}\sigma_2$$
$$\Pi_i = \lambda_{i1}B_{i1}^* + \lambda_{i2}B_{i2}^* \qquad (i = L, K)$$

---

† Since at present we are trying to assess the effect of a change in ω on the input–output coefficients as of a given technology, the notation used for dC_{ij}/C_{ij} is A_{ij}^* instead of C_{ij}^*, which actually denotes the rate of total change in C_{ij}.

and

$$\Pi_j = \theta_{Lj}B^*_{Lj} + \theta_{Kj}B^*_{Kj} \qquad (j = 1,2).$$

Before we proceed further with the analysis, a few explanatory remarks concerning β_i, Π_i and Π_j are in order. If production co-efficients are fixed, $\sigma_j = 0$, in which case β_i also equals zero. In the general case of variable coefficients, however, β_i reflects the percentage change in the use of the ith factor per unit of output that occurs in both commodities as a result of a change in the wage/rental ratio alone. By contrast, Π_i represents the percentage reduction in the ith factor that occurs owing to the occurrence of technical progress in both commodities when the wage/rental ratio is kept constant; for example,

$$\Pi_L = \lambda_{L1}B^*_{L1} + \lambda_{L2}B^*_{L2}.$$

Consequent upon technical improvements, the percentage reduction in the use of labour per unit of output in the first commodity equals B^*_{L1}, but $\lambda_{L1}B^*_{L1}$ gives the total saving in the use of labour, made possible by the improvement, to produce the original output of X_1. Similarly, $\lambda_{L2}B^*_{L2}$ represents the saving in the use of labour required to produce the pre-technical change level of X_2. When such savings in the use of labour in each commodity are added up, we get Π_L, which represents the overall labour-saving character of technical progress. Similar explication also applies to Π_K.

On the other hand, Π_j is a measure of the rate of technical advance in the jth commodity; for instance,

$$\Pi_1 = \theta_{L1}B^*_{L1} + \theta_{K1}B^*_{K1}.$$

The incidence of technical improvement is to lower the unit cost of production; $\theta_{L1}B^*_{L1}$ then reflects the reduction in the labour cost, whereas $\theta_{K1}B^*_{K1}$ exhibits the reduction in the capital cost in the production of one unit of X_1. The total reduction in the unit cost of production is therefore given by Π_1. Similar remarks apply to Π_2. It is worth pointing out that Π_i and Π_j are defined to be non-negative.

Turn now to equations (2.6) and (2.7). Differentiating them totally, we get

$$D^*_1 = \quad \alpha_1(p^*_2 - p^*_1) + \eta_1 Y^* \tag{2.27}$$

$$D^*_2 = -\alpha_2(p^*_2 - p^*_1) + \eta_2 Y^* \tag{2.28}$$

where $\alpha_1 = (p/D_1)(\partial D_1/\partial p)$ and $\alpha_2 = -(p/D_2)(\partial D_2/\partial p)$ are the price elasticities of demand, and $\eta_1 = (Y/D_1)(\partial D_1/\partial Y)$ and $\eta_2 = (Y/D_2)(\partial D_2/\partial Y)$ are the income elasticities of demand for the first and the second commodity, respectively. In the absence of inferior goods, $\eta_j > 0$.

For expository purposes, another relation may now be introduced on the demand side, namely, the elasticity of demand substitution, σ_D, which is defined as

$$\sigma_D = \frac{p}{(D_1/D_2)} \cdot \frac{\partial(D_1/D_2)}{\partial p} = p\left[\frac{1}{D_1}\frac{\partial D_1}{\partial p} - \frac{1}{D_2}\cdot\frac{\partial D_2}{\partial p}\right]$$
$$= \alpha_1 + \alpha_2 > 0.$$

Subtracting equation (2.27) from (2.28) gives us

$$D_2^* - D_1^* = -\sigma_D(p_2^* - p_1^*) + (\eta_2 - \eta_1)Y^*. \qquad (2.29)$$

By now we have collected the full complement of ingredients needed to derive general equations showing the effects of a change in all parameters on the variables of the system, so that the implications of a change in any particular parameter can be analysed as a special case of the general solution. By subtracting equation (2.23) from (2.24), and (2.26) from (2.25), utilising equations (2.21), (2.22) and the $|\lambda|$ and $|\theta|$ determinants from (2.17*), we have

$$|\lambda|(X_2^* - X_1^*) = (K^* - L^*) + (\Pi_K - \Pi_L) - (w^* - r^*)(\beta_K + \beta_L) \qquad (2.30)$$

$$|\theta|(w^* - r^*) = [(p_1^* - p_2^*) + (\Pi_1 - \Pi_2)]. \qquad (2.31)$$

The substitution of $(w^* - r^*)$ from (2.31) in (2.30) yields

$$(X_2^* - X_1^*) = \frac{(K^* - L^*) + (\Pi_K - \Pi_L)}{|\lambda|}$$
$$+ \sigma_s[(p_2^* - p_1^*) + (\Pi_2 - \Pi_1)]. \qquad (2.32)$$

where $\sigma_s = (X_2^* - X_1^*)/(p_2^* - p_1^*) = (\beta_K + \beta_L)/(|\lambda||\theta|)$ is the elasticity of substitution between commodities on the supply side, that is, it is the elasticity of commodity substitution along the transformation curve.† The mutual interaction of demand and supply in a closed economy requires that $D_j^* = X_j^*$. The right-hand sides of equations (2.29) and (2.32) are therefore the same in equilibrium. Making use of this equality then gives us the expression for the change in the commodity-price ratio:

$$p_1^* - p_2^* = \frac{(K^* - L^*) + (\Pi_K - \Pi_L)}{|\lambda|(\sigma_D + \sigma_s)}$$
$$+ \frac{\sigma_s(\Pi_2 - \Pi_1)}{(\sigma_D + \sigma_s)} + \frac{Y^*(\eta_1 - \eta_2)}{(\sigma_D + \sigma_s)}. \qquad (2.33)$$

2.4 Commodity and Factor Prices

Equation (2.31) exhibits a relationship among the commodity-price ratio (p), the wage/rental ratio (ω) and the rate of technical advance in the two commodities. This equation may be rewritten to obtain

$$(p_1^* - p_2^*) = |\theta|(w^* - r^*) + (\Pi_2 - \Pi_1). \qquad (2.31^*)$$

Consider first the case where technical progress is absent in both industries. The relationship between p and ω is then determined solely by $|\theta|$, which, from (2.17), is positive if $k_2 > k_1$, but negative if $k_2 < k_1$. In other words, in the absence of technical progress a decline in p leads to a rise in ω if the first commodity is labour-intensive, but to a decline in ω if the first commodity is capital-intensive. Furthermore, the relationship between p and ω is mutually dependent. In other words, a change in ω results in a change in p, and conversely.

This result can be very simply derived from the unit isoquant diagram presented in the previous chapter. The only difference now is that the diagram will have to include unit isoquants in both commodities. This is accomplished in Fig. 2.1, where X_2 and X_1 are respectively the unit isoquants of the second and the first commodity; the slope of AB displays the wage/rental ratio and, corresponding to AB, the

---

† This elasticity was first introduced by Jones [2]. Along any transformation curve, factor supplies and the level of technology are given, so that $K^* = L^* = \Pi_L = \Pi_1 = \Pi_2 = 0$. Then, from equation (2.32),

$$\frac{(X_2^* - X_1^*)}{p_2^* - p_1^*} = \sigma_s.$$

In the absence of market distortions, σ_s, which also equals $[(\beta_L + \beta_K)/(|\lambda||\theta|)]$, is positive, because $\beta_L > 0$, $\beta_K > 0$ and $|\lambda|$ and $|\theta|$ always possess the same sign.

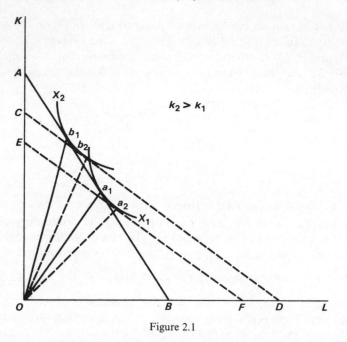

Figure 2.1

equilibrium capital/labour ratio in X_2 is given by the slope of Ob_1 and in X_1 by the slope of Oa_1. As shown in the previous chapter, the price of each commodity can be expressed exclusively in terms of the cost of labour or capital. Suppose capital is selected to be the numéraire. Then $p_1 = p_2 = r.OA$, so that $p = p_2/p_1 = 1$. It is not difficult to see that the reason for a unit value of p lies in the fact that both unit isoquants lie on the same isocost line. Now suppose there is a decline in ω, so that AB is replaced by the two parallel lines CD and EF, both of which exhibit a smaller wage/rental ratio. Two changes take place. First, the capital/labour ratio in each industry declines – in X_2 from the slope of Ob_1 to Ob_2 and in X_1 from the slope of Oa_1 to Oa_2. Second, $p_2 = r.OC$ and $p_1 = r.OE$, which means that p, now equal to OC/OE, has risen above its previous level of unity. It may be observed that the diagram depicts X_2 to be capital-intensive relative to X_1 at all wage/rental ratios, as is evident from the fact that the slope of Ob_1 and Ob_2 exceeds that of Oa_1 and Oa_2, respectively. Inherent in this construction also is the fact that factor intensities are non-reversible. This, as we shall see later, is

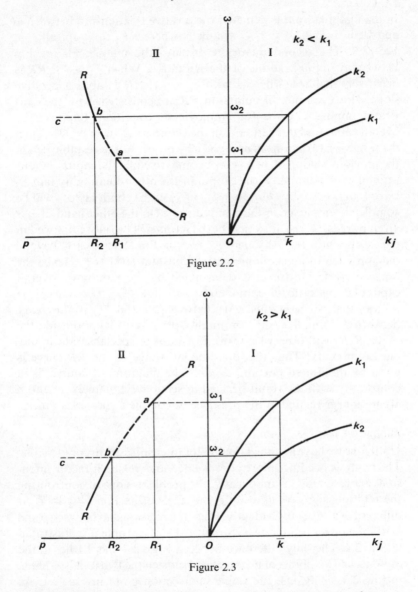

Figure 2.2

Figure 2.3

attributable to the fact that the unit isoquants intersect only once. A similar diagram can be drawn for the case where $k_2 < k_1$.

The 'one-to-one' relationship between ω and p on the one hand, and between ω and k_j on the other, is depicted in Figs. 2.2 and 2.3.

In the first quadrant is depicted the positive relationship between ω and k_j. In Fig. 2.2, $k_2 < k_1$ at any ω, whereas $k_2 > k_1$ for all ω in Fig. 2.3. The second quadrant displays the unique relationship between p and ω in terms of the RR curve. When $k_2 > k_1$, RR is negatively inclined, whereas with $k_2 < k_1$, RR exhibits a positive slope. However, not all points on RR are consistent with the constraint imposed by the full-employment condition. Suppose the overall capital/labour ratio (k) in the economy is given by $O\overline{k}$. Then the range for variations in ω is given by $\omega_1\omega_2$. For, as established in the previous section, if, at any ω, k comes to equal the capital/labour ratio in any commodity, the output of the other commodity falls to zero. If ω is given by $O\omega_1$, then $k = k_1$, so that both factors will be completely employed in the first industry. On the other hand, if ω is given by $O\omega_2$, $k = k_2$, so that both factors will be fully employed in the second industry. Any ω above $O\omega_1$ in Fig. 2.3 is clearly beyond the approach of an economy with a constant level of k. Hence the range of variation for ω is determined by the economy's overall capital/labour ratio in conjunction with the Ok_1, Ok_2 curves. It follows that, since ω must vary between ω_1 and ω_2, p must vary between R_1 and R_2. Any commodity-price ratio lying outside the range R_1R_2 will otherwise result in complete specialisation in any one commodity. Thus the 'operational' range of the RR curve is given by the dotted portion, ω_1abc. The diagram, of course, is in conformity with the result derived in section 2.2, namely, ω and p are no longer related in the presence of complete specialisation.

Factor-Intensity Reversals
Until now we have assumed that factor intensities are non-reversible. The analysis becomes more complicated and vexing if factor intensities are reversible. Symbolically, the problem is one of confronting the multiple signs of $|\theta|$ at different levels of ω. For if $k_2 \gtrless k_1$ at different ω's, $|\theta| \gtrless 0$. Evidently, then, the relationship between p and ω will no longer be unique. Geometrically, the problem is illustrated in Fig. 2.4. The only difference between Figs. 2.4 and 2.1 lies in the presence of two points of intersection between the two unit isoquants in Fig. 2.4, as against the single intersection point in Fig. 2.1. As before, we commence with the isocost line AB and a unit commodity-price ratio (p). As the wage/rental ratio declines, we find that X_2 becomes labour-intensive relative to X_1 because Ob_2 is less steep than Oa_2, although in the initial situation X_2 was capital-intensive

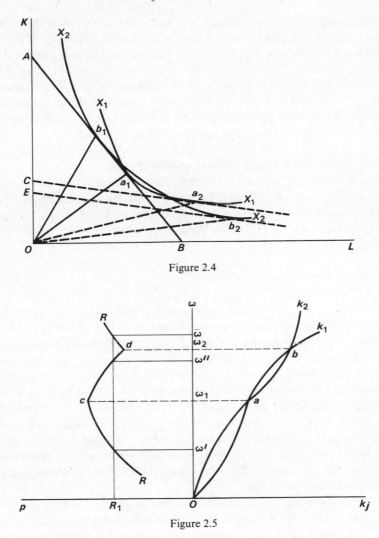

Figure 2.4

Figure 2.5

relative to X_1. In other words, factor intensities have been reversed in the new situation. Moreover, in contrast to the situation depicted in Fig. 2.1, p has now declined to the level given by $OE/OC < 1$.

The implications of the factor-intensity reversals for the commodity-price ratio are pictured in Fig. 2.5, where, as before, the first quadrant portrays the unique relationship between ω and k_j, but where, unlike the previous diagrams, factor intensities get reversed at points such as a and b. If ω lies between O and ω_1, $k_1 > k_2$; if it lies between ω_1 and ω_2, $k_1 < k_2$; and beyond ω_2, $k_1 > k_2$ again. In the presence of the factor-intensity reversals, the slope of the RR curve is also altered at points such as c and d corresponding, respectively, to a and b. It can be easily seen now that the relationship between p and ω is no longer unique. For example, to one price ratio OR_1 there correspond three values of ω (ω', ω'' and $\bar{\omega}$).

2.5   Factor Endowment and Commodity Prices

The relationship between the commodity-price ratio and the overall capital/labour ratio (k) can be ascertained from equation (2.33). Here again, we assume that the level of technology is given, so that $\Pi_K = \Pi_L = \Pi_2 = \Pi_1 = 0$. With this simplification, equation (2.33) reduces to

$$-p^* = p_1^* - p_2^* = \frac{K^* - L^*}{|\lambda|(\sigma_D + \sigma_s)} + \frac{Y^*(\eta_1 - \eta_2)}{(\sigma_D + \sigma_s)}. \qquad (2.33^*)$$

Since σ_D and σ_s are both non-negative, the sign of $(p_1^* - p_2^*)$ depends crucially on the signs of $|\lambda|$, and $(\eta_1 - \eta_2)$. Further simplification can be achieved if we assume that the community preferences are homothetic, so that both income elasticities of demand are identically equal to unity.† Under these circumstances, a rise in $k(K^* - L^* > 0)$ will lead to a decline in $p(p_2^* - p_1^* < 0)$ if $|\lambda| > 0$, which from (2.17) means that $k_2 > k_1$. On the other hand, if $|\lambda| < 0$, so that $k_2 < k_1$, k and p are positively related. These two cases are diagrammatically depicted in Figs. 2.6 and 2.7. However, if factor intensities are reversible, so that $|\lambda|$ is positive for some levels of ω but negative for others, the relationship between k and p will no longer be unique.

What happens if community preferences are not homothetic, so that neither η_1 nor η_2 equals unity? For expository purposes, let us assume that the change in k is effected by a change in K alone, without being accompanied by a change in L, so that $L^* = 0$. This implies that k^* and Y^* are positively related. A rise in k shifts the transformation curve away from the origin, resulting thereby in a higher

---

† By homothetic preferences we mean that the communities' taste pattern is described by a homothetic social utility function, so that the commodity-price ratio is exclusively determined by the ratio between the output levels of the two commodities.

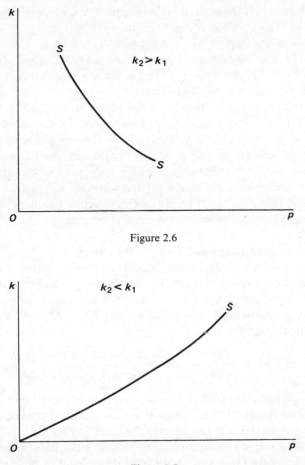

Figure 2.6

Figure 2.7

level of national income. The introduction of the possibility of non-homothetic preferences, however, may or may not alter the complexion of the analysis. If $|\lambda| < 0$, that is, if the second commodity is labour-intensive relative to the first commodity, the relationship between k and p is reinforced, provided $\eta_2 > \eta_1$. Stated differently, a rise in k will now result in a greater rise in p than the case would be if η_1 and η_2 were equal. The reason is not difficult to pinpoint. If the relative price of the second commodity rises as a result of a rise in k in the presence of homothetic preferences, the rise in p will be even greater if the demand change due to the income change was biased in favour of the second commodity, that is if $\eta_2 > \eta_1$. The same reasoning applies to the case of a decline in k.

The relationship between k and p continues to be unique if $|\lambda| > 0$, that is, $k_2 > k_1$, and $\eta_2 < \eta_1$. Here a rise in k will result in a larger decline in p than before, and conversely.

The picture becomes blurred if the terms on the right-hand side of (2.33*) possess opposite signs. This will be the case if (i) $|\lambda| < 0$ but $\eta_2 < \eta_1$, or (ii) $|\lambda| > 0$ but $\eta_2 > \eta_1$. To say the least, the relationship between k and p is now weakened. Furthermore, the previous relationship between k and p may be reversed; that is to say, if k and p were positively related when $\eta_1 = \eta_2$, they may be negatively related when the influence of differing income elasticities of demand is taken into account, and conversely.

2.6 Technical Change and Commodity Prices

The implications of technical progress for the commodity-price ratio can be explored as a special case of the general solution provided by equation (2.33). For the sake of convenience, let us assume that factor endowments are given, so that $K^* = L^* = 0$. Equation (2.33) then simplifies to

$$-p^* = p_1^* - p_2^* = \frac{\Pi_K - \Pi_L}{|\lambda|(\sigma_D + \sigma_s)} + \frac{\sigma_s(\Pi_2 - \Pi_1)}{(\sigma_D + \sigma_s)} + \frac{Y^*(\eta_1 - \eta_2)}{(\sigma_D + \sigma_s)}. \quad (2.33')$$

At first glance, equation (2.33') is not amenable to simple and unambiguous interpretation. Even if we assume that preferences are homothetic so that the last term in the equation disappears, myriad possibilities suggest themselves, and all may be equally plausible on *a priori* grounds. Drastic simplification is needed if we wish to derive unambiguous results of some kind. The analysis will become more manageable if we rewrite the expressions for Π_i and Π_j presented in section 2.3. Thus

$$\Pi_i = \lambda_{i1} B_{i1}^* + \lambda_{i2} B_{i2}^* \qquad (i = L, K)$$
$$\Pi_j = \theta_{Lj} B_{Lj}^* + \theta_{Kj} B_{Kj}^* \qquad (j = 1, 2).$$

If we assume that technical progress is Hicks-neutral, then $B_{Lj}^* = B_{Kj}^*$. Using this relationship and expression (2.17*), we can show that

$$\Pi_K - \Pi_L = |\lambda|(\Pi_2 - \Pi_1).$$

Substituting this in equation (2.33'), we obtain

$$p_1^* - p_2^* = \frac{(1+\sigma_s)(\Pi_2 - \Pi_1)}{(\sigma_D + \sigma_s)} + \frac{Y^*(\eta_1 - \eta_2)}{(\sigma_D + \sigma_s)}. \qquad (2.34)$$

As before, matters are simplified if we assume that preferences are homothetic, so that $\eta_1 = \eta_2 = 1$. The change in the commodity-price ratio is then simply determined by Π_j, the rate of technical advance in the jth industry. If technical progress occurs at a uniform rate in both industries, that is, $\Pi_2 = \Pi_1$, the commodity-price ratio remains unaltered, for then $p_1^* = p_2^*$. On the other hand, if $\Pi_1 > \Pi_2$, that is, if the first commodity enjoys a greater rate of technical improvement than the second commodity, the commodity-price ratio rises ($p_1^* < p_2^*$), and conversely.

When income effects are introduced, the relationship between p and Π_1/Π_2 may be reinforced or weakened. If $\eta_2 > \eta_1$, the relationship is strengthened; if $\eta_2 < \eta_1$, the relationship may be either weakened, or actually become negative.

2.7 Other Properties of the Model

Sections 2.4 and 2.5 in the foregoing analysis of this chapter have been concerned, respectively, with the implications of changes in the factor-price ratio and the overall capital/labour ratio for the commodity-price ratio in a closed economy. The equations of change that were used to analyse these effects can also be used to examine some other related theorems, of great intrinsic interest and importance, which deal directly with the impact of a change in any particular parameter on the individual variables rather than their ratios.

The Stolper-Samuelson Theorem

Consider first the implications of a change in commodity prices for real factor rewards. A categorical analysis of this problem was first provided by Stolper and Samuelson in a pioneering article [5]. *According to Stolper and Samuelson, a rise in the price of a commodity results in a rise in the real reward of its intensive factor and a decline in the real reward of its unintensive factor,* and vice versa. For a demonstration of this result we go back to equations (2.25) and

(2.26), which in conjunction with (2.17*) can be solved for given factor endowments and technological levels to furnish

$$w^* - p_j^* = \frac{\theta_{Kj}(p_1^* - p_2^*)}{|\theta|} \tag{2.35}$$

$$r^* - p_j^* = \frac{-\theta_{Lj}(p_1^* - p_2^*)}{|\theta|} \qquad (j = 1,2). \tag{2.36}$$

Clearly, the impact of a change in the commodity-price ratio on the factor rewards in terms of any commodity price is determined by the sign of $|\theta|$. Suppose the first commodity is the labour-intensive of the two, so that $k_2 > k_1$ and $|\theta| > 0$. Then a rise in the relative price of the first commodity, implying that $(p_1^* - p_2^*) > 0$, promotes a rise in the wage rate, which is the reward of its intensive factor, and a decline in the rental of capital, which is the price paid to its un-intensive factor. Since the wage rate increases and the rental rate declines in terms of both commodity prices, the real reward of labour increases and the real reward of capital decreases unambiguously. If $|\theta|$ were negative, that is, if $k_2 < k_1$, then labour would un-ambiguously suffer but capital would benefit as a result of a decline in p, and conversely. It should be obvious by now that this result derives directly from the one-to-one relationship established in section 2.4 between the wage/rental ratio and the commodity-price ratio. Here, as before, incomplete specialisation is a necessary con-dition for the full validity of the Stolper–Samuelson theorem.

For a geometrical proof of this theorem, we revert to Fig. 2.1, which is drawn under the assumption that $k_2 > k_1$. It may be recalled that the relative price of the second commodity associated with the wage/rental ratio given by the isocost line AB equals unity, but that associated with the lower wage/rental ratio furnished by the slope of CD, parallel to EF, equals $OC/OE > 1$. This of course brings us back to the result that a rise in p has resulted in a decline in ω. In addition, however, the real wage rate declines, but the real reward of capital rises. For prior to the rise in p, real reward of labour in both industries was given by $1/OB$, and the real reward of capital by $1/OA$, but after the rise in p the real wage rate has declined to $1/OF$ in terms of the first commodity and to $1/OD$ in terms of the second commodity, whereas the real rental has risen to $1/OE$ in terms of the first and to $1/OC$ in terms of the second commodity. The effects of a decline in p are symmetrically opposite.

The Rybczynski Theorem

Another remarkable theorem is associated with T. M. Rybczynski [3], who showed *that a rise in the supply of a factor at constant commodity prices promotes expansion of the commodity which utilises the expanding factor relatively intensively and contraction of the other commodity.* The economic explanation of this theorem is rather straightforward. Suppose there is an increase in the supply of capital alone. At constant commodity prices, factor rewards and hence factor proportions in each industry are unaltered. Under the full-employment constraint the additional capital stock must be absorbed in the economy, and this, with the constant capital/labour ratio in each industry, requires an expansion in the output of the capital-intensive commodity. Since both factors are indispensable in the production process, the additional labour needed by the capital-intensive commodity in order to utilise the additional capital stock must, with the constant labour endowment, be withdrawn from the other commodity, which means that the output of the labour-intensive good must decline.

A simple algebraic demonstration of this phenomenon follows directly from the solution of (2.23) and (2.24) and the use of (2.17*), so that

$$X_1^* = \frac{\lambda_{K2} L^* - \lambda_{L2} K^*}{|\lambda|} \tag{2.37}$$

$$X_2^* = \frac{\lambda_{L1} K^* - \lambda_{K1} L^*}{|\lambda|}. \tag{2.38}$$

With a rise in the supply of capital alone, $K^* > 0$ but $L^* = 0$. The proof of the Rybczynski theorem then follows directly by observing that

$$X_1^* \lessgtr 0, \qquad X_2^* \gtrless 0 \quad \text{for} \quad |\lambda| \gtrless 0, \quad \text{or} \quad k_2 \gtrless k_1.$$

A simple diagrammetic derivation of the Rybczynski theorem can be accomplished by utilising the box diagram presented in the previous chapter. Consider Fig. 2.8, where the factor supplies are measured along the axes merging in the origins O_1 and O_2 and the outputs by the distance of the production point from the respective origins. Suppose A is the initial production point lying on the contract curve $O_1 A O_2$, so that the capital/labour ratio in each industry is given by the slope of $O_1 A$ and $O_2 A$, reflecting that the first commodity is labour-intensive relative to the second commodity, and

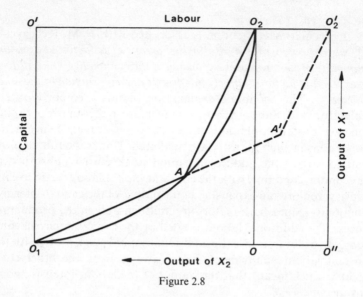

Figure 2.8

the output of X_1 and X_2 equals O_1A and O_2A, respectively. The supply of capital and labour constraining the contract curve O_1AO_2 is given, respectively, by O_1O' and O_1O. Now suppose the supply of labour increases by OO'' to O_1O''. Since the capital/labour ratio in each commodity is unaltered at constant commodity prices, the new production point is given by A', which lies on the extension of O_1A and O'_2A', drawn parallel to O_2A. The new production point, which lies on the new contract curve (not drawn), shows that the output of the labour-intensive commodity, X_1, rises to O_1A' and the output of the capital-intensive commodity, X_2, declines to O'_2A'. The diagram can be easily adapted to the case where the supply of capital, instead of labour, has increased.

Duality and the Magnification Effect

The formulation of the model in terms of equations (2.1)–(2.4) serves to reveal the fundamental duality that exists between the Stolper–Samuelson and the Rybczynski theorems. Moreover, the effects of variations in commodity prices on factor rewards and in factor endowments on individual outputs at constant commodity prices are magnified to show that a change in the price of a commodity alters the factor rewards in a greater proportion, whereas a change in the supply of any factor gives rise to a more than proportionate change in the two outputs. This so-called *magnification effect*, which further emphasises the dual relationship between the theorems described in this section, becomes vivid when equations (2.35)–(2.38) are written in the following manner:

$$\frac{w^*}{p_1^*} = 1 + \frac{\theta_{K1}}{|\theta|} \qquad (2.35^*)$$

$$\frac{r^*}{p_1^*} = 1 - \frac{\theta_{L1}}{|\theta|} \qquad (2.36^*)$$

$$\frac{X_1^*}{L^*} = 1 + \frac{\lambda_{L2}}{|\lambda|} \qquad (2.37^*)$$

$$\frac{X_2^*}{L^*} = 1 - \frac{\lambda_{L1}}{|\lambda|}. \qquad (2.38^*)$$

Equations (2.35*) and (2.36*) are derived under the condition that only the price of the first commodity changes, e.g. $p_2^* = 0$, whereas the condition behind (2.37*) and (2.38*) is that $K^* = 0$. It may now be evident that the link provided by $|\theta|$ between commodity prices and factor rewards is symmetrical to the link provided by $|\lambda|$ between factor endowments and the individual outputs. Furthermore, each equation serves to show the magnification effect. For example, suppose that $k_2 > k_1$ so that both $|\lambda|$ and $|\theta|$ are positive. Then a rise in the price of the labour-intensive commodity (implying that $p_1^* > 0$) stimulates, at constant k, a more than proportionate rise in the reward of labour, whereas a rise in the supply of labour alone at constant p results in a more than proportionate increase in the output of the labour-intensive commodity (see equations (2.35*) and (2.37*)). On the other hand, if $k_2 < k_1$, i.e. if $|\lambda|$ and $|\theta|$ are negative, the magnification and the dual effects are reflected in equations (2.36*) and (2.38*).†

---

† Any remaining doubts concerning the dual relationship may be dispelled by observing that, if $p_2^* = K^* = 0$, then the substitution of (2.17) in (2.35) and (2.37) yields

$$\frac{dw}{dp_1} = \frac{dX_1}{dL} = \frac{k_2}{C_{L1}(k_2 - k_1)}.$$

On the other hand, if $p_1^* = L^* = 0$, then

$$\frac{dr}{dp_2} = \frac{dX_2}{dK} = \frac{1}{C_{L2}(k_2 - k_1)}.$$

2.8 Autarky Equilibrium

By definition, the equilibrium under autarky is reached when demand and supply for all goods are equal. If we assume that the community behaves like a single consumer, the problem may be formulated as one of maximising an aggregate utility function U subject to the constraint imposed by available factor supplies, a constraint inherent in the construction of the transformation curve which describes that $X_1 = X_1(X_2)$. If the community welfare is a function of the aggregate consumption of the two commodities, then the aggregate utility function may be written as

$$U = U(D_1, D_2).$$

The problem is then to maximise U subject to

$$D_j = X_j$$

and

$$X_1 = X_1(X_2).$$

This is accomplished by forming a Lagrangian H as $H = U(D_1, D_2) - \lambda_1[D_1 - X_1(X_2)] - \lambda_2(D_2 - X_2)$, where λ_1 and λ_2 are the Lagrangian multipliers. The first-order conditions for an interior maximum are

$$\frac{\partial H}{\partial D_1} = U_1 - \lambda_1 = \frac{\partial H}{\partial D_2} = U_2 - \lambda_2 = \frac{\partial H}{\partial X_2} = \lambda_1 \frac{\partial X_1}{\partial X_2} + \lambda_2 = 0$$

where $U_j = \partial U / \partial D_j$ is the marginal utility of the jth commodity. The solution of these equations furnishes

$$\frac{U_2}{U_1} = \frac{\lambda_2}{\lambda_1} = -\frac{\partial X_1}{\partial X_2}.$$

Under perfect competition in all markets we know that $-\partial X_1/\partial X_2 = U_2/U_1 = p$. Hence welfare is maximised when p equals the slope of the transformation curve as well as the community indifference curve, which is a geometrical counterpart of the aggregate utility function. This is achieved in Fig. 2.9 at S, the point of self-sufficiency equilibrium.

2.9 The Community Indifference Curve

In the preceding section, the concept of community indifference has been used to illustrate how the closed-economy equilibrium is

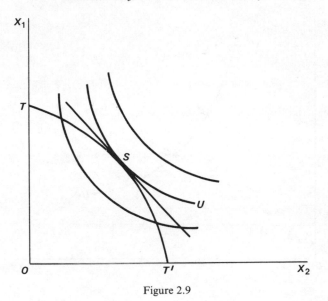

Figure 2.9

attained. The uniqueness of the autarky equilibrium in Fig. 2.9 is attributable to the existence of a well-behaved, non-intersecting community indifference map which ensures that there is only one point such as S where a community indifference curve is tangential to the transformation curve. In other words, it is only when the community indifference map is a national counterpart of the individual indifference map that it is possible to obtain a unique equilibrium point. This procedure, however, gives rise to several vexing questions, a definite answer to which, contrary to the popular impression, is not yet in sight. If all individuals constituting a community or nation possess identical tastes and incomes, there is no problem in deriving the aggregate utility function that will have the properties of individual utility functions. But to postulate this condition is to beg the question entirely. Where in the world can we find a society enjoying such a 'pure' form of communism? The assumption that individual preferences are identical is certainly not outrageous, but the assumption that people have identical incomes certainly is.

Let us first see how a community indifference curve is constructed. A community indifference curve, as defined by Scitovsky [4], is a locus of quantities demanded at various commodity prices and a

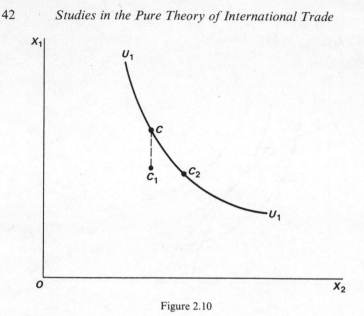

Figure 2.10

given constant distribution of *utilities* among individuals. Consider a community of individuals exchanging among themselves two commodities, X_1 and X_2, which are respectively measured along the abscissa and ordinate in Fig. 2.10, and suppose that the initial consumption point, for given tastes and incomes, is given by C. Now suppose that the price of X_1 rises, inducing members of the community to forgo a certain quantity of it, and move vertically down to the consumption point given by C_1. In principle, we can ascertain how much extra X_2 will be needed to make every member of the community just as well off as he was prior to the price change. The new consumption point, if this compensating substitution does occur, will lie to the south-east of C. Suppose C_2 is such a consumption point. By varying the amount of the initial price change, an infinity of points such as C_2 can be derived. The locus of these points, Scitovsky asserts, makes up a community indifference curve such as $U_1 U_1$ in Fig. 2.10, which has the same geometrical properties as the underlying individual preference maps.

The important fact to remember about Scitovsky's construction is that it assumes a fixed utility (or income) distribution throughout. In general, as recognised by Scitovsky himself, an infinite number of community indifference curves pass through any point in the commodity space, each one corresponding to a different initial income distribution. Thus in order to obtain a well-behaved, non-intersecting community indifference map such as the one depicted in Fig. 2.9, the initial underlying income distribution must be kept constant. This is not an easy task, especially in an economy with more than one factor of production where different goods utilise factors in different proportions. If there was only one factor of production, or if the factor proportions were similar in all activities of production, the income distribution would be invariant as we moved along the resultant straight-line transformation curve in order to obtain the autarky equilibrium point. The community indifference map would then be just as well behaved as the individual indifference maps. However, the picture is more complicated and baffling when factor proportions differ in each industry. Here the movement along the transformation curve would induce changes in commodity prices, which in turn, from the Stolper–Samuelson theorem, would alter the complexion of income distribution, say between wage-earners and owners of capital. The situation becomes particularly serious if the tastes of the wage-earners are biased towards the consumption of the labour-intensive good and those of the rental earners are biased towards the consumption of the capital-intensive good. In order to find a way out of this dilemma, recourse must be made to two conditions succinctly described by Chipman ([1], p. 695):

> To summarise, we may say that if utility functions of all people are positive homogeneous, and if either (1) all people have identical tastes, or (2) all people have a distribution of resources proportionate to the aggregate distribution, then their behaviour can be represented by a single utility function. Since these two conditions are independent, and each one of them is sufficient, obviously neither one of them is necessary in itself.

As recognised by Chipman, these are sufficient, though not necessary, conditions for the existence of an aggregate utility function. More important, however, is the fact that if only one of the two conditions (1) and (2) holds, the resulting community indifference curves will describe merely the *consumption behaviour* of the society, but will have no welfare connotation. In other words, aggregate demand functions can be derived from the indifference curves, although we cannot say that the community is indifferent among the various output bundles along any one of these curves as the latter are not uniquely related to a single distribution of utilities among individuals. However, if individual utility functions are homothetic and if conditions (1) and (2) are simultaneously satisfied, then the community indifference curves obtained will constitute a genuine counterpart of each individual's indifference curves both in the behavioural and in the welfare sense.

2.10 Summary

The purpose of this chapter was to analyse factors that affect the commodity-price ratio in a closed economy. We studied how the commodity-price ratio changes under the thrust of changes in factor prices, factor endowments and levels of technology in the two industries. Using a two-commodity, two-factor model with perfect competition, neo-classical production functions, full employment and non-reversible factor intensities, etc., the following results were derived:

1. At constant factor endowment and technology, there exists a unique relationship between the commodity-price ratio and the factor-price ratio. This relationship is, however, no longer unique if factor intensities are reversible. Furthermore, a rise in the price of a commodity leads to a more than proportionate rise in the reward of its intensive factor and a decline in the reward of its unintensive factor, and conversely. The latter result is usually called the Stolper–Samuelson theorem.
2. Under unchanged technology and homothetic preferences, there exists a unique relationship between the overall capital-labour ratio (k) and the commodity-price ratio (p). However, when income effects are introduced, that is, when community preferences are non-homothetic, or when factor intensities are reversible, the relationship between k and p may no longer be monotonic, in which case there arises a strong possibility of multiple equilibria.
3. At constant technology and commodity prices, a rise in the supply of a factor results in a more than proportionate rise in the output of the commodity utilising the expanded factor intensively at the expense of the output of the other commodity, and vice-versa. This is the so-called Rybczynski theorem.
4. For any k and homothetic preferences, there exists a monotonic

relationship between changes in p and relative rates of Hicks technical advance in the two industries. However, this relationship may not be monotonic when income effects are also taken into account.

5. There exists a dual relationship between the Stolper–Samuelson and the Rybczynski theorems.

These are some of the properties of the model which have been extensively utilised in the current literature on trade theory. It may be stated without any fear of exaggeration that the model yields conclusive, elegant and straightforward theorems. These properties will be utilised again and again in the analysis of subsequent chapters. For the time being, however, we wish to emphasise that the elegant properties of the model depend crucially upon the assumptions made at the beginning of this chapter, assumptions the true significance of which will be revealed only as we proceed with the analysis in succeeding chapters.

REFERENCES

[1] Chipman, J. S., 'A Survey of the Theory of International Trade: Part 2, the Neo-Classical Economy', *Econometrica*, XXXIII (Oct 1965) 685–760.

[2] Jones, R. W., 'The Structure of Simple General Equilibrium Models', *Journal of Political Economy*, LXXIII (Dec 1965) 557–72.

[3] Rybczynski, T. M. 'Factor Endowment and Relative Commodity Prices', *Economica*, XXII (Nov 1955) 336–41.

[4] Scitovsky, T., 'A Reconsideration of the Theory of Tariffs', *Review of Economic Studies*, IX (summer 1942) 89–110.

[5] Stolper, W. F., and Samuelson, P. A., 'Protection and Real Wages', *Review of Economic Studies*, IX (Nov 1941) 58–73.

3   The Basis of International Trade

3.1   Introduction

In the last chapter we studied how changes in the commodity-price ratio occur under the thrust of variations in the factor-price ratio, the overall capital/labour ratio and the relative rate of technical advance in the two industries. Any theory attempting to explain the basis of international trade must always commence with the theory of resource allocation and production in a closed economy. This task having been accomplished in the previous chapters, we are now in a position to pinpoint the factors that determine a country's pattern of trade. The issue is what goods a country will export and import. Stated differently, is it possible to predict a country's configuration of exports and imports just by examining the characteristics of a closed economy? Seeking a clear-cut answer to this query constitutes the subject-matter of this chapter.

The traditional answer to the question of why a particular country exports a particular commodity is simply that, owing to the handiwork of nature or man, it is able to produce that commodity at a lower comparative cost than the rest of the world, usually taken to represent a single entity in the community of nations. International trade occurs because countries stand to benefit by the exchange of goods that are produced at dissimilar relative costs and hence at different relative prices. It is desirable, therefore, to go deeper and unearth the causes responsible for inter-country disparities in the comparative cost or the commodity-price ratios. The reasons, quite ostensibly, must be sought in the international differences in factor endowments, tastes or levels of technology, because, as established in the preceding chapter, these are the forces which influence the commodity-price ratio in autarky. However, before we get involved in a detailed examination of the theories identifying themselves with these forces, it is imperative that the necessary conditions preventing the occurrence of international trade be expressly spelt out.

3.2 Conditions for the Absence of Trade

If countries were identical in all respects in the absence of the opportunity to trade, the commodity-price ratios would be similar everywhere and there would be no incentive to trade even if such an opportunity was available. Obviously, this situation requires the fulfilment of the following conditions:

1. Production functions are similar internationally.
2. Factor endowments are the same internationally.
3. Tastes are similar in all countries.
4. Production functions are neo-classical.
5. All markets are universally characterised by perfect competition.

This set of conditions is sufficient to generate inter-country identity on both the demand and the supply side, resulting thereby in similar autarky prices and, as a consequence, precluding any possibility of mutually profitable trade. Clearly, then, the relaxation of any of these five requirements could provide a basis for international trade. In other words, there are five different ways in which an 'international economy' could be simulated by the trade theorist. However, from the viewpoint of propositions concerning the pattern of trade, the two most widely known simulations are those of Ricardo [11] and Heckscher–Ohlin [3, 10], who, respectively, formulated their theorems in terms of relaxing conditions (1) and (2). Needless to say, if one of these conditions is relaxed in order to forecast the pattern of trade, the remaining four assumptions must be retained if the trade pattern is to follow the prediction under all circumstances.

3.3 The Ricardian Theory

The classical economists were concerned primarily with the demonstration of the welfare proposition that trade is beneficial, and only occasionally with isolating the crucial variables that could explain the pattern of trade by means of a formal, determinate model. Yet a general model of trade and resource allocation can be formulated directly from the insights of Ricardo [11] and Mill [9]. There is little doubt about the plausibility of the former viewpoint. None the less, the foundations of most of the early expositions of the comparative cost doctrine lie in a definite structural model, however primitive to the modern writer, that can be used to explain the pattern of international specialisation.

On this latter interpretation, the Ricardian theory of comparative advantage can be constructed directly from Ricardo's famous numerical example concerning unit costs of production in England and Portugal. According to the Ricardian theorem, *a country exports that commodity which has higher comparative factor productivity and imports the commodity which has lower comparative factor productivity than the other country.*

Let us assume that the world consists of only two countries, one home country (H) and one foreign country (F), each producing the two commodities, X_1 and X_2. Following Ricardo, suppose further that there exists only one factor of production, say labour, and that returns to scale are constant. As established in Chapter 1, the transformation curve under the postulated conditions is given by a negatively inclined straight line whose slope reflects the ratio of labour productivities. It can be shown directly from equations (2.3) and (2.4), presented in the previous chapter, that the autarky commodity-price ratio $(p = p_2/p_1)$ is determined exclusively by the output-input ratios, provided labour (or capital) is the only factor of production. Hence, with $C_{K1} = C_{K2} = 0$, p, from (2.3) and (2.4), is given by

$$p = \frac{C_{L2}}{C_{L1}} = \frac{a_1}{a_2} \qquad (3.1^*)$$

where $a_j = 1/C_{Lj}$ is the average productivity of labour in the jth commodity. Thus the pre-trade commodity-price ratio in the Ricardian model is determined neither by factor supply nor by demand, but only by the state of technology hidden behind the output/labour ratios. If we postulate an identical model for both countries, it follows that the reason for the disparity in the two countries' autarky price ratios and hence for the existence of international trade must be ascribed to international differences in the relative output/labour ratios or in the state of technology. Put another way, the basis for international trade lies in international differences in production functions – a violation of condition (1) stated in the previous section. To consider a specific example, suppose that the comparative labour productivity in the first industry is higher in the home country; that is,

$$(a_1/a_2)_h > (a_1/a_2)_f \qquad (3.1)$$

where the subscripts f and h respectively denote countries F and H.

(In what follows, the subscripts h and f will be introduced wherever it is necessary to distinguish between the variables in the two countries. If these subscripts do not appear, the variables will be taken to refer to the home country, except when specified otherwise.) It follows immediately from this relationship that

$$p_h > p_f \tag{3.2}$$

so that the relative price of the second commodity in country H is higher than that in country F. It is now relatively simple to deduce that H will export the first commodity in which her comparative labour productivity is higher, and import the second commodity in which her comparative labour productivity is lower than that in F. This is the proof of the Ricardian theory of comparative advantage.

Geometry will perhaps throw further light on the issues involved in the Ricardian theorem. Consider Fig. 3.1, where HH' and FF' are, respectively, the linear transformation curves in countries H and

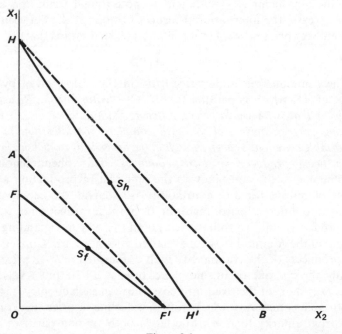

Figure 3.1

F, with their slopes reflecting the autarky price ratios satisfying the relation expressed by (3.2). If we assume that there are no transport costs and no impediments to the free international flow of goods, there prevails only one commodity-price ratio in the free trade equilibrium. The reason is that the consumer in each country consumes the importable goods at the price charged by producers in the other country. As a result, the commodity-price ratio is the same in both countries in the free trade equilibrium with no transport costs. Even so, the common terms of trade prevailing in the international trade market are normally different from the autarky price ratios, except in the singular case where the gigantic size of one of the trading partners prevents the trade with the relatively small country from having any impact on its own domestic prices, in which case the common international terms of trade are given by the large country's autarky price ratio. This latter possibility will not be pursued here, but will be taken up again in the chapters on gains from trade. Nor shall we examine the factors that go into the determination of the international terms of trade. For the time being it is sufficient to note that, barring the large country case, the international terms of trade (p') lie between the two autarky price ratios. Under relation (3.2), it means that

$$p_h > p' > p_f.$$

The common free trade price ratio in Fig. 3.1 is given by the slope of AF' which is parallel to BH. *One feature of the Ricardian model is that, with world prices differing from autarky prices, each trading partner must end up with complete specialisation in the exportable commodity, even though in the absence of trade both goods were being produced in both countries.* This phenomenon is attributable to the constancy in the unit cost of production at all levels of output for any commodity, so that as the economy is exposed to different prices resulting from the introduction of trade, the producers find it profitable to go all the way in expanding the output of the commodity whose relative price has risen. Conversely, the producers of the commodity with diminished relative price are totally thrown out of business, because at all output levels the price falls short of the fixed unit cost. Since in each country it is the importable commodity which suffers a decline in price, the transition from autarky to free trade lands both trading partners in a situation where only their respective exportable good is produced.

The self-sufficiency equilibrium point in the two countries is given by S_h and S_f, but the free trade production points are given by H in the home country and F' in the foreign country.

The Role of Demand

We have seen above that the factor supply and commodity demand conditions play no role in the determination of the autarky price ratio. This perhaps led to the long-held belief that the demand conditions do not enter into the determination of the trade pattern in a Ricardian world. The fallacy of this view has been recently pointed out by Bhagwati [1]. His proof consists in the demonstration that, even if the autarky price ratios were everywhere the same, international trade in the Ricardian simulation of the world economy could still occur because of the possibility of multiple production equilibria stemming directly from the prevalence of the linear transformation curve. A neat exposition of this point emerges from Fig. 3.2, where HH' and FF' are the transformation curves belonging, as before, to H and F, but unlike the case in Fig. 3.1 HH' and FF' are parallel, showing that the autarky price

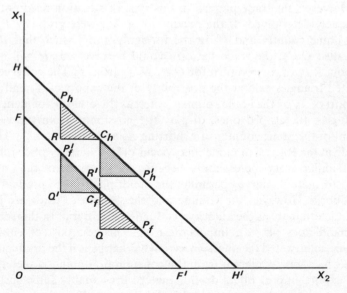

Figure 3.2

ratios are similar in both countries. Suppose that country H selects consumption at C_h and country F at C_f. For the sake of visual clarity, points C_f and C_h are vertically lined. Owing to the constancy of the unit production cost, the production point in each country may lie anywhere on its transformation curve. If the home production point lies at C_h and the foreign production point at C_f, there is no disparity in the demand–supply position in both countries, so that there will be no need for international trade. Suppose, however, that the production point in the home country is given by P_h whereas in the foreign country it is given by P_f, such that the distances RC_h and QP_f are equal. The domestic needs of each country can be satisfied only through trade. For in the absence of trade the demand–supply equilibrium may never be achieved without some kind of government intervention. Under constant prices and incomes, consumers certainly have no reason to alter their demands. Similarly, in the face of given prices, producers have no incentive to alter the composition of their output, unless, of course, the government requires them to do so. The only solution to this impasse may then be the introduction of international trade. In the example just presented, the home country exports RP_h of X_1 in exchange for QP_f of X_2.

However, the trade pattern in this type of situation need not be uniquely determined. If the production point were given by P'_h in the home country and P'_f in the foreign country, such that $R'P'_h$ equalled $Q'C_f$, the trade pattern would be reversed: H will now export $R'P'_h$ of X_2 in return for $Q'P'_f$ of X_1 from F. The congruent, dotted triangles exhibit the possibility of the export of X_2 and the import of X_1 by the home country, whereas the other set of identical triangles, the striped ones, display the possibility from the viewpoint of the home country of exporting X_1 and importing X_2. Thus trade in the Ricardian model may occur even if autarky price ratios are similar everywhere simply because the presence of the linear transformation curve permits the multiplicity of production equilibria. However, the volume and the pattern of trade are just as indeterminate as the autarky production equilibria. In this sense, demand does play an important role. This analysis, of course, leaves unanswered the question as to what happens if the production in each country, different from the consumption point, is such that the export–import offers do not match. Presumably some sort of governmental intervention would then be unavoidable.

Bhagwati [1] provides yet another demonstration where the lack of restrictions on demand conditions may give rise to the invalidity of the Ricardian theorem even if autarky price ratios between the two countries were different. The villain now lies in such demand conditions as may result in multiple self-sufficiency equilibria. The discussion on the concept of community indifference in the previous chapter made it clear that the multiple self-sufficiency equilibria could occur in the absence of well-behaved, non-intersecting community indifference curves. In such a case, it is possible that there may be no trade in spite of the international differences in production functions. Consider Fig. 3.3, where the transformation curve of country F is omitted for the sake of simplicity. Let us suppose that, in the absence of trade, the self-sufficiency equilibrium is given by S_h, where the home transformation curve is tangential to the community indifference curve $U_1 U_1$. As the closed economy is opened to free trade the commodity-price ratio is given by the slope of BH and the home production shifts to point H. Now if the community preference map were well behaved, the consumption point will shift to a point such as C, the home country will export HG of X_1 and import GC of X_2, and

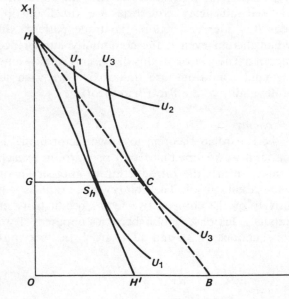

Figure 3.3

the home welfare would improve to the level indicated by U_3U_3, which, as can be seen, does not intersect U_1U_1. However, if the community preference map is not well behaved, the new consumption point could lie anywhere on BH including the point H. This latter case is depicted in the diagram, where the price line BH touches the community indifference curve U_2H at H and there is no possibility of any trade, because even at the price ratio given by BH, production and consumption are the same. Thus the Ricardian theorem may not be valid if certain restrictions are not placed on demand conditions. Fortunately, these restrictions transpire to be insignificant. Since income distribution, as established in the previous chapter, remains constant in a single-factor economy, all we need to assume, in order to secure well-behaved community indifference curves, is that the individual indifference curves are well behaved, a restriction certainly not serious if we remember the formidable difficulties that stand in the way of obtaining the well-behaved community preference map in a multi-factor economy where it may be impossible to keep the initial income distribution unaltered. An alternative and equally lenient restriction could be to assume that both goods are demanded in each country at all commodity prices, so that the extremities of the transformation curve as possible self-sufficiency equilibria are ruled out by assumption. Under this later restriction, the trade pattern will follow the Ricardian dictum even if the community indifference curves were to intersect. The gist of all this discussion is that some restrictions on demand conditions are desirable if we wish to demonstrate the full validity of the Ricardian theorem.

The Two-Factor Economy

The extension of the Ricardian theorem to a two-factor model is a rather simple matter if we assume that factor proportions in each industry are the same. In fact the introduction of another factor does not modify the results at all. The autarky price ratio is still determined exclusively by the comparative factor productivity of any one of the inputs. This observation becomes apparent if we rewrite the price equations (2.3) and (2.4) from the previous chapter; thus

$$wC_{L1} + rC_{K1} = p_1 \qquad (2.3)$$

$$wC_{L2} + rC_{K2} = p_2 \qquad (2.4)$$

Dividing (2.4) by (2.3), we obtain

$$p = \frac{wC_{L2}[1+(r/w)(C_{K2}/C_{L2})]}{wC_{L1}[1+(r/w)(C_{K1}/C_{L1})]} \tag{3.3}$$

so that with

$$(C_{K1}/C_{L1}) = (C_{K2}/C_{L2}) \tag{3.4}$$

$$p = \frac{C_{L2}}{C_{L1}} = \frac{a_1}{a_2} \tag{3.5}$$

which is exactly the same as equation (3.1*) derived in the single-factor case. From (3.4), (3.3) can also be written as

$$p = \frac{C_{K2}}{C_{K1}} = \frac{b_1}{b_2} = \frac{C_{L2}}{C_{L1}} = \frac{a_1}{a_2} \tag{3.6}$$

where b_j denotes the average productivity of capital in the jth industry ($j = 1,2$). Equations (3.5) and (3.6) make it clear that if each industry possesses the same capital/labour ratio, as is implicit in (3.4), the autarky price ratio (p) is determined solely by the comparative factor productivity of either input. Thus the Ricardian theory of comparative advantage remains intact in a two-factor economy, provided both commodities employ the two factors in the same proportion.

The complexion of the analysis changes substantially if factor proportions in each commodity are dissimilar, for then (a_1/a_2) is no longer equal to (b_1/b_2), so that it may be impossible to achieve consistent comparisons between comparative factor productivities in the two countries. Furthermore, the autarky price ratio will now be governed by factor supplies and demand conditions also.

Therefore, in order that inter-country technological differences retain their prominence as the basis of international trade, we must now assume that factor endowments and demand conditions are similar internationally. Matters may be further simplified by assuming that production functions concerning X_2 are similar internationally but those concerning X_1 differ. This situation is then equivalent to the one where technical progress in X_1 has occurred in one country alone. More specifically, suppose that technology in the foreign country is unchanged, but that Hicks-*neutral* technical improvement occurs in X_1 in the home country. Under these circumstances we can show that the home country will export X_1

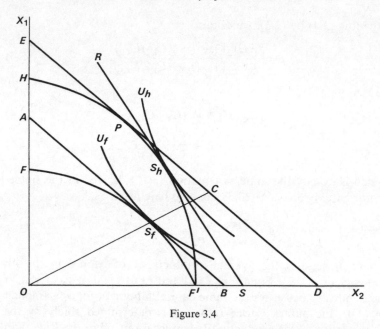

Figure 3.4

and import X_2 from the foreign country. This can be established readily from an examination of Fig. 3.4, where FF' is the transformation curve in the foreign country, U_f is its highest attainable community indifference curve under autarky and S_f is its self-sufficiency equilibrium point, with the autarky price ratio given by the slope of AB. If the home country were identical to the foreign country in all respects, it would possess the same factor endowments, the same technology in all industries, the same transformation curve, the same community indifference curves and the same autarky price ratio. There would then be no basis for trade. Instead, assume that in the home country X_1 alone comes to enjoy a Hicks-neutral technical improvement, so that its transformation curve shifts to HF', which lies outside of FF' at all production points except F' where no X_1 is produced. At the same commodity-price ratio given by the slope of DE, which is parallel to AB, the production point in the home country is given by P. *Now if the consumption pattern is the same internationally, then in both countries the two goods are consumed in the same proportion at the same commodity–price ratio. This, of course, implies that community preferences in the two countries are not only identical, but that they are also homothetic.*† Under these circumstances, the consumption point in the home country would be given by C, if the commodity prices were to remain unchanged. But then the home economy would not be in self-sufficiency equilibrium, for C is not identical with P. In other words, under the postulated conditions and the absence of trade, the commodity-price ratio in the home country cannot be the same as that in the foreign country. Since at the price ratio given by the slope of DE the home country produces relatively less of X_2 than it consumes, the relative price of the second commodity must rise to bring about the demand–supply equilibrium. This also implies that the self-sufficiency equilibrium in the home country must lie on HF' to the right of P but somewhere to the north-west of C. In Fig. 3.4 the home self-sufficiency equilibrium point is given by S_h and the home autarky price ratio is given by the slope of RS, which, since it is steeper than AB, shows that

$$p_h > p_f$$

which means that the home country will export X_1 and import X_2 from the foreign country. It is also clear that international trade occurs only because of international differences in production functions.

Now the kind of Hicks-neutral efficiency differences in international production functions assumed in our analysis ensures that the comparative productivity of both factors in the first commodity is higher in the home country than in the foreign country. The Richardian theorem may then be restated for the case of a two-factor economy. *A country exports the commodity which possesses a higher comparative productivity of all factors and imports the commodity where the comparative productivity of both factors is lower than that in the other country.*

Until now we have assumed that community preferences are homothetic and similar internationally. What if the homothety assumption is dropped? If the two countries have different levels of income, then non-homothety of preference may seriously compromise the validity of the Richardian theorem even if community preferences in the two countries are similar. This possibility will

---

† It was not necessary to make this assumption in the simple Ricardian formulation because factor supply and demand conditions played no role in the determination of the autarky price ratio.

not be pursued here, but its significance will become clear later when we examine the validity of the Heckscher–Ohlin theorem.

3.4   The Heckscher–Ohlin Theory

The theory explaining the basis of international trade which has earned literally universal acceptability among modern trade theorists is popularly known as the Heckscher–Ohlin theory. Associated with the names of two distinguished writers, Heckscher [3] and Ohlin [10], this theory asserts that *a country exports the commodity which uses intensively its relatively abundant factor and imports the commodity which is intensive in the use of its relatively scarce factor.* Two definitions of factor scarcity (or abundance), namely, the *price* and the *physical* definition, have gained wide currency in the literature on trade theory. According to the price definition due initially to Heckscher and Ohlin, country H is capital-abundant (or labour-scarce) relative to country F if

$$\omega_h > \omega_f \tag{3.7}$$

where it may be reminded that ω denotes the wage/rental ratio. According to the physical definition due initially to Leontief [7], H is capital-abundant relative to F if

$$k_h > k_f \tag{3.8}$$

where $k = K/L$. If the Heckscher–Ohlin dictum is true, then the capital-rich country H will export the capital-intensive commodity and import the labour-intensive commodity from the labour-rich country F. For the full validity of the Heckscher–Ohlin (henceforth called H.O.) theory, it is necessary to assume that production functions for each commodity are different within a country (so that factor proportions differ in each industry) but similar internationally. We also assume that factors are perfectly mobile internally but completely immobile externally.

The Price Definition

The proof of the H.O. theorem in terms of the price definition is rather simple and requires the use of the one-to-one relationship, established in the previous chapter, that exists between p and ω in the absence of factor-intensity reversals. Consider Fig. 3.5, which reproduces parts of Figs. 2.2 and 2.3 presented in the previous chapter. The first quadrant of Fig. 3.5 portrays a negative

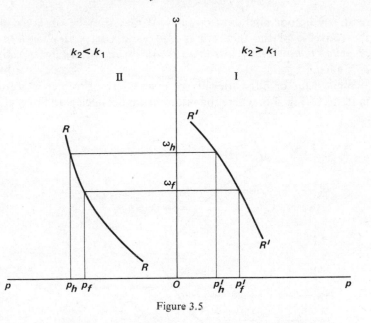

Figure 3.5

relationship between p and ω in terms of the $R'R'$ curve under the condition that $k_2 > k_1$ at all ω, whereas the second quadrant depicts the positive relationship between p and ω in terms of the RR curve drawn for the case where $k_2 < k_1$ at all ω. Owing to the international similarity of production functions, RR and $R'R'$ curves describe the nature of the relationship between p and ω in both countries. $O\omega_h$ exceeds $O\omega_f$ to reflect the inter-country factor-endowment relationship expressed in (3.7), so that if

$$k_2 < k_1, \quad \text{then} \quad p_h > p_f \qquad (3.9)$$

which implies that the home country will export the capital-intensive commodity X_1 and import the labour-intensive commodity X_2 from the foreign country, and if

$$k_2 > k_1, \quad \text{then} \quad p_h' < p_f' \qquad (3.10)$$

and the home country will export X_2 and import X_1, but X_2 is now capital-intensive relative to X_1. Thus, whatever the factor-intensity relationship between the two commodities, the relatively capital-abundant country exports the relatively capital-intensive commodity and imports the relatively labour-intensive commodity from the relatively labour-abundant country. It may now be observed that the converse of the theorem is also valid. *A country's relatively abundant factor is the one utilised relatively intensively by its exportable good.*

What if factor intensities are reversible? The problem is studied in terms of Fig. 3.6, where the relationship between p and ω is given

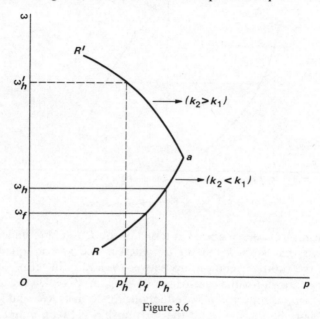

Figure 3.6

by RaR', a being the factor-intensity reversal point. The Ra portion of the curve indicates that $k_2 < k_1$, whereas the $R'a$ portion shows that $k_2 > k_1$ over the corresponding ranges of ω. If the inter-country factor-abundance relationship is given by ω_h and ω_f, we are operating in that portion of the RR' curve where $k_2 < k_1$ and

$$p_h > p_f$$

which is the same as (3.9), so that the H.O. theorem still holds. On the other hand, suppose that the autarky ω in the home country is given by ω'_h, then we find that for the home country $k_2 > k_1$, but for the foreign country $k_2 < k_1$. Furthermore,

$$p'_h < p_f.$$

It is evident that the H.O. theorem continues to hold in the case of the home country, but not in the case of the foreign country, which, despite being a relatively labour-abundant country, exports *its* capital-intensive commodity X_1. From this discussion we may conclude that *if the autarky wage/rental ratios of the two countries lie on one side of the factor-intensity reversal point, the H.O. theorem is valid; but if they lie on different sides, at least one of the countries violates the H.O. dictum.* The H.O. logic is demolished because of the fact that the same commodity is intensive in the use of different factors in the two countries.

The Role of Demand
One may be tempted to conclude that the H.O. theorem is valid in the absence of factor-intensity reversals. At least, this was the popular belief until the recent appearance of two studies, one by Bhagwati [1] and the other by Inada [4]. Both have shown that the validity of the H.O. theorem in terms of the price definition may be compromised if suitable restrictions on community preferences are not placed. We have already shown in the context of the Ricardian model that if the community indifference curves are not well behaved, there may be multiple self-sufficiency equilibria which may preclude the possibility of trade even if production functions were non-identical internationally. However, in the H.O. two-factor model where the transformation curve is concave to the origin, the existence of intersecting community indifference curves may not only prevent the occurrence of international trade in spite of inter-country disparities in factor endowments, but may also lead to a pattern of trade contradicting the H.O. theorem.

Consider Fig. 3.7 for a possible demonstration of these results. Suppose factor intensities are non-reversible and $k_2 > k_1$, so that from (3.10) $p_f > p_h$; suppose further that p' denotes the free trade terms of trade such that $p_f > p' > p_h$. If the H.O. theorem is to hold, the home country should export X_2 and import X_1. Assume that the self-sufficiency equilibrium point for the home country is given by S_h in Fig. 3.7 and the autarky price ratio is furnished by the line $p_h p_h$, which is tangential to both the home transformation curve HH' and its community indifference curve $U_1 U_1$ at point S_h. In the free trade situation, the production point shifts to P where the $p'p'$ line, whose slope displays the international terms of trade,

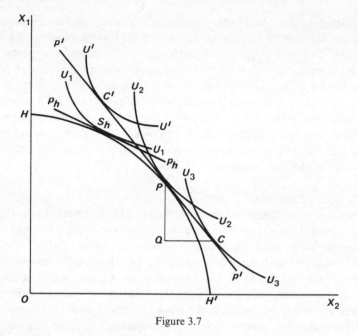

Figure 3.7

is tangential to the transformation curve. If X_2 is to be exported, the new consumption point should lie on $p'p'$ but to the left of the production point P. Such a consumption point is given by C', but note that the corresponding community indifference curve $U'U'$ does not intersect U_1U_1. However, if the community indifference map is not as well behaved as the one just depicted, the new consumption point could lie anywhere on $p'p'$. If it lies on P, which requires that U_2U_2 be tangential to the transformation curve at P, there will be no trade, a case illustrated by Bhagwati [1]; if it lies on $p'p'$ to the right of P, say on C where the line $p'p'$ is tangential to U_3U_3, the pattern of trade runs contradictory to the H.O. hypothesis, a result pointed out by Inada [4]. With point C, for example, the capital-rich home country exports the labour-intensive commodity X_1 and imports the capital-intensive commodity X_2 from the labour-rich foreign country. Thus some restrictions on demand conditions are needed even if the H.O. theorem is to be proved in terms of the price definition of relative factor abundance. *It is sufficient to assume that the community preferences are well behaved, or, what is the same thing, that each country behaves like a single rational consumer.* This restriction eliminates the possibility of multiple equilibria and, with it, ensures the validity of the H.O. theorem.†

The Physical Definition

The proof of the H.O. theorem in terms of the physical definition of relative factor abundance is slightly more involved, for here, in addition to the international identity of production functions, it is necessary to assume the international similarity of consumption patterns. At the same time, one may regard the physical definition as the only acceptable definition of inter-country factor abundance. It may be argued that proving the H.O. theorem in terms of the price definition borders on truism because the autarky factor prices themselves, when the theorem is valid, are different because commodity prices are different. Furthermore, the starting-point should not begin with factor prices because the latter are determined through a complicated interaction of many economic forces, like demand and supply, and not by physical factor endowments, alone, so that the price and the physical definition may run counter to each under some circumstances. A more objective definition, it appears, would take into account the availability of factor supplies in physical amounts.

At the outset, we assume that community preferences internationally are not only similar but also homothetic, so that in each country the income elasticity of demand for each commodity (η_j) is identically equal to unity. Under these conditions, there exists a unique relation between the overall K/L ratio (k) and the commodity-price ratio (p), as established in the previous chapter. If factor-intensity reversals are ruled out, this relationship is depicted in Fig. 3.8, which replicates Figs. 2.6 and 2.7 from the previous chapter. The first quadrant of Fig. 3.8 depicts the case where $k_2 > k_1$ and the relation between k and p in both countries is given by the negatively inclined curve SS; the second quadrant on the other hand represents the case where $k_2 < k_1$ so that the

† Some of the autarky equilibria will be unstable. However, the absence of unstable autarky equilibria is not sufficient to ensure the general validity of the H.O. theorem. Since income distribution in the H.O. model varies with the variations in commodity prices, there are numerous autarky equilibria, not all of which are unstable. In particular, there may be more than one stable autarky equilibrium. For further details on these points, see Inada [4] and Kemp [6].

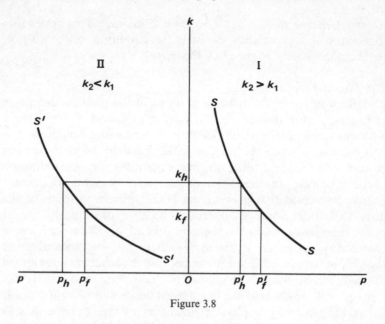

Figure 3.8

relationship between k and p is given by the positively inclined curve $S'S'$; k_h is placed above k_f to show that the home country is capital-abundant relative to the foreign country. In order to prove the H.O. theorem, we wish to derive relations (3.9) and (3.10) from the physical definition described by the relation (3.8). The autarky price configurations corresponding to this factor-abundance specification are given by

$$(1) \quad k_2 < k_1 \quad \text{and} \quad p_h > p_f$$
$$\text{and} \quad (2) \quad k_2 > k_1 \quad \text{and} \quad p'_h < p'_f$$

which accord exactly with expressions (3.9) and (3.10), respectively. This proves the H.O. theorem in terms of the physical definition.

An alternative proof of the H.O. theorem in terms of the physical definition turns out to be more rewarding. We can establish the theorem in exactly the same manner as we demonstrated the validity of the Ricardian theorem in terms of Fig. 3.4. Consider Fig. 3.9, where FF' is the foreign transformation curve, U_f is its community indifference curve, S_f is its self-sufficiency equilibrium point and AB reflects its autarky price ratio. Suppose now that

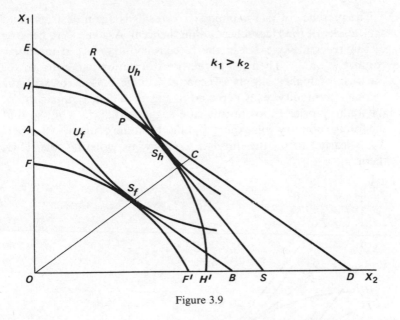

Figure 3.9

there is an increase in the supply of capital alone and that $k_1 > k_2$. The transformation curve then shifts out to HH' which lies outside FF' at all production points, showing that greater output of one or both goods can be produced with the help of increased factor supply. However, since X_1 is capital-intensive relative to X_2, and the factor with the expanded supply is capital, the outward shift of the transformation curve is biased towards the capital-intensive good. Let us now suppose that HH' belongs to the home country which has been assumed to be relatively capital-abundant. At the price ratio given by the slope of DE (parallel to AB) the home production point is given by P, but its consumption point is given by C. Proceeding in the same manner as we did while discussing Fig. 3.4, we can argue that the home self-sufficiency equilibrium will be given by a point like S_h, with an autarky price ratio given by the slope of, say, RS. Since RS is steeper than AB,

$$p_h > p_f$$

which in turn ensures that the home country will export X_1 and import X_2 in accordance with the dictates of the H.O. theorem.

The presence of factor-intensity reversals is again destructive of the validity of the Heckscher–Ohlin theorem. Assume that, because of this reversal, $k_1 > k_2$ in the foreign country, but in the home country $k_1 < k_2$. Then the home transformation curve drawn for the case of higher supply of capital will be biased towards the second commodity, as is depicted in Fig. 3.10. The comparison of the autarky price ratios in this case suggests that $p_f > p_h$, so that the foreign country will export X_1 and the home country will export X_2. Clearly, then, the foreign country is violating the H.O. theorem.

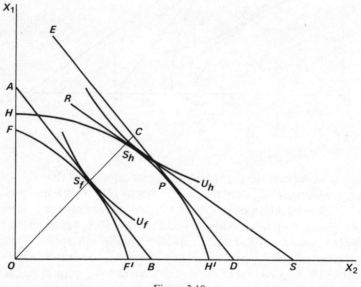

Figure 3.10

The Role of Demand

Demand conditions assume the most significant role in the derivation of the H.O. theorem in terms of the physical definition. We have already seen that international similarity of taste patterns is crucial to the validity of the theorem. To see the significance of this assumption, all we have to do is to conceive that each country (or one country alone) has a strong preference for the consumption of the commodity that is intensive in the use of its relatively abundant factor. Going back to Fig. 3.9, let us suppose that the home consumption pattern is strongly biased towards the first good. Then at the price ratio reflected by DE (and AB), the home consumption point would lie on DE to the left of C; but so long as this consumption point lies between P and C, it is easy to see that the point S_h would lie on HH' to the right of P, so that the H.O. theorem would continue to hold. However, if the home consumption point at the commodity-price ratio reflected by DE lies to the left of P, the point S_h would lie on HH' to the left of P, and the relationship between the autarky price ratios would be reversed, so that the H.O. theorem would not hold. Thus, in the absence of international similarity of consumption patterns, the H.O. theorem may not be valid even if all other requirements are satisfied. As argued before, for the intercountry similarity of consumption patterns it is not sufficient that the community preferences be identical; it is also necessary that in each country they be homothetic. The significance of this desideratum in the case where national incomes differ has been demonstrated by Romney Robinson [12]. The tenor of his argument is quite simple. If the community preference map of each country is identical but not homothetic, the income elasticities of demand for the goods differ, but the countries will still consume the two goods in the same proportion at a given commodity-price ratio if the national incomes are the same everywhere. Otherwise the proportion in which the two goods are consumed by each country at any price ratio will differ even if their community indifference curves are non-intersecting; and this, as we have seen above, could seriously compromise the validity of the Heckscher–Ohlin theorem.

3.5 A Comparison

In the last two sections we have examined in detail the Ricardian and the Heckscher–Ohlin theories explaining a country's pattern of trade. This places us in a strong position to combine and collate the various issues involved in the establishment of the two theorems.

Perhaps the only similarity between the two theories consists in the obvious fact that both tend to explain the basis of trade in terms of international disparities in comparative costs. Otherwise the two theories are poles apart, because of the following points of difference:

1. The Ricardian theory relies on international differences in production functions in order to explain the causality of international trade, whereas the H.O. theorem explicitly assumes the international similarity of production functions.
2. The original Ricardian formulation assumed the existence of a single factor of production, and this along with the presence of constant returns to scale ensured the constancy of unit costs along the transformation curve. By contrast, the H.O. theorem postulates two productive factors, and this along with the inter-commodity dissimilarity of production functions gives rise to increasing unit costs along the transformation curve. Another implication of this difference is that demand conditions play a much more important role in the H.O. logic, expounded in terms of any definition of relative factor abundance, and as a consequence necessitate much more stringent restrictions than those needed in the Ricardian world.
3. As a result of the difference enumerated above, the introduction of trade in the Ricardian model leads the trading partners to complete specialisation, whereas in the H.O. framework trade may or may not result in complete specialisation, as will be clear from a glance at Fig. 3.7.

These, then, are some of the substantive differences, as far as the positive aspects are concerned, that exist between the Ricardian and the H.O. simulations of the world economy. These points perhaps conceal some of the similarities that can be shown to exist when the two theorems are applied to the 'normative' analysis of international trade. For instance, in terms of both frameworks it is possible to show that free trade is beneficial. A detailed exploration of these points is, however, beyond the domain of this chapter.

3.6   Equilibrium in International Trade

The next important question, after a country's pattern of trade has been determined, concerns the characteristics of equilibrium in international trade. Here we assume that there is no interference in the free inter-country flow of commodities and that returns to scale are constant. Equilibrium in international trade simply signifies a situation where the value of a country's exports equals the value of its imports and the commodity prices thus obtained furnish the equilibrium terms of trade. In order to facilitate comprehension of how this equilibrium is reached, it is necessary to derive what is well known as a country's offer curve, which may be defined simply as the locus in two-dimensional space of various quantities of a commodity offered by a country in exchange for the varying offers of another commodity by its trading partner. Because it simultaneously indicates the export supply that reciprocates for the import demand, the offer curve is also called the reciprocal demand curve.

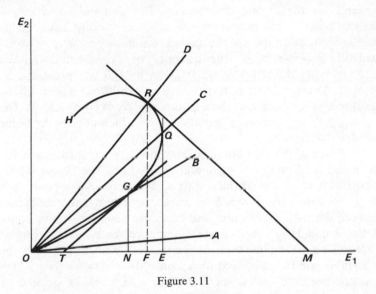

Figure 3.11

The derivation of a country's offer curve proceeds as follows. Consider Fig. 3.11, where the home country's exports of the first commodity, given by $E_1 = X_1 - D_1$, are measured along the abscissa and its imports of the second commodity, given by $E_2 = D_2 - X_2$, are measured along the ordinate. The slope of any ray through the origin represents the ratio between the international prices of exportables and importables. For example, the slope of OA furnishes, from the home country's viewpoint, a certain ratio between the export price and the import price, and as the ray from the origin becomes steeper, the terms of trade become more favourable to the home country. Now at a certain price ratio the home country is in self-sufficiency equilibrium, that is to say, its consumption and production points lie identically on its transformation curve. Suppose such a price ratio is indicated by the ray OA; clearly, the starting-point of the offer curve is the origin, where no trade occurs. At another price ratio, reflected by the slope of OB, the home country produces more but consumes less of the first commodity and at the same time produces less and consumes more of the second commodity. Thus at this new price ratio the home country faces excess supply of the first commodity and excess demand for the second commodity. The demand–supply equilibrium requires the export of the first commodity equal to its excess supply and import of the second commodity equal to its excess demand. Suppose, then, the quantity of exports and imports accompanying the terms of trade given by OB is represented by point G. At other levels of terms of trade exhibited respectively by the slopes of OC and OD these points are given by Q and R. The locus of all such 'exchange' points is OH, which depicts the home country's offer curve.

The shape of the offer curve is determined by the transformation curve and the community's preference function. The export supply is positively related to its relative price, but only up to a point such as Q, because export supply is an excess supply, the difference between domestic production and domestic demand. The response of the demand for exportables to improvements in the terms of trade (which is the same thing as the rise in the relative price of the exportable good) can be split into a pure substitution effect, which is always negative, and an income effect, which may be positive or negative. In the case of non-inferior goods the rise in income resulting from an improvement in the terms of trade tends to raise the domestic demand for the exportable good, and if this effect is very pronounced, the export supply could decline as a result of the rise in its relative price. Such a possibility is depicted by the RQ segment of the offer curve. In the extreme case it is possible that the offer curve may bend backwards, as shown by the HR segment of the offer curve. But this would in turn imply that the imported commodity is a Giffen good, for as a result of a decline in its relative price the home consumers would be consuming less of it.

A question related to the shape of the offer curve concerns the elasticity of demand for imports by the home country (a_h), where by definition $a_h = -(dE_2/dp)(p/E_2)$ and where $p = p_2/p_1 = E_1/E_2$, so that†

$$a_h = -[dE_2/d(E_1/E_2)](E_1/E_2^2) = \frac{-E_1 dE_2}{E_2 dE_1 - E_1 dE_2}$$

$$= \frac{-dE_2/dE_1}{(E_2/E_1) - (dE_2/dE_1)}$$

after differentiation. Now dE_2/dE_1 is the slope of the offer curve at any point, say G, and equals GN/TN, and $(E_2/E_1) = GN/ON$, so that $a_h = ON/OT > 1$, because, as may be observed, the offer curve has a positive slope at G. Similarly, at Q where the offer curve has just begun to change its slope, $a_h - 1$, and at R where the offer curve is negatively inclined, $a_h = OF/OM < 1$.

In a similar fashion, one can construct the offer curve of the foreign country. The volume and the terms of trade in equilibrium are determined by the point of intersection between the two countries' offer curves, OH and OF, as depicted in Fig. 3.12 where the equilibrium terms of trade are indicated by the slope of OE, and where the home country exports OQ amount of the first commodity in exchange for EQ amount of the second commodity from the foreign country.

Stability of Equilibrium
How is one to ensure that the international trade equilibrium schematised in Fig. 3.12 is stable? For example, if the home offer curve was given by OH' instead of OH, there would be three points of intersection and hence three possible equilibria, E, E' and E''. However, it can be shown that equilibrium at E is unstable if the offer curves are given by OF and OH', but stable if the home offer curve is given by OH. The demonstration consists in differentiating the balance-of-payments (B) equation

$$B = E_1 - pE_2$$

† Since each point on the offer curve represents by definition a certain level of export supply or import demand, at every point $p_2 E_2 = p_1 E_1$. However, the latter equality should not be misconstrued as the equilibrium condition at this point. It merely suggests what a country is willing to import in return for some exports at certain terms of trade. The equality becomes an equilibrium condition only when one country's import demand is exactly matched by the other country's willingness to meet that demand at certain terms of trade.

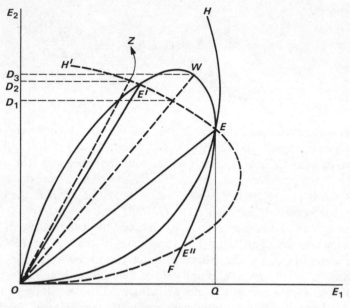

Figure 3.12

with respect to p and in observing that the stability of equilibrium requires that an improvement in a country's terms of trade, which is equivalent to a decline (rise) in the relative price of importables (exportables) in the foreign trade market, must lead to a deficit in its balance of payments, that is, $dB/dp > 0$. Carrying out the differentiation of B with respect to p yields

$$\frac{dB}{dp} = \frac{dE_1}{dp} - p\frac{dE_2}{dp} - E_2.$$

If, initially, trade is in balance, so that $B = 0$,

$$\frac{dB}{dp} = E_2\left[\frac{p}{E_1}\cdot\frac{dE_1}{dp} - \frac{p}{E_2}\frac{dE_2}{dp} - 1\right] = E_2(a_f + a_h - 1)$$

where $E_2 > 0$, and a_f and a_h are respectively the foreign and home elasticities of demand for imports. Evidently, stability is ensured if $a_f + a_h > 1$, that is, if the sum of the two elasticities of import demand exceeds unity.† Reverting to Fig. 3.12, it is now easy to see

† Quite frequently, this condition is referred to as the Marshall–Lerner condition for stability.

why E is unstable and E' and E'' stable when the two offer curves are given by OF and OH'. For example, with E', if the terms of trade shift in favour of the home country from OE' to OZ, its balance of payments runs into a deficit of D_1D_2 in terms of the imported commodity, which in turn means that $dB/dp > 0$. However, with E, a similar favourable shift in the home country's terms of trade to OW brings about a balance-of-payments surplus of D_1D_3, so that $dB/dp < 0$. Here, then, the equilibrium is unstable. The stability of E'' can be established analogously. This analysis simply echoes Marshall's view [8] that an unstable equilibrium point must be flanked by points of stable equilibria, and that the number of equilibrium points must be odd. It follows then that a unique (single intersection) equilibrium must be stable.

It is possible to derive the stability condition in terms of only one commodity and in the process obtain more information. Since the export of a commodity by one country must in equilibrium equal the import demand of the other country,

$$E_1 = E_{1f} \quad \text{and} \quad E_2 = E_{2f}$$

where E_{1f} and E_{2f} are respectively the quantities imported and exported by the foreign country. The balance of payments in terms of one commodity can be written as

$$B = E_1 - E_{1f} = (X_1 - D_1) - (D_{1f} - X_{1f})$$
$$= (X_1 + X_{1f}) - (D_1 + D_{1f}) = x_1 - d_1$$

where x_1 and d_1 are respectively the world supply and demand for the first commodity. Any discrepancy between x_1 and d_1 causes disequilibrium and sets into motion changes in the terms of trade. We are interested in finding conditions which cure this situation of disequilibrium. Stability in terms of the world market of the first commodity requires that $dB/dp < 0$, that is, a rise in the world relative price of the first commodity causes an excess supply, or a rise in B, and conversely. Differentiating B and remembering that with initial trade equilibrium $x_1 = d_1$, we get

$$\frac{dB}{dp} = -(b_1 + c_1)\frac{x_1}{p}$$

where $b_1 = -(p/x_1)(dx_1/dp)$ and $c_1 = (p/d_1)(dd_1/dp)$ are respectively the elasticities of world supply and demand for the first commodity. Similarly,

$$B = (D_2 + D_{2f}) - (X_2 + X_{2f}) = -(x_2 - d_2)$$

and

$$\frac{dB}{dp} = -(b_2 + c_2)\frac{x_2}{p}$$

where $b_2 = (p/x_2)(dx_2/dp)$ and $c_2 = -(p/d_2)(dd_2/dp)$. Stability conditions expressed in terms of the second commodity again require that $dB/dp < 0$, that is, a fall in the world relative price of the second commodity must lead to a situation of excess demand, and vice versa. It may be observed that, in the absence of decreasing costs and Giffen goods, $dB/dp < 0$ in terms of both markets. However, if either the opportunity costs are decreasing or the goods are of the Giffen variety, the equilibrium may be unstable. It is interesting to observe that, in the presence of positively sloped supply curves, the necessary condition for instability is that the commodities be Giffen goods. Unless otherwise specified, the equilibrium point will be assumed to be stable.

Equilibrium in the Ricardian World

In the Ricardian simulation of the world where unit costs are constant, the mechanism of attaining equilibrium and the stability conditions remain the same, except that the shapes of the offer curves differ. Instead of the smooth curves depicted in Figs. 3.11 and 3.12, the offer curves in the Ricardian economy contain a kink at the point of complete specialisation. This is pictured in Fig. 3.13, where the home and the foreign offer curves exhibit kinks at K and

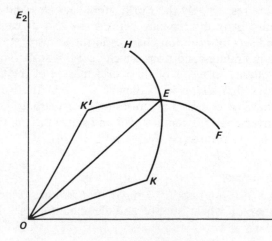

Figure 3.13

K' respectively. The existence of these kinks is attributable to the fact that, until the point of complete specialisation, each country can satisfy the additional demand for its exportables by just shifting its production point without any increase in the price of the exportable good. However, after complete specialisation has been attained, further increases in export surplus call forth a decrease in local demand and hence a rise in the price of the exportable good. In other words, after the attainment of complete specialisation, the offer curves assume the shape and properties of those depicted before, so that the equilibrium is reached at E, the point of intersection between the two offer curves.

Factor-Price Equalisation
One striking property of the Heckscher–Ohlin model is that under certain conditions factor prices in the free trade equilibrium get completely equalised in the trading countries. Despite undertones of unrealism, the so-called factor-price equalisation theorem has held remarkable fascination with trade theorists, if only because the theorem is in fact valid under some admittedly stringent conditions. Although the controversy over the theorem has raged for more than twenty years, the underlying logic of the theorem is very simple.

We have already shown that in a two-commodity, two-factor, constant returns to scale model, there is a unique relationship between the commodity-price ratio and the wage/rental ratio, provided factor intensities are non-reversible and both commodities are produced. Now under free trade and the absence of transport costs there prevails only one commodity-price ratio in the trading countries, so that if production functions are internationally similar, there will be only one wage/rental ratio (ω) prevailing in both countries, which in turn implies that each commodity will utilise the same capital/labour ratio everywhere. It follows then that the marginal product and hence real reward of each factor must under free trade be the same in both countries.

It is thus seen that the underlying logic of the factor-price equilisation theorem is very simple. Yet the long controversy that this theorem has sparked belies this impression. There are two issues here, which, in view of the earlier debate, deserve examination in detail. What are the roles played by (i) incomplete specialisation and (ii) the non-reversibility of factor intensities in the attainment

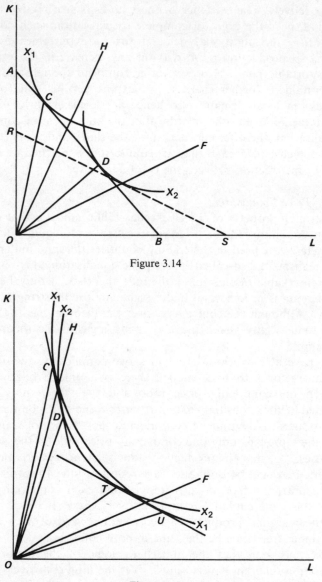

Figure 3.14

Figure 3.15

of international factor-price equalisation? A satisfactory answer
to this question requires recourse to Figs. 3.14 and 3.15.

Consider any equilibrium international price ratio. By the normalisation rule, such units of traded quantities can be selected as yield the unit price ratio. If at this unit price ratio both commodities are to be produced in a country, then two conditions must simultaneously be satisfied. First, there must exist an isocost line tangential to the unit isoquants of both commodities,† and second, the overall capital/labour ratio must lie between the capital/labour ratios of each commodity.‡ All this is depicted in Fig. 3.14, where the isocost line *AB* is tangential to the unit isoquants X_1 and X_2 at *C* and *D* respectively, and where *OH* is the endowment ray, the slope of which indicates the overall capital/labour ratio in the home country. Rays *OC* and *OD* form what Chipman [2] calls the 'cone of diversification', which in the diagram is given by the cone *COD*. Thus if the endowment ray *OH* lies within the cone of diversification, as it clearly does in Fig. 3.14, then at the wage/rental ratio reflected by the slope of *AB* both commodities are produced and both factors can be shown to be fully employed.

Let us now introduce the endowment ray of the labour-abundant foreign country, *OF*. If *OF* lies within the cone of diversification, there will be incomplete specialisation in both countries, the cone of diversification will coincide, and factor prices will be the same. If *OF* lies on *OD*, factor prices will still be similar internationally, although the foreign country will be specialised completely in the production of the labour-intensive commodity X_2. However, if *OF* lies outside the cone *COD*, as it does in the diagram, not only will the foreign country be completely specialised in X_2, but factor rewards will also be dissimilar. This is because the wage/rental ratio required to effect full employment in the foreign country will be given by the slope of the isocost line *RS*, which is different from the wage/rental ratio prevailing in the home country.

What if the relationship between *p* and ω is not unique, that is, what if the factor intensities are reversible as in Fig. 3.15, where, because of multiple intersections of the isoquants, two isocost lines are shown to be tangential to the unit isoquants, giving rise to two

† For the sake of illustration, suppose that the isocost line is tangential only to one unit isoquant and that the other unit isoquant lies above it. Evidently, then, only one commodity will be produced, because the unit cost of the other commodity exceeds its price.

‡ This was established in section 2.2 of the previous chapter.

cones of diversification, *COD* and *TOU*. Clearly, then, if both the endowment rays lie in one of the two cones, factor-price equalisation is inevitable. However, if they lie in different cones, equalisation is impossible in spite of the prevalence of incomplete specialisation in both countries. With *OH* flanked by *COD* and *OF* by *TOU*, one can see that the isocost lines in the two countries possess different slopes and hence reflect unequal wage/rental ratios. *Thus we conclude that the necessary and sufficient condition for the validity of the factor-price equalisation theorem, among others, is that the two endowment rays lie within or coincide with the same cone of diversification, irrespective of whether or not the factor intensities are reversible.* In other words, the unique relationship between p and ω is neither necessary nor sufficient for factor-price equalisation; nor is incomplete specialisation in any country a necessary condition.†

What is the effect of international trade on factor rewards in the event of the violation of this condition? There is no categorical answer to this question, except in the case where factor intensities are not reversible and the autarky equilibria are unique, which is, of course, one of the sufficient conditions for the validity of the Heckscher–Ohlin theorem. The introduction of trade then at least moves the international factor prices closer together than before the opening of the trade. If factor intensities are reversible, this effect is indeterminate. As shown by Johnson [5], the answer is determined in part by the number of intersections between the unit isoquants, whether two, three, or more and whether this number is odd or even.

Arbitrary Number of Commodities and Factors
A good deal of the literature in trade theory is concerned with the validity of the factor-price equalisation theorem in the realistic case where there are more than two commodities and two factors. An illuminating discussion of this issue has been provided by Chipman [2] and Kemp [6] among many others. It turns out that if the other sufficient conditions upholding the Heckscher–Ohlin theorem are maintained, the general rule for equalisation established

† Suppose the endowment ray of the home country coincides with *OC* and that of the foreign country coincides with *OD* in Figs. 3.14 or 3.15. Then both countries will be completely specialised but factor-price equalisation will still prevail, for the wage/rental ratio in each country will be given by the slope of *AB*.

above applies regardless of the number of commodities and factors. Suppose that there are r factors and n commodities, something of which is produced in the world, though not necessarily in each country. Given a vector of n world equilibrium commodity prices, what are the conditions which will ensure that each of r factors of production receives the same reward in each country?

As before, given the price vector, commodity units can be so chosen that all price ratios will be equal to unity. Corresponding to these unit product-price ratios, we can define n unit isoproduct surfaces, which may or may not possess a common tangent isocost plane. If a common tangent plane does not exist, factor-price equalisation, as before, is impossible. If such a plane exists, equalisation is possible but not necessary. For factor prices to be equalised internationally, it is necessary that the endowment ray of each country lie within the cone of diversification specified by n points of tangency. For otherwise the relative factor prices associated with the common tangent plane may not be consistent with the full employment of all factors.

What about the uniqueness of the common tangent plane? In the two-by-two case, this uniqueness implies the non-reversal of factor intensities. In the n by r case, where it may be extremely difficult, if not impossible, to define relative factor intensities, one of the necessary conditions for uniqueness is that $n = r$. If $n \neq r$, uniqueness is impossible, for then the number of equations does not match the number of unknowns. However, we have shown in the two-by-two case that uniqueness is not a necessary condition for the international equalisation of factor rewards. This is also true with the n-by-r case. *All that is necessary and sufficient to ensure the equalisation of factor prices in the two countries is that each country's endowment ray be flanked by the cone of diversification defined by the points of tangency between the common tangent isocost plane and the unit isoproduct surfaces.* This rule applies to all cases defined by $n \gtreqless r$.

REFERENCES

[1] Bhagwati, J., 'The Proofs of the Theorems on Comparative Advantage', *Economic Journal*, LXXVII (Mar 1967) 75–83.
[2] Chipman, J. S., 'A Survey of the Theory of International Trade: Part 3, The Modern Theory', *Econometrica*, XXXIV (Jan 1966) 18–76.

[3] Heckscher, E. F., 'The Effect of Foreign Trade on the Distribution of Income', in *Readings in the Theory of International Trade*, ed. H. S. Ellis and L. A. Metzler (Philadelphia: Blakiston, 1949).

[4] Inada, K., 'A Note on the Heckscher–Ohlin Theorem', *Economic Record*, XLIII (Mar 1967) 88–96.

[5] Johnson H. G., 'Factor Endowments, International Trade and Factor Prices', *Manchester School of Economic and Social Studies*, XXV (Sep 1957) 270–83.

[6] Kemp, M. C., *The Pure Theory of International Trade* (Englewood Cliffs, N.J.: Prentice-Hall, 1964).

[7] Leontief, W. W., 'Domestic Production and Foreign Trade: The American Capital Position Re-examined', *Proceedings of the American Philosophical Society*, XCVII (Sep 1953) 332–49.

[8] Marshall, A., *The Pure Theory of Foreign Trade* (London: London School of Economics and Political Science, 1949).

[9] Mill, J. S., *Principles of Political Economy with Some of their Applications to Social Philosophy*, 3rd ed. (London: Parker & Co., 1852).

[10] Ohlin, B., *Interregional and International Trade* (Cambridge, Mass.: Harvard U.P., 1933).

[11] Ricardo, D., *On the Principles of Political Economy and Taxation* (London: John Murray, 1817).

[12] Robinson, R., 'Factor Proportions and Comparative Advantage', *Quarterly Journal of Economics*, LXX (May 1956) 169–92.

4 Gains from Trade

The theory of gains from trade is almost as old as economics itself. Early contributions in trade theory were motivated by the desire to demonstrate the speciousness of protectionist policies advocated by the Mercantilist School. Adam Smith was among the first to point out the beneficial effects of international trade because it provided expanded opportunities for 'division of labour', or for what the modern writers call 'specialisation'.

In this chapter we are interested in a rigorous demonstration and evaluation of some of the welfare propositions that have been advanced by various economists under the standard assumptions which are necessary to ensure the existence of the Paretian optimum, at least within each trading country. Such cases where Pareto optimality conditions cannot be satisfied will be examined in subsequent chapters.

The first prerequisite in any discussion of welfare propositions calls for a prior agreement on the welfare criterion to be used in evaluating the merits of the suggested policy devices. Unfortunately, here we have to traverse very slippery grounds because of the nature of the analysis itself. For the introduction of trade is bound to cause a change in commodity prices, and, from the Stolper–Samuelson theorem established in Chapter 2, we know that some factors will lose and some will gain. On what basis then can we say that the community as a whole is better off in one situation than in the other? Furthermore, what type of income distribution is desirable and, maybe, socially acceptable?

The discussion on this question in welfare economics is voluminous, and we shall not explore its subtleties and intricacies, if only because no satisfactory technique commanding universal concurrence has as yet been devised. Some progress, of course, has been achieved by the discovery of what is now familiar as the compensation principle. According to this principle, a policy change is recommendable if, in the new situation, gainers can more than compensate the losers, so that everyone can be better off than before. The question of whether the compensation should actually take place is an ethical one for which the economist has no pronouncement. The important point is that some 'desired' type of income distribution can always be maintained if the state is ready to adopt a policy of lump-sum transfers. In this spirit we assume throughout our analysis of the gains from trade the existence of a community welfare function which is a function of the quantities of various products consumed by the community and which possesses properties that are parallel to individual utility functions.† Under this approach the desired level of income distribution becomes inherent in the choice of the utility function. Most of the assumptions made in Chapter 2 are retained, except that, in the interest of generality, we assume any arbitrary number of commodities and factors of production. Thus production functions are still assumed to be homogeneous of the first degree, all goods are non-inferior and factors are fully employed and inelastically supplied. The supply curves for all commodities are upward-sloping; all markets are perfect and factors of production are fully mobile internally but immobile between countries;‡ furthermore, unless otherwise specified, the country under analysis is assumed to be a small country. This last assumption implies that international prices are unaffected by the policies followed by the country under question, simply because the trade volume of this country constitutes a tiny fraction of the total volume of world trade in any commodity. The foreign offer curve in the two-good setting then becomes a ray from the origin, so that whatever the position of the home offer curve, the terms of trade are unaltered.

Under this setting the economy can be described by the following equations:

$$U = U(D_1, D_2, D_3, \ldots, D_n) \qquad (4.1)$$

$$X_i = F_i(K_i, L_i, N_i) \quad (i = 1, 2, \ldots, n) \qquad (4.2)$$

† The exact conditions under which the community utility function enjoys the properties of the individual utility functions have been established by Samuelson [11].

‡ This assumption is not necessary and will be relaxed in the chapter on international investment. Furthermore, the assumption of inelastic factor supplies is made only for simplifying the exposition.

$$a_1 = pa_2 = p_3a_3 = \ldots p_na_n \tag{4.3}$$

$$b_1 = pb_2 = p_3b_3 = \ldots p_nb_n \tag{4.4}$$

$$e_1 = pe_2 = p_3e_3 = \ldots p_ne_n \tag{4.5}$$

$$K_1 + K_2 + K_3 \ldots + K_n = K \tag{4.6}$$

$$L_1 + L_2 + L_3 \ldots + L_n = L \tag{4.7}$$

$$N_1 + N_2 + N_3 \ldots + N_n = N \tag{4.8}$$

and

$$X_1 + pX_2 + p_3X_3 + \ldots p_nX_n = D_1 + pD_2 + p_3D_3 + \ldots p_nD_n \tag{4.9}$$

where U = utility, D = demand, X = output, K_i, L_i and N_i are respectively the factors of production – capital, labour and land – used in the production of the ith commodity, a, b and e are respectively the marginal productivities of capital, labour and land, and the subscript i denotes the ith commodity.† The price of each commodity is expressed in terms of the first. Thus p is the world price of the second commodity in terms of the first, p_3 is the world price of the third commodity in terms of the first, and similarly for $p_4, p_5, \ldots, p_n$. The community's utility function is described by (4.1), its production functions by (4.2), and its full-employment relations by (4.6)–(4.8). Under perfect competition, the value of the marginal product of each factor is the same in all industries. This equilibrium situation is described by (4.3)–(4.5), where factor prices are expressed in terms of the first commodity. Equation (4.9) states the economy's budget constraint in terms of foreign prices, namely, the value of production expressed in terms of the first commodity equals the value of consumption. In the absence of trade, $D = X$, whereas in the presence of international trade the demand for some commodities differs from their local supplies. Note that it is not necessary that all goods be traded; it is sufficient if at least two are. For non-traded goods, D_j and X_j simply cancel out from (4.9), where j denotes the jth non-traded commodity ($j \leq n-2$).

† For the sake of expository convenience only three factors are explicitly shown in the production function. However, the number of factors, as we shall see later, is immaterial.

In the two-good framework, we demonstrated that (dX_1/dX_2) $= -p$, or $dX_1 + pdX_2 = 0$. In the general setting, we can show that

$$dX_1 + pdX_2 + p_3dX_3 + \ldots p_ndX_n = 0.\dagger \qquad (4.10)$$

4.1   The Optimality of Free Trade

To begin with, we demonstrate that under the stipulated conditions free trade is the optimal policy, where the criterion for optimality is the maximisation of social welfare. Although several protagonists of this view can be found in the eighteenth and nineteenth centuries, the first rigorous demonstration of the theorem was provided by Samuelson in 1939 [10]. Free trade is defined as a situation where the local and the world prices of all traded goods are the same, assuming, of course, the absence of transport costs. Our method of analysis in proving this theorem is this. We seek an expression for the change in welfare resulting from a slight deviation from the initial situation of *laissez-faire*. If this expression is non-zero, then an increase in welfare could be secured by introducing a suitable policy; otherwise the initial free trade situation is optimal.

Differentiating (4.1) totally, we obtain

$$dU = U_1 \left[dD_1 + \frac{U_2}{U_1} dD_2 + \frac{U_3}{U_1} dD_3 + \ldots \frac{U_n}{U_1} dD_n \right] \quad (4.11)$$

where $U_i = \partial U/\partial D_i$ is the marginal utility of the ith commodity.

† For simplicity, we derive this expression for the three-good, three-factor case; the extension to arbitrary numbers of goods and factors, not necessarily equal, follows the same procedure.

Differentiating (4.2) totally, we have

$$dX_i = a_i dK_i + b_i dL_i + e_i dN_i.$$

Similarly, from (4.6)–(4.8),

$$dK_1 + dK_2 + dK_3 = dL_1 + dL_2 + dL_3 = dN_1 + dN_2 + dN_3 = 0$$

because K, L and N are all inelastically supplied. Taking this and (4.3)–(4.5) into account, the expression for dX_1 can be written as

$$
\begin{aligned}
dX_1 = a_1 dK_1 + b_1 dL_1 + e_1 dN_1 &= -p[a_2(dK_2 + dK_3) + b_2(dL_2 + dL_3) \\
&\quad + e_2(dN_2 + dN_3)] \\
&= -p\left[dX_2 + \frac{p_3}{p}(a_3 dK_3 + b_3 dL_3 + e_3 dN_3) \right] \\
&= -p\left[dX_2 + \frac{p_3}{p} dX_3 \right].
\end{aligned}
$$

Hence $dX_1 + pdX_2 + p_3dX_3 = 0$.

Assuming the absence of satiation in consumption, $U_i > 0$. Since $U_2/U_1 = p$, $U_3/U_1 = p_3$ and so on, (4.11) becomes

$$dU = U_1(dD_1 + pdD_2 + p_3dD_3 + \ldots p_ndD_n). \qquad (4.12)$$

Under the small country assumption, $p, p_3, \ldots, p_n$ are all given. Therefore, from (4.9),

$$dX_1 + pdX_2 + \ldots p_ndX_n = dD_1 + pdD_2 + \ldots p_ndD_n \qquad (4.13)$$

which from (4.10) equals zero. Hence $dU = 0$ under the initial situation of *laissez-faire*. In other words, no other policy can lead to an improvement in welfare. Stated differently, *free trade is the optimal policy*.

When the country in question is not small, but is large enough to influence world prices by manipulating the volume of its trade, that is, when the country possesses monopoly power in international trade,† the optimality of free trade cannot be established, but, as Kemp [7] has shown, free trade still turns out to be superior to no trade, a situation where the state intervention is so high that no commodity can be imported and hence exported. The economic explanation of the superiority of free trade over no trade is this. By restricting its trade, the country enjoying monopoly power in trade can cause an improvement in its terms of trade and thus secure higher welfare. This will be rigorously established in the next chapter. But when trade is completely prohibited, this benefit evaporates, because there are no longer any foreign terms of trade. Hence the complete prohibition of trade leads merely to a mis-allocation of resources without any compensating benefits. In what follows, we retain the small country assumption and assume that the international prices are unaffected by the home country's commercial policy.

A geometrical demonstration of the optimality of free trade turns out to be very rewarding in terms of clarity and exposition. Let us assume that the home country produces only two commodities, X_1 and X_2, each utilising two factors in the production process. In other words, we are reverting to the transformation curve geometry that

† Note that this situation does not imply monopoly or imperfect competition at home.

we have worked with in previous chapters. Consider Fig. 4.1, where HH' is the home country's transformation curve and the slope of FP reflects the exogenously given free trade terms of trade, so that the production point is given by P.

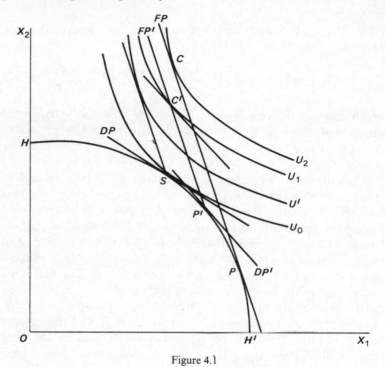

Figure 4.1

In demonstrating the superiority of free trade over no trade, it is not necessary to show just how this FP line is determined. Whether the country in question is a price-taker or possesses monopoly power in trade, the availability (or the consumption possibility) frontier under free trade is given by the foreign price line, because now the country has the choice to select any consumption point along FP. Without trade, however, the availability frontier is given by the transformation curve HH'. Since the free trade availability frontier lies uniformly outside the no-trade frontier (except for the border-line case at P), the consumption bundle available with free international exchange of goods is superior to the one attainable in the absence of trade. Note that, in arriving at this result, we have not made use of the small country assumption. It is a relatively simple matter now to demonstrate that the community welfare under free trade is superior to the one without trade.

As before, we assume that the home country imports the second commodity, so that its social indifference curve lies at C on FP to the north-west of P, with the level of welfare in free trade given by U_2. Now suppose trade is completely restricted by means of, say, a prohibitive tariff which raises the domestic price of the importable good to such an extent that its local consumption falls and is entirely satisfied by the increased local production. At this tariff, nothing need be imported and hence exported. In the diagram, DP indicates the tariff-inclusive domestic-price ratio, self-sufficiency equilibrium is at S and the level of welfare is at U_0 which lies below the free trade level, U_2. Hence free trade is necessarily superior to no trade.

The total gain in welfare resulting from the introduction of free trade can be divided into two components. First, the switch from no trade to free trade enables the consumers to consume the importable good at lower relative prices, and this results in what Johnson [6] calls the 'consumption gain'. This gain arises purely from the international exchange of goods and does not take into account any secondary change in welfare which may occur owing to the change in the production point. In terms of Fig. 4.1, the consumption gain is given by the improvement in welfare from U_0 to U'. Second, the switch from no-trade to free trade prices calls for a shift in the production point. Any gain arising from this shift is termed by Johnson the 'production gain'. In Fig. 4.1 this gain is given by the improvement in welfare from U' to U_2. Thus the total change in welfare resulting from the introduction of free trade is the sum of the consumption and the production gains.

Next, we show that for a small country free trade is necessarily superior to restricted trade, which may be effected by a consumption tax on the importable, or a production subsidy to the importable, or a non-prohibitive tariff. Actually, free trade can be shown to be superior to any kind of trade intervention which may reduce the volume of trade or promote its expansion.

Consider Fig. 4.2, where the incidence of the consumption tax on X_2 is considered. It is important to remember that a consumption tax under the small country assumption changes the commodity-price ratio to the consumer but leaves it unchanged to the producers.

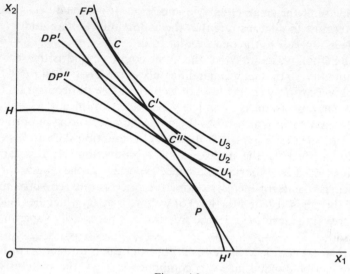

Figure 4.2

Consequently, only the consumption point is affected, and the production point is not. In Fig. 4.2, as a result of the consumption tax the relative price of X_2 facing the consumers is indicated by DP', the consumption point shifts from the initial free trade point C to C', the production point remains unchanged, and welfare declines to U_2.

By contrast, a production subsidy changes the commodity-price ratio to the producers but leaves it unaltered to the consumers. The implications of the production subsidy to the importable good are examined in Fig. 4.3, where the commodity-price ratio facing the producers changes to DP', production shifts to P', consumption to C' which lies on FP' parallel to FP, and welfare declines to U_1.

A tariff, on the other hand, alters the commodity-price ratio to both producers and consumers. In Fig. 4.1 a non-prohibitive tariff results in a domestic-price ratio exhibited by the slope of DP', production shifts to P', consumption to C', and welfare declines to U_1. It may be observed that with a tariff, unlike with a consumption tax or a production subsidy, both the marginal rate of substitution and the marginal rate of transformation are different from their free trade levels. In all three cases we find that free trade is superior to restricted

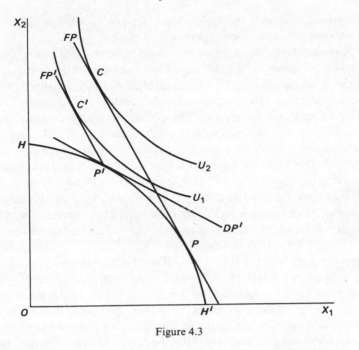

Figure 4.3

trade. Similarly, it can be shown that free trade is superior to any other type of trade intervention, even if it promotes the expansion of trade. *Hence free trade is the optimal policy for a small country.*

4.2 Higher Trade Intervention versus Lower Trade Intervention

From the practical and policy viewpoints, the comparison between various levels of intervention in free trade is the most important. For free trade seldom prevails in the real world, and the architects of commercial policy are frequently faced with the choice between a higher versus a lower tariff or a higher versus a lower consumption tax and so on. Kemp [7] has shown that less restricted trade is superior to more restricted trade, where trade restriction is measured by the divergence between international and local prices. Kemp limits his discussion to tariffs, quotas and exchange controls. However, it can be shown that any form of trade intervention would give rise to his results regardless of whether the intervention is trade-increasing or trade-decreasing. A rigorous demonstration of the proposition *that the higher trade intervention is inferior to the lower level of intervention* is presented below.†

Suppose the home country interferes with the free operation of markets by imposing a tariff or a consumption tax on the imports of the second commodity, or by granting a production subsidy to its local production. Here we assume that all goods entering into the budget constraint are traded. The problems arising from the non-traded goods will be dealt with in a subsequent chapter. Let t, c and s denote respectively the tariff, the consumption tax and the production subsidy. Then the local relative price of the second commodity equals $p(1+t)$ with the tariff, that facing the consumers alone equals $p(1+c)$ with the consumption tax, and the one facing only the producers is given by $p(1+s)$. The marginal rate of substitution between the second and the first commodity must then reflect either the tariff-inclusive price or the price ratio facing the consumers, depending on whether it is the tariff or the consumption tax that is the subject of analysis. Similarly, the marginal rate of transformation must either reflect the tariff-inclusive prices or the price ratio facing the producers. It must be noted, however, that with the production subsidy, for example, the marginal rate of substitution remains unchanged. Suppose now the level of trade intervention is slightly increased. Differentiating the utility function totally with respect to t, we obtain

$$\frac{dU}{dt} = U_1\left[\frac{dD_1}{dt} + p(1+t)\frac{dD_2}{dt} + p_3\frac{dD_3}{dt} + \ldots p_n\frac{dD_n}{dt}\right]. \quad (4.14)$$

Repeating the similar differentiation with respect to c, we get

$$\frac{dU}{dc} = U_1\left[\frac{dD_1}{dc} + p(1+c)\frac{dD_2}{dc} + p_3\frac{dD_3}{dc} + \ldots p_n\frac{dD_n}{dc}\right]. \quad (4.15)$$

With the production subsidy, however,

$$\frac{dU}{ds} = U_1\left[\frac{dD_1}{ds} + p\frac{dD_2}{ds} + p_3\frac{dD_3}{ds} + \ldots p_n\frac{dD_n}{ds}\right]. \quad (4.16)$$

† This is a more general version of Kemp's theorem and is free from any trade-restricting connotations.

Using the budget constraint (4.9), (4.14)–(4.16) can be expressed in terms of the outputs; (4.10) can then be utilised to obtain simple expressions for a change in welfare resulting from a rise in the level of trade intervention. With the consumption tax (4.10) is unaltered; but with the tariff or the production subsidy, p in (4.10) is replaced either by $p(1+t)$ or by $p(1+s)$. Keeping this discussion in view, and following the procedure outlined above, (4.14)–(4.16) can be written as

$$\frac{1}{U_1} \cdot \frac{dU}{dt} = tp\left[\frac{dD_2}{dt} - \frac{dX_2}{dt}\right] = tp\,\frac{dE_2}{dt} \qquad (4.17)$$

$$\frac{1}{U_1} \cdot \frac{dU}{dc} = cp\,\frac{dD_2}{dc} \qquad (4.18)$$

and

$$\frac{1}{U_1} \cdot \frac{dU}{ds} = -sp\,\frac{dX_2}{ds}. \qquad (4.19)$$

In the absence of inferior goods, an increase in t or c leads to a decline in the demand for imports or for the importable commodity, so that both dE_2/dt and dD_2/dc are negative. With the supply curve rising, $dX_2/ds > 0$. It follows from this discussion that all of the dU/dt, dU/dc and dU/ds are negative. In other words, a slight increase in trade intervention of any form culminates in a decline in welfare.† Equations (4.17) and (4.18) also confirm Bhagwati's results [1] that, in the presence of inferior goods, the higher tariff (or consumption tax) may be superior to the lower tariff (or consumption tax).

The geometric presentation of these results in the two-good case follows the technique developed before. In Fig. 4.4 the domestic-price ratio with the initial tariff is indicated by DP. The increase in the tariff shifts it to DP', production moves from P to P', consumption

---

† It is worth noting here that in the discussion of the consumption tax or the production subsidy, it is not necessary to specify whether a commodity is exported or imported. Thus whether D_2 in (4.18) and X_2 in (4.19) are respectively the consumption and the production of the importable or the exportable good is immaterial to the theorem in question. The theorem permits easy extension to other forms of intervention in free trade, including the consumption tax or subsidy and the production tax or subsidy on the exportable good.

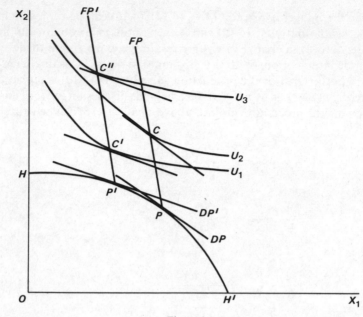

Figure 4.4

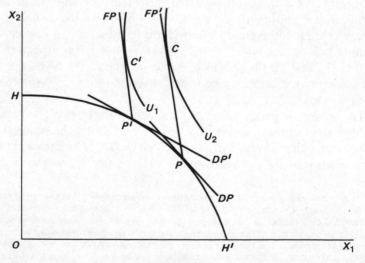

Figure 4.5

from C to C', and welfare declines from U_2 to U_1. Note that the foreign-price ratio is unchanged at FP parallel to FP' and the import volume declines as a result of the shift from C to C'. Note further that if the exportable is the inferior good, the import volume may rise with the tariff, consumption may switch to C'', and welfare may improve to U_3.

In the case of the consumption tax, we can go back to Fig. 4.2. As the consumption tax is raised, the domestic-price ratio facing the consumers shifts from DP' to DP'', consumption from C' to C'', production is unchanged, and welfare declines from U_2 to U_1. However, if the export good is an inferior good, the import demand may increase with the consumption tax and welfare may rise. (This is not shown in the diagram.)

With the production subsidy, the marginal rate of substitution remains unchanged as in Fig. 4.5, where the higher subsidy to X_2 moves production from P to P', consumption shifts from C to C', and welfare declines from U_2 to U_1. It is worth noting perhaps that, since trade takes place along the international prices, each consumption point must lie on FP.

However, the proposition that the higher trade intervention is *necessarily* inferior to the lower level of intervention in the absence of inferior goods does not hold under realistic situations where tariffs or other forms of intervention may exist on the imports of several commodities. The theorem transpires to be valid only when the intervention occurs in the international market for only one commodity. If, say, tariffs exist on the imports of two or more goods, the theorem is no longer tenable.

In this spirit, assume the imports of, say, the third good are also subject to a tariff t_3, so that its local price expressed in terms of the first good is given by $p_3(1+t_3)$. Equation (4.14) is then superseded by

$$\frac{dU}{dt} = U_1\left[\frac{dD_1}{dt}+p(1+t)\frac{dD_2}{dt}+p_3(1+t_3)\frac{dD_3}{dt}+ \ldots p_n\frac{dD_n}{dt}\right] (4.20)$$

and (4.10) by

$$dX_1+p(1+t)dX_2+p_3(1+t_3)dX_3+ \ldots p_ndX_n = 0. \quad (4.21)$$

Differentiating the budget constraint and using (4.21), (4.20) becomes

$$\frac{1}{U_1}\frac{dU}{dt} = tp\frac{dE_2}{dt} + t_3 p_3 \frac{dE_3}{dt} \qquad (4.22)$$

which means that unless $dE_3/dt \leq 0$, the sign of dU/dt is ambiguous. Normally, an increase in the tariff on one commodity, with unchanged tariffs on others, will raise the import demand of the other commodity, so that $dE_3/dt > 0$.† In other words, there is clearly no *a priori* reason to believe that a higher tariff on one imported commodity is inferior to a lower tariff when tariffs on other importables are constant even in the absence of inferior goods. The same result applies to other forms of trade intervention.‡

4.3   Trade Intervention versus No Trade

It is a relatively simple matter now to compare the welfare implications of trade intervention with the complete absence of trade. Kemp [7] subscribes to the view that some trade is superior to no trade at all, whereas Bhagwati [1] has recently demonstrated that this proposition is valid only if trade intervention takes the form of tariffs, quotas or exchange control, policies which give rise to the divergence between foreign prices and domestic prices facing both the consumers and the producers. Stated differently, if the interference in the free inter-country flow of goods is such as to disrupt the equality between foreign prices and the domestic prices facing either the consumers or the producers, but not both, Kemp's theorem that some trade is necessarily superior to no trade may no longer be valid. In other words, Kemp's theorem is tenable only for

---

† This is necessarily true if all imports are gross substitutes.

‡ With the corresponding consumption tax on the third commodity (c_3) already in existence, we have

$$\frac{1}{U_1}\frac{dU}{dc} = cp\frac{dD_2}{dc} + c_3 p_3 \frac{dD_3}{dc}.$$

Similarly, in the presence of a production subsidy to the third commodity (s_3) a rise in the production subsidy to the second good yields

$$\frac{1}{U_1}\frac{dU}{ds} = -\left[sp\frac{dX_2}{ds} + s_3 p_3 \frac{dX_3}{ds} \right].$$

The reader may derive his own conclusions from these expressions.

the class of the trade restrictions he considered, namely tariffs, etc., but it cannot be generalised to all forms of trade intervention.

That the tariff-ridden trade is superior to no trade is apparent from one glance at Fig. 4.1, Where U_1, the level of welfare associated with a non-prohibitive tariff, is superior to U_0, the welfare level prevailing in the presence of a prohibitive tariff. This is a simple demonstration of Kemp's viewpoint.

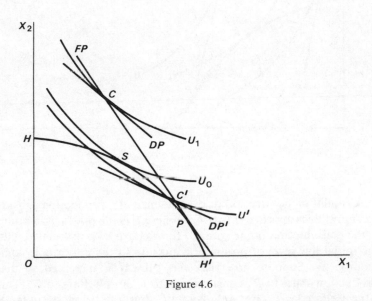

Figure 4.6

A simple counter-example when trade intervention consists in the imposition of a consumption tax on the importable commodity, X_2, is presented in Fig. 4.6. The domestic-price ratio facing the consumers at a low level of the consumption tax is indicated by DP; consumption is at C and welfare at U_1. A higher consumption tax which shifts DP to DP' not only lowers welfare to U' but lowers it below the autarky level U_0. It may be noted that some trade exists even with the higher consumption tax, because the consumption point, C', differs from the production point, P. The necessary condition for this result is that the consumption of importables after the introduction of the consumption tax be less than the corresponding level in autarky.

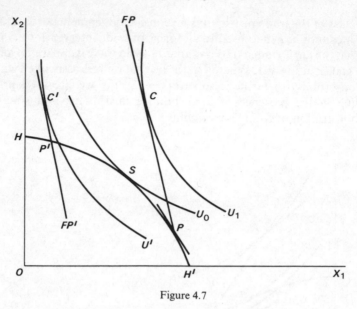

Figure 4.7

A similar demonstration in the presence of a production subsidy to importables appears in Fig. 4.7, where P is the production point, C the consumption point, and U_1 the welfare level associated with the initial low level of production subsidy to the importable commodity, X_2. Suppose now that this subsidy is increased so that production shifts to P', consumption to C' and welfare to U'. This latter welfare level is not only below U_1 but also below the autarky level given by U_0. The necessary condition for this result is that the local production of importables associated with the higher subsidy be higher than the production of importables in autarky.

The trade intervention depicted in these two counter-examples tends to restrict the volume of trade, as can be observed from Figs. 4.6 and 4.7. However, these results are valid even if the intervention tends to expand the quantum of trade. For example, it can be shown that increasing doses of production subsidy to the exportable commodity (X_1) would continue to move the production point towards the H' extremity of the transformation curve, promote the expansion of trade, and lead to a continuous decline in social welfare which, at some level of subsidy, might decline even below the autarkic level.

4.4 Tariffs, Subsidies and Taxes

The analysis of the previous sections can be used to compare the welfare implications of tariffs with those of production subsidies and consumption taxes. Corden [4] has shown that a tariff is inferior to an equivalent production subsidy, where equivalence is defined here in terms of the equality between the protective effect generated by the two policies on the production of the importable commodity. Suppose trade intervention occurs in the world market for the second commodity only. Then the equivalence between the tariff and the subsidy is defined by

$$s = t, \; ds = dt, \quad \text{and} \quad \frac{dX_2}{dt} = \frac{dX_2}{ds}$$

that is to say, we compare those rates of the tariff and the production subsidy which result in an equal rise in the output of the second commodity.

Corden's theorem can be demonstrated simply by subtracting (4.19) from (4.17), so that

$$G = \frac{1}{U_1} \left[\frac{dU}{dt} - \frac{dU}{ds} \right] = p \left[t \frac{dE_2}{dt} + s \frac{dX_2}{ds} \right]$$

$$= p \left[t \left\{ \frac{dD_2}{dt} - \frac{dX_2}{dt} \right\} + s \frac{dX_2}{ds} \right].$$

For Corden's theorem to be valid, $G < 0$. With $s = t$ and $dX_2/dt = dX_2/ds$ under the definition of equivalence,

$$G = tp \frac{dD_2}{dt} < 0$$

in the absence of inferior goods, for then a rise in the tariff rate would lead to a decline in the local demand for the importable good.

The two-commodity case permits a simple geometrical demonstration of this proposition. In Fig. 4.8, P is the initial production point and P' the production point as a result of the introduction of the tariff which results in a domestic-price ratio indicated by the slope of DP. An equivalent production subsidy which also shifts the production point from P to P' furnishes a welfare level of U_s. However, with the tariff, the welfare level is given by U_t, which lies below U_s. Hence the tariff is shown to be inferior to the equivalent production subsidy. The reason is not far to seek. The introduction of a

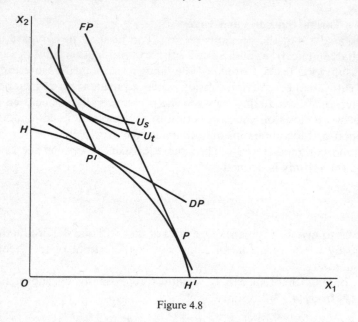

Figure 4.8

tariff creates a divergence between the given foreign-price ratio (*FP*) and the domestic marginal rate of transformation and the marginal rate of substitution, both of which are reflected by *DP* in Fig. 4.8, and hence generates distortions on the production as well as the consumption side. However, a production subsidy gives rise to an equivalent distortion on the production side only, and hence results in a lower decline in welfare than the tariff.

Next, we turn to the relative welfare implication of tariffs and consumption taxes. Bhagwati and Srinivasan [3] have recently shown that a consumption tax is superior to an equivalent tariff when the community's objective is to restrict the consumption of the importable good at a certain level. Equivalence is here defined by $t dD_2/dt = c dD_2/dc$.

Subtracting (4.18) from (4.17), we have

$$Q = \frac{1}{U_1}\left[\frac{dU}{dt} - \frac{dU}{dc}\right] = p\left[t\frac{dE_2}{dt} - c\frac{dD_2}{dc}\right]$$

$$= p\left[t\left\{\frac{dD_2}{dt} - \frac{dX_2}{dt}\right\} - c\frac{dD_2}{dc}\right].$$

For the validity of the theorem by Bhagwati and Srinivasan, we require that $Q < 0$. With $cdD_2/dc = tdD_2/dt$ under the definition of equivalence,

$$Q = -tp\frac{dX_2}{dt} < 0$$

because $dX_2/dt > 0$.

For a geometrical demonstration, consider Fig. 4.9, where welfare with the tariff is given by U_t and that with the equivalent consumption tax by U_c. The equivalence of the two policies is reflected by the fact that c and c_t are horizontally aligned, so that the consumption of X_2 is the same in both cases. Since U_c lies above U_t, the superiority of the consumption tax over the equivalent tariff is clear.

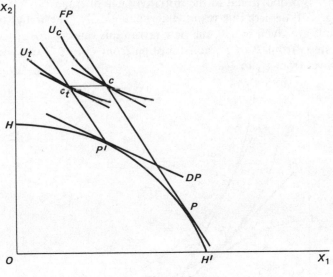

Figure 4.9

4.5 The Terms of Trade and Welfare

The classical economists frequently used the terms of trade as an indicator of a country's gains from trade. A rigorous demonstration to this effect has recently been provided by Krueger and Sonnenschien [8]. Assuming that the country is a price-taker in the world markets, what is the effect of an exogenous change in one foreign-price ratio, with all the other terms of trade remaining constant? For example, suppose there is a change in p alone. Differentiating (4.1) and (4.9) totally with respect to p, using (4.10) and remembering that the initial situation is one of free trade, we obtain

$$\frac{1}{U_1} \frac{dU}{dp} = X_2 - D_2 = -E_2 \qquad (4.23)$$

which is less than zero, because $E_2 > 0$. In other words, there is an inverse relationship between the level of welfare and p. Now a decline in p, with all other foreign prices constant, implies an improvement in the terms of trade and vice versa. Thus we conclude that an improvement in the terms of trade results in an improvement in welfare, and conversely. Note that it was not necessary to assume the absence of non-traded goods. Note further that the change in welfare is proportional to the initial volume of trade.

Fig. 4.10 depicts this result diagrammatically. The initial terms of trade are given by FP, the new favourable ones by FP', production shifts from P to P', consumption from C to C', and welfare improves from U_1 to U_2.

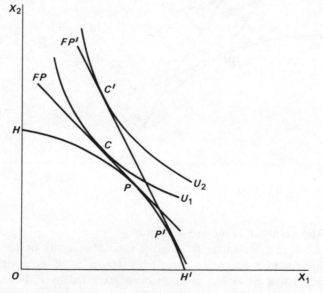

Figure 4.10

The relationship between the terms of trade and welfare is no longer predictable when more than one terms of trade change exogenously. For example, suppose the first commodity is exported and the second and the third are imported. Assume further that both p and p_3 change exogenously. Following the procedure indicated above, we can derive

$$\frac{1}{U_1} \frac{dU}{dp} = -\left[E_2 + E_3 \frac{dp_3}{dp} \right].$$

Now if all terms of trade alter in the same direction, there is no problem. For example, if dp_3 and dp have the same sign, dU/dp is unambiguously negative. The trouble arises when dp_3 and dp have different signs, so that the sign of dU/dp is not predictable in the absence of information concerning the extent of the shifts in each terms of trade and the initial volumes of the two imports. It is worth pointing out, however, that the sign of dU/dp may be indeterminate not because of the presence of more than two traded goods, but because the two terms of trade may not change in the same direction and it may then be impossible to speak of an improvement or a deterioration in the terms of trade.

4.6 Discriminatory Tariffs: The Theory of Customs Union

Some sections of this chapter have been devoted to the examination of welfare implications of tariffs which were implicitly assumed to be non-discriminatory. The analysis presented there can be directly used to explore the welfare implications of discriminatory tariffs, or what is commonly called the customs union. The tariff discrimination can occur in two ways. A country may impose different taxes on the imports of the same commodity from different countries. This is called country discrimination. Alternatively, a country may impose different rates of duty on the imports of different commodities. This is called commodity discrimination. 'The theory of customs union', in Lipsey's words, 'may be defined as that branch of tariff theory which deals with the effects of geographically discriminatory changes in trade barriers' ([9] p. 496). Prior to a pioneering contribution by Viner [12], the theory of customs union attracted little attention, the popular belief being that customs union will always be welfare-increasing simply because it involves reductions in tariffs and hence constitutes a movement towards freer trade. This result was challenged by Viner who demonstrated that customs union can be welfare-decreasing. His demonstration consisted in the introduction of the now familiar concepts of trade diversion and trade creation. In the nature of the anlysis, a customs union involves at least three countries. In this spirit, then, suppose that there are three countries, the home country (H), its union partner, country B, and another country, F, each of which produces two commodities, X_1 and X_2. Suppose further that F is the least-cost and H the highest-cost producer of the second commodity the import of which is prevented by a prohibitive tariff by the home country. If now the home country forms a customs union with B, she will be better off than before. This is an example of trade creation. However, if initially the home tariff was non-prohibitive and non-discriminatory, she would be importing the second commodity from its least-cost producer, country F. Now suppose the home country enters into an agreement with B, and removes its tariff on B's goods such that to the home importers F is no longer the least-cost supplier. This is an example of trade diversion where the home country switches its imports from the lower-cost producer to the higher-cost producer. According to Viner, trade-creating customs union results in a gain in welfare, whereas trade-diverting union leads to a welfare loss. Viner thus assailed the then traditional view that customs union was generally welfare-improving.

Although Viner's logic appears impeccable, his main proposition that trade diversion is necessarily welfare-decreasing is open to some serious objections. Gehrels [5] and Lipsey [9], accusing Viner of ignoring the substitution possibilities on the consumption side, have shown that trade diversion need not lead to a welfare loss when such possibilities are taken into account. Lipsey, however, ignores the substitution effects on the production side, and if such effects are operative, which they must be in the absence of complete specialisation, Viner's proposition may not be valid, even if the substitution effects on the consumption side are ignored. Lipsey's rendition of Viner has recently been challenged by Bhagwati [2] who, while building his case on the substitution possibilities on the production side, argues that the implicit assumption made by Viner in demonstrating the welfare-reducing potential of the trade-diverting union is concerned not with the constancy of the consumption pattern but with the constancy of the level of imports. Bhagwati's interpretation appears all the more plausible when we remember that the absence of substitutability on the consumption side alone is not a sufficient condition for trade diversion to be detrimental to social welfare, provided the specialisation is incomplete. All these points emerge clearly from a formula derived in the following, which determines the conditions under which trade diversion can be shown to be beneficial.

The trade-diverting customs union in general gives rise to two conflicting pulls, one tending to raise and the other tending to lower welfare. On the one hand, the repeal of the tariff by the home country on (potential)† imports from B works for an increase in welfare; on the other hand, the switch from the lower-cost producer to the higher-cost producer, equivalent to a deterioration in the terms of trade, serves to lower welfare. In this spirit we may write

$$U = U(t,p) = U(D_1,D_2)$$

where, as before, t is the non-prohibitive, non-discriminating home tariff on its imports and p is the exogenously determined terms of trade between the home country and its trading partner. In other words, the home welfare becomes a function of concomitant changes in t and p when the home country decides to form a customs union. Furthermore,

$$D_1 + pD_2 = X_1 + pX_2 \quad \text{and} \quad dX_1 + p(1+t)\, dX_2 = 0$$

so that

$$\frac{dD_1}{dt} + p(1+t)\frac{dD_2}{dt} = tp\frac{dE_2}{dt} - E_2\frac{dp}{dt}.$$

Differentiating the utility function totally with respect to t, we have

$$\frac{1}{U_1}\frac{dU}{dt} = \frac{dD_1}{dt} + p(1+t)\frac{dD_2}{dt} = tp\frac{dE_2}{dt} - E_2\frac{dp}{dt}$$

or

$$dU = U_1 pE_2 (E_t - A_p)\, dt \qquad (4.24)$$

† Assuming, of course, that the relative price at which B offers its goods is lower' than the tariff-inclusive price of the goods which the home country imports in the absence of the customs union from country F.

where $E_t = (t/E_2)(dE_2/dt)$ is the total home elasticity of demand for imports with respect to the tariff,† and $A_p = (1/p)(dp/dt)$ is the proportionate change in the terms of trade as the home country switches its trade from country F to country B.‡ The home country's agreement to form a customs union implies that $dt < 0$. The signs of E_t and A_p, however, depend on the characteristics of the union. In general, dp is negative with the trade-creating union, but positive with the trade-diverting union. However, in our example, where the *small* home country initially trades with country F, the trade creation can be represented by a simple removal of the tariff, with no accompanying change in the terms of trade. This suggests that with trade creation $dt < 0$ and $A_p = 0$, but with trade diversion $dt < 0$ and $A_p < 0$. Like the sign of A_p, the sign of E_t is also determined by the nature of the customs union. Under trade creation, where $dp \leq 0$, the repeal of the tariff must lead to a rise in the demand for the importable good. In other words, dE_2/dt and hence E_t are negative.§ Now for the customs union to be beneficial to welfare, $dU > 0$. It is at once clear from (4.24) that with $A_p = 0$ and $E_t < 0$, the trade-creating union leads to a rise in social welfare.

The sign of E_t is not so apparent when the union is of the trade-diverting type. Since $A_p < 0$ under trade diversion, (4.24) suggests that the necessary condition for $dU > 0$ is that $E_t < 0$. Lipsey postulated a Ricardian economy where any amount of profitable trade results in complete specialisation in the exportable good. Under Lipsey's setting, then, $dX_2/dt = 0$, so that dE_2/dt reduces to dD_2/dt. Thus, if E_t is to be negative, dD_2/dt must be negative. This

† E_t is the total home elasticity of demand for imports because it represents the effects on the home demand for imports of a simultaneous change in both t and p that occurs as a result of the formation of customs union.

‡ The reader may be reminded here that the change in the terms of trade resulting from the formation of the trade-diverting union is not because the home country comes to possess natural monopoly power in trade and ceases to be a small country, but because of the exogenous and once-for-all shift in the terms of trade consequent upon the home country's decision to form the union with B and thus accept the given terms at which B will offer its goods.

§ This can be seen immediately by differentiating $E_2 = E_2(t,p)$ totally with respect to t to obtain

$$\frac{dE_2}{dt} = \frac{\partial E_2}{\partial t} + \frac{\partial E_2}{\partial p} \cdot \frac{dp}{dt}$$

so that with $\partial E_2/\partial t < 0$, $\partial E_2/\partial p < 0$ and $dp/dt \geq 0$ under trade creation, dE_2/dt and hence E_t are negative.

means that the formation of the customs union must give rise to a decline in the relative price of the importable good facing the consumers in the home country. For the unfavourable movement in the terms of trade that accompanies the trade-diverting union is bound in the presence of complete specialisation to lower the value of home production (or national income measured in terms of outputs), and this factor tends to make dD_2 negative and dD_2/dt positive. For dD_2 to be positive, therefore, the necessary condition is that the trade-diverting union contribute to a decline in the relative price of the second good. This latter condition can also be seen to be necessary if the trade diversion is ever to lead to an improvement in welfare. For if $dD_2 > 0$ and hence $dD_2/dt < 0$, $E_t < 0$, and if $|E_t| > |A_p|$, dU may be positive. However, if the substitution effects on the consumption side are ignored, dD_2 must be negative, dD_2/dt and hence E_t must be positive, and with $A_p < 0$, dU must be negative.† In other words, if the goods are consumed in a given proportion, trade diversion must lead to a loss in welfare. This is Lipsey's interpretation. He accuses Viner of implicitly assuming that the consumption pattern is constant, for otherwise trade diversion may also contribute to an improvement in welfare.

Lipsey's critique, however, is open to a serious objection in that he postulates a Ricardian economy and ignores the substitution possibilities on the production side. Let us then examine these issues when $dX_2 \neq 0$. If the formation of the union results in a decline in the relative price of the importable good (which, as we have seen

---

† The validity of this argument becomes vivid if we differentiate $D_2 = D_2$ $[p(1+t), Y]$ with respect to t to obtain

$$\frac{dD_2}{dt} = \frac{\partial D_2}{\partial[p(1+t)]} \cdot \frac{dp(1+t)}{dt} + \frac{m_2}{p(1+t)} \cdot \frac{dY}{dt} \qquad \text{(a)}$$

where m_2 is the home marginal propensity to consume the second good. We assume that $0 < m_2 < 1$. Substituting this expression in (4.24), equating $(1/U_1)(dU/dt)$ with dY/dt and remembering that under Lipsey's formulation $dE_2 = dD_2$ and $E_2 = D_2$, we obtain

$$dY\left[1 - \frac{m_2 t}{1+t}\right] = p\left[\frac{t\partial D_2}{\partial[p(1+t)]} \cdot \frac{dp(1+t)}{dt} - D_2 A_p\right] dt.$$

Since $m_2 t/(1+t) < 1$, $dY < 0$ if $\partial D_2/\partial[p(1+t)] = 0$, because under trade diversion A_p and dt are both negative. In other words, if the substitution possibilities are ignored on the consumption side, trade diversion in Lipsey's model leads to a decline in welfare. It may also be seen from expression (a) that with $dY/dt > 0$ when the substitution effect is ignored, $dD_2/dt > 0$; this is what has been intuitively argued in the text.

above, is the necessary condition for trade diversion to be beneficial in Lipsey's formulation), then $dX_2 < 0$, so that $dX_2/dt > 0$. This suggests that $(dE_2/dt) = (dD_2/dt) - (dX_2/dt)$ may be negative even if dD_2/dt is positive. Thus even if the consumption pattern is fixed, so that $dD_2/dt > 0$, E_t (whose sign is the same as that of dE_2/dt) may be negative, and if this effect is sufficiently pronounced, dU from (4.24) will be positive and trade diversion would lead to a rise in welfare. Hence Lipsey's contention that Viner implicitly assumed the constancy of the consumption pattern in order to demonstrate the inferiority of trade diversion is not tenable, because the alleged implicit assumption is not sufficient to rule out the beneficial effects of the trade-diverting union.

Taking these facts into account, Bhagwati [2] has presented a more convincing interpretation of Viner's analysis. He suggests that Viner implicitly assumed the constancy of the level of imports, rather than the constancy of the proportion in which the two goods are consumed, for under the former assumption the detrimental effects of the trade-diverting union can be unambiguously demonstrated. This follows vividly from an examination of (4.24), for if the imports are given, then $E_t = 0$, and with $A_p < 0$ and $dt < 0$, $dU < 0$. In fact, so long as $E_t \geq 0$, Viner's proposition that trade diversion is welfare-decreasing is valid. This serves to confirm Bhagwati's view that, so long as $dE_2 \leq 0$, the trade-diverting union is welfare-decreasing. However, although Bhagwati's condition is weaker than the one suggested by Lipsey, it is not as weak as the one suggested by our formula (4.24). As a matter of fact our formula also furnishes a necessary and sufficient condition for trade diversion to be welfare-increasing. The two factors that determine the welfare implications of customs union are the home elasticity of demand for imports with respect to the tariff, and the extent of the deterioration in her terms of trade resulting from the formation of the customs union. It is clear from (4.24) that $dU \gtreqless 0$ if $|E_t| \lesseqgtr |A_p|$.

These results are illustrated geometrically in Fig. 4.11, where HH' is the home transformation curve, DP indicates the domestic-price ratio, FP represents the terms of trade between the home country and F, and at the initial consumption point given by C, which lies on the social indifference curve U, the marginal rate of substitution equals the domestic-price ratio. Clearly, then, the initial situation describes the case of a non-prohibitive tariff by the home country, but since F is the least-cost producer of the second commodity, she

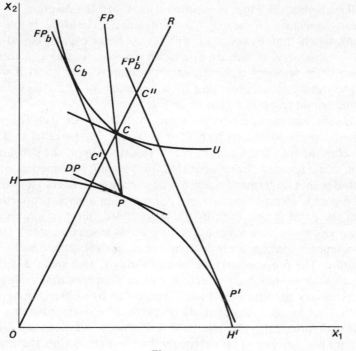

Figure 4.11

is also the only supplier of the home imports. Now suppose the home country and B form a union which eliminates the importation of the F goods by any union partner. The new terms of trade facing the home country are then given by FP_b which are less favourable to the home country than those reflected by FP, ensuring that the union is trade-diverting. If, following Lipsey, we ignore the substitution effects on the consumption side, the consumption point in every case must lie on a given ray from the origin. Suppose this ray is given by OR and the initial consumption point lies on it. If the substitution effect on the production side is also ignored, then the production point remains unchanged in spite of the shift in the relative prices from DP to FP_b. Under this setting, the new consumption point is given by C' which is clearly inferior to the initial point C. This is how Lipsey interprets Viner. He argues that if substitution is allowed on the consumption side, the new consumption point will be different from C' and the level of welfare attained will be higher than that associated with C'. In the diagram, FP_b is drawn tangential to the original indifference curve at C_b. It follows immediately that, by consuming at C_b, the home country can attain the original level of welfare even with the customs union. Clearly, then, if the terms of trade between the home country and B were slightly more favourable than those reflected by FP_b, the customs union would result in a gain in welfare.

If substitution is permitted on the production side also, the production point will shift from P to P' where FP_b' (parallel to FP_b) touches the transformation curve. If substitution on the consumption side is ignored, the new consumption point C'' is superior to the initial point C in terms of welfare. The welfare gain, of course, would be higher if commodities are not consumed in a given proportion. But the point is that even if this is conceded, substitution on the production side itself may nullify Lipsey's assertion that with a given consumption pattern trade diversion necessarily leads to a decline in welfare. The proposition of general validity is that welfare with a trade-diverting union may decline, rise, or even remain unchanged. A necessary condition for trade diversion to be welfare-improving is that the union terms of trade (FP_b) must be intermediate to the domestic-price ratio (DP) and FP. Likewise, a sufficient condition for trade diversion to be detrimental to welfare is that the union terms of trade are such as to raise the output of the importable good or leave it unchanged. This can be verified easily from the diagram.

In the course of our analysis, the reader may have noticed the intimate relationship that exists between the propositions established in this section and Kemp's theorem that a higher tariff is inferior to a lower tariff. We have already shown that Kemp's theorem may not hold when more than one import is subject to the tariff. It follows then that our customs union results also cannot be extended beyond the narrow domain of two traded goods.

REFERENCES

[1] Bhagwati, J., 'The Gains from Trade Once Again', *Oxford Economic Papers*, XX (July 1968) 137–48.
[2] ———, 'Customs Unions and Welfare Improvement', *Economic Journal*, LXXXI (Sept 1971) 580–7.
[3] ———, and Srinivasan, T. N., 'Optimal Intervention to Achieve Non-Economic Objectives', *Review of Economic Studies*, XXXVI (Jan 1969) 27–38.
[4] Corden, W. M., 'Tariffs, Subsidies and the Terms of Trade', *Economica*, XXIV (Aug 1957) 235–42.

[5] Gehrels, F., 'Customs Unions from a Single Country Viewpoint', *Review of Economic Studies*, XXIV (Jan 1956) 61–4.

[6] Johnson, H. G., 'Optimal Intervention in the Presence of Domestic Distortions', in *Trade, Growth and the Balance of Payments* (Chicago: Rand McNally, 1965).

[7] Kemp, M. C., *The Pure Theory of International Trade and Investment* (New Jersey: Prentice-Hall, 1969) chap. 12.

[8] Krueger, A. O., and Sonnenschien, H., 'The Terms of Trade, the Gains from Trade and Price Divergence', *International Economic Review*, VIII (Feb 1967) 121–7.

[9] Lipsey, R., 'The Theory of Customs Unions: A General Survey', *Economic Journal*, LXX (Sep 1960) 496–513.

[10] Samuelson, P. A., 'The Gains from International Trade', *Canadian Journal of Economics and Political Science*, V (May 1939) 195–205.

[11] ——, 'Social Indifference Curves', *Quarterly Journal of Economics*, LXX (Feb 1956) 1–21.

[12] Viner, J., *The Customs Union Issue* (New York: Carnegie Endowment for International Peace, 1950).

5 The Theory of Nominal Tariffs

Because of its long chronicle, the theory of nominal tariffs has earned a pivotal place in the literature on the pure theory of international trade. Historically, the main concern of this theory has been with the implications of tariffs on the imports of final products, and it is only recently that the trade theorist has begun to explore the implications of tariffs on the imports of intermediate products, despite their existence in practice for centuries. The fast-proliferating literature concerned with the latter question is surveyed in the chapter on effective protection; the present chapter is concerned solely with the issues arising from the imposition of nominal tariffs.

The theory of nominal tariffs figured prominently in the classical writings of Mill [11], Marshall [8] and Graham [1, 2], among others, and as with the gains from trade, the theory of tariffs branched directly out of the controversy over free trade and protectionism. Some of the normative aspects of tariffs were examined in the previous chapter. Here our main concern will be with the positive analysis of tariffs. Although the analysis of tariff dates back to the classical tradition, interest in the nominal tariffs has been kept alive by two pioneering contributions, one by Stolper and Samuelson [13] and the other by Metzler [10], whose basic analytical framework was cast in the modern Heckscher–Ohlin mould. The seminal results of Metzler have been more recently challenged by Södersten and Vind [12], but Jones [4] has effectively demonstrated the spurious nature of their critique. The analysis in this chapter parallels closely the illuminating discussion provided by Jones.

5.1 The Analytical Framework
For our analytical tool-kit, we return to the two-country, two-commodity, two-factor framework outlined in Chapters 2 and 3. The generalised multi-commodity, multi-factor framework ex-

pounded in the previous chapter is not suitable for the issues discussed in the present chapter.

In the presence of tariffs, each country's demand for imports depends on the international terms of trade, p, and the level of its tariff. As before, $E_2 = D_2 - X_2$ is the import demand by the home country for the second commodity, and $E_{1f} = D_{1f} - X_{1f}$ is the foreign country's import demand for the first commodity. Let t_h and t_f be the tariffs imposed respectively by the home and the foreign country and let $T_h = (1 + t_h)$ and $T_f = (1 + t_f)$. Then

$$E_2 = E_2(p, T_h) \tag{5.1}$$

and

$$E_{1f} = E_{1f}(p, T_f). \tag{5.2}$$

Furthermore,

$$E_2 = D_2(p_h, Y) - X_2(p_h) \tag{5.3}$$

and

$$E_{1f} = D_{1f}(p_f, Y_f) - X_{1f}(p_f) \tag{5.4}$$

where $p_h = pT_h$ and $p_f = p/T_f$ are respectively the domestic-price ratios in the home and the foreign country, Y is national income in the home country and Y_f is national income in the foreign country. For our purposes it is the change in the real income affecting the change in demand that is relevant. If the change in social welfare is an index of the change in real income, then for the two-commodity case we may write

$$\frac{dU}{U_1} = dY = dD_1 + p_h dD_2 \tag{5.5}$$

which expresses the change in the home real income in terms of the first commodity and is free from any cardinal utility restrictions. Similarly,

$$dY_f = dD_{1f} + p_f dD_{2f}. \tag{5.6}$$

In the absence of tariffs, the budget constraint, as in the previous chapter, simply shows that the value of consumption equals the value of production. However, in the presence of the tariffs the complications arising from the distribution of tariff proceeds have also to be taken into account. Here there are several alternatives.

The government may just collect tariff revenue without spending it, in which case the value of consumption expressed in terms of domestic prices is still restricted by the value of production. On the other hand, the government may spend the tariff proceeds in the manner that private consumers would; this procedure also causes little trouble. However, if the government's spending proclivities are different from those of the private sector, the analysis becomes quite complicated, for now we also have to consider separate demand functions for the government. The simplest way of handling the problem arising from the disposal of tariff proceeds is to assume that the government hands the tariff revenue back to the private sector in a lump-sum fashion. In this last alternative, which is the one adopted here, the value of consumption expressed in terms of domestic prices is restricted by the value of production as well as tariff proceeds.

Another issue that deserves consideration here concerns the way the tariff revenue is to be expressed. For the home country which imports the second commodity, the tariff revenue simply equals

$$p_h E_2 - p E_2 = E_2(p_h - p) = t_h p E_2 = (T_h - 1) p E_2.$$

However, with the foreign country importing the first commodity, which has all along been taken to be the numéraire, the expression is not so simple. If p_{1f} is the absolute local price of the first commodity in the foreign country and p_1 is the corresponding world price, then the tariff proceeds are given by

$$E_{1f}(p_{1f} - p_1) = t_f p_1 E_{1f}$$

but since $p_{1f} = p_1(1 + t_f)$, the tariff revenue equals

$$t_f p_{1f} E_{1f}/(1 + t_f)$$

so that when expressed in terms of the first commodity, the tariff revenue is given by

$$t_f E_{1f}/(1 + t_f) = (T_f - 1)E_{1f}/T_f.$$

With all this information at hand, the budget constraint in each country, expressed in terms of domestic prices, is given by

$$D_1 + p_h D_2 = X_1 + p_h X_2 + (T_h - 1)p E_2 \tag{5.7}$$

and

$$D_{1f} + p_f D_{2f} = X_{1f} + p_f X_{2f} + (T_f - 1)E_{1f}/T_f. \tag{5.8}$$

Finally, the balance-of-payments constraint is described by

$$pE_2 = E_1 \tag{5.9}$$

or

$$pE_{2f} = E_{1f}. \tag{5.10}$$

5.2 Tariffs and the Terms of Trade

In order to determine the effects of tariffs on the terms of trade, the system of equations presented above needs to be differentiated. As before, let an asterisk denote the relative rate of change. The analytical procedure followed here, and actually to be followed later in all questions of comparative statics in trade theory, runs parallel to the procedure employed in the derivation of stability conditions. First, we examine the impact of any change in the system on the excess demand for importables at constant terms of trade. If the change in this excess demand is not zero, then the prices in the system will have to change to restore the equilibrium situation.

In this spirit, differentiate (5.1) and (5.2) totally to obtain

$$E_2^* = -a_h p^* - A_h T_h^* \tag{5.11}$$

and

$$E_{1f}^* = a_f p^* - A_f T_f^* \tag{5.12}$$

where $a_h = -(p/E_2)(\partial E_2/\partial p)$ and $a_f = (p/E_{1f})(\partial E_{1f}/\partial p)$ are the familiar elasticities of demand for imports, $A_h = -(T_h/E_2)(\partial E_2/\partial T_h)$ and $A_f = -(T_f/E_{1f})(\partial E_{1f}/\partial T_f)$ are respectively the home and the foreign elasticities of import demand with respect to the tariff. Equations (5.11) and (5.12) state that the change in each country's demand for imports can be divided into two parts, the first relating to the change in the import demand along the offer curve for a given tariff and the second arising from the shift in the offer curve itself as a result of the change in the tariff for given terms of trade. A_h and A_f have been defined to be non-negative to signify that the rise in the tariff leads to a decline in the demand for imports at a given p. The justification for this will be provided later.

For the sake of simplicity and convenience, let us limit our differentiation to the home country. From (5.3),

$$E_2^* = -e_h p_h^* + \frac{m_h}{p_h E_2} dY - s_h p_h^* \qquad (5.13)$$

where $e_h = -(p_h/E_2)(\partial D_2/\partial p_h)$ describes the substitution effect of a change in p_h on D_2 at a constant real income, $s_h = (p_h/E_2)$ (dX_2/dp_h) captures the substitution effect on the production side as output changes along the transformation curve,† and $m_h = p_h(\partial D_2/\partial Y)$ equals the home marginal propensity to consume the importable good. Differentiating (5.7) and using (5.5), we have

$$dY = -E_2 dp_h + (T_h-1)pdE_2 + (T_h-1)E_2 dp + pE_2 dT_h. \qquad (5.14)$$

Differentiating $p_h = pT_h$, we get

$$dp_h = T_h dp + pdT_h \qquad (5.15)$$

and substituting in (5.14), we obtain

$$dY = -E_2 dp + (T_h-1)pdE_2. \qquad (5.16)$$

Substituting (5.16) and from (5.15) the relation

$$p_h^* = p^\lambda + T_h^*$$

in (5.13), we derive

$$E_2^* = \frac{-p^*[e_h + s_h + m_h/T_h] - T_h^*(s_h + e_h)}{(1 - m_h t_h/T_h)}. \qquad (5.17)$$

The comparison of (5.17) with (5.11) suggests that

$$a_h = \frac{[e_h + s_h + m_h/T_h]}{(1 - m_h t_h/T_h)} \qquad (5.18)$$

---

† The substitution effect on the production side represents the change in the output of the commodities that accompanies the change in commodity prices. This substitution effect depends, among other things, on the elasticities of factor substitution in the sectors. For further discussion of this effect, see Jones [4].

and

$$A_h = \frac{(s_h + e_h)}{(1 - m_h t_h / T_h)}. \tag{5.19}$$

Since $t_h / T_h < 1$, and for non-inferior goods $0 < m_h < 1$, the denominator of (5.17)–(5.19) is positive; (5.18) furnishes the factors that influence the elasticity of demand for imports as we move along the offer curve. In view of the construction of the offer curves described in Chapter 3, it is not surprising to find that a_h depends upon the substitution effects on the consumption and the production side as well as the marginal propensity to consume importables; in addition, the initial level of tariff also affects the magnitude of the elasticity of the import demand. The expression $(1 - m_h t_h / T_h)$, as Jones ([4] p. 420) has observed, is similar to the Keynesian type of multiplier, and this indeed is the case. Let us call the term $1/(1 - m_h t_h / T_h)$ the *tariff multiplier*. If initially there is no tariff, so that $t_h = 0$, this multiplier phenomenon disappears. In the presence of an initial tariff, however, this multiplier, as with the Keynesian system, has a multiple effect. The major difference is that, unlike in the Keynesian framework where the multiple effect is on national income, the multiplier in the barter-trade model has a pronounced effect on the demand for imports. It affects both a_h and A_h. For example, suppose that with a tariff already existing there is an exogeneous increase in p so that E_2 declines. Now a decline in E_2 lowers the community's receipts from the tariff proceeds, which leads to a further decline in the demand for imports, and so on. Therefore the final decline in E_2 equals the initial decline in E_2 multiplied by the tariff multiplier $1/(1 - m_h t_h / T_h)$, and similarly for the term A_h. For a given p and an initial tariff, any further rise in the tariff serves to lower the import demand by raising the domestic production of the importable good as well as by lowering its domestic consumption. These two effects show themselves in the numerator of (5.19). The same multiplier effect appears once again. The initial decline in the import spending serves to lower the community's receipts from the tariff proceeds, which in turn leads to a further decline in the import demand and so on, so that eventually the tariff multiplier again has a cumulative effect on A_h. If initially there is free trade, the introduction of the tariff at constant p causes no change in the national income, as is evident from (5.16) where with $p^* = 0$ and $T_h = 1$, dY also equals zero. It may be noted that this is why there will then be no income term in (5.19).† The income term (m_h) does appear when $t_h > 0$, but only via the tariff multiplier.

Enough has been said on the factors determining the demand for imports by the home country. By following essentially the same, but a little more involved, procedure, an analogous expression for E_{1f}^* can be obtained:‡

$$E_{1f}^* = \frac{p^*[e_f + s_f + m_f/T_f] - T_f^*(e_f + s_f)}{(1 - m_f t_f/T_f)}. \tag{5.20}$$

The next step involves the differentiation of the market adjustment condition (5.9), so that

$$p^* + E_2^* = E_1^*. \tag{5.21}$$

Substituting (5.11) and (5.12) in (5.21) then furnishes

$$p^* = \frac{A_f T_f^* - A_h T_h^*}{a_f + a_h - 1}. \tag{5.22}$$

The denominator of (5.22) is positive for the foreign trade market to be stable. Hence the relationship between p and the tariff is determined by the signs of A_f and A_h, both of which, in the absence of inferior goods or a positive initial tariff, are positive. It is now a simple matter to observe that, unless one of the a_f and a_h is infinity, an increase in the tariff rate by any country results in an improvement in its terms of trade. With the home country, for example, an increase in its tariff ($T_h^* > 0$, $T_f^* = 0$) will lead to a decline in p and hence to a shift in the terms of trade in its favour. This result is attributable to the existence of the negative relationship between E_2 and T_h when terms of trade are kept constant. From (5.17) it is apparent that with $p^* = 0$, $E_2^*/T_h^* < 0$ irrespective of whether initially the tariff is positive or zero, provided, of course, that inferior goods are non-existent. Since at constant terms of trade an increase in the tariff results in a decline in the demand for imports, the international relative price of the importable good must eventually decline to restore equilibrium in the foreign trade market. However, if the exportables are inferior in social consumption or if the im-

---

† This merely confirms our result derived in the previous chapter, that with initial free trade and given terms of trade, *laissez-faire* is the optimal policy.

‡ It may be recalled here that $E_1^* = E_{1f}^*$, and that e_f, s_f and m_f carry the same meaning in the foreign country as their counterparts in the home country.

portables are the luxury goods, so that $m_h > 1$, it is possible that a rise in the tariff rate may lead to a rise in the demand for imports. Evidently, this possibility requires that

$$m_h > \frac{T_h}{t_h} = \frac{1+t_h}{t_h} > 1 \qquad (5.23)$$

which implies that $m_h > 1$ is the necessary condition. It is obvious now that if inequality (5.23) is satisfied, a rise in the rate of tariff will result in a deterioration in the terms of trade of the tariff-raising country.

However, (5.23) is a condition for instability. As Kemp ([5] p. 37) has pointed out, the system's reaction to the increase in the tariff would be explosive. For an increase in the rate of tariff would generate a further rise in imports and hence in tariff proceeds, which in turn would give rise to a further increase in import spending and so on. Hence if we rule out instability, a tariff increase must cause an improvement in the terms of trade. Finally, it may be emphasised again that if initially there is free trade, the introduction of the tariff always results in a shift in the terms of trade in favour of the tariff-imposing country.

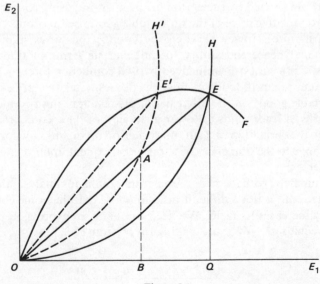

Figure 5.1

Given that tariffs normally result in an improvement in the terms of trade, the improvement will be smaller, the greater are the elasticities of demand for imports in the two countries. In the limiting case where the foreign offer curve is perfectly elastic so that $a_f = \infty$, there will be no change in the terms of trade at all.

The implications of tariffs on the terms of trade are geometrically depicted in Fig. 5.1, where the introduction of the tariff by the home country shifts its offer curve from OH to OH', and as a result the terms of trade move in its favour from the slope of OE to that of OE'. Notice that at initial terms of trade reflected by the slope of OE, the imposition of the tariff results in a decline in the import demand from EQ to AB.

5.3   Tariffs and the Domestic-Price Ratio

The effects of tariffs on the domestic-price ratio are not as straight-forward as may appear at first glance. Indeed, until the pioneering contribution by Metzler [10], the problem was not even considered, it being taken for granted that the imposition of the tariff would raise the domestic-relative price of the importable commodity. In the small country case this is undoubtedly true, for then, with the terms of trade unaffected by the action of the tariff-imposing country, the domestic-relative price of the importable good rises in proportion to the tariff rate. However, when the country possesses monopoly power and hence the ability to influence its terms of trade, the domestic-price ratio is influenced by two conflicting forces. On the one hand, the tariff tends to raise the domestic-relative price of the importable good; on the other hand, the resultant improvement in the terms of trade tends to lower it. In view of these countervailing factors, the derivation of a suitable criterion predicting categorically the change in the domestic-price ratio consequent upon the tariff is in order.

Fortunately, with the necessary paraphernalia for analysis already collected, this is not a difficult task. Suppose that the home country slightly increases its tariff. We need to obtain an expression for p_h^* which equals $p^* + T_h^*$. Substituting for p^* from (5.22), we get

$$p_h^* = \frac{A_f T_f^* + T_h^*(a_f + a_h - 1 - A_h)}{a_f + a_h - 1}.$$

Substituting for a_h and A_h from (5.18) and (5.19), we obtain

$$p_h^* = \frac{A_f T_f^* + T_h^* \left[a_f + \dfrac{m_h}{T_h(1 - m_h t_h/T_h)} - 1 \right]}{a_f + a_h - 1}. \tag{5.24}$$

With no change in the foreign tariff, so that $T_f^* = 0$, and with the denominator of (5.24) positive to ensure the market stability,

$$\frac{p_h^*}{T_h^*} \gtreqless 0, \quad \text{if} \quad a_f + \frac{m_h}{T_h(1 - m_h t_h/T_h)} \gtreqless 1. \tag{5.25}$$

If initially there is free trade, it is clear that $T_h(1 - m_h t_h/T_h) = 1$, so that $p_h^*/T_h^* < 0$ only if $a_f + m_h < 1$. In other words, if the sum of the foreign elasticity of demand for imports and the home marginal propensity to consume importables falls short of unity, the introduction of the tariff will lead to a decline in the domestic-relative price of the importable commodity. This is the Metzler paradox. Alternatively, this paradox requires that a_f be less than the home marginal propensity to consume exportables ($= 1 - m_h$). *Evidently, the necessary condition for the Metzler paradox in the absence of inferior goods is that the foreign import demand be inelastic.* On the other hand, if the importable good is inferior, so that $m_h < 0$, the Metzler paradox may occur even if the foreign import demand is elastic.

The economic explanation of this result requires consideration of changes in each country's local markets at constant local prices that occur as a result of the introduction of the tariff by the home country. The improvement in the terms of trade resulting from the home tariff leads to a rise in the home real income, a part of which at the unchanged p_h goes into the increased demand for the home exportable commodity. This latter effect is reflected by $1 - m_h$. There is no other change in the home country, because with p_h held constant no substitution effects on the production as well as the consumption side take place. In the foreign country, by contrast, the improvement in the terms of trade leads to a decline in the demand for the home exports. This is represented by a_f. If the increase in the home demand for its exportable good, $1 - m_h$, exceeds the decrease in the foreign demand for the same good, given by a_f, there occurs an excess demand for the home exportable good at initial p_h. Equilibrium is

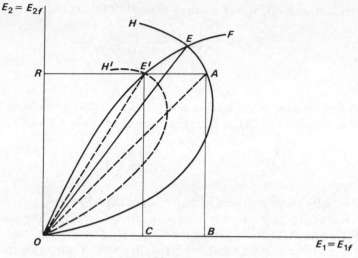

Figure 5.2

eventually restored by a rise in the domestic-relative price of the home exportable good, or, what is the same thing, by a decline in the domestic-relative price of the importable good.

This much has been known since the appearance of Metzler's path-breaking article in 1949. What has not been realised is that there are alternative and perhaps weaker necessary conditions available. All we need to do is to substitute for a_f from (5.20) in (5.25). By analogy to the breakdown of E_2^*, E_{1f}^* can be split into the coefficients of p^* and T_f^* to obtain

$$a_f = \frac{e_f + s_f + m_f/T_f}{1 - m_f t_f/T_f}.$$

The substitution of this in (5.25) yields the following conditions under the initial situation of free trade:

$$\frac{p_h^*}{T_h^*} \gtrless 0, \quad \text{if} \quad e_f + s_f + m_f + m_h \gtrless 1.$$

An interesting condition now suggests itself. Evidently, *the necessary condition for the validity of the Metzler paradox is that the sum of the marginal propensities to consume importables in the two countries falls short of unity.* The condition can alternatively be stated in terms of one good only. *The foreign marginal propensity to consume the first*

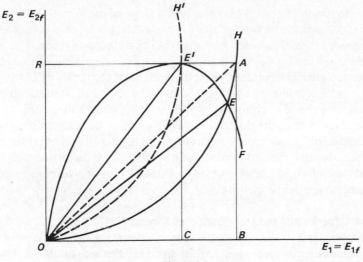

Figure 5.3

commodity (*its importable good*) *should be less than the home marginal propensity to consume the first commodity* (*its exportable good*).

A further comprehension of these results may be gained from an examination of Figs. 5.2 and 5.3. Fig. 5.2 depicts the case of an elastic foreign offer curve, OF, whereas in Fig. 5.3 OF is inelastic in the neighbourhood of initial equilibrium point E and the post-tariff equilibrium point E', which is generated by the intersection of OF and the tariff-distorted home offer curve OH', with the pre-tariff home offer curve given by OH. The post-tariff terms of trade are given by the slope of OE', and at the new international prices the foreign country offers OR of the second good in exchange for RE' of the first commodity; the home producers offer RA, so that the difference AE' is collected by the government as tariff revenue in terms of the first commodity. The rate of tariff in terms of the first commodity therefore is $AE'/E'R$. The domestic-price ratio in the home country can be computed simply from the formula that

$$p(1+t_h) = p_h$$

or

$$\frac{OC}{E'C}\left(1+\frac{AE'}{E'R}\right) = \frac{OC}{E'C}\cdot\frac{AR}{OC} = \frac{OB}{AB}$$

which is nothing but the inverse of the slope of the dotted ray OA. In Fig. 5.2, where the foreign offer curve is shown to be elastic, OA is less steep than OE, which indicates the initial terms of trade. This implies that the domestic-relative price of the exportable commodity has declined as a result of the introduction of the tariff. By contrast, in Fig. 5.3, where the foreign offer curve is drawn inelastic in the neighbourhood of equilibrium points, OA is steeper than OE, showing thereby that the domestic-relative price of the exportable good (importable good) has risen (declined) in the post-tariff equilibrium. Thus the diagrams demonstrate the necessary condition for the validity of the Metzler paradox, namely, that the foreign import demand should be inelastic.

5.4   Tariffs and the Distribution of Income

In Chapter 2 it was established that a rise in the relative price of a commodity resulted in a rise in the real reward of its intensive factor, and we termed this result the Stolper–Samuelson theorem. Although this is essentially the quintessence and more recent interpretation of their results, Stolper and Samuelson formulated their proposition in terms of the effects of tariffs on the internal distribution of income. With the help of the Heckscher–Ohlin framework, where the importable good is intensive in the use of the relatively scarce factor, they were able to demonstrate that protection raises the real and the relative reward of the scarce factor. Prior to the Stolper–Samuelson contribution, the solution to the incidence of tariffs on factor prices had been thwarted by the so-called 'index number' problem. The classical economists, who perhaps because of the intractability of the problem paid little attention to the effects of the tariffs on income distribution, were able to show only that protection benefited a factor relatively, though not necessarily absolutely. By a careful choice of assumptions, Stolper and Samuelson [13] solved this problem by showing that protection necessarily alters the distribution of income in favour of the scarce factor. The tenor of their argument must have been palpable by now. They assumed a small country where a tariff necessarily raises the domestic-relative price of the importable good. Under perfect competition, full employment, constant returns to scale, perfect internal factor mobility and incomplete specialisation, the rise in this relative price would result in a rise in the real reward of the factor intensively employed in the local production of the importable good, and since in the Heckscher–Ohlin model this is the relatively scarce factor, protection necessarily raises the absolute and hence the relative reward of the scarce factor. If the Heckscher–Ohlin theory is not valid, the essential logic of the Stolper–Samuelson argument is not affected. It is still true that the introduction of the tariff would necessarily alter the real reward of *any* factor and hence the complexion of income distribution.

Expressed in this manner, the Stolper–Samuelson theorem is valid even when the tariff-imposing country possesses monopoly power, except in the singular case where, as we have seen above, the foreign elasticity of demand for imports equals the home marginal propensity to consume importables, so that the domestic-price ratio and hence the factor rewards remain unaltered.

Over the years since the appearance of the Stolper–Samuelson contribution, the theorem has been extended to the case of three commodities and three factors by Kemp and Wegge [6], but beyond the three-by-three case the difficulty in defining the factor intensities of the commodities stands in the way of deriving any simple and meaningful conclusions.

5.5 The Optimum Tariff

We have already seen above that the terms of trade move in favour of the tariff-imposing country if the latter possesses monopoly power in trade. This has interesting ramifications for social welfare, which now gets subjected to two conflicting pulls. On the one hand, the improvement in the terms of trade consequent upon the tariff tends to raise social welfare, and this welfare gain increases with the tariff; on the other hand, the introduction of the tariff impairs productive efficiency and tends to lower welfare, and this welfare loss increases with the rise in the tariff. It follows then that there is a certain rate of tariff at which social welfare is maximised. This tariff is the optimum tariff. Evidently, then, free trade is not the optimal policy in the presence of variable terms of trade. The reason can be intuitively appreciated. When the terms of trade are constant, free trade equalises the foreign- and the domestic-price ratios. Under these conditions, the foreign-price ratio (FP) reflects both the foreign marginal rate of transformation ($FMRT$) and the foreign average rate of transformation ($FART$). On the other hand, the domestic-price ratio (DP) under competitive conditions reflects the domestic marginal rate of transformation ($DMRT$) and domestic marginal rate of substitution ($DMRS$). Hence under free trade with constant foreign prices

$$FMRT = FP = DP = DMRT = DMRS$$

which constitutes a necessary condition for welfare maximisation. However, when terms of trade are variable, $FP = FART \neq FMRT$. Hence under free trade $DMRT$ and $DMRS$ are equalised to $FART$ but not to $FMRT$. Only a tariff, which creates a divergence between FP and DP, can effect such equalisation. This solution derives from the general principle that the cure should be directed to where the malady is. Since the violation of the optimality conditions stems from the variability of the terms of trade, the cure should aim at eliminating the distortion occurring in the foreign trade market. Hence any policy which concentrates on the local markets like production or consumption subsidies (taxes) will be inferior to an appropriate tariff in the presence of variable terms of trade.

The optimum tariff formula can be derived simply by equating dY to zero. From the balance-of-payments equilibrium condition, $pdE_2 = dE_{1f} - E_2 dp$. Substituting this in (5.16), we get

$$dY = (T_h - 1)dE_{1f} - T_h E_2 dp.$$

Using (5.12), we then obtain

$$dY = E_{1f}(T_h - 1)(a_f p^* - A_f T_f^*) - T_h p E_2 p^*$$
$$= E_{1f}[p^*\{t_h(a_f - 1) - 1\} - t_h A_f T_f^*]. \qquad (5.26)$$

For the given foreign tariff ($T_f^* = 0$), the home welfare is maximised if the coefficient of p^* equals zero. The optimum tariff (t_0) formula is then given by

$$t_0 = \frac{1}{a_f - 1}. \qquad (5.27)$$

It is evident that the existence of the positive optimum tariff ($t_0 > 0$) requires the foreign offer curve to have some range where $a_f > 1$.

A simple geometric derivation of this formula is depicted in Fig. 5.4, where U_1, U_2, U_3, etc., curves represent the levels of social

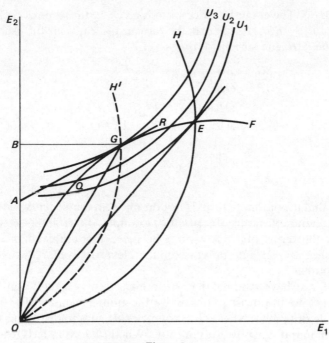

Figure 5.4

welfare in increasing order;† *E* is the point of equilibrium under free trade, and the level of welfare is indicated by U_1 which is tangential at *E* to the free trade terms of trade line *OE*. The introduction of the tariff by the home country moves the trade equilibrium point along the foreign offer curve, *OF*, and as a result trade indifference curves also move upwards. For example, if the level of tariff is such as to make the new home offer curve intersect *OF* at *R*, the trade indifference curve moves to U_2, which, however, does not represent the highest attainable level of welfare, simply because at *R* the trade indifference curve intersects the foreign offer curve, so that the *DMRS* still does not equal *FMRT*, which in turn is reflected by the slope of *OF*. Maximum welfare is achieved when the trade indifference curve, U_3, touches *OF* at *G*, so that *FMRT* is equated

† Here U_1, U_2 and U_3 are trade indifference curves; for further details on their derivation, see Johnson [3].

to *DMRS*. The domestic-price ratio is given by the slope of *OF*, *AG*, so that $p_h = BG/AB$, whereas the foreign-price ratio is furnished by $p = BG/OB$, and since $p_h = p(1 + t_0)$,

$$\frac{BG}{AB} = \frac{BG}{OB}(1 + t_0)$$

$$t_0 = \frac{OB}{AB} - 1 = \frac{OA}{AB} = \frac{OA}{OB - OA}$$

$$= \frac{1}{\dfrac{OB}{OA} - 1} = \frac{1}{a_f - 1}.$$

Note that the optimum tariff is not the one that is associated with the most favourable terms of trade. For example, if *OH'* intersected *OF* at *Q*, the terms of trade would be more favourable than those furnished by *G*; but the concomitant level of welfare would be suboptimal.

So far we have assumed that the foreign country takes no action in response to the tariff imposed by the home country. The more realistic situation is where both countries attempt to reap gains from their monopolistic positions in trade. When each country is ready to retaliate against the imposition of the tariff by the other, the optimum tariff argument loses much of its appeal. Both countries obviously cannot gain by imposing tariffs, and if retaliatory measures continue, both may lose in the final equilibrium. In all likelihood both countries would then be better off with the free trade policy, although, as Johnson [3] has shown, one country under certain conditions may be able to benefit by restricting its trade at the expense of the other even if the latter takes retaliatory measures.

5.6   The Symmetry between the Import and Export Taxes

It has been shown by Lerner [7] that the effects of import and export taxes are symmetrical, provided the government disposal of the tax proceeds is not affected by the type of the tax. This follows directly from the barter character of our model and is readily explained with the help of Fig. 5.2, where, it may be recalled, the imposition of the tariff rate equal to *AE'/RE'* shifted the home offer curve from *OH* to *OH'*. The foreign producers in the case of the home import tax offer *AB* of the second commodity and receive *RE'* of the first, whereas the home producers offer *RA* of the first commodity, the difference AE' being the tariff revenue collected by the government. Let us now consider an export tax imposed at a rate equal to AE'/RE'. The foreign importers now receive RE'', the home exporters offer RA in exchange for AB and the customs revenue in terms of the first commodity again equals AE'. Hence the extent of the shift of OH is the same in both types of taxes. Evidently, then, the terms of trade, imports, exports, domestic production and consumption are the same in both cases; the only difference is that in one case the tax is paid by the importers, whereas in the other it is paid by exporters.

A simple algebraic proof of Lerner's symmetry theorem is given as follows. Let t_e be the export tax imposed by the home country, so that

$$p_h/(1+t_e) = p$$

which is clearly the same as the relative price structure associated with the import tax, namely,

$$p_h = p(1+t_h)$$

given, of course, that $t_h = t_e$. This implies that the home outputs are also the same in both cases. However, the demand for each commodity depends not only on relative prices, but also on real income. Hence for the symmetry theorem it is necessary to show that real incomes are also the same under both taxes. Note that, in the case of the tariff, real income expressed in terms of local prices is given by

$$Y = X_1 + p_h X_2 + t_h p E_2$$

whereas that in the case of the export tax is given by

$$Y_e = X_1 + p_h X_2 + \frac{t_e}{1+t_e} E_1.$$

It is interesting to note that the tariff revenue in the two cases looks different, but is in reality the same. The apparent difference is attributable to the choice of the numéraire. Therefore, after adjusting for the different absolute prices, $t_h p E_2 = t_e E_1/(1+t_e)$. Hence $Y = Y_e$, which, with similar relative price structure, implies that production, consumption and imports are the same under both types of taxes.

REFERENCES

[1] Graham, F. D., 'Some Aspects of Protection Further Considered', *Quarterly Journal of Economics*, XXXIX (Feb 1925) 324–30.

[2] ——, *The Theory of International Values* (Princeton U.P., 1948).

[3] Johnson, H. G., *International Trade and Economic Growth* (London: Allen & Unwin, 1958) chap. ii.

[4] Jones, R. W., 'Tariffs and Trade in General Equilibrium: Comment', *American Economic Review*, LIX (June 1969) 418–24.

[5] Kemp, M. C., *The Pure Theory of International Trade* (Englewood Cliffs, N.J.: Prentice-Hall, 1964).

[6] ——, *The Pure Theory of International Trade and Investment* (Englewood Cliffs, N.J.: Prentice-Hall, 1969).

[7] Lerner, A. P., 'The Symmetry between Import and Export Taxes', *Economica*, III (Aug 1936) 306–13.

[8] Marshall, A., *The Pure Theory of Foreign Trade* (London: London School of Economics and Political Science, 1949).

[9] ——, *Money, Credit, and Commerce* (London: Macmillan, 1923).

[10] Metzler, L. A., 'Tariffs, the Terms of Trade, and the Distribution of National Income', *Journal of Political Economy*, LVII (Feb 1949) 1–29.

[11] Mill, J. S., *Principles of Political Economy* (London: Longmans, Green, 1909).

[12] Södersten, B., and Vind, K., 'Tariffs and Trade in General Equilibrium', *American Economic Review*, LVIII (June 1968) 394–408.

[13] Stolper, W. F., and Samuelson, P. A., 'Protection and Real Wages', *Review of Economic Studies*, IX (Nov 1941) 58–73.

6 Economic Expansion and the Terms of Trade

6.1 Introduction

The analysis of interrelations between economic expansion and the terms of trade cannot boast of a long, uninterrupted history. Here and there one may come across a few scattered references to terms of trade in studies of the incidence of technological innovations on the growing country's net gain from growth in the works of Mill [18], Edgeworth [9], Bastable [2] and Ohlin [19]; of the desirability of the policy of protection in the wake of technical improvements in what is known as the German tariff controversy;† of the celebrated transfer problem sparked primarily by Thornton [22] and Hume [14] and subsequently resurrected by Taussig [21] and Keynes [17] (in the famous debate over the German reparations problem); finally, of the impact of international capital movements featuring in the works of Fanno [10], Iverson [15] and Ohlin [19]. But the avowed application of the tools of general equilibrium analysis to the diagnosis of the behaviour of the terms of trade consequent upon growth is only a post-war phenomenon. Whatever ingenuity the problem of shifts in inter-country commodity prices elicited from the economist in the pre-war era was, with a few exceptions,‡ incidental; it arose not because of an interest in the application of economic theory to the problem of economic development, which itself never figured prominently in neo-classical writings, but was due to the economist's preoccupation with some other issues of current importance wherein considerations of the terms of trade were unavoidable.

Like many other fields of economics, trade theory has welcomed the dent made in it by the theory of economic growth pioneered by

---

† See, for example, Wagner [23] and Dietzel [8].
‡ Mill's work [18] constitutes an important exception.

Sir Roy Harrod.† The evolution of this branch of theory has been further accentuated by two other burning issues: (1) the problem of international liquidity, of which the apprehensions concerning the long-run shortage of dollars in the world markets constituted but one phase, for since 1958 the dollar paucity has turned into the dollar glut; and (2) the question of the secular deterioration in the terms of trade of the countries producing primary products.

Until the middle of the 1950s it was quite fashionable among trade theorists to argue that the dollar difficulties of the post-war period constituted a legacy of the pre-war years; that there was in fact a long-run tendency for the U.S. balance of payments to run into surplus, only to create cumulative difficulties for the non-dollar world. A variety of reasons for the tendency were advanced. Balogh [1] and others took the faster growth of the U.S. productivity than that in other countries as granted, with the result that the increasingly cheaper U.S. exports were displacing the exports of other countries. Hicks [13] suggested, in addition, that innovations in the U.S. tended to be 'import-biased', that is, they were concentrated in those goods which competed with American imports.

So overwhelming was the economist's obsession with the secular shortage of dollars until even the late 1950s that Keynes's sole dissension that 'in the long run more fundamental forces may be at work, . . . tending towards equilibrium', so that 'the chances of the dollar becoming dangerously scarce in the course of the next five to ten years [were] not very high',‡ proved only a distant cry in the wilderness. From the strength of hindsight Keynes once again proved right, although the affirmation of his prophecy came almost a decade after his demise. As of 1950, the U.S. balance of payments has displayed chronic deficits; the entire situation has been so transformed that strong equivocations are now cast in some quarters as to the very stability of the dollar. The post-war international monetary crises, climaxed by the recent Smithsonian accord leading to the

---

† To be sure, Harrod [12] did not address himself to the trade problems arising from growth; but he did succeed in opening new vistas for the trade theorist to explore. His references to growth stemming from technical progress and capital accumulation may be deemed partly responsible for the assiduity with which the economist has engaged himself to unravel the interrelation between growth and the terms of trade.

‡ Quoted from Clement *et al.* ([5] p. 352). The bracketed expression is theirs.

realignment of world currencies in 1971, demonstrate how the strength of the dollar has been steadily eroded over the last twenty-five years.

Similarly, in explaining the ubiquity of abject poverty in the underdeveloped countries, the emphasis placed by Prebisch [20] and others on the deterioration in the terms of trade of countries exporting primary products due to the presence of strong monopolistic elements in advanced Western economies has also turned out to be misplaced. The underdeveloped world has been deriving large intangible gains from trade with the advanced nations, although these benefits, direct or indirect, cannot fully, on account of their complexity, be incorporated in the theorist's abstract model. All that can be conceded in fairness to the adherents of the Prebisch hypothesis is that the distribution of the gains from trade between the underdeveloped and the developed nations may not have been equitable.

These two hypotheses – the secular shortage of the dollar and the secular deterioration of the terms of trade of the underdeveloped areas – have thus transpired to be based on specious arguments. The dramatic investigations and research aroused by these issues have turned out to be their own nemesis. A large section of economists have become disenchanted with these views and doubtful of their empirical validity.

'But', as Corden rightly contends, 'out of the discussion and especially out of Hicks's argument that technical progress in the U.S. is import-biased and that this has an adverse effect on the terms of trade of other countries, has come an advance in theory of lasting value.' ([6], p. 36).

The purpose of this chapter is to survey some of the major issues that have been raised in this field. Our task in this respect is simplified by recalling that some of the equations and results developed in Chapter 2 can be used directly in our analysis here.

6.2   Economic Expansion

For the sake of simplicity and without loss of generality, we assume that only the home country experiences growth, whereas its trading partner, the foreign country, remains stationary. This implies that the foreign offer curve is given, whereas the home offer curve may shift its position in response to economic expansion. For the time being it is immaterial to our analysis just how this economic growth may come about; later we shall have occasion to identify major factors that may account for growth of one type or another.

Let G denote the expansionary (growth) agent. In addition to the terms of trade, each country's import demand should now become a function of the growth agent, but since the foreign country is assumed to be stationary, only the home demand for imports will be related to G. That is, the balance of payments equilibrium equation will now look as follows:

$$E_1(p) - pE_2(p,G) = 0. \qquad (6.1)$$

Differentiating (6.1) totally with respect to G and utilising the fact that in equilibrium $E_2 = E_1/p$, we obtain

$$p\frac{\partial E_2}{\partial G} = \frac{dp}{dG}\left[\frac{dE_1}{dp}\cdot\frac{p}{E_1} - \frac{\partial E_2}{\partial p}\cdot\frac{p}{E_2} - 1\right]E_2$$

$$= \frac{dp}{dG}(a_f + a_h - 1)E_2$$

where a_f and a_h are as defined in the previous chapter. Now commodity units can be so chosen that p is initially equal to unity. The change in the terms of trade consequent upon growth can then be written as

$$\frac{dp}{dG} = \frac{\partial E_2/\partial G}{(a_f + a_h - 1)E_2}. \qquad (6.2)$$

Stability in the foreign trade market demands that $a_f + a_h - 1 > 0$. Since $E_2 > 0$, it follows from (6.2) that $dp/dG \gtreqless 0$ if $\partial E_2/\partial G \gtreqless 0$. In other words, the sign of the change in the terms of trade depends solely on the sign of the change in the home demand for imports. Since $\partial E_2/\partial G$ represents the partial derivative of E_2 with respect to G, and since E_2 is a function only of p and G, the evaluation of the change in the home demand for imports arising from growth must be done at constant terms of trade. The economic rationale behind such evaluation is that in order to determine the impact of growth on the growing country's terms of trade, one first needs to ascertain the impact of growth on the growing country's demand for imports at unchanged terms of trade. This determines the manner in which the home offer curve will shift in response to growth. The terms of trade of the growing country will eventually deteriorate, improve or

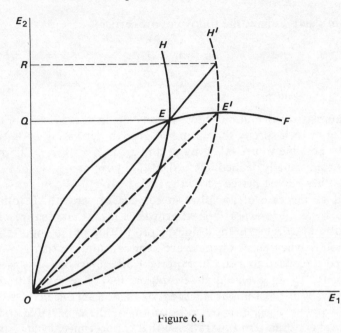

Figure 6.1

remain unchanged depending on whether its demand for imports, at constant terms of trade, has increased, decreased or remained unaltered as a result of growth. For example, in Fig. 6.1 the home offer curve, OH, shifts outwards to OH', the home import demand, at old terms of trade reflected by OE, rises from OQ to OR and, as a consequence, its terms of trade deteriorate to those indicated by the slope of OE' in the new equilibrium. Now

$$E_2 = D_2(p, Y) - X_2(p, G) \tag{6.3}$$

or

$$\frac{\partial E_2}{\partial G} = \frac{\partial D_2}{\partial Y} \cdot \frac{\partial Y}{\partial G} - \frac{\partial X_2}{\partial G} = \frac{\partial Y}{\partial G}(m_h - z_h) \tag{6.4}$$

where $m_h = p\partial D_2/\partial Y = \partial D_2/\partial Y$ is the marginal propensity to consume importables in the home country and $z_h = (\partial X_2/\partial G)/(\partial Y/\partial G)$ measures the rate of change in the output of importable goods as a proportion of the rate of change in income. Let

$$m_1 = \frac{\partial D_1}{\partial Y} \quad \text{and} \quad z_1 = \frac{\partial X_1}{\partial G} \bigg/ \frac{\partial Y}{\partial G}.$$

Then m's and z's have the following properties:

$$m_h + m_1 = 1 \qquad (6.5)$$

$$z_h + z_1 = 1. \qquad (6.6)$$

A number of definitions have sprung up in the contemporary literature which specify the nature of growth depending upon the various possible values taken by z_1 and z_h. If $z_h < 0$, $z_1 > 1$: this case is traditionally defined in Corden's [7] terminology as the case of an 'ultra-export-biased' growth; if $z_h > 1$, $z_1 < 0$: this case is termed as the case of an 'ultra-import-biased' growth. In other words, by an ultra-export-biased growth is meant one that results in an absolute decline in the domestic production of the importable commodity when terms of trade are kept constant, so that growth must perforce lead to a rise in exports if inferior goods are absent and hence to an eventual deterioration in the terms of trade. Similarly, by an ultra-import-biased growth is meant one that results in an absolute decline in the production of the exportable commodity at constant terms of trade, so that exports must decline, and hence in the new equilibrium the terms of trade must improve. It may be noted here that only ultra-biased types of growth admit of determinate results; other types where z_h and z_1 may be positive fractions do not yield any *a priori* conclusions. Substituting (6.4) in (6.2), we obtain

$$\frac{dp}{dG} = \frac{(\partial Y/\partial G)(m_h - z_h)}{E_2(a_f + a_h - 1)}. \qquad (6.7)$$

This last equation furnishes the standard formula which will come to our assistance throughout in determining the effect of growth on the terms of trade. One glance at (6.7) is sufficient to reveal that $dp/dG \gtreqless 0$, if $m_h \gtreqless z_h$.

Matters may be further simplified by observing that, from our assumption of the absence of inferior goods, m_h is only a positive fraction. Thus if z_h happens to assume either a negative value or a value greater than unity, the implications of growth on the terms of trade can be immediately predicted. For example, if z_h comes out to be negative, m_h must exceed z_h, so that the home terms of trade must deteriorate (i.e. its price of imports relative to the price of its exports, p, must rise); if, on the other hand, z_h exceeds or equals unity, it must also exceed m_h, so that p must fall, or to say the same thing in different words, the home terms of trade must improve.

From (6.4) three possibilities emerge, to wit, $m_h \gtreqless z_h$. These are depicted by Fig. 6.2. Growth is represented by an outward shift of the transformation curve from HH' to GG'; changes in the outputs and the demands for X_1 and X_2 are evaluated at unaltered terms of trade, as may be evident from the fact that the pre-growth terms of trade given by FP are the same as those in the post-growth situation given by FP' (FP is parallel to FP'). As a consequence of growth, the production point shifts from P to P'. Now if the consumption point shifts from C to C', that is, if PP' is parallel to CC', z_h equals m_h. The home offer curve does not shift in this case, so that the terms of trade will remain unaltered. If the consumption point moves to anywhere towards the left of C', say $\bar{C}$, z_h falls short of m_h, so that the terms of trade will move against the home country; if to anywhere towards the right of C', say C'', z_h exceeds m_h and the terms of trade will switch in favour of the home country.

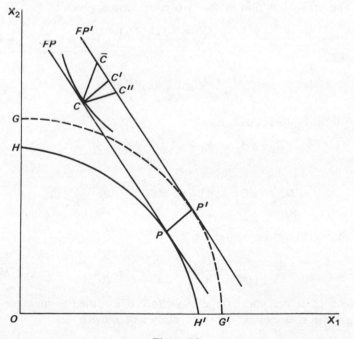

Figure 6.2

6.3 Immiserising Growth

The case in which the terms of trade deteriorate while the foreign country benefits from the home expansion is of special interest. For, as first noted by Edgeworth [9], it suggests the possibility that the home country might find itself in a worse position after growth than before if the worsening in its terms of trade is large enough to wipe out the gain in its output as a result of growth. What needs to be comprehended here is the distinction between growth in the form of expanded output against an increase in its real income. If the terms of trade remain constant, the growth in the home country output will be the same as the growth in its real income; if the terms of trade improve, the rise in the home real income will exceed the rise in its output; if they deteriorate, the rise in the home real income will fall short of the rise in its output, the changes in the home output in all three cases being assessed at constant commodity prices. Is it then possible that the home real income may actually decline as a result of growth? The following criterion for the change in real income will determine the answer.

The utility function in the two-good case is given by

$$U = U(D_1, D_2)$$

so that

$$\frac{1}{U_1} \frac{dU}{dG} = \frac{dD_1}{dG} + p \frac{dD_2}{dG}. \tag{6.8}$$

From the budget constraint

$$D_1 + pD_2 = X_1 + pX_2$$

and

$$\frac{dD_1}{dG} + p \frac{dD_2}{dG} = \frac{dX_1}{dG} + p \frac{dX_2}{dG} + X_2 \frac{dp}{dG} - D_2 \frac{dp}{dG}$$

so that (6.8) can be written as

$$\frac{dY}{dG} = \frac{dX_1}{dG} + p \frac{dX_2}{dG} - E_2 \frac{dp}{dG} \tag{6.9}$$

where, as before, the change in welfare is assumed to measure the change in real income. In the presence of growth

$$X_i = X_i(p, G) \quad \text{where} \quad i = 1, 2$$

so that

$$\frac{dX_1}{dG}+p\,\frac{dX_2}{dG} = \frac{dp}{dG}\left[\frac{\partial X_1}{\partial p}+p\,\frac{\partial X_2}{\partial p}\right]+\frac{\partial X_1}{\partial G}+p\,\frac{\partial X_2}{\partial G}.$$

Remembering that $(\partial X_1/\partial p + p\partial X_2/\partial p) = 0$, (6.9) can be written as

$$\frac{dY}{dG} = \frac{\partial X_1}{\partial G}+p\,\frac{\partial X_2}{\partial G}-E_2\,\frac{dp}{dG}. \tag{6.10}$$

The first two terms in the right-hand side of (6.10) represent the change in the value of production resulting from growth at constant terms of trade, and hence equal $\partial Y/\partial G$. Therefore

$$\frac{dY}{dG} = \frac{\partial Y}{\partial G}-E_2\,\frac{dp}{dG}. \tag{6.11}$$

Substituting for dp/dG from (6.7) we obtain

$$\frac{dY}{dG} = \frac{\partial Y}{\partial G}\left[1-\frac{m_h-z_h}{a_f+a_h-1}\right] \tag{6.12}$$

Since $\partial Y/\partial G > 0$, it is clear from (6.12) that for the home real income to decline as a result of growth

$$m_h-z_h > a_f + a_h - 1$$

or, from (6.6),

$$m_h+z_1 > a_f+a_h. \tag{6.13}$$

In other words, if the sum of the home country's marginal propensity to consume importables and the rate of change in the output of its exportable goods as a proportion of its change in its total output exceeds the sum of the two countries' price elasticities of demand for imports, the home real income will actually decline as a result of economic expansion. The criterion can be further concretised by utilising Slutsky's decomposition of price effects into income effects and substitution effects. A price elasticity of demand can always be written as the sum of a 'compensated' (i.e. pure substitution) elasticity and an income propensity. Let a'_h be the income-compensated elasticity of demand for imports (i.e. an elasticity compensated by changes in income) in the home country; then

$$a_h = a'_h + m_h. \tag{6.14}†$$

Utilising (6.14), inequality (6.13) may be written as

$$z_1 > a_f + a'_h. \tag{6.15}$$

The presentation of the criterion for what Professor Bhagwati [3] calls 'immiserising growth' in the form (6.15) helps in singling out the key factor that may be accountable for the home country's immiserisation due to growth. Evidently, the key factor, given the foreign total elasticity and the home compensated elasticity of demand for imports, lies in the pattern of growth. For if the latter is concentrated heavily in the exportable industry, the value of z_1 may be large enough to satisfy inequality (6.15), in which case the home real income would decline.

This somewhat paradoxical result is illustrated diagrammatically in Fig. 6.3. The level of home welfare in the pre-growth situation is given by the social indifference curve U_1 which lies on line (1); if the terms of trade remain constant after the outward shift of the transformation curve, welfare improves to U_2 which lies on line (2), parallel to line (1), the rise in real income being commensurate with the rise in output; if the terms of trade improve and are indicated by the slope of line (3), home welfare improves further to U_3; finally, if the terms of trade deteriorate, the home welfare declines below U_2, and if the deterioration in the terms of trade is as high as the one reflected by the switch to line (4), welfare declines to U_0 which is actually below the original, pre-growth level of welfare. This is immiserising growth.

---

† Differentiating $E_2 = E_2(p, Y)$ totally with respect to p, we obtain

$$\frac{dE_2}{dp} = \frac{\partial E_2}{\partial p} + \frac{\partial E_2}{\partial Y}\frac{dY}{dp}.$$

But $(\partial E_2/\partial Y) = \partial D_2/\partial Y$ and $dY/dp = -E_2$. Therefore

$$\frac{p}{E_2}\frac{dE_2}{dp} = \frac{p}{E_2}\frac{\partial E_2}{\partial p} - \frac{p\partial D_2}{\partial Y}$$

or

$$a_h = a'_h + m_h.$$

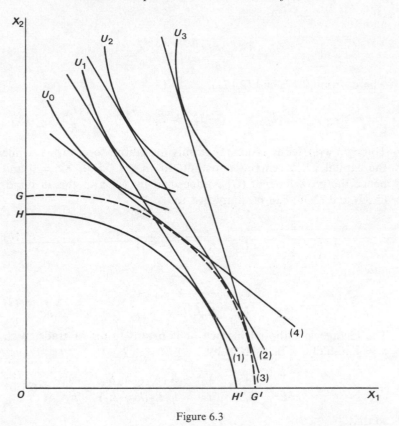

Figure 6.3

6.4 Factor Accumulation

It is high time that we introduced the specific sources of economic expansion. We begin with factor accumulation, whose implications for the closed-economy prices were first explored in the second chapter. The pioneering contribution in this field is credited to Rybczynski, whose theorems have already been expounded. In order to determine the impact of factor accumulation on the terms of trade, we first need to derive the effects of factor growth on the two outputs at constant terms of trade. Such expressions are given by (2.37) and (2.38). Thus

$$X_1^* = \frac{\lambda_{K2} L^* - \lambda_{L2} K^*}{|\lambda|} \tag{2.37}$$

and

$$X_2^* = \frac{\lambda_{L1}K^* - \lambda_{K1}L^*}{|\lambda|} \tag{2.38}$$

where, from (2.17) and (2.17*),

$$|\lambda| = \lambda_{L1}\lambda_{K2} - \lambda_{K1}\lambda_{L2} = \lambda_{L1} - \lambda_{K1} = \lambda_{K2} - \lambda_{L2} = \frac{L_1 L_2}{LK}(k_2 - k_1).$$

To begin with, let us assume that only the labour force grows, while the capital stock remains constant, so that $L^* > 0$, $K^* = 0$ and hence the growth agent (G) is identified by L. With this in mind, (2.37) and (2.38) can be simplified to

$$\frac{\partial X_1}{\partial L} = \frac{X_1 K_2}{L_1 L_2 (k_2 - k_1)} \tag{6.16}$$

and

$$\frac{\partial X_2}{\partial L} = \frac{-X_2 K_1}{L_1 L_2 (k_2 - k_1)}. \tag{6.17}$$

The change in national income at constant terms of trade, with $p = 1$ initially, is then given by

$$\frac{\partial Y}{\partial L} = \frac{\partial X_1}{\partial L} + \frac{\partial X_2}{\partial L} = \frac{X_1 K_2 - X_2 K_1}{L_1 L_2 (k_2 - k_1)} = \frac{w}{p_1} \tag{6.18}†$$

so that

$$\frac{\partial X_2}{\partial L} \bigg/ \frac{\partial Y}{\partial L} = z_L = \frac{X_2 K_1}{X_2 K_1 - X_1 K_2} = \frac{\theta_{K1}}{\theta_{K1} - \theta_{K2}} \tag{6.19}$$

where z_L measures the change in X_2 as a proportion of the change in national income at constant terms of trade. Evidently, the place of z_h in (6.7) is now taken by (z_L). It can be readily seen that z_L is either negative or greater than unity, given of course that factor intensities in the two industries differ to ensure that the denominator of (6.19) is non-zero. For example, if $X_2 K_1 > X_1 K_2$, or $(K_1/X_1) > (K_2/X_2)$,

---

† Solving the two price equations in Chapter 2 and remembering that $p = 1$ initially, we obtain

$$w = \frac{p_1(X_1 K_2 - X_2 K_1)}{L_1 L_2 (k_2 - k_1)}$$

then, with p initially unity, it means that the relative share of capital in the first commodity exceeds that in the second commodity, that is, the first commodity is capital-intensive relative to the second. With the denominator of (6.19) positive, $z_L > 1$; on the other hand, if this denominator is negative, that is, if the first commodity is labour-intensive relative to the second, $z_L < 0$. Thus it is clear that the economic expansion resulting from labour growth alone is ultra-biased. It is ultra-import-biased if the importable good (the second good) is labour-intensive, and ultra-export biased if it is capital-intensive relative to the other commodity. The terms of trade facing the growing home country will eventually improve in the former case but deteriorate in the latter case. The reason follows directly from the Rybczynski theorem, according to which an increase in the supply of labour alone results at constant terms of trade in a rise in the output of the labour-intensive commodity at the expense of the output of the other commodity. Hence if the labour-intensive commodity happens to be the importable good, labour expansion is ultra-import-biased; if the exportable good, it is ultra-export-biased.

Similar results can be obtained if it is capital which is the expanding factor while the labour force remains unchanged. In other words, economic expansion is necessarily ultra-biased if only one factor experiences an increase in supply.

The geometric exposition of the effects of an increase in the supply of one factor on the two outputs at constant commodity prices was presented in Chapter 2 in terms of the box diagram. Here we utilise an alternative diagrammatic technique which turns out to be of great help in the ensuing discussion of technological change.

Consider Fig. 6.4, where AB gives the wage/rental ratio, x_1 and x_2 are the unit isoquants of the two commodities with their points of equilibrium at v and s respectively, and point E indicates the factor-endowment ratio (K/L). For the sake of simplicity, the diagram shows that the aggregate output in the economy equals one unit of the first commodity (Ov) plus one unit of the second commodity (Os), and that since the unit isoquants lie on the same isocost line (AB), the commodity-price ratio equals unity. It is worth pointing out that a good grasp of the way this diagram is drawn is essential for comprehending the present and subsequent analysis. For example, note that the level of the two outputs is ascertained by drawing from E lines parallel to Ok_1 and Ok_2, the slopes of which indicate the capital/labour ratios in the two industries. Point E,

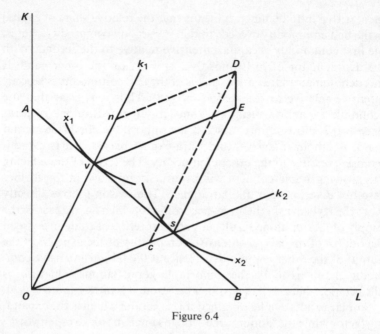

Figure 6.4

which may be construed to have been determined by the summation of the two vectors (Os and Ov), reflect that the economy's factor endowment is fully absorbed by the unit level of output of each commodity.[†]

Now suppose there occurs an increase in the supply of capital alone, such that the factor-endowment point moves vertically from E to D. We seek to explore the direction of change in the two outputs in the new situation, keeping the terms of trade and hence k_1 and k_2 constant. If we draw from D lines parallel to k_1 and k_2 (so that Dn is parallel to k_2 and Dc to k_1), it can be observed that the output of X_1 rises from Ov to On and that of X_2 declines from Os to Oc. This is then an alternative proof of the Rybczynski theorem.

So far we have confined our analysis to those cases where the supply of only one factor increases while the supply of the other factor remains unchanged. The more realistic case is where both factor supplies expand and contribute to a country's economic growth. The effects on the two outputs in the latter situation depend

[†] This is assumed purely for diagrammatic simplicity.

not only on the inter-industry ranking on the basis of factor intensities, but also on the relationship between each industry's capital/labour ratio and the incremental capital/labour ratio, dK/dL. For example, suppose that the first industry is capital-intensive relative to the second, as is the case in Fig. 6.4. In this case $|\lambda| < 0$, so that from (2.37)

$$X_1^* = \frac{\lambda_{L2}L^*[(\lambda_{K2}/\lambda_{L2}) - K^*/L^*]}{|\lambda|} \leq 0$$

only if $\lambda_{K2}/\lambda_{L2} \geq K^*/L^*$, or $k_2 \geq dK/dL$. In other words, if the capital/labour ratio of the labour-intensive commodity (X_2) exceeds the incremental capital/labour ratio, the output of the capital-intensive commodity (X_1) will decline. On the other hand, from (2.38),

$$X_2^* = \frac{\lambda_{L1}L^*[(K^*/L^*) - \lambda_{K1}/\lambda_{L1}]}{|\lambda|} \leq 0$$

only if $K^*/L^* \geq \lambda_{K1}/\lambda_{L1}$, or $dK/dL \geq k_1$. In other words, if the incremental capital/labour ratio exceeds the capital intensity of the capital intensive commodity, the output of the labour-intensive commodity will decline. It follows that, if the incremental capital/labour ratio lies between the capital/labour ratios in the two industries, the output of both commodities will rise. Indeed, if both factors grow at the same rate, both outputs will rise at this rate. This is clear from the fact that, with $K^* = L^*$,

$$X_1^* = X_2^* = L^*$$

because it may be recalled that

$$|\lambda| = \lambda_{K2} - \lambda_{K1} = \lambda_{L1} - \lambda_{K1}.$$

These results will gain further clarification from Fig. 6.5, which is constructed on the same principle as Fig. 6.4. It can be observed that if factor growth follows the growth path sE, parallel to k_1, there will be no change in the output of X_2; this depicts the case where $dK/dL = k_1$. For example, if the factor-endowment point shifts from E to G, the output of X_1 rises from Ov to On, without any change in the output of X_2 (equal to Os). It follows, therefore, that if factor growth were to follow a path steeper than sE, say ER

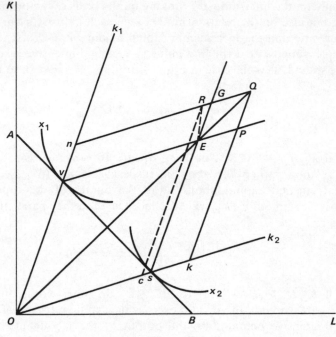

Figure 6.5

(here $dK/dL > k_1$), the output of X_1 would again rise to On, but that of X_2 would decline from Os to Oc. Similarly, it can be easily demonstrated that if factor growth followed the growth path EP (i.e. $dK/dL = k_2$), the output of X_2 would rise without any change in the output of X_1; if it were to follow a path flatter than $vE(dK/dL < k_2)$, the rise in the output of X_2 would be accompanied by a decline in the output of X_1. Finally, if the growth path followed by the factors is OE, that is, if the factor-endowment point shifts from E to Q, the output of both commodities will rise in the same proportion; for the output of X_1 rises to On and that of X_2 to Ok and it can be easily seen that $sk/Os = vn/Ov$.

The impact of growth in both factors on the home terms of trade can be determined as before. It may be observed that only those cases admit of *a priori* conclusions where $dK/dL \geq k_1$, or $k_2 \geq dK/dL$; in other cases results will depend on many additional factors such as the magnitude of the home marginal propensity to consume importables, etc.

6.5 Technological Change

Another major source of economic expansion is the occurrence of technical improvements in one industry or both. Here again the basic groundwork has already been laid in Chapter 2. As usual, we wish to determine the ramifications of technical advance on the two outputs at constant terms of trade, assuming that the other major source of expansion, namely factor supply, is unchanged. This last assumption is made merely to simplify the analysis.

Various types of technical improvements in the Hicksian sense were introduced in Chapter 1. These definitions will now be slightly modified to suit the two-good character of our model. We continue to define neutral technical progress in any commodity as one which leaves the capital/labour ratio of the commodity unchanged at the old wage/rental ratio. However, instead of the labour-using or labour-saving nomenclature that we used earlier, we introduce two different definitions of non-neutral improvements, namely, the 'intensive-factor-using' and the 'intensive-factor-saving' types of technical advance.† In the former case, technical progress in a commodity promotes a relatively larger use of its intensive factor, whereas with the latter the relative use of the intensive factor declines at the original wage/rental ratio. For example, suppose the capital/labour ratio in X_1 declines at the old wage/rental ratio owing to the technical advance. If X_1 is capital-intensive, the technical advance is intensive-factor-saving; if it is labour-intensive, the technical advance is intensive-factor-using.

To be specific, let us assume that technical progress occurs only in one industry, say X_2. Let us now go back to Chapter 2 and rewrite in the following some of the equations presented there:

$$\lambda_{L1}X_1^* + \lambda_{L2}X_2^* = \pi_L + \beta_L(w^* - r^*) \tag{2.23}$$

$$\lambda_{K1}X_1^* + \lambda_{K2}X_2^* = \pi_K - \beta_K(w^* - r^*) \tag{2.24}$$

$$\theta_{L1}w^* + \theta_{K1}r^* = p_1^* \tag{2.25}$$

$$\theta_{L2}w^* + \theta_{K2}r^* = p_2^* + \pi_2 \tag{2.26}$$

where β_L and β_K are positive, and

$$\pi_i = \lambda_{i1}B_{i1}^* + \lambda_{i2}B_{i2}^* \qquad (i = L, K)$$
$$\pi_j = \theta_{Lj}B_{Lj}^* + \theta_{Kj}B_{Kj}^* \qquad (j = 1, 2)$$

† This nomenclature is borrowed from Johnson [16].

and where B_{ij}^* indicates the effect of technical progress on the use of the ith input in the jth output. In rewriting these equations, we have made use of the assumption that $L^* = K^* = \pi_1 = 0$. If the terms of trade are constant, $p_1^* = p_2^* = 0$. Remembering this, and solving (2.25) and (2.26), we obtain

$$w^* = -\frac{\pi_2 \theta_{K1}}{|\theta|} \tag{6.20}$$

$$r^* = \frac{\pi_2 \theta_{L1}}{|\theta|} \tag{6.21}$$

and

$$w^* - r^* = -\frac{\pi_2}{|\theta|}. \tag{6.22}$$

Substituting (6.22) in (2.23) and (2.24), and solving, we obtain

$$X_1^* = \frac{(\lambda_{K2}\pi_L - \lambda_{L2}\pi_K)|\theta| - \pi_2(\lambda_{K2}\beta_L + \lambda_{L2}\beta_K)}{|\lambda||\theta|} \tag{6.23}$$

and

$$X_2^* = \frac{(\lambda_{L1}\pi_K - \lambda_{K1}\pi_L)|\theta| + \pi_2(\lambda_{L1}\beta_K + \lambda_{K1}\beta_L)}{|\lambda||\theta|}. \tag{6.24}$$

In the absence of technical progress in the first commodity, $\pi_L = \lambda_{L2}B_{L2}^*$ and $\pi_K = \lambda_{K2}B_{K2}^*$. Making these substitutions in (6.23) and (6.24), we get

$$X_1^* = \frac{\lambda_{K2}\lambda_{L2}(B_{L2}^* - B_{K2}^*)|\theta| - \pi_2(\lambda_{K2}\beta_L + \lambda_{L2}\beta_K)}{|\lambda||\theta|} \tag{6.25}$$

$$X_2^* = \frac{(\lambda_{L1}\lambda_{K2}B_{K2}^* - \lambda_{K1}\lambda_{L2}B_{L2}^*)|\theta| + \pi_2(\lambda_{L1}\beta_K + \lambda_{K1}\beta_L)}{|\lambda||\theta|}. \tag{6.26}$$

Neutral Technical Progress

A number of results can now be derived from (6.25) and (6.26). Let us first consider the effects of neutral technical progress, which implies that $B_{L2}^* = B_{K2}^*$.† Since $|\lambda|$ and $|\theta|$ have the same sign, $|\lambda||\theta| > 0$. It is immediately clear then that $X_1^* < 0$. The sign of

† The reader is advised to go back to Chapter 2 for verification.

X_2^* is not evident at first glance, but if we substitute for $|\lambda| = \lambda_{L1}\lambda_{K2} - \lambda_{K1}\lambda_{L2}$, (6.26) reduces to

$$X_2^* = B_{K2}^* + \frac{\pi_2(\lambda_{L1}\beta_K + \lambda_{K1}\beta_L)}{|\lambda||\theta|} > 0.$$

Thus we conclude that neutral technical progress is ultra-biased; it raises the output of the industry in which it occurs and lowers the output of the other commodity when terms of trade are kept constant. This result has been derived by many authors, including Bhagwati [4], Corden [7] and Findlay and Grubert [11] among others.

The economic rationale behind this result is not so obvious, but becomes clear when the effects of technical progress in the second industry alone on factor prices are analysed. The neutral improvement in X_2 alone lowers the unit cost of production in X_2, thereby lowering the original commodity-price ratio (p). In order to maintain the previous commodity prices, the price of the factor employed intensively by X_2 should rise and that of the factor employed unintensively by it should fall. Given that labour enters more intensively and capital less intensively in the production of X_2, i.e. $k_2 < k_1$ and $|\theta| < 0$, the wage rate of labour needs to rise whereas the rental of capital needs to fall so as to restore the pre-improvement commodity prices. That this is what happens is clear from (6.20) and (6.21) where, with $|\theta| < 0$, $w^* > 0$ and $r^* < 0$. The rise in the wage/rental ratio induces the substitution of capital for labour in both industries, so that the capital/labour ratio increases in both commodities, which in turn creates a situation of excess demand for capital and an excess supply of labour. To maintain full employment, the output of X_2, the industry which can absorb labour more rapidly, will rise and that of X_1, the industry which is in a better position to release capital, will decline. This is how a Hicks-neutral improvement in any commodity raises the output of the 'progressive' commodity at the expense of the output of the other when terms of trade are kept constant. Clearly, then, neutral technical advance in one commodity alone is ultra-biased, and for this reason it must have definite implications for the terms of trade, a task which, in the light of earlier developments in this chapter, we leave to the reader.

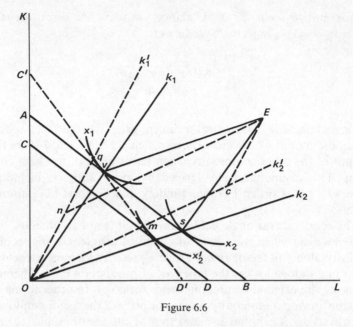

Figure 6.6

The analysis presented above can be clarified further by a resort to simple geometry first developed by Findlay and Grubert [11]. Consider Fig. 6.6, where x_1 and x_2 are our familiar unit isoquants with national income equalling one unit of X_1 (Ov) plus one unit of X_2 (Os), and the factor-endowment ratio is given by E. Recall that the level of output in each industry is determined by drawing Ev parallel to k_2 and Es parallel to k_1. Since the unit isoquants lie on the same isocost line AB, the terms of trade (p) equal unity. Now suppose X_2 comes to enjoy a neutral improvement so that its unit isoquant shifts towards the origin to x'_2, signifying a reduction in its unit cost; k_2 is unaltered at the unchanged wage/rental ratio (AB is parallel to CD) to demonstrate the neutrality of the technical advance. Now since x'_2 lies on an isocost line (CD) below the one (AB) on which lies the unit isoquant of X_1, the commodity-price ratio falls below unity. In order to maintain the previous one-to-one price parity between the two commodities, x'_2 and x_1 should be made to lie on the same isocost line. This is accomplished by drawing $C'D'$ tangential to both x_1 and x'_2 at q and m respectively. It is noteworthy that unit outputs in X_1 and X_2 now become Oq and Om respectively, and that the capital/labour ratio rises in both X_1 and

X_2 to k'_1 and k'_2. The next step, of course, is to draw from E lines parallel to the new factor-intensity rays, so that En is parallel to k'_2 and Ec to k'_1. It may be observed that the output of X_2 rises from its pre-expansion unit level of output (now equal to Om) to Oc, whereas the output of X_1 declines from Oq to On. In other words, neutral technical progress in X_2 is ultra-import-biased. A similar diagram can be constructed to show that a neutral improvement in X_1 alone will be ultra-export-biased.

Intensive-Factor-Saving Technical Progress

Suppose now that the improvement in X_2, the labour-intensive industry, is labour-saving. Evidently, this is a case of intensive-factor-saving technical progress. With technical progress in the second industry tending to bring about a greater saving in the use of labour than capital, $B^*_{L2} > B^*_{K2}$. The implications for X_1 are evident from a glance at (6.25); with $|\theta| < 0$, the output of X_1 declines even more than was the case with the neutral improvement in X_2 alone, for now an additional negative term $|\theta|\lambda_{K2}\lambda_{L2}(B^*_{L2} - B^*_{K2})$ is added to

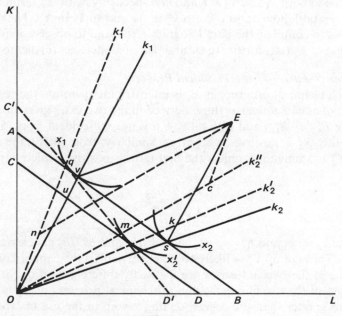

Figure 6.7

X_1^* in (6.25). By the same token, the rise in the output of X_2 exceeds that which resulted from the neutral improvement. For with $|\lambda| < 0$, $\lambda_{L1}\lambda_{K2} < \lambda_{L2}\lambda_{K1}$, so that with $B_{K2}^* < B_{L2}^*$ and $|\theta| < 0$, the first term on the right-hand side of (6.26) is positive. If π_2 is the same in the case of the neutral or the intensive-factor-saving improvement, that is, the unit cost reduction is the same with both types of improvement, the rise in the output of X_2 is greater now than before. Thus we conclude that the intensive-factor-saving technical progress in X_2 alone is more ultra-import-biased. Consequently, it will exert a more pronounced effect on the terms of trade. Similarly, a capital-saving improvement in X_1 alone will be more ultra-export-biased.

The diagrammatic exposition of this result proceeds in the same manner as before. Consider Fig. 6.7, where the unit X_2 isoquant shifts towards the origin to x_2' in such a manner that its capital/labour ratio rises from k_2 to k_2' at the old wage/rental ratio. The immediate result is a rise in the output of X_2 from its unit level to Ok and a fall in the output of X_1 from its unit level to Ou, as can be seen by drawing Eu (not drawn) paràllel to k_2'. Once again, in order to restore the original price parity between X_1 and X_2, we draw $C'D'$ tangential to both x_1 and x_2' at q and m respectively, with the result that the capital/labour ratio rises to k_2'' in X_2 and to k_1' in X_1. The next step is to complete the parallelogram $EnOc$ and to observe that the output of X_2 rises further to Oc and that of X_1 declines further to On.

Intensive-Factor-Using Technical Progress

When technical progress in X_2 is intensive-factor-using, the results are not as categorical as those derived in the two cases given above. Here $B_{K2}^* > B_{L2}^*$, and with $|\theta| < 0$ it is not self-evident from (6.25) whether X_1^* is positive or negative. Similarly, from (6.26), the sign of X_2^* is ambiguous, unless the first term is positive, which implies that

$$\frac{k_2}{k_1} < \frac{B_{L2}^*}{B_{K2}^*}. \tag{6.27}$$

Since $k_2 < k_1$ and $B_{L2}^* < B_{K2}^*$, both k_2/k_1 and B_{L2}^*/B_{K2}^* are less than one. The sign of X_2^* is likely to be positive if (i) the capital/labour ratios in the two industries are markedly different, and/or (ii) the saving in the use of capital due to technical progress in X_2 is not much greater than the corresponding saving in the use of labour, that is, B_{L2}^*/B_{K2}^* is close to unity. On the other hand, if the capital/labour ratios in the two industries are sufficiently close so

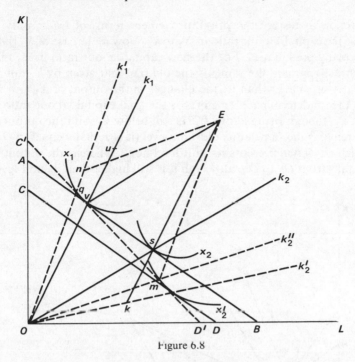

Figure 6.8

that k_2/k_1 is close to unity, and B^*_{L2}/B^*_{K2} falls considerably short of unity so that inequality (6.27) is violated, X^*_2 may be negative. The crux of the whole matter is that the intensive-factor-using technical progress may or may not be ultra-biased and that it may raise the output of both commodities or only the output of the commodity which is not subject to technical improvements. These possibilities are diagrammatically depicted in Fig. 6.8, where at the same factor-price ratio the capital/labour ratio declines as a result of the shift of x_2 down to x'_2. The immediate result in this case is a rise in the output of X_1 from Ov to Ou, as can be seen by drawing Eu (not shown) parallel to k'_2 – a case exactly opposite to the case of intensive-factor-saving improvements;† $C'D'$ is again the tangent drawn

---

† There appears to be some confusion on this point in contemporary literature. Findlay and Grubert ([11] p. 119), for example, assert that an intensive-factor-using technical progress must in the immediate period lower the output of the commodity in which it has occurred. This is what is pictured in Fig. 6.8, but it is by no means certain. It depends on the extent of the technical advance and its factor-using bias. For example, if technical progress in X_2 were only slightly labour-using, the immediate effect would be a rise in the output of both commodities. This possibility is shown in Fig. 6.9.

common to restore the pre-improvement terms of trade, only to raise the capital/labour ratio in X_1 to k_1'. Now in the case of X_2 there are many possibilities. For the new capital/labour ratio in X_2 may eventually remain the same as the old (i.e. that given by k_2), or be greater or smaller than it; the changes in the output of X_1 and X_2 are then indeterminate. In Fig. 6.8 the final capital/labour ratio in X_2, k_2'', though rising above k_2', is still below k_2; and the output of X_2 remains the same at its old unit level (it is actually equal to Om, which anyway represents its unit level now), whereas the output of X_1 falls from Ou to On, although it is still higher than its unit level.

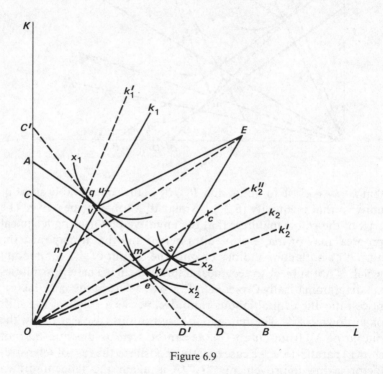

Figure 6.9

However, we could have obtained an entirely different result just as well. Consider Fig. 6.9, where the final capital/labour ratio X_2, given by k_2'', lies above k_2. As Ec is drawn parallel to k_1' and En to k_2'', the output of X_1 can be seen to have declined to On and that of X_2 to have risen to Oc. Thus an intensive-factor-using technical progress in any commodity may have any impact on the two outputs; its effect on the terms of trade, accordingly, cannot be prognosticated.

REFERENCES

[1] Balogh, T., *The Dollar Crisis: Causes and Cure* (Oxford: Blackwell, 1949).

[2] Bastable, C. F., *The Theory of International Trade*, 4th ed. (London: Macmillan, 1903).

[3] Bhagwati, J., 'Immiserizing Growth: A Geometric Note', *Review of Economic Studies*, xxv (June 1958) 201–5.

[4] ——, 'Growth, Terms of Trade and Comparative Advantage', *Economia Internazionale*, xii (Aug 1959) 393–418.

[5] Clement, M. D., Pfister, R. L., and Rothwell, K. J., *Theoretical Issues in International Economics* (Boston: Houghton Mifflin, 1967).

[6] Corden, W. M., *Recent Developments in the Theory of International Trade* (Princeton: International Finance Section, Princeton University, 1965).

[7] ——, 'Economic Expansion and International Trade: A Geometric Approach', *Oxford Economic Papers*, viii (Sep 1956) 223–8.

[8] Dietzel, H., 'The German Tariff Controversy', *Quarterly Journal of Economics*, xvii (May 1903) 365–416.

[9] Edgeworth, F. Y., 'On a Point in the Pure Theory of International Trade', *Economic Journal*, ix (March 1899) 125–8.

[10] Fanno, M., *Normal and Abnormal International Capital Transfers* (Minneapolis: Univ. of Minnesota Press, 1939).

[11] Findlay, R., and Grubert, H., 'Factor Intensities, Technological Progress, and the Terms of Trade', *Oxford Economic Papers*, xi (Feb 1959) 111–21.

[12] Harrod, R. F., *Towards a Dynamic Economics* (London: Macmillan, 1948).

[13] Hicks, J. R., 'An Inaugural Lecture: The Long-Run Dollar Problem', *Oxford Economic Papers*, v (June 1953) 117–35.

[14] Hume, D., *Writings on Economics*, ed. E. Rotwein (Madison: Univ. of Wisconsin Press, 1955).

[15] Iverson, C., *Some Aspects of the Theory of International Capital Movements* (Copenhagen: Levin & Munksgaard, 1936).

[16] Johnson, H. G., 'Effects of Changes in Comparative Costs as Influenced by Technical Change', in R. Harrod and D. Hague (eds), *International Trade in a Developing World* (London: Macmillan, 1963) chap. 4.

[17] Keynes, J. M., 'The German Transfer Problem', in *Readings in the Theory of International Trade* (Philadelphia: Blakiston, 1950).

[18] Mill, J. S., *Principles of Political Economy*, ed. Sir W. J. Ashley (London: Longmans, Green, 1909) bk iii.

[19] Ohlin, B., *Interregional and International Trade* (Cambridge, Mass.: Harvard U.P., 1933).

[20] Prebisch, R., 'Commercial Policy in the Underdeveloped Countries', *American Economic Review*, xlix (May 1959) 251–73.

[21] Taussig, F. W., *International Trade* (New York: Macmillan, 1927).

[22] Thornton, H., *An Enquiry into the Nature and Effects of the Paper Credit of Great Britain* (London: Allen & Unwin, 1939).

[23] Wagner, A., 'Agrarian State versus Manufacturing State', in F. W. Taussig (ed.), *Selected Readings in International Trade and Tariff Problems* (Boston: Ginn, 1921).

7 Intermediate Products: The Inter-Industry Flows

Until now we have assumed that goods are produced with the help of primary factors only, but since in practice much of the production activity would come to a halt if there were no intermediate products – goods which are produced to be used as inputs in other goods – this assumption, although a convenient one, is very unrealistic. There is hardly any justification for this assumption, even though the bulk of trade theory has ignored the presence of material inputs which constitute a very large proportion of the total volume of world trade.† It is only recently that trade theorists have come to recognise the importance of intermediate products in the production process, but even here the general tendency has been to defend the neglect of the treatment of material inputs in the earlier literature. In his book on trade theory, for example, Kemp ([7], p. 148), citing Vanek [10], defends the neglect of the incorporation of intermediate goods in earlier trade theory. In some respect, this neglect may be justified. Many properties of the general equilibrium model presented in the previous chapters carry over to the model with intermediate goods. However, there are some crucial differences which have not been recognised before. The analysis of such similarities and differences is the subject-matter of this chapter.

Within the discussion on intermediate products, the earlier analyses have been disproportionately concentrated on the implications of inter-industry flows, goods that serve the dual role of intermediate as well as final products. However, it cannot be denied that there exist several types of goods which are used not at all for consumption, but are produced solely to be used as inputs in other final goods. These may be called 'pure' intermediate products. In this chapter we are concerned only with the inter-

† See, for example, Yates [11].

industry flows. The latter type of intermediate goods is analysed in the next chapter.

7.1 The Model with Inter-Industry Flows

It is assumed that there are two commodities (X_1 and X_2), each of which requires in the production process two primary factors, L and K, as well as the use of the other good. Other assumptions concerning production functions, perfect competition, etc., made at the beginning of Chapter 2, remain the same.

Let X_{ij} denote the amount of ith good used as an input in the production of the jth good, and let x_j be the net output of the jth good ($i, j = 1, 2$). The production functions for the two commodities may then be written as

$$X_1 = x_1 + X_{12} = F_1(K_1, L_1, X_{21}) \tag{7.1}$$

and

$$X_2 = x_2 + X_{21} = F_2(K_2, L_2, X_{12}) \tag{7.2}$$

where X_j now becomes the gross output of the jth good. The expressions for unit outputs then become

$$F_1\left(\frac{K_1}{x_1+X_{12}}, \frac{L_1}{x_1+X_{12}}, \frac{X_{21}}{x_1+X_{12}}\right) = F_1(C_{K1}, C_{L1}, C_{21}) = 1$$

and

$$F_2\left(\frac{K_2}{x_2+X_{21}}, \frac{L_2}{x_2+X_{21}}, \frac{X_{12}}{x_2+X_{21}}\right) = F_2(C_{K2}, C_{L2}, C_{12}) = 1$$

where C_{ij}, as before, denotes the *direct* requirement of the ith input per unit of the jth good. Full employment of the primary factors implies that

$$C_{L1}(x_1+X_{12})+C_{L2}(x_2+X_{21}) = L \tag{7.3}$$

and

$$C_{K1}(x_1+X_{12})+C_{K2}(x_2+X_{21}) = K. \tag{7.4}$$

It is convenient, however, to express the full-employment conditions in terms of net outputs only. Solving for X_{12} and X_{21} from the following two equations:

$$C_{12} = X_{12}/(x_2+X_{21})$$

and

$$C_{21} = X_{21}/(x_1 + X_{12})$$

we obtain

$$X_{12} = \frac{C_{12}(x_2 + C_{21}x_1)}{1 - C_{12} \cdot C_{21}} \quad \text{and} \quad X_{21} = \frac{C_{21}(x_1 + C_{12}x_2)}{1 - C_{12} \cdot C_{21}}.$$

Substituting these in the full-employment equations, (7.3) and (7.4), we get

$$\left[\frac{C_{L1} + C_{L2} \cdot C_{21}}{1 - C_{12} \cdot C_{21}} \right] x_1 + \left[\frac{C_{L2} + C_{L1} \cdot C_{12}}{1 - C_{12} \cdot C_{21}} \right] x_2 = L \qquad (7.5)$$

and

$$\left[\frac{C_{K1} + C_{K2} \cdot C_{21}}{1 - C_{12} \cdot C_{21}} \right] x_1 + \left[\frac{C_{K2} + C_{K1} \cdot C_{12}}{1 - C_{12} \cdot C_{21}} \right] x_2 = K. \qquad (7.6)$$

The coefficients of x_1 and x_2 in the last two equations reflect the *total* (or true) requirements of primary factors per unit of net outputs. For example, $(C_{L1} + C_{L2} \cdot C_{21})/(1 - C_{12} \cdot C_{21})$ represents the amount of labour which directly enters the production of a unit of X_1 plus the amount of labour embodied in that quantity of X_2 which X_1 uses as an input. To complete the description of the model, we need add only two equations for product prices, which under perfect competition reflect unit costs. Thus

$$C_{L1}w + C_{K1}r + C_{21}p_2 = p_1 \qquad (7.7)$$

and

$$C_{L2}w + C_{K2}r + C_{12}p_1 = p_2. \qquad (7.8)$$

Substituting for p_2 in (7.7) and for p_1 in (7.8), we obtain

$$\left(\frac{C_{L1} + C_{L2} \cdot C_{21}}{1 - C_{12} \cdot C_{21}} \right) w + \left(\frac{C_{K1} + C_{K2} \cdot C_{21}}{1 - C_{12} \cdot C_{21}} \right) r = p_1 \qquad (7.9)$$

and

$$\left(\frac{C_{L2} + C_{L1} \cdot C_{12}}{1 - C_{12} \cdot C_{21}} \right) w + \left(\frac{C_{K2} + C_{K1} \cdot C_{12}}{1 - C_{12} \cdot C_{21}} \right) r = p_2. \qquad (7.10)$$

The basic difference between the full-employment and price equations presented here and the corresponding equations presented in Chapter 2 where inter-industry flows were ignored must now be apparent. If each of C_{12} and C_{21} equals zero, we obtain the simple two-good model without intermediate goods. In the presence of material inputs, however, the model not only becomes more complicated, but it is also no longer certain whether the system has a solution. *For the production of any positive net amount of the goods is possible if and only if* $(1 - C_{12} \cdot C_{21}) > 0$, *a requirement which is similar to the so called Simon–Hawkins condition well familiar to students of linear programming*; and there is no guarantee that this condition will be satisfied with arbitrarily chosen production functions. Thus, in this respect at least, the existence of inter-industry flows modifies the model without intermediate products. In what follows, we assume that $C_{12} \cdot C_{21} < 1$.

Let R_{ij} denote the total requirement of the ith primary factor per unit of the jth good. Then the full-employment and price equations can be written as

$$R_{L1}x_1 + R_{L2}x_2 = L \tag{7.11}$$
$$R_{K1}x_1 + R_{K2}x_2 = K \tag{7.12}$$
$$R_{L1}w + R_{K1}r = p_1 \tag{7.13}$$

and

$$R_{L2}w + R_{K2}r = p_2. \tag{7.14}$$

Let R denote the matrix of production coefficients contained in (7.11) and (7.12). Then

$$R = \begin{bmatrix} R_{L1} & R_{L2} \\ R_{K1} & R_{K2} \end{bmatrix}.$$

The determinant of $[R]$ is given by

$$|R| = R_{L1}R_{K2} - R_{K1}R_{L2} = R_{L1}R_{L2}[(R_{K2}/R_{L2}) - (R_{K1}/R_{L1})]$$

whose sign, it may be surprising to note, is the same as the sign of $|C|$ obtained in Chapter 2, for

$$\frac{R_{K2}}{R_{L2}} - \frac{R_{K1}}{R_{L1}} = \frac{C_{K2} + C_{K1}C_{12}}{C_{L2} + C_{L1}C_{12}} - \frac{C_{K1} + C_{K2}C_{21}}{C_{L1} + C_{L2}C_{21}}$$
$$= \frac{(1 - C_{12}C_{21})(C_{L1}C_{K2} - C_{K1}C_{L2})}{(C_{L2} + C_{L1}C_{12})(C_{L1} + C_{L2}C_{21})}.$$

Since $C_{12}C_{21} < 1$ by assumption, and since $|C| = C_{L1}C_{K2} - C_{K1}C_{L2}$, the sign of $|R|$ is the same as the sign of $|C|$.† The sign of $|C|$ reflects the factor-intensity ranking of the two commodities in terms of 'apparent' or *net* production coefficients, whereas the sign of $|R|$ expresses the factor-intensity ranking in terms of 'true' or *gross* production coefficients. The conclusion is unmistakable. In the inter-industry flow model, the gross and the net factor-intensity rankings of commodities are identical. In other words, if a commodity appears to be, say, capital-intensive relative to the other, then it will remain capital-intensive even when account is taken of the amounts of the primary factors embodied in the production of those quantities of a good which are used in the production of the other. This identity suggests that at least those theorems, usually derived in the absence of intermediate products, that depend exclusively on the inter-industry factor-intensity ranking will hold without any qualitative modification even in the presence of inter-industry flows. As will be shown later, this indeed turns out to be the case. But first we attend to the properties associated with the transformation curve in the present model.

7.2   The Transformation Curve
The important questions associated with any discussion of the transformation curve concern its slope as well as its shape. It can be readily shown that, just like the model without intermediate products, the marginal rate of transformation between net outputs equals the commodity-price ratio. Similarly, the transformation curve concerning net outputs is concave to the origin, although that concerning gross outputs may have any shape. The discussion in this section is devoted to an examination of these two questions.

Since the total value of net output equals the sum of factor payments,

$$p_1 x_1 + p_2 x_2 = wL + rK.$$

Differentiating this totally and keeping in mind that L and K are in inelastic supply,

$$(p_1 dx_1 + p_2 dx_2) + (x_1 dp_1 + x_2 dp_2) = Ldw + Kdr. \qquad (7.15)$$

Taking the factor prices as given in competitive factor markets, the

---

† See the expression for $|C|$ in Chapter 2.

entrepreneur minimises its unit cost by setting the first derivative of $(wR_{Lj}+rR_{Kj})(j = 1, 2)$ to zero; that is,

$$wdR_{Lj}+rdR_{Kj} = 0. \tag{7.16}$$

From (7.11) and (7.12),

$$Ldw + Kdr = (R_{L1}x_1+R_{L2}x_2)dw+(R_{K1}x_1+R_{K2}x_2)dr$$
$$= x_1(R_{L1}dw+R_{K1}dr)+x_2(R_{L2}dw+R_{K2}dr).$$

Using (7.13), (7.14) and (7.16),

$$Ldw + Kdr = x_1dp_1+x_2dp_2.$$

Substituting this in (7.15) yields

$$p_1dx_1+p_2dx_2 = 0$$

or

$$\frac{dx_1}{dx_2} = -\frac{p_2}{p_1} \tag{7.17}$$

which accords with the slope of the transformation curve obtained in the model without intermediate products.

Coming now to the shape of the transformation curve, we begin with the observation that in models where (7.17) holds, the shape of the transformation curve can be directly inferred from the response of the outputs to changes in their relative prices. Specifically, if the supply curves are upward-sloping, the underlying transformation curve is concave to the origin; if they are downward-sloping, the transformation curve will be locally or globally convex to the origin. Therefore, what we need now are expressions for output response to changes in prices. For this purpose, the full-employment and price equations should be transformed into equations of relative change. Totally differentiating (7.11)–(7.14), we get

$$\lambda_{L1}x_1^*+\lambda_{L2}x_2^* = L^*-(\lambda_{L1}R_{L1}^*+\lambda_{L2}R_{L2}^*) \tag{7.18}$$

$$\lambda_{K1}x_1^*+\lambda_{K2}x_2^* = K^*-(\lambda_{K1}R_{K1}^*+\lambda_{K2}R_{K2}^*) \tag{7.19}$$

$$\theta_{L1}w^*+\theta_{K1}r^* = p_1^* \tag{7.20}$$

and

$$\theta_{L2}w^*+\theta_{K2}r^* = p_2^* \tag{7.21}$$

where λ_{ij} denotes the proportion of the total endowment of the ith primary factor used directly and indirectly in the jth sector (for example, $\lambda_{L1} = R_{L1}x_1/L$), and θ_{ij} stands for the *total* distributive share of the ith primary factor in the jth sector (for example, $\theta_{L1} = R_{L1}w/p_1$). As usual, in obtaining (7.20) and (7.21) use has been made of the cost-minimising condition (7.16). There is yet another way of writing (7.20) and (7.21), one which for some problems turns out to be more useful. Differentiating (7.7) and (7.8), we get

$$\rho_{L1}w^* + \rho_{K1}r^* + \rho_{21}p_2^* = p_1^* \tag{7.20*}$$

and

$$\rho_{L2}w^* + \rho_{K2}r^* + \rho_{12}p_1^* = p_2^* \tag{7.21*}$$

where ρ_{ij} is the *net* relative share of the ith factor ($i = L, K, 1, 2$) used in the production of the jth product; for example, $\rho_{L1} = C_{L1}w/p_1$. Evidently, then, $\rho_{L1} + \rho_{K1} + \rho_{21} = 1$, and so on. Solving (7.20) and (7.21) simultaneously, we obtain

$$w^* = (\theta_{K2}p_1^* - \theta_{K1}p_2^*)/|\theta| \tag{7.22}$$

$$r^* = (-\theta_{L2}p_1^* + \theta_{L1}p_2^*)/|\theta| \tag{7.23}$$

and

$$(w^* - r^*) = -(p_2^* - p_1^*)/|\theta| \tag{7.24}$$

where
$$|\theta| = \begin{vmatrix} \theta_{L1} & \theta_{K1} \\ \theta_{L2} & \theta_{K2} \end{vmatrix}.$$

It can be readily seen that the sign of $|\theta|$ is the same as the sign of $|R|$, so that if $k_2 \gtrless k_1, |\theta| \gtrless 0$.

Each direct input–output coefficient C_{ij}, and thus each total input–output coefficient R_{ij}, is a function of the prices of productive inputs. Therefore, we may write

$$C_{ij} = C_{ij}(w, r, p_i) \quad (i = L, K, 1, 2; j = 1, 2; i \neq j).$$

However, since commodity prices from (7.24) are related to factor prices, the total input–output coefficients are uniquely determined solely by w and r.

It is shown in the appendix (section 7.6) that

$$R^*_{L1} = -\frac{(\alpha + \rho_{21}\beta)}{\Omega_L}(w^* - r^*)$$

$$R^*_{L2} = -\frac{(\beta + \rho_{12}\alpha)}{\eta_L}(w^* - r^*)$$

$$R^*_{K1} = \frac{(\alpha + \rho_{21}\beta)}{\Omega_K}(w^* - r^*)$$

$$R^*_{K2} = \frac{(\beta + \rho_{12}\alpha)}{\eta_K}(w^* - r^*)$$

where

$$\alpha = \rho_{L1}\rho_{21}\theta^2_{K2}\sigma^1_{L2} + \rho_{K1}\rho_{21}\theta^2_{L2}\sigma^1_{K2} + \rho_{L1}\rho_{K1}\sigma^1_{LK}$$

$$\beta = \rho_{L2}\rho_{12}\theta^2_{K1}\sigma^2_{L1} + \rho_{K2}\rho_{12}\theta^2_{L1}\sigma^2_{K1} + \rho_{L2}\rho_{K2}\sigma^2_{LK}$$

$$\Omega_L = \rho_{L1} + \rho_{L2}\rho_{21} > 0, \quad \Omega_K = \rho_{K1} + \rho_{K2}\rho_{21} > 0,$$

$$\eta_L = \rho_{L2} + \rho_{L1}\rho_{12} > 0, \quad \eta_K = \rho_{K2} + \rho_{K1}\rho_{12} > 0,$$

and where σ^j_{ik} denotes the partial elasticity of substitution between factors i and k in the jth sector.†

We normally expect a rise in the wage/rental ratio to lower the labour coefficients and raise the capital coefficients. A sufficient condition for these results to hold is that both α and β be unambiguously positive. Where only two primary factors are used in the production of the two goods, or where intermediate products are used in fixed proportions, so that $\sigma^1_{L2} = \sigma^1_{K2} = \sigma^2_{L1} = \sigma^2_{K1} = 0$, the elasticity of substitution between labour and capital in each sector is necessarily positive, i.e. $\sigma^j_{LK} > 0$. It then follows that $(\alpha, \beta) > 0$. With three factors of production, however, the sign of the various elasticities of substitution is indeterminate, although it can be established that at most one partial elasticity may be negative.‡ If all factors are gross substitutes, all elasticities of substitution are positive, in which case a simple glance reveals that both α and β are positive. However, if any two factors are complementary to each other, some elasticities of substitution are negative; the signs of α and β appear to be ambiguous in this case. However, it turns out that if production functions are linearly homogeneous, something we have

† For further remarks on σ^j_{ik}, see the appendix.
‡ See the appendix for further details.

assumed all along, there are certain restrictions on σ_{ik}^j which are sufficient to ensure the positive signs of α and β. This complicated and lengthy task is taken up in the appendix. Returning to (7.18) and (7.19), let

$$\gamma_L = -(\lambda_{L1}R_{L1}^* + \lambda_{L2}R_{L2}^*)/(w^* - r^*)$$

and

$$\gamma_K = (\lambda_{K1}R_{K1}^* + \lambda_{K2}R_{K2}^*)/(w^* - r^*).$$

Then γ_L and γ_K are necessarily positive because α and β are positive. Substituting these expressions in (7.18) and (7.19), and setting L^* and K^* to zero, we obtain

$$\lambda_{L1}x_1^* + \lambda_{L2}x_2^* = \gamma_L(w^* - r^*) \tag{7.25}$$

and

$$\lambda_{K1}x_1^* + \lambda_{K2}x_2^* = -\gamma_K(w^* - r^*). \tag{7.26}$$

We have now gathered all the ingredients necessary to investigate the response of net outputs to changes in the commodity-price ratio as well as the shape of the locus of competitive outputs in the inter-industry flows model. Solving (7.25) and (7.26) simultaneously for x_1^* and x_2^*, we get

$$x_1^* = \frac{(\lambda_{K2}\gamma_L + \lambda_{L2}\gamma_K)}{|\lambda|}(w^* - r^*) \tag{7.27}$$

and

$$x_2^* = \frac{-(\lambda_{K1}\gamma_L + \lambda_{L1}\gamma_K)}{|\lambda|}(w^* - r^*) \tag{7.28}$$

where

$$|\lambda| = \begin{vmatrix} \lambda_{L1} & \lambda_{L2} \\ \lambda_{K1} & \lambda_{K2} \end{vmatrix}.$$

The sign of $|\lambda|$ clearly depends on the ranking of the two commodities in terms of their capital/labour ratios. It is readily shown that $|\lambda|$ always possesses the same sign as $|\theta|$ or $|R|$. Since we are concerned with the response of outputs to changes in commodity prices, we may substitute for $(w^* - r^*)$ from (7.24) in (7.27) and (7.28) to obtain

$$x_1^* = \frac{(\lambda_{K2}\gamma_L + \lambda_{L2}\gamma_K)}{|\lambda| \cdot |\theta|}(p_1^* - p_2^*) \tag{7.29}$$

and

$$x_2^* = \frac{-(\lambda_{K1}\gamma_L + \lambda_{L1}\gamma_K)}{|\lambda| \cdot |\theta|}(p_1^* - p_2^*).$$ (7.30)

Since γ_L and γ_K are positive and since $|\lambda| \cdot |\theta| > 0$, $x_1^*/(p_1^* - p_2^*) > 0$ and $x_2^*/(p_1^* - p_2^*) < 0$. In other words, a rise in the relative price of the first commodity leads to a rise in its net output and a decline in the net output of the second commodity, and conversely. The result is similar to the one derived in the model without inter-industry flows.

As suggested earlier, if the tangency condition expressed in (7.17) holds, the shape of the transformation curve can be inferred from the direction of the response of outputs to changes in the commodity-price ratio. This can be seen by differentiating (7.17) with respect to x_2 to obtain

$$\frac{d^2 x_1}{dx_2^2} = -\frac{d(p_2/p_1)}{dx_2}.$$

Now (7.30) implies that $d(p_2/p_1)/dx_2 > 0$, so that $d^2 x_1/dx_2^2 < 0$. In other words, the transformation curve between net outputs is strictly concave to the origin.†

The Geometrical Exposition

One special case where the material inputs are utilised in fixed proportions is of further interest, for it permits the geometrical derivation of the net transformation curve from the gross transformation curve. This derivation was first accomplished by Vanek [10], while Guisinger [6] and Batra and Pattanaik [2] later on provided certain qualifications to Vanek's technique.

Consider Fig. 7.1, where TT'' is the transformation between gross outputs of X_1 and X_2 drawn under the assumption that $C_{12} = C_{21} = 0$; TT' is thus derived in the absence of inter-industry flows. If any of C_{12} and C_{21} is not zero, the new transformation curve will lie within the area enclosed by TT'. Consider any point such as E on TT'; draw EX and EY parallel respectively to the X_2 axis and the X_1 axis; next, draw two straight lines from E, the slopes of which with reference to the new axes (EX and EY)

---

† It may be noted here that it is the net output of each good which is positively related to its price. The gross output of the commodity may behave in any way. For this reason, there is nothing to guarantee that the gross transformation curve would also be concave to the origin. For further details, see Ethier [5].

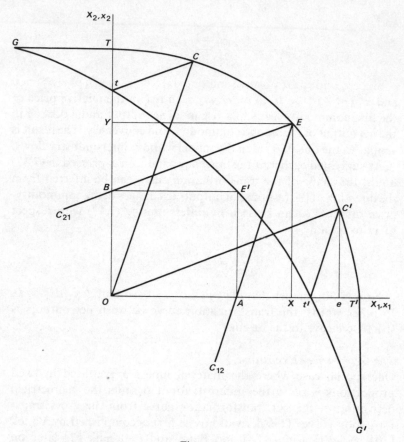

Figure 7.1

equal C_{12} and C_{21}, that is, the slope of EC_{12} intersecting OX_1 at A, and that of EC_{21} intersecting OX_2 at B, represent, respectively, the requirement of X_1 per unit of X_2 and of X_2 per unit of X_1; OA is then the net output of X_1 and OB the net output of X_2, and these two furnish a point E' that corresponds to E on the gross transformation curve TT'. In other words, AX of X_1 and BY of X_2 serve the role of material inputs in producing net outputs equal to OA and OB. By repeating such construction for other points on TT', we derive all the points on the net transformation tt' except its corner points, t and t'. For example, t' is obtained by drawing from the origin a ray OC', parallel to EC_{21} and intersecting TT' at C'; drawing $C't'$ parallel to EC_{12} then furnishes one of the corner points of the new transformation curve. In other words, et' amount of X_1 is utilised by eC' amount of X_2, which in turn is fully utilised by X_1, so that the net output of X_2 is zero and that of X_1 is Ot'. It may be noted that t' does not correspond to T' but to C' and is derived from the latter in a manner different from the derivation of E' from E, in order to ensure that the net supply of X_2 is zero. Similarly, we can derive the other corner point of tt' by drawing first OC parallel to EC_{12} and then Ct parallel to EC_{21}. Thus the net transformation curve tt' corresponds only to the CC' segment of the gross transformation curve TT'. As rigorously established above, tt' must be strictly concave to the origin.

An interesting possibility emerges if the economy is exposed to international trade, for then a part or all of the imported good can be used as an input in the production of the exportable good. When this possibility is admitted, the net transformation curve extends its frontier to the negative quadrants and is actually given by GG'; here the corner points G and G' are aligned respectively to T and T'. For example, point G implies a maximum net output of X_2 equal to OT which is produced with the help of the inelastically supplied primary factors, plus GT amount of X_1 which is obtained from abroad. A similar explication applies to G'. Thus if material inputs can be imported, the net transformation curve extends to the negative quadrants. Now if material inputs are used in fixed proportions, the net transformation curve has corner points such as G and G'. But if all factors are used in variable proportions, the net transformation curve has virtually no limits, for if any amount of the material input can be imported from abroad, the output of the exportable good can be increased without limit by continued addition of the imported input to the fixed domestic primary factors. The limits on the output of the exportable good are then provided only by the availability of the world export surplus.

7.3 Some Standard Trade Theorems

Let us now see whether some of the standard trade theorems continue to be valid in the presence of intermediate products.

To begin with, let us re-examine the Stolper–Samuelson theorem which is concerned with the impact of commodity prices on real factor rewards. From (7.22) and (7.23),

$$w^* - p_j^* = \frac{\theta_{Kj}(p_1^* - p_2^*)}{|\theta|} \qquad (7.31)$$

and

$$r^* - p_j^* = \frac{-\theta_{Lj}(p_1^* - p_2^*)}{|\theta|}. \tag{7.32}$$

If the first commodity is capital-intensive, $|\theta| < 0$. Clearly, then, a rise in its relative price ($p_1^* > p_2^*$) causes a rise in the reward of its intensive factor, capital, and a decline in the reward of the other factor, labour, in terms of both commodity prices, showing that the Stolper–Samuelson theorem remains unscathed by the introduction of the intermediate products.

Next we turn to the Rybczynski theorem, which deals with the effects of changes in factor supplies on the outputs at constant commodity prices. The latter stipulation implies that factor rewards and hence the input–output coefficients are constant. In other words, the expressions in the parentheses of the right-hand side of (7.18) and (7.19) reduce to zero. Solving them simultaneously then yields

$$x_1^* = \frac{\lambda_{K2}L^* - \lambda_{L2}K^*}{|\lambda|} \tag{7.33}$$

and

$$x_2^* = \frac{\lambda_{L1}K^* - \lambda_{K1}L^*}{|\lambda|}. \tag{7.34}$$

With X_1 capital-intensive relative to X_2, $|\lambda| < 0$. A rise in the supply of, say, capital alone then raises the net output of the capital-intensive commodity, x_1, and lowers the net output of the other commodity, x_2, to show that the Rybczynski theorem continues to hold in the presence of material inputs. However, the theorem holds only qualitatively, because the magnitude of the changes in the net outputs is different in the presence of intermediate goods. In the case where only the labour force is growing, for example, we may write from (7.33) and (7.34) that

$$\frac{dx_1}{dL} = \frac{C_{K2} + C_{K1}C_{12}}{C_{L1}C_{K2} - C_{L2}C_{K1}} \tag{7.35}$$

and

$$\frac{dx_2}{dL} = \frac{-(C_{K1} + C_{K2}C_{21})}{C_{L1}C_{K2} - C_{L2}C_{K1}}. \tag{7.36}$$

Given that the denominator of (7.35) and (7.36) is negative, the decline in the net output of X_1 and the rise in the net output of X_2 resulting from labour growth alone will be greater in the presence of intermediate goods (so that C_{12} and C_{21} are positive) than would otherwise be the case. In other words, the economic expansion resulting from labour growth becomes more ultra-biased in the presence of inter-industry flows. This is because, with the increase in the output of one commodity, additional units of output of the other commodity must be withdrawn from final consumption, a factor that vanishes in the absence of intermediate products. It follows then that the magnitude of the changes in the terms of trade consequent upon the increase in labour supply will also be more pronounced in the presence of inter-industry flows.

Thus we see that the Stolper–Samuelson and the Rybczynski theorems are unaffected qualitatively by the incorporation of inter-industry flows. It is now a simple matter to show that the magnification effect and the fundamental duality that were found to exist between these two theorems also remain unaltered. A simple proof consists in the observation that equations (7.31)–(7.34) are exactly the same as the corresponding equations (2.35)–(2.38) in Chapter 2, except that $|\lambda|$ and $|\theta|$ in each chapter are different in magnitude but not in sign.

7.4 Technical Progress

We have shown in the previous chapter that neutral technical progress in any commodity is ultra-biased, because at constant commodity prices it promotes the expansion of the 'progressive' commodity at the expense of the output of the other commodity. We now wish to examine whether this theorem holds in the presence of inter-industry flows without any additional qualification. The extension of this theorem to the case of inter-industry flows has recently been provided by Casas [3], and our analysis here runs parallel to his discussion. In the presence of technical change

$$C_{ij} = C_{ij}(w, r, p_i, t) \tag{7.37}$$

where t denotes the technical improvement. To be more specific, we assume that only the first industry experiences a Hicks-neutral improvement at a rate T^*, where

$$T^* = -\frac{1}{\partial C_{i1}} \frac{\partial C_{i1}}{\partial t} \, dt > 0 \quad (i = L, K, 2). \tag{7.38}$$

Assuming that the factor supplies are unchanged, so that $L^* = K^* = 0$, equations (7.13) and (7.14) then change to

$$\lambda_{L1}x_1^* + \lambda_{L2}x_2^* = -(\lambda_{L1}R_{L1}^* + \lambda_{L2}R_{L2}^*)$$
$$+ \frac{\lambda_{L1}(1 + C_{12}x_2/x_1)T^*}{(1 - C_{12}C_{21})} \quad (7.39)$$

$$\lambda_{K1}x_1^* + \lambda_{K2}x_2^* = -(\lambda_{K1}R_{K1}^* + \lambda_{K2}R_{K2}^*)$$
$$+ \frac{\lambda_{K1}(1 + C_{12}x_2/x_1)T^*}{1 - C_{12}C_{21}} \quad (7.40)$$

where R_{ij}^* again denotes the change in R_{ij} resulting from a change in the wage/rental ratio only. Similarly, (7.15) and (7.16) are now replaced by

$$\theta_{L1}w^* + \theta_{K1}r^* = p_1^* + \frac{T^*}{(1 - C_{12}C_{21})} \quad (7.41)$$

and

$$\theta_{L2}w^* + \theta_{K2}r^* = p_2^* + \frac{\rho_{12}T^*}{(1 - C_{12}C_{21})} \quad (7.42)$$

where ρ_{ij} and θ_{ij} are defined as before. If commodity prices are kept constant, $(p_1^* - p_2^*) = 0$ so that, by subtracting (7.42) from (7.41), we obtain

$$(w^* - r^*) = \frac{(1 - \rho_{12})T^*}{|\theta|(1 - C_{12}C_{21})}. \quad (7.43)$$

As before, the first expression on the right-hand side of (7.39) and (7.40) can be expressed in terms of γ_L and γ_K, although, since $(w^* - r^*)$ is now different, their values will be different. Substituting (7.43) in the expressions for γ_L and γ_K, the resultant γ_L and γ_K in (7.39) and (7.40), and then solving the latter two equations simultaneously, we obtain

$$x_1^* = \frac{T^*}{(1 - C_{12}C_{21})}$$
$$\times \left[(1 + C_{12}x_2/x_1) + \frac{(1 - \rho_{12})(\lambda_{K2}\gamma_L + \lambda_{L2}\gamma_K)}{|\lambda||\theta|} \right] \quad (7.44)$$

$$x_2^* = \frac{-T^*}{(1 - C_{12}C_{21})} \left[\frac{(1 - \rho_{12})(\lambda_{K1}\gamma_L + \lambda_{L1}\gamma_K)}{|\lambda||\theta|} \right]. \quad (7.45)$$

Our conclusions in this section, just like the ones derived in the section on the transformation curve, depend chiefly on the signs of γ_L and γ_K. Recalling that both γ_L and γ_K are positive, and given our assumption that $C_{12}C_{21} < 1$, it can be seen that $x_1^* > 0$ and $x_2^* < 0$. In other words, the output of the commodity enjoying the technical improvement rises and that of the other commodity declines when terms of trade are kept constant. Thus neutral technical progress in any commodity is ultra-biased even when inter-industry flows are present.

7.5 The Gains From Trade

The existence of inter-industry flows has very interesting and important implications for gains from trade. It has been argued by Chipman ([4] pp. 509–11) and McKinnon ([8] pp. 601–10), among others, that the existence of trade in intermediate products tends to raise a country's gains from trade and hence its social welfare. A simple demonstration of this result involves the use of Fig. 7.2, where HH' is the home net transformation curve in the absence of trade in intermediate products. That is to say, if the imported good is used only for final consumption and not as an intermediate product, the maximum possible net output of the exportable good, x_1, equals OH'. However, if the importable good is also used as a material input, the transformation curve, as argued before, extends to the negative quadrants. Let us first consider the case where the importable good is used for final consumption only. For any country, large or small, the maximum level of social welfare under free trade is the one that is associated with complete specialisation in the exportable commodity. Let us assume that world prices are such that the home country does in fact produce only its exportable commodity in the free trade equilibrium. Such a world-price ratio is given by FP, production is at H', consumption at C, and social welfare is given by U_1. Now let us suppose that the imported good is used not only for final consumption but also for the production of the exportable good. If FP is such that it is just sufficient to take the production point to H', that is to say, if FP just equals the marginal rate of transformation in the neighbourhood of H', there will be no change in the output of x_1 even though the transformation frontier now extends to the negative quadrants. At the same time there will be no change in welfare. However, if FP is greater than the marginal

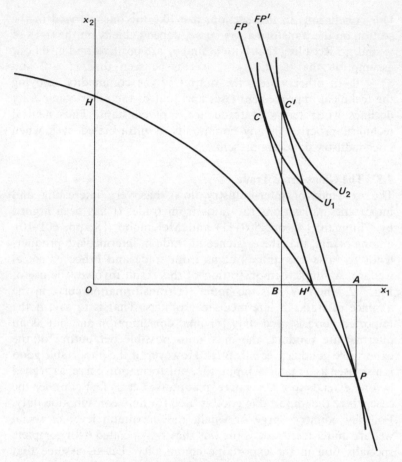

Figure 7.2

rate of transformation in the neighbourhood of H', the production point will change when the imported good can be used in the production of the exportable good and welfare will improve. Such a possibility is depicted in Fig. 7.2, where the foreign-price line FP', parallel to FP, takes the production point to P, the net output of X_1 equals OA, consumption is at C', and welfare is at U_2, which is higher than the welfare level attained when X_2 cannot be used as an intermediate product. The total amount of X_2 imported equals $C'B$ which is used for final consumption, plus AP which is used as an input in the production of X_1. This is how the existence of trade in intermediate products leads to an increase in gains from trade and hence to an increase in social welfare.

However, this is not the end of the story. Melvin [9] has raised an interesting point which, in the present context, serves as a note of warning against hasty generalisations. Introducing inter-industry flows in a Ricardian, single-primary-factor framework, he shows that even though world welfare as a whole goes up when inter-mediate products are traded, it is no longer certain that each individual country will gain from trade. In order to comprehend the subtleties of Melvin's argument, it is necessary first to derive the transformation curve when inter-industry flows are introduced in the Ricardian model. The derivation is much simpler than that in the case of the two-primary-factor world, and requires the use of total product curves for each good. Consider Fig. 7.3, where Of_2 and Of_1 are, respectively, the total product curves for X_2 and X_1, and where the production of each good requires the use of

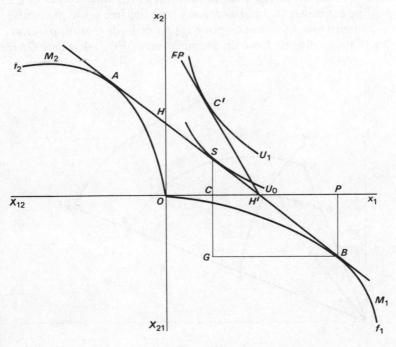

Figure 7.3

labour and the other good. Each of Of_2 and Of_1 are drawn under
the constraint of full employment of labour, which in Melvin's
words implies that 'all possible production points must be convex
combinations of points on f_1 and f_2' ([9] p. 142). In Fig. 7.3, inputs
are measured along the negative axes and outputs along the
positive axes; M_1 and M_2 are the points where f_1 and f_2 respectively
approach their maxima. Let AB be the common tangent drawn to
f_1 and f_2. Then $M_2AHH'BM_1$ is the net transformation curve. In
autarky, or in the case where the imported good is used only for
consumption, the transformation curve is given by the segment
HH'. If the home country is a small country and faces a given
world-price ratio different from that given by the slope of HH',
then, of course, the home country will benefit by the introduction
of trade. It also follows, from the argument presented above in the
two-primary-factor case, that the gains from trade will be higher
if the world-price ratio is such as to take the production point to
the negative quadrant. However, if the equilibrium world-price
ratio is obtained through the interaction of the offer curves of the
trading countries, it is not necessary that the free trade price ratio
will differ from the autarky price ratios of both trading partners.
This follows directly from an examination of Fig. 7.4, where OKH

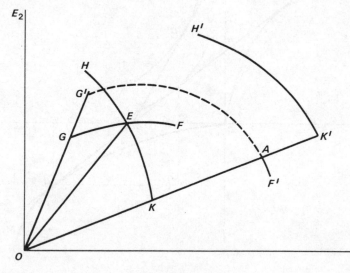

Figure 7.4

and *OGF* are the home and foreign offer curves of the Ricardian model if the imported goods are not used as inputs. Thus *K* and *G*, as in Chapter 3, indicate the points of complete specialisation in the home and the foreign countries respectively. Point *K*, for example, conforms to point *H'* in Fig. 7.3. However, if the imported goods are not only used for consumption but also for production, the points of production are no longer limited to either *H* or *H'*; as suggested, they extend to the negative quadrants. This means that the kinks in the offer curves in Fig. 7.4 also occur at higher volumes of trade. Now if the foreign offer curve extends only to *OG'F'* and the home offer curve undergoes a large shift to *OK'H'*, the free trade equilibrium will then occur at *A* instead of at *E*, which is the point of intersection between the two offer curves in the absence of trade in intermediate products. The reader may notice a clear difference in the two situations. If intermediate goods are not traded, the free trade price ratio (*OE*) differs from the home autarky price ratio (*OK*), whereas in the presence of trade in intermediate products the free trade price ratio and the home autarky price ratio do not differ, as is the case in Fig. 7.4. In the former situation the home country definitely benefits from trade, as is described in Fig. 7.3, where *FP* is the world price ratio corresponding to *OE*, production moves from the self-sufficiency equilibrium point *S* to *H'*, consumption to *C'*, and social welfare improves from U_0 to U_1. In the latter situation, where the autarky price ratio reflected by the slope of *AB* remains unchanged, production moves from *S* to any point on *H'B* to the south east of *H'* (but it cannot go beyond *B* because the price ratio is unchanged), consumption remains at *S*, again because of the absence of any change in autarky prices, and welfare is unchanged at U_0, which lies clearly below U_1, the welfare level that could be attained if the imported good was not an intermediate good. In Fig. 7.3 the actual production point in free trade is given by *B*, the net output of X_1 equals *OP*, the import of X_2 equals *GS*, part of which, *SC*, is used for consumption and the other part, *CG*, in the production of X_1. This is how Melvin shows that the introduction of trade in intermediate goods may not be gainful to both countries. The converse of this result is also true. In Melvin's words, 'a situation which results in a gain for only one country when there is trade in consumption goods only, may very well result in gains for both countries when trade in intermediate goods is allowed' ([9] p. 151).

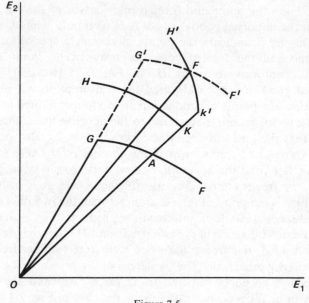

Figure 7.5

This argument is illustrated in Fig. 7.5. In the initial situation of trade in final consumption goods only, the home offer and the foreign offer curves are such that the home autarky price ratio remains unchanged at OA, so that the home country derives no benefit from trade. If the imported goods can also be used for production, the two offer curves shift to $OK'H'$ and $OG'F'$ in such a way that the free trade equilibrium price ratio is given by the slope of OE, which is different from OA. Obviously, here the home welfare will benefit from trade.

7.6 Appendix

Since each production coefficient is a function of input prices, we can write $C_{ij} = C_{ij}(w,r,p_i)(i = L,K,1,2; j = 1,2; i \neq j)$. Differentiating this totally, and remembering that p_1 does not affect the input choice in the first commodity, we have

$$C_{L1}^* = \rho_{L1}\sigma_{LL}^1 w^* + \rho_{K1}\sigma_{LK}^1 r^* + \rho_{21}\sigma_{L2}^1 p_2^*$$
$$C_{K1}^* = \rho_{L1}\sigma_{LK}^1 w^* + \rho_{K1}\sigma_{KK}^1 r^* + \rho_{21}\sigma_{K2}^1 p_2^* \qquad \text{(A7.1)}$$
$$C_{21}^* = \rho_{L1}\sigma_{L2}^1 w^* + \rho_{K1}\sigma_{K2}^1 r^* + \rho_{21}\sigma_{22}^1 p_2^*.$$

Intermediate Products: The Inter-Industry Flows   175

Similarly,

$$C_{L2}^* = \rho_{L2}\sigma_{LL}^2 w^* + \rho_{K2}\sigma_{LK}^2 r^* + \rho_{12}\sigma_{L1}^2 p_1^*$$
$$C_{K2}^* = \rho_{L2}\sigma_{LK}^2 w^* + \rho_{K2}\sigma_{KK}^2 r^* + \rho_{12}\sigma_{K1}^2 p_1^* \qquad \text{(A7.2)}$$
$$C_{12}^* = \rho_{L2}\sigma_{L1}^2 w^* + \rho_{K2}\sigma_{K1}^2 r^* + \rho_{12}\sigma_{11}^2 p_1^*$$

where σ_{ik}^j denotes the partial elasticity of substitution between the ith and the kth factor in the jth industry. For instance, σ_{LK}^1 is the partial elasticity of substitution in the first industry between the pair of factors labour and capital against the intermediate product. If there are only two factors of production, each elasticity of factor substitution (as defined, for example, in Chapter 1) must be positive. This requirement follows from the assumption of linearly homogeneous and quasi-concave production functions.[†] However, when there are more than two productive inputs, this linear homogeneity is compatible with the negative sign of some elasticities of substitution. In the presence of inter-industry flows, each industry utilises three factors and possesses six elasticities of substitution out of which three may be called 'own' elasticities and three 'cross' elasticities. For example, in the first industry, σ_{LL}^1, σ_{KK}^1, σ_{22}^1 are the 'own' elasticities which are all negative, whereas σ_{LK}^1, σ_{L2}^1 and σ_{K2}^1 are the 'cross' elasticities. The negative sign of the own elasticities arises from the fact that the demand for a factor varies inversely with the change in its price when other factor prices are kept constant. Only one of the three cross-elasticities may be negative if the production functions are quasi-concave.[‡] If the two inputs are gross substitutes, then the corresponding cross-elasticity of substitution is positive; if they are complements, it is negative. The linear homogeneity in our three-factor case thus requires that a factor may be complementary with only one other input, or that all may be substitutes.

With these remarks in mind, equation (A7.1) and (A7.2) can be simplified by noting that

$$p_1^* = \theta_{L1}w^* + \theta_{K1}r^* \qquad \text{(A7.3)}$$
$$p_2^* = \theta_{L2}w^* + \theta_{K2}r^* \qquad \text{(A7.4)}$$

[†] This is also proved in Chapter 1.
[‡] See Allen ([1] pp. 504–8) for further details.

where the θ's are, as before, the gross share of the relevant primary factor. If all factor prices change in the same proportion, the production coefficients remain unchanged. Thus if $w^* = r^* = p_1^* = p_2^*$, $C_{ij}^* = 0$. This implies that

$$-\rho_{L1}\sigma_{LL}^1 = (\rho_{K1}\sigma_{LK}^1 + \rho_{21}\sigma_{L2}^1) > 0 \tag{A7.5}$$

$$-\rho_{L2}\sigma_{LL}^2 = (\rho_{K2}\sigma_{LK}^2 + \rho_{12}\sigma_{L1}^2) > 0 \tag{A7.6}$$

$$-\rho_{K1}\sigma_{KK}^1 = (\rho_{L1}\sigma_{LK}^1 + \rho_{21}\sigma_{K2}^1) > 0 \tag{A7.7}$$

$$-\rho_{K2}\sigma_{KK}^2 = (\rho_{L2}\sigma_{LK}^2 + \rho_{12}\sigma_{K1}^2) > 0 \tag{A7.8}$$

$$-\rho_{21}\sigma_{22}^1 = (\rho_{L1}\sigma_{L2}^1 + \rho_{K1}\sigma_{K2}^1) > 0 \tag{A7.9}$$

$$-\rho_{12}\sigma_{11}^2 = (\rho_{L2}\sigma_{L1}^2 + \rho_{K2}\sigma_{K1}^2) > 0. \tag{A7.10}$$

The positive sign of all the expressions in (A7.5)–(A7.10) follows from the fact that the own elasticities of substitution are all negative. Substituting (A7.3)–(A7.10) in (A7.1) and (A7.2) yields

$$C_{L1}^* = -(\rho_{21}\theta_{K2}\sigma_{L2}^1 + \rho_{K1}\sigma_{LK}^1)(w^* - r^*)$$
$$C_{K1}^* = (\rho_{21}\theta_{L2}\sigma_{K2}^1 + \rho_{L1}\sigma_{LK}^1)(w^* - r^*) \tag{A7.11}$$
$$C_{21}^* = (\rho_{L1}\theta_{K2}\sigma_{L2}^1 - \rho_{K1}\theta_{L2}\sigma_{K2}^1)(w^* - r^*)$$

and

$$C_{L2}^* = -(\rho_{12}\theta_{K1}\sigma_{L1}^2 + \rho_{K2}\sigma_{LK}^2)(w^* - r^*)$$
$$C_{K2}^* = (\rho_{12}\theta_{L1}\sigma_{K1}^2 + \rho_{L2}\sigma_{LK}^2)(w^* - r^*) \tag{A7.12}$$
$$C_{12}^* = (\rho_{L2}\theta_{K1}\sigma_{L1}^2 - \rho_{K2}\theta_{L1}\sigma_{K1}^2)(w^* - r^*).$$

It will be recalled that R_{L1} was defined as

$$R_{L1} = \frac{C_{L1} + C_{L2}C_{21}}{(1 - C_{12}C_{21})}.$$

Hence

$$R_{L1}^* = \frac{dR_{L1}}{R_{L1}} = \frac{C_{L1}C_{L1}^* + C_{21}R_{L2}C_{21}^* + C_{21}(C_{L2}C_{L2}^* + C_{12}R_{L1}C_{12}^*)}{C_{L1} + C_{L2}C_{21}}$$
$$= \frac{\rho_{L1}C_{L1}^* + \rho_{21}\theta_{L2}C_{21}^* + \rho_{21}(\rho_{L2}C_{L2}^* + \rho_{12}\theta_{L1}C_{12}^*)}{\rho_{L1} + \rho_{L2}\rho_{21}}.$$

Substituting from (A7.11) and (A7.12), and noting that $\theta_{L1}+\theta_{K1} = \theta_{L2}+\theta_{K2} = 1$

$$R_{L1}^* = -\left[\frac{(\rho_{L1}\rho_{21}\theta_{K2}^2\sigma_{L2}^1+\rho_{K1}\rho_{21}\theta_{L2}^2\sigma_{K2}^1+\rho_{K1}\rho_{L1}\sigma_{LK}^1)}{(\rho_{L1}+\rho_{L2}\rho_{21})}\right.$$
$$\left.+\frac{\rho_{21}(\rho_{L2}\rho_{12}\theta_{K1}^2\sigma_{L1}^1+\rho_{K2}\rho_{12}\theta_{L1}^2\sigma_{K1}^1+\rho_{K2}\rho_{L2}\sigma_{LK}^2)}{(\rho_{L1}+\rho_{L2}\rho_{21})}\right](w^*-r^*)$$
$$= -\frac{(\alpha+\rho_{21}\beta)}{\Omega_L}(w^*-r^*).$$

In a similar fashion, it can be shown that

$$R_{L2}^* = -\frac{(\beta+\rho_{12}\alpha)}{\eta_L}(w^*-r^*)$$

$$R_{K1}^* = \frac{(\alpha+\rho_{21}\beta)}{\Omega_K}(w^*-r^*)$$

$$R_{K2}^* = \frac{(\beta+\rho_{12}\alpha)}{\eta_K}(w^*-r^*)$$

where

$$\alpha = \rho_{L1}\rho_{21}\theta_{K2}^2\sigma_{L2}^1+\rho_{K1}\rho_{21}\theta_{L2}^2\sigma_{K2}^1+\rho_{L1}\rho_{K1}\sigma_{LK}^1$$
$$\beta = \rho_{L2}\rho_{12}\theta_{K1}^2\sigma_{L1}^1+\rho_{K2}\rho_{12}\theta_{L1}^2\sigma_{K1}^1+\rho_{L2}\rho_{K2}\sigma_{LK}^2$$
$$\Omega_L = \rho_{L1}+\rho_{L2}\cdot\rho_{21}, \quad \Omega_K = \rho_{K1}+\rho_{K2}\cdot\rho_{21}$$
$$\eta_L = \rho_{L2}+\rho_{L1}\cdot\rho_{12}, \quad \eta_K = \rho_{K2}+\rho_{K1}\cdot\rho_{12}.$$

It is clear that the signs of the R_{ij}^*'s depend crucially on the signs of α and β; we shall now proceed to show that, given our assumptions with respect to the production functions, both α and β are positive.

(A7.5) can be rewritten as:

$$\sigma_{LL}^1 = \left(\frac{-\rho_{K1}}{\rho_{L1}}\right)\sigma_{LK}^1+\left(\frac{-\rho_{21}}{\rho_{L1}}\right)\sigma_{L2}^1.$$

Substituting for σ_{LK}^1 from (A7.7) and for σ_{L2}^1 from (A7.9), we get

$$\sigma_{LL}^1 = \frac{1}{\rho_{L1}^2}(\rho_{K1}^2\sigma_{KK}^1+2\rho_{K1}\rho_{21}\sigma_{K2}^1+\rho_{21}^2\sigma_{22}^1).$$

This, in turn, may be rewritten in matrix notation as

$$\sigma_{LL}^1 = \frac{1}{\rho_{L1}^2} \begin{bmatrix} \rho_{K1} & \rho_{21} \end{bmatrix} \begin{bmatrix} \sigma_{KK}^1 & \sigma_{K2}^1 \\ \sigma_{K2}^1 & \sigma_{22}^1 \end{bmatrix} \begin{bmatrix} \rho_{K1} \\ \rho_{21} \end{bmatrix}. \qquad \text{(A7.13)}$$

We have previously argued that under the assumption that production functions exhibit constant returns to scale and are quasi-concave, the 'own' partial elasticities of substitution are negative, which implies that the quadratic form on the R.H.S. of (A7.13) must be negative definite. This constraint is satisfied if (i) $\sigma_{KK}^1 < 0$, (ii) $\sigma_{22}^1 < 0$, and (iii) $\sigma_{KK}^1\sigma_{22}^1 - (\sigma_{K2}^1)^2 > 0$. The first two conditions have already been assumed to be valid, while the third may be written as

$$\sigma_{KK}^1\sigma_{22}^1 - (\sigma_{K2}^1)^2 = \frac{\rho_{L1}\sigma_{LK}^1(\rho_{L1}\sigma_{L2}^1 + \rho_{K1}\sigma_{K2}^1) + \rho_{21}\rho_{L1}\sigma_{L2}^1\sigma_{K2}^1}{\rho_{K1}\rho_{21}} > 0$$

which is possible only if

$$\sigma_{LK}^1 > \frac{-\rho_{21}\sigma_{L2}^1\sigma_{K2}^1}{(\rho_{L1}\sigma_{L2}^1 + \rho_{K1}\sigma_{K2}^1)}.$$

Remembering that

$$\alpha = \rho_{21}\rho_{L1}\theta_{K2}^2\sigma_{L2}^1 + \rho_{21}\rho_{K1}\theta_{L2}^2\sigma_{K2}^1 + \rho_{L1}\rho_{K1}\sigma_{LK}^1$$

we can now write that

$$\alpha > \rho_{21}\rho_{L1}\theta_{K2}^2\sigma_{L2}^1 + \rho_{21}\rho_{K1}\theta_{L2}^2\sigma_{K2}^1 - \frac{\rho_{L1}\rho_{K1}\rho_{21}\sigma_{L2}^1\sigma_{K2}^1}{(\rho_{L1}\sigma_{L2}^1 + \rho_{K1}\sigma_{K2}^1)}$$

or

$$\alpha > \frac{\rho_{21}}{(\rho_{L1}\sigma_{L2}^1 + \rho_{K1}\sigma_{K2}^1)}\{\rho_{L1}^2\theta_{K2}^2(\sigma_{L2}^1)^2 + \rho_{K1}^2\theta_{L2}^2(\sigma_{K2}^1)^2 + \rho_{L1}\rho_{K1}\sigma_{L2}^1\sigma_{K2}^1(\theta_{L2}^2 + \theta_{K2}^2 - 1)\}$$

or

$$\alpha > \frac{\rho_{21}}{(\rho_{L1}\sigma_{L2}^1 + \rho_{K1}\sigma_{K2}^1)}\{\rho_{L1}^2\theta_{K2}^2(\sigma_{L2}^1)^2 + \rho_{K1}^2\theta_{L2}^2(\sigma_{K2}^1)^2 - 2\rho_{L1}\rho_{K1}\theta_{L2}\theta_{K2}\sigma_{L2}^1\sigma_{K2}^1\}$$

or

$$\alpha > \frac{\rho_{21}}{(\rho_{L1}\sigma_{L2}^1 + \rho_{K1}\sigma_{K2}^1)}(\rho_{L1}\theta_{K2}\sigma_{L2}^1 - \rho_{K1}\theta_{L2}\sigma_{K2}^1)^2. \qquad \text{(A7.14)}$$

Since the right-hand side of (A7.14) is positive, $\alpha > 0$. In a similar fashion, we can establish the positive sign of β.

REFERENCES

[1] Allen, R. G. D., *Mathematical Analysis for Economists* (London: Macmillan, 1938).

[2] Batra, R. N., and Pattanaik, P. K., 'Economic Growth, Intermediate Products, and the Terms of Trade', *Canadian Journal of Economics*, IV (May 1971) 225–37.

[3] Casas, F. R., 'The Theory of Intermediate Products, Technical Change and Growth', *Journal of International Economics*, II (May 1972).

[4] Chipman, J. S. 'A Survey of the Theory of International Trade: Part 3, The Modern Theory', *Econometrica*, XXXIV (Jan 1966) 18–76.

[5] Ethier, W., 'Input Substitution and the Concept of the Effective Rate of Protection', *Journal of Political Economy*, LXXX (Jan–Feb 1972) 34–47.

[6] Guisinger, S. E., 'Negative Value Added and the Theory of Effective Protection', *Quarterly Journal of Economics*, LXXXIII (Aug 1969) 415–33.

[7] Kemp, M. C., *The Pure Theory of International Trade and Investment* (Englewood Cliffs, N.J.: Prentice-Hall 1969) chap. 7.

[8] McKinnon, R. I., 'Intermediate Products and Differential Tariffs: A Generalization of Lerner's Symmetry Theorem', *Quarterly Journal of Economics*, LXXX (Nov 1966) 584–615.

[9] Melvin, J. R., 'Intermediate Goods, the Production Possibility Curve, and the Gains from Trade', *Quarterly Journal of Economics*, LXXXIII (Feb 1969) 141–51.

[10] Vanek, J., 'Variable Factor Proportions and Inter-Industry Flows in the Theory of International Trade', *Quarterly Journal of Economics*, LXXVII (Feb 1963) 129–42.

[11] Yates, P. L., *Forty Years of Foreign Trade* (London: Allen & Unwin, 1959).

SUPPLEMENTARY READINGS

[12] Warne, R. D., 'Intermediate Goods in International Trade with Variable Proportions and Two Primary Inputs', *Quarterly Journal of Economics*, LXXXV (May 1971) 225–36.

8　Pure Intermediate Products

In the previous chapter our analysis focused entirely on the implications of inter-industry flows for various theorems in trade theory. As noted there, most of the trade literature on intermediate products concerns the commodities which serve the dual role of goods used for final consumption and as productive inputs. However, there exists another class of intermediate goods which are produced solely to be used as productive inputs and not for final consumption at all. Such goods may be called pure intermediate goods, and include produced inputs like raw materials, spare parts, steel, etc. The current literature in trade theory pays scant attention to the implications of such products. If the ramifications of pure intermediate products ran closely parallel to those of inter-industry flows, the current neglect of the former could be easily vindicated. However, as will be demonstrated in this chapter, there are important differences between the implications of the two types of material inputs, crucial among them being the fact that, unlike with the inter-industry flows, the gross and net factor-intensity rankings need not be identical in the presence of pure intermediate products. This implies that those traditional theorems in trade theory that depend exclusively on the nature of the differences between the factor intensities in the two final products may no longer be valid in the model that allows for the presence of pure intermediate products, even though these theorems continued to be valid in the model with inter-industry flows.

In some respects, of course, the two types of intermediate goods give rise to identical consequences for certain variables in the economy. For example, the number of productive factors rises from two to three, so that with both classes of intermediate goods there arises the possibility of complementarity among inputs, although, as with inter-industry flows, this in itself introduces no qualitative modification to the results.

These and some other interesting points emerge vividly from the subsequent discussion, which also highlights the need for a full-fledged and separate analysis of pure intermediate products.

8.1 The Model with Pure Intermediate Goods

It is assumed that the economy under consideration consists of three goods, two final goods, X_1 and X_2, and one intermediate product, M, which is produced solely to be used as an input in the production of the final products. There are no inter-industry flows as far as the final goods are concerned, that is, none of X_1 and X_2 serves the role of an intermediate good. Relaxing this assumption adds only to complications without altering substantially any of the results derived from the simpler model. In all other respects, however, the assumptions of this chapter are the same as those of the previous one.

Full-employment equations now become

$$C_{L1}X_1 + C_{L2}X_2 + C_{LM}M = L \tag{8.1}$$

$$C_{K1}X_1 + C_{K2}X_2 + C_{KM}M = K \tag{8.2}$$

and

$$C_{M1}X_1 + C_{M2}X_2 = M \tag{8.3}$$

where C_{Mj} is the requirement of the intermediate good per unit of the jth final good ($j = 1,2$). These three equations can be reduced to two equations by substituting (8.3) in (8.1) and (8.2) to obtain

$$(C_{L1} + C_{LM}C_{M1})X_1 + (C_{L2} + C_{LM}C_{M2})X_2 = L$$

and

$$(C_{K1} + C_{KM}C_{M1})X_1 + (C_{K2} + C_{KM}C_{M2})X_2 = K$$

where the terms in the parentheses represent total factor requirements per unit of the final product. Denoting R_{ij} as the total requirement of the ith primary factor per unit of the jth final good ($i = L,K$; $j = 1,2$), these equations can be written as

$$R_{L1}X_1 + R_{L2}X_2 = L \tag{8.1*}$$

and

$$R_{K1}X_1 + R_{K2}X_2 = K. \tag{8.2*}$$

Similarly, the price equations are given by

$$C_{L1}w + C_{K1}r + C_{M1}p_M = p_1 \tag{8.4}$$

$$C_{L2}w + C_{K2}r + C_{M2}p_M = p_2 \tag{8.5}$$

and

$$C_{LM}w + C_{KM}r = p_M \tag{8.6}$$

or by

$$R_{L1}w + R_{K1}r = p_1 \tag{8.4*}$$

and

$$R_{L2}w + R_{K2}r = p_2 \tag{8.5*}$$

where p_M is the price of the intermediate good.

At this stage it is necessary to introduce a distinction between *gross* and *net* capital/labour ratios in the final-good industry in our model with pure intermediate products. The net or apparent capital/labour ratio in the jth final good is as usual given by $k_j = K_j/L_j$, whereas the gross capital/labour ratio (k'_j) equals the ratio between the amounts of capital and labour utilised directly and indirectly by the final product. For example, the gross amount of capital employed in the jth final good (K'_j) equals the amount of capital utilised directly (K_j) plus the amount of capital used by the intermediate good (K_M) multiplied by the proportion of the intermediate good used in the production of the jth final good; that is,

$$K'_j = K_j + (M_j/M)K_M$$

so that the gross capital/output coefficient is given by

$$\frac{K'_j}{X_j} = \frac{K_j}{X_j} + \frac{(M_j/M)K_M}{X_j} = C_{Kj} + C_{Mj}C_{KM} = R_{Kj}.$$

Similarly, the gross labour/output coefficient is given by R_{Lj}. Let R be the matrix of gross production coefficients presented in (8.1*) and (8.2*). Evidently, then, the sign of the determinant of R determines the gross factor-intensity ranking for each commodity, that is,

$$\frac{R_{K1}}{R_{L1}} \gtrless \frac{R_{K2}}{R_{L2}}, \text{ or } k'_1 \gtrless k'_2, \text{ only if } |R| = (R_{L1}R_{K2} - R_{K1}R_{L2}) \lessgtr 0.$$

Whether or not the factor-intensity ranking in the gross sense will be identical to that in the net sense is determined by the expansion of $|R|$ in terms of the net input–output coefficients. Thus $|R| \lessgtr 0$ implies that

$$C_{L1}C_{L2}\left[\frac{C_{K1}}{C_{L1}} - \frac{C_{K2}}{C_{L2}}\right] + C_{M1}C_{LM}C_{L2}\left[\frac{C_{KM}}{C_{LM}} - \frac{C_{K2}}{C_{L2}}\right]$$
$$+ C_{M2}C_{LM}C_{L1}\left[\frac{C_{K1}}{C_{L1}} - \frac{C_{KM}}{C_{LM}}\right] \gtrless 0$$

or

$$C_{L1}C_{L2}(k_1 - k_2) + C_{M1}C_{LM}C_{L2}(k_M - k_2)$$
$$+ C_{M2}C_{LM}C_{L1}(k_1 - k_M) \gtrless 0 \quad (8.7^*)$$

where k_j is the apparent capital/labour ratio in the jth commodity $(j = 1,2,M)$. For the sake of illustration, suppose that the first industry is relatively capital-intensive in the net sense, that is, $k_1 > k_2$. Now it will be truly capital-intensive only if $k'_1 > k'_2$ or if (8.7^*) is positive. It is clear at a glance that $(k_1 - k_2)$ may not have the same sign as $(k'_1 - k'_2)$, that is, the net and the gross factor-intensity rankings may not be identical in the presence of pure intermediate products. This, incidentally, is one of the basic differences between the implications of the pure intermediate products and those of the inter-industry flows analysed in the previous chapter. However, we can derive the sufficient conditions that will ensure the identity between the net and the gross factor-intensity rankings. For example, if k_M lies between k_1 and k_2, one can observe that the sign of $(k_1 - k_2)$ is the same as the sign of $(k'_1 - k'_2)$. Thus sign $(k_1 - k_2) = $ sign $(k'_1 - k'_2)$ if $k_1 \gtrless k_M \gtrless k_2$. This identity continues to hold if k_M does not lie between k_1 and k_2, but $C_{M2}C_{L1} = C_{M1}C_{L2}$, which implies that both final products possess the same intensity of use of the intermediate product, that is, $(C_{M2}/C_{L2}) = (C_{M1}/C_{L1})$. The problem arises in the non-trivial case where this latter equality does not hold. There are two other possibilities: (i) $k_1 \gtrless k_2 \gtrless k_M$, and (ii) $k_2 \gtrless k_1 \gtrless k_M$. It may be observed that $(k_1 - k_2)$ has the same sign as $(k'_1 - k'_2)$ if the last two terms in (8.7^*) have the same sign as the first term. It turns out that in case (i) this requires that $C_{M2}/C_{L2} > C_{M1}/C_{L1}$, whereas in case (ii) it is sufficient if $C_{M2}/C_{L2} < C_{M1}/C_{L1}$. Take, for example, the possibility where $k_1 > k_2 > k_M$.

Here $(k_1 - k_2) > 0$, and if $C_{M2}/C_{L2} > C_{M1}/C_{L1}$ so that $C_{M2}C_{L1} > C_{M1}C_{L2}$, one can see that

$$C_{M2}C_{L1}(k_1 - k_M) > C_{M1}C_{L2}(k_2 - k_M)$$

because $(k_1 - k_M) > (k_2 - k_M)$, which in turn implies that the first and the last two terms in (8.7*) have identical signs. From all this discussion, the following lemma may be derived:

Lemma 1. The factor-intensity rankings of the final products in the net and the gross sense are identical if (1) k_M lies between k_1 and k_2, or (2) the commodity whose capital/labour ratio lies between the capital/labour ratios of the intermediate product and the other final product is at least as intensive in the use of the intermediate product as the other final product. Any one of these conditions is also sufficient to generate an unambiguous sign of $|R|$.

The intensity in the use of the intermediate product is defined by $C_{Mj}/C_{Lj} = M_j/L_j$. If condition (2) in Lemma 1 is not satisfied, there arises the possibility of a conflict between the factor-intensity rankings in the net and the gross sense; that is to say, a commodity may be relatively capital-intensive in the net sense, but relatively labour-intensive in the gross sense, and vice versa. Stated differently, the sign of $(k_1 - k_2)$ may be opposite to the sign of $(k'_1 - k'_2)$, in which case the sign of $|R|$ will be ambiguous.

To summarise, the basic difference between the model with inter-industry flows developed in the previous chapter and the one with pure intermediate products is that the gross and net factor-intensity rankings of the final products are not necessarily identical if some goods are produced solely for the sake of further production in the final products. As stated earlier, this has significant ramifications for those theorems which depend crucially on the inter-industry factor-intensity rankings. Otherwise the present model can be developed in much the same manner as the one presented in the preceding chapter. This similarity enables us to present the equations of change without recording detailed explanations.

8.2 The Structural Relations

Proceeding in precisely the same manner as we did in the previous chapter, the following equations can be derived by differentiating the system of equations presented in the foregoing section:

$$\lambda_{L1}X_1^* + \lambda_{L2}X_2^* = L^* - (\lambda_{L1}R_{L1}^* + \lambda_{L2}R_{L2}^*) \tag{8.7}$$

$$\lambda_{K1}X_1^* + \lambda_{K2}X_2^* = K^* - (\lambda_{K1}R_{K1}^* + \lambda_{K2}R_{K2}^*) \tag{8.8}$$

$$\rho_{L1}w^* + \rho_{K1}r^* + \rho_{M1}p_M^* = p_1^* \tag{8.9}$$

$$\rho_{L2}w^* + \rho_{K2}r^* + \rho_{M2}p_M^* = p_2^* \tag{8.10}$$

$$\rho_{LM}w^* + \rho_{KM}r^* = p_M^* \tag{8.11}$$

where, as before, λ_{ij} is the proportion of the gross amount of the ith primary factor used in the production of the jth final good, and the ρ's refer to the net relative share of the relevant factor. Substituting (8.11) in (8.9) and (8.10),

$$\theta_{L1}w^* + \theta_{K1}r^* = p_1^* \tag{8.12}$$

and

$$\theta_{L2}w^* + \theta_{K2}r^* = p_2^* \tag{8.13}$$

where θ_{ij} is the gross relative share of the ith primary factor in the jth final good. As in the previous chapter, the expressions for R_{ij}^* ($i = L,K; j = 1,2$) can be obtained by differentiating

$$C_{ij} = C_{ij}(w,r,p_M) \qquad (i = L,K; j = 1,2)$$
and $$C_{iM} = C_{iM}(w,r).$$

It is shown in the appendix (section 8.8) that

$$R_{L1}^* = -\frac{(\alpha + \xi)}{\theta_{L1}}(w^* - r^*)$$

$$R_{L2}^* = -\frac{(\beta + \delta)}{\theta_{L2}}(w^* - r^*)$$

$$R_{K1}^* = \frac{(\alpha + \xi)}{\theta_{K1}}(w^* - r^*)$$

$$R_{K2}^* = \frac{(\beta + \delta)}{\theta_{K2}}(w^* - r^*)$$

where

$$\alpha = \rho_{L1}\rho_{K1}\sigma_{LK}^1 + \rho_{KM}^2\rho_{L1}\rho_{M1}\sigma_{LM}^1 + \rho_{LM}^2\rho_{K1}\rho_{M1}\sigma_{KM}^1 > 0$$
$$\beta = \rho_{L2}\rho_{K2}\sigma_{LK}^2 + \rho_{KM}^2\rho_{L2}\rho_{M2}\sigma_{LM}^2 + \rho_{LM}^2\rho_{K2}\rho_{M2}\sigma_{KM}^2 > 0$$
$$\xi = \rho_{LM}\rho_{KM}\rho_{M1}\sigma_{LK}^M > 0$$
$$\delta = \rho_{LM}\rho_{KM}\rho_{M2}\sigma_{LK}^M > 0.$$

8.3   Some Properties of the Model

To begin with, we show that the transformation curve between the final goods in the model with pure intermediate goods has the same properties as the model where the intermediate goods are absent. This result, then, is in line with the one obtained in the inter-industry flows model developed in the previous chapter.

Since the total value of production in each sector equals the sum of factor payments,

$$p_1 X_1 = wL_1 + rK_1 + p_M M_1$$
$$p_2 X_2 = wL_2 + rK_2 + p_M M_2$$

and

$$p_M M = wL_M + rK_M$$

so that

$$p_1 X_1 + p_2 X_2 = w(L_1 + L_2) + r(K_1 + K_2) + p_M M$$
$$= w(L_1 + L_2 + L_M) + r(K_1 + K_2 + K_M) = wL + rK.$$

Differentiating this totally,

$$(p_1 dX_1 + p_2 dX_2) + (X_1 dp_1 + X_2 dp_2) = Ldw + Kdr. \quad (8.14)$$

However, from (8.1*) and (8.2*) and (8.12) and (8.13),

$$Ldw + Kdr = X_1[R_{L1}dw + R_{K1}dr] + X_2[R_{L2}dw + R_{K2}dr]$$
$$= X_1 dp_1 + X_2 dp_2.$$

Substituting this in (8.14), we obtain

$$\frac{dX_1}{dX_2} = -\frac{p_2}{p_1}$$

which, of course, shows that the commodity-price ratio reflects the marginal rate of transformation between the final goods.

The shape of the transformation curve can as usual be inferred from the price–output response. Solving (8.7) and (8.8) simultaneously, utilising R_{ij}^* and (8.12) and (8.13), and setting L^* and K^* to zero, we derive

$$X_1^* = \frac{(\lambda_{K2}\gamma_L + \lambda_{L2}\gamma_K)}{|\lambda| \cdot |\theta|} (p_1^* - p_2^*)$$

and

$$X_2^* = -\frac{(\lambda_{K1}\gamma_L + \lambda_{L1}\gamma_K)}{|\lambda| \cdot |\theta|} (p_1^* - p_2^*)$$

where

$$\gamma_L = -(\lambda_{L1}R_{L1}^* + \lambda_{L2}R_{L2}^*)/(w^* - r^*) > 0$$

and

$$\gamma_K = (\lambda_{K1}R_{K1}^* + \lambda_{K2}R_{K2}^*)/(w^* - r^*) > 0.$$

It is clear that $X_1^*/(p_1^* - p_2^*) > 0$ and $X_2^*(p_1^* - p_2^*) < 0$, because both $|\lambda|$ and $|\theta|$ have the same sign as $|R|$:

$$|\lambda| = \begin{vmatrix} \lambda_{L1} & \lambda_{L2} \\ \lambda_{K1} & \lambda_{K2} \end{vmatrix} = \begin{vmatrix} \dfrac{R_{L1}X_1}{L} & \dfrac{R_{L2}X_2}{L} \\ \dfrac{R_{K1}X_1}{K} & \dfrac{R_{K2}X_2}{K} \end{vmatrix} = \frac{X_1 X_2}{LK} |R|$$

and

$$|\theta| = \begin{vmatrix} \theta_{L1} & \theta_{K1} \\ \theta_{L2} & \theta_{K2} \end{vmatrix} = \begin{vmatrix} \dfrac{R_{L1}w}{p_1} & \dfrac{R_{K1}r}{p_1} \\ \dfrac{R_{L2}w}{p_2} & \dfrac{R_{K2}r}{p_2} \end{vmatrix} = \frac{wr}{p_1 p_2} |R|.$$

All this suggests that the transformation curve is strictly concave to the origin.†

8.4 The Standard Trade Theorems

Let us now examine the Rybczynski and the Stolper–Samuelson theorems in our model incorporating the pure intermediate product. With $R_{ij}^* = 0$ at unchanged commodity prices, the solution of (8.7) and (8.8) yields

$$X_1^* = \frac{\lambda_{K2}L^* - \lambda_{L2}K^*}{|\lambda|}$$

† For further details concerning the shape and the properties of the transformation curve in the presence of pure intermediate products, see Batra and Casas [1].

and
$$X_2^* = \frac{\lambda_{L1} K^* - \lambda_{K1} L^*}{|\lambda|}.$$

If factor intensities are defined in the gross sense, $|\lambda|$, which has the same sign as $|R|$, has a definite sign; if they are specified in the net sense, then again $|\lambda|$ (or $|R|$) has an unambiguous sign only if the net and the gross factor-intensity rankings are identical. *It follows then that the Rybczynski theorem is necessarily valid only if factor · intensities are defined in the gross sense; if they are specified in the net sense the theorem may not be valid.* For example, with $L^* > 0$ and $K^* = 0$, $X_1^* > 0$ and $X_2^* < 0$ if $|\lambda| > 0$ or if the second industry is capital-intensive relative to the first in the gross sense. However, if X_1 is labour-intensive relative to X_2 in the net sense, that is, if $k_1 < k_2$, but it is capital-intensive in the gross sense, so that $k_1' > k_2'$, the Rybczynski theorem does not hold, because then the output of the apparently labour-intensive commodity will decline as a result of a rise in the supply of labour alone when terms of trade are kept constant.

In the similar fashion, the Stolper–Samuelson theorem may not be valid if the gross and the net factor-intensity rankings are not identical. This can be seen by solving (8.12) and (8.13) to obtain

$$w^* - p_j^* = \frac{\theta_{Kj}(p_1^* - p_2^*)}{|\theta|}$$

and
$$r^* - p_j^* = \frac{-\theta_{Lj}(p_1^* - p_2^*)}{|\theta|}.$$

Since again $|\theta|$ (or $|R|$) may not have the same sign as $(k_1 - k_2)$, the Stolper–Samuelson theorem may not be valid in terms of the net or the apparent factor-intensity rankings.

8.5   Technical Progress in the Final Good

We have seen above that the theorems by Rybczynski and Stolper and Samuelson do not hold if there is a conflict between gross and net factor-intensity rankings of the final products. This kind of conflict, however, does not interfere with the traditional results concerning the implications of neutral technical progress in any final product. A rigorous demonstration of this result has been provided by Casas [2].

As in the previous chapter, let

$$T^* = \frac{-1}{C_{i1}} \frac{\partial C_{i1}}{\partial t} dt \quad (i = L, K, M)$$

be the rate of Hicks-neutral technical progress in the first industry. The two equations of change (8.7) and (8.8) are now replaced by

$$\lambda_{L1} X_1^* + \lambda_{L2} X_2^* = -(\lambda_{L1} R_{L1}^* + \lambda_{L2} R_{L2}^*) + \lambda_{L1} T^* \quad (8.15)$$

and $$\lambda_{K1} X_1^* + \lambda_{K2} X_2^* = -(\lambda_{K1} R_{K1}^* + \lambda_{K2} R_{K2}^*) + \lambda_{K1} T^* \quad (8.16)$$

where R_{ij}^* now indicates the change in the input–output coefficients resulting from the change in factor prices alone. Similarly, (8.12) is now replaced by

$$\theta_{L1} w^* + \theta_{K1} r^* = p_1^* + T^* \quad (8.17)$$

whereas (8.13) is unaltered because no technical improvement occurs in the second industry. At constant commodity prices, the solution of (8.13) and (8.17) yields

$$w^* - r^* = \frac{T^*}{|\theta|}. \quad (8.18)$$

Solving (8.15) and (8.16), and using (8.18) and the expressions for R_{ij}^* presented in the preceding section, we obtain

$$X_1^* = \left[1 + \frac{\lambda_{K2} \gamma_L + \lambda_{L2} \gamma_K}{|\lambda| \cdot |\theta|} \right] T^* > 0$$

and $$X_2^* = -\frac{\lambda_{K1} \gamma_L + \lambda_{L1} \gamma_K}{|\lambda| \cdot |\theta|} \cdot T^* < 0$$

which shows clearly that neutral technical progress in a final-good industry raises the output of that good and lowers the output of the other final product when commodity prices are kept constant.

8.6 Technical Progress in the Intermediate Product

So far we have assumed that technical progress occurs in a final product. What happens if technical progress occurs in the industry producing the intermediate product, a possibility which does not arise in the inter-industry flow model? This section is devoted to an examination of the implications of this type of technical advance for the output of the final goods, when commodity prices are unchanged.

The implications of a Hicks-neutral technical improvement in M are more complex than a superficial glance might suggest. Such a technical change has the effect of lowering the unit cost of production in all three commodities, where the extent of the unit cost reduction in the two final products depends on the rate of technical advance in the intermediate good and the two material input–output coefficients, C_{Mj}. This amounts to the occurrence of technical improvements in the jth final product in proportion to the initial level of C_{Mj}, and one may argue that the entire question could be treated in the same way as that presented in the previous section. However, a technical improvement in the intermediate good also tends to raise the supply of the material input, because the same output level of this product can now be produced by smaller quantities of capital and labour. The rise in the supply of the material input in turn has its own repercussions on the output of the final products. The final outcome depends on these two forces, which may be contradictory or complementary to each other. Let

$$T_M^* = -\frac{1}{C_{iM}}\frac{\partial C_{iM}}{\partial t}\, dt \quad (i = L, K)$$

be the rate of technical advance in M. Differentiating (8.1)–(8.3), we have

$$\lambda_{L1}X_1^* + \lambda_{L2}X_2^* = \gamma_L(w^* - r^*) + \phi_{LM}T_M^* \qquad (8.19)$$

and

$$\lambda_{K1}X_1^* + \lambda_{K2}X_2^* = -\gamma_K(w^* - r^*) + \phi_{KM}T_M^* \qquad (8.20)$$

where ϕ_{LM} and ϕ_{KM} are, respectively, the proportion of the labour force and the capital stock employed in M. Similarly, differentiating (8.4)–(8.6) yields

$$\theta_{L1}w^* + \theta_{K1}r^* = p_1^* + \rho_{M1}T_M^* \qquad (8.21)$$

and

$$\theta_{L2}w^* + \theta_{K2}r^* = p_2^* + \rho_{M2}T_M^*. \qquad (8.22)$$

From (8.21) and (8.22), with $p_1^* = p_2^* = 0$, we have

$$w^* - r^* = \frac{(\rho_{M1} - \rho_{M2})T_M^*}{|\theta|}. \qquad (8.23)$$

Using (8.23), (8.19) and (8.20) can be solved to obtain

$$\frac{X_1^*}{T_M^*} = \frac{(\lambda_{K2}\gamma_L + \lambda_{L2}\gamma_K)(\rho_{M1} - \rho_{M2})}{|\lambda|\cdot|\theta|} + \frac{\lambda_{K2}\phi_{LM} - \lambda_{L2}\phi_{KM}}{|\lambda|} \qquad (8.24)$$

$$\frac{X_2^*}{T_M^*} = -\frac{(\lambda_{K1}\gamma_L + \lambda_{L1}\gamma_K)(\rho_{M1} - \rho_{M2})}{|\lambda| \cdot |\theta|} + \frac{\lambda_{L1}\phi_{KM} - \lambda_{K1}\phi_{LM}}{|\lambda|}.$$

$$(8.25)$$

Let 'cost effect' denote the effect of technical progress in the intermediate product on the unit costs of the two final goods, and let 'factor-supply effect' be the effect of such a technical change on the total supply of the material input. The cost effect depends on the relative share of the intermediate good in the total cost of each final product, or simply on ρ_{M1} and ρ_{M2}. If $\rho_{M1} = \rho_{M2}$, unit costs in both commodities decline in the same proportion. If $\rho_{M1} > \rho_{M2}$, the cost effect is equivalent to a higher rate of technical advance in X_1 than X_2, and vice versa. Consider the case where $\rho_{M1} > \rho_{M2}$, so that the unit cost in X_1 declines relative to the unit cost in X_2. If commodity prices are to be kept constant, then the relative price of the primary factor employed intensively by X_1 must rise. That this is the case follows clearly from (8.23) where, with $|\theta| > 0$, implying that X_2 is capital-intensive relative to X_1 in the gross sense, $(w^* - r^*) > 0$. This in turn will lead to a rise in the gross capital/labour ratio in both final products, and eventually to a decline in the output of the capital-intensive industry, X_2, and a rise in the output of the labour-intensive industry, X_1, if full employment is to be maintained. This is the cost effect of a technical change in the intermediate product on the two final outputs and is given by the first term in (8.24) and (8.25).

The second term in these two equations arises from the factor-supply effect. If the output of the intermediate good is kept constant, then depending on the rate of technical advance in M, capital and labour are released from M in the proportion k_M. Therefore, if k_M lies between k_1 and k_2, the output of both final goods will rise from the factor-supply effect. If $k_1 < k_M < k_2$, then $|R|$ and hence $|\lambda|$ are positive, which implies that (i) $(\lambda_{K2}/\lambda_{L2}) > (\lambda_{K1}/\lambda_{L1})$ and (ii) $(\lambda_{K2}/\lambda_{L2}) > (\phi_{KM}/\phi_{LM}) > (\lambda_{K1}/\lambda_{L1})$.[†] Clearly, then, both the numerator and the denominator of the second term in (8.24) and (8.25) are positive. In the opposite case where $k_1 > k_M > k_2$, both of these are negative. Hence the second term in both of the equations is positive when k_M lies between k_1 and k_2. However, if the latter condition is not fulfilled, $|\lambda|$ may not have a definite sign and the

† This is because $\phi_{KM}/\phi_{LM} = k_M$.

signs of the numerator and the denominator of the second term in one of the two equations (8.24) and (8.25) may be opposite. For example, suppose that $|\lambda| > 0$ so that $(\lambda_{K2}/\lambda_{L2}) > (\lambda_{K1}/\lambda_{L1})$. However, (ϕ_{KM}/ϕ_{LM}) may be greater than $(\lambda_{K2}/\lambda_{L2})$ and less than $(\lambda_{K1}/\lambda_{L1})$ if k_M does not lie between k_1 and k_2. In this case the second term is negative in (8.24) but positive in (8.25).

The overall effect of the technical progress in the intermediate good on the two final outputs is the sum of the cost effect and the factor-supply effect, which is determinate only if both effects have the same sign. On the basis of the discussion in this section, the following theorem can be derived:

Theorem 8.1. If the capital/labour ratio of the intermediate product lies between the capital/labour ratio of the final products, then technical progress in the intermediate good raises the output of the commodity which has the higher material cost component, given that the terms of trade are constant; the effect on the output of the other commodity is indeterminate.

If k_M does not lie between k_1 and k_2, then the output of X_1 may actually decline and that of X_2 rise even if $\rho_{M1} > \rho_{M2}$, or the output of both X_1 and X_2 may rise.

8.7 Trade in Intermediate Products

In the previous chapter we showed that the introduction of trade in intermediate products resulted in a rise in world welfare. This result, derived from an inter-industry flow model, cannot be extended to the present model where intermediate products are produced solely for the sake of further production in the final products. Until now we have tacitly assumed that the intermediate product is not traded, so that its local supply always equals its local demand. If we introduce trade in the intermediate product in addition to the trade in final products, the model becomes indeterminate, for if all prices, p_1, p_2 and p_M, are determined exogenously, we would have three independent price equations (8.4), (8.5) and (8.6) to determine two variables w and r. With the number of equations exceeding the number of unknowns there will be inconsistency in the model. On the other hand, if the intermediate product is non-traded, we can visualise the attainment of equilibrium in a situation where any arbitrary level of world prices p_1 and p_2 determines w and r from

(8.4) and (8.5), and w and r in turn determine p_M in (8.6) in such a way that the output of all three industries is positive. Another way out of the indeterminacy would be to assume that one of the final products is non-traded. Under no alternative, however, is it possible to compare the level of gains from trade which a country derives in two situations, one where the intermediate good is traded and the other where it is not. All we can show is that, for a small country, free trade is the optimal policy irrespective of the type of goods that are traded.†

The Pattern of Trade
It is fashionable nowadays to explain the pattern of trade between two countries in terms of the Heckscher–Ohlin theorem according to which a country exports the commodity which uses intensively its relatively abundant factor, and imports the commodity which is intensive in the use of its relatively scarce factor. Previously, the validity of this theorem has been shown to depend crucially upon the validity of the Stolper–Samuelson and the Rybczynski theorems. Unfortunately, in our model where three goods are produced, the pattern of trade turns out to be indeterminate if all three goods are to be traded, even if the Rybczynski and the Stolper–Samuelson theorems hold unambiguously.

Suppose initially no trade in M is allowed. If we assume that international production functions are identical, then the Heckscher–Ohlin theorem follows directly from the validity of the Stolper–Samuelson theorem. If, in addition, we assume that consumption patterns are also identical internationally, then the Heckscher–Ohlin theorem derives from the validity of the Rybczynski theorem. If all three goods continue to be produced in free trade equilibrium, factor prices are equated between countries; M also commands the same price between countries, and there is no incentive to trade M once the prohibition to such trade is lifted.

None the less, trade *could* take place in either direction. World outputs and world demand for final products are unaffected, because the free trade equilibrium gives rise to a given set of world prices. But each country's transformation curve shifts–outwards for the country importing M and inwards for the other. Suppose there are two countries, the home country and the foreign country,

---

† This can be shown easily by following the procedure developed in Chapter 4.

and suppose further that the former is relatively capital-abundant and that $k_1 > k_M > k_2$. If M is exported by the home country, at free trade prices the home production of both X_1 and X_2 declines (and rises abroad). Thus the home country might eventually import *both* X_1 and X_2 in exchange for M, although the Heckscher–Ohlin theory would require the home country to *export* X_1. Alternatively, if the home country imports M, it might (i) be an exporter of X_1 and an importer of X_2, or (ii) export both X_1 and X_2 and import M. Thus without further restrictions it is impossible to pick out *any* commodity and state whether it will be imported or exported by the home country.

The solution that we wish to propose must have become obvious. by now. If one of the three goods is non-traded, not only do we solve the indeterminacy problem in the model, but we can also salvage the Heckscher–Ohlin theory. Note that our solution does not require that the non-traded good be the intermediate good only.

Let us define the home country to be capital-abundant relative to the foreign country if

$$\omega_h > \omega_f$$

where $\omega = w/r$ is the wage/rental ratio and the subscripts h and f refer, respectively, to the home and foreign countries. If the intermediate good is not traded, all that we need to demonstrate in order to prove the Heckscher–Ohlin theorem is that $(d\omega/dp)$ has an unambiguous sign. From (8.12) and (8.13),

$$\frac{\omega^*}{p^*} = \frac{-1}{|\theta|} \quad (p^* = p_2^* - p_1^*). \tag{8.26}$$

From (8.26) it is clear that the relationship between ω and p is unique only if $|\theta|$ has an unambiguous sign. If $|\theta| < 0$, then with $\omega_h > \omega_f$ it is clear that

$$p_h > p_f$$

where p_j is the autarky-relative price of the second good in terms of the first in the jth country $(j = h, f)$. The home country will then export X_1 and import X_2. On the other hand, if $|\theta| > 0$, then with $\omega_h > \omega_f$

$$p_h < p_f$$

so that the home country will export X_2 and import X_1. In general, with the intermediate good non-traded, the Heckscher–Ohlin theorem will hold if sign $|\theta| = $ sign $(k_1 - k_2)$, and we already know that a sufficient condition for this is that k_M lie between k_1 and k_2.

Let us now consider the other case where one of the final goods is the non-traded good. Let X_1 be such a good. For the demonstration of the Heckscher–Ohlin theorem, we now need an expression relating p_M/p_2 with ω. From (8.12) and (8.13),

$$w^* = \frac{\theta_{K2}p_1^* - \theta_{K1}p_2^*}{|\theta|} \tag{8.27}$$

and

$$r^* = \frac{\theta_{L1}p_2^* - \theta_{L2}p_1^*}{|\theta|}. \tag{8.28}$$

Similarly, from (8.13) and (8.11) and (8.27) and (8.28),

$$p_M^* - p_2^* = \frac{(\theta_{L2} - \rho_{LM})p^*}{|\theta|} \tag{8.29}$$

so that by using (8.26), we obtain

$$\frac{p_2^* - p_M^*}{\omega^*} = \theta_{L2} - \rho_{LM} = \rho_{L2}\rho_{KM} - \rho_{LM}\rho_{K2} \tag{8.30}$$

$$= \frac{r\rho_{L2}\rho_{LM}}{w}(k_M - k_2)$$

where, in obtaining (8.29) and (8.30), we have made use of the fact that $\rho_{LM} + \rho_{KM} = \theta_{Kj} + \theta_{Lj} = 1$ $(j = 1,2)$ and that $|\theta| = \theta_{K2} - \theta_{K1} = \theta_{L1} - \theta_{L2}$. If $\omega_h > \omega_f$ and $k_2 > k_M$, then from the Heckscher–Ohlin theorem we should expect the home country to export X_2 and import M. For this pattern of trade to take place, we require that

$$\frac{p_2^* - p_M^*}{\omega^*} < 0$$

so that $(p_2/p_M)_h < (p_2/p_M)_f$ when $\omega_h > \omega_f$. Evidently, this condition is satisfied if $k_2 > k_M$. From this we conclude that if one of the final goods is treated as a non-traded good, the Heckscher–Ohlin theorem continues to hold.

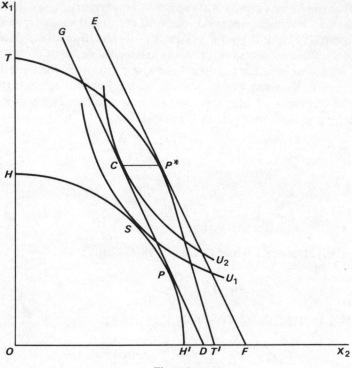

Figure 8.1

The Nature of the Free Trade Equilibrium

Given that one commodity is not traded, what is the nature of equilibrium in free trade? If the non-traded good is the intermediate product, the answer is very simple and conforms to the traditional graphical explanations, where the world prices in conjunction with the transformation curve determine the free trade production point, and where the consumption point is determined by the demand conditions. The problem is not so simple when the non-traded good is one of the final commodities. The free trade consumption point relating to final goods is, as before, determined by the demand conditions, but the production point is determined not only by world prices but also by the volume of trade.

As an illustration, consider Fig. 8.1, which depicts the case of the home country exporting X_2 and importing M while treating X_1 as the non-traded good. As previously seen, such a pattern would arise if $\omega_h > \omega_f$ under autarky and $k_2 > k_M$. In Fig. 8.1, HH' is the home country's net transformation curve and S is the point of self-sufficiency equilibrium which is determined by the tangency of the social indifference curve U_1 with HH'. Since the home country exports X_2 and imports M, the switch from autarky to free trade causes a rise in p and a decline in p_M/p_1, with all prices expressed in terms of the non-traded good. For the time being, assume that no M is imported. Then the rise in p as a result of the introduction of trade shifts production from S to P where GD, the price line prevailing in the free trade equilibrium, is tangential to the *net* transformation curve, and consumption moves from S to C which lies on a higher indifference curve U_2. P, however, is not the final equilibrium production point, for the imports of M will shift the transformation curve outwards, the extent of this shift depending upon the volume of M imported. Such a transformation curve is given by TT' and the final production point is given by P^*, where the price line EF, parallel to GD, touches the new transformation curve.

Several points deserve further exposition. First, the free trade equilibrium production point P^* is horizontally aligned with the consumption point C, showing that the supply of and the demand for X_1 are equal. Second, the output of X_2 corresponding to P^* may be smaller or larger than that corresponding to P. This follows from the fact that the import of M is equivalent to the injection of capital and labour into the home country in the proportion C_{KM}/C_{LM} $= k_M$. However, if $k_2 > k_1 > k_M$, the import of M will result in a decline in the output of X_2 and a rise in the output of X_1 at the free trade prices if X_2 is capital-intensive in gross terms,† and vice versa.

† If we rewrite equation (8.3) as

$$M = C_{M1}X_1 + C_{M2}X_2 - E_M$$

where E_M denotes the imports of the intermediate good, then at constant world prices and with fixed supplies of primary factors, it is readily shown that

$$\frac{\partial X_1}{\partial E_M} = \frac{X_1 X_2 C_{L2} C_{LM}(k_2 - k_M)}{LK|\lambda|}$$

and

$$\frac{\partial X_2}{\partial E_M} = -\frac{X_1 X_2 C_{L1} C_{LM}(k_1 - k_M)}{|\lambda|}.$$

If $k_2 > k_1 > k_M$ and if X_2 is capital-intensive in gross terms relative to X_1, then $|\lambda| > 0$ and $\partial X_1/\partial E_M > 0$ and $\partial X_2/\partial E_M < 0$. Under these conditions the import of M causes a rise in the output of X_1 and a decline in the output of X_2 at given world prices. On the other hand, if $k_2 > k_M > k_1$, then both outputs rise as a result of the importation of M when $|\lambda| > 0$. Hence the new production point P^* may or may not reflect the decline in the output of X_2.

For this reason, if we assume that sign $|\lambda| = \text{sign}(k_1 - k_2)$, it follows that the shift in the transformation curve from HH' to TT' will be biased towards X_1. Third, the length CP^* measures the value of the imports of M in terms of the second commodity and, in equilibrium, this equals the value of the exports of X_2. This follows from the fact that the change in the value of home production, equal to CP^* in Fig. 8.1, must be equal to the amount of the increase in the availability of the intermediate input multiplied by its price. Expressed in terms of the second commodity, this equals $p_M E_M / p_2$, where E_M is the amount of M imported; that is,†

$$CP^* = p_M E_M / p_2.$$

But $p_M E_M / p_2$ is nothing but the value of the imports of M expressed in terms of the second commodity. With balanced trade, this must equal the export of X_2 which, in Fig. 8.1, is also given by CP^*. In other words, the location of the final production point P^* satisfies the balance-of-trade equilibrium condition, namely, $p_M E_M = p_2 E$, where E is the amount of X_2 exported. *In toto*, Fig. 8.1 shows that as a result of the switch from autarky to free trade, production moves from S to P^*, consumption moves from S to C, and welfare improves from U_1 to U_2.

An analogous but opposite procedure can be followed for the case where the home country is an exporter of M and an importer of X_2. Here, $k_2 < k_M$ with $\omega_h > \omega_f$ under autarky. This case is pictured in Fig. 8.2, where the switch from autarky to free trade takes production from S to P^*, consumption from S to C, and welfare from U_1 to U_2. CP^* here equals the imports of X_2 as well as the value of the exports of M expressed in terms of the second commodity, with the demand for X_1 equal to the domestic production of X_1.

---

† At constant prices, the increase in the total value of domestic output resulting from the importation of E_M units of the intermediate good is given by

$$\left[\frac{\partial X_1}{\partial E_M} + p \frac{\partial X_2}{\partial E_M} \right] E_M.$$

This can be easily seen to be equal to $p_M E_M / p_1$ in terms of the first commodity, and hence to $p_M E_M / p_2$ in terms of the second.

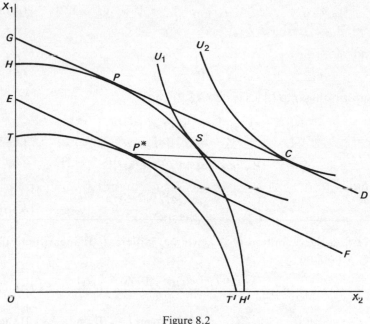

Figure 8.2

8.8 Appendix

With σ_{ik}^{j} denoting the partial elasticity of substitution between factors i and k in the jth sector, and ρ_{ij} the *direct* share of the ith factor per dollar of the jth good, the differentiation of $C_{ij} = C_{ij}(w,r,p_M)$ yields

$$C_{Lj}^* = \rho_{Lj}\sigma_{LL}^{j}w^* + \rho_{Kj}\sigma_{LK}^{j}r^* + \rho_{Mj}\sigma_{LM}^{j}p_M^*$$
$$C_{Kj}^* = \rho_{Lj}\sigma_{LK}^{j}w^* + \rho_{Kj}\sigma_{KK}^{j}r^* + \rho_{Mj}\sigma_{KM}^{j}p_M^* \qquad \text{(A8.1)}$$
$$C_{Mj}^* = \rho_{Lj}\sigma_{LM}^{j}w^* + \rho_{Kj}\sigma_{KM}^{j}r^* + \rho_{Mj}\sigma_{MM}^{j}p_M^*$$

where $j = 1,2$. Similarly, from $C_{iM} = C_{iM}(w,r)$ $\quad (i = L,K)$,

$$C_{LM}^* = \rho_{LM}\sigma_{LL}^{M}w^* + \sigma_{KM}\sigma_{LK}^{M}r^*$$
$$C_{KM}^* = \rho_{LM}\sigma_{LK}^{M}w^* + \rho_{KM}\sigma_{KK}^{M}r^*. \qquad \text{(A8.2)}$$

Equations (A8.1) and (A8.2) may be simplified by noting that

$$p_M^* = \rho_{LM}w^* + \rho_{KM}r^* \qquad \text{(A8.3)}$$
$$\rho_{Lj}\sigma_{LL}^{j} = -(\rho_{Kj}\sigma_{LK}^{j} + \rho_{Mj}\sigma_{LM}^{j}) < 0 \qquad (j = 1,2) \qquad \text{(A8.4)}$$
$$\rho_{Kj}\sigma_{KK}^{j} = -(\rho_{Lj}\sigma_{LK}^{j} + \rho_{Mj}\sigma_{KM}^{j}) < 0 \qquad (j = 1,2) \qquad \text{(A8.5)}$$

$$\rho_{Mj}\sigma_{MM}^j = -(\rho_{Lj}\sigma_{LM}^j + \rho_{Kj}\sigma_{KM}^j) < 0 \qquad (j = 1,2) \qquad \text{(A8.6)}$$

$$\rho_{LM}\sigma_{LL}^M = -\rho_{KM}\sigma_{LK}^M < 0 \qquad\qquad\qquad\qquad \text{(A8.7)}$$

and

$$\rho_{KM}\sigma_{KK}^M = -\rho_{LM}\sigma_{LK}^M < 0. \qquad\qquad\qquad\qquad \text{(A8.8)}$$

Substituting into (A8.1) and (A8.2) gives

$$
\begin{aligned}
C_{Lj}^* &= -(\rho_{Kj}\sigma_{LK}^j + \rho_{Mj}\rho_{KM}\sigma_{LM}^j)(w^* - r^*) \\
C_{Kj}^* &= (\rho_{Lj}\sigma_{LK}^j + \rho_{Mj}\rho_{LM}\sigma_{KM}^j)(w^* - r^*) \\
C_{Mj}^* &= (\rho_{Lj}\rho_{KM}\sigma_{LM}^j - \rho_{Kj}\rho_{LM}\sigma_{KM}^j)(w^* - r^*)
\end{aligned} \qquad \text{(A8.9)}
$$

and

$$
\begin{aligned}
C_{LM}^* &= -\rho_{KM}\sigma_{LK}^M(w^* - r^*) \\
C_{KM}^* &= \rho_{LM}\sigma_{LK}^M(w^* - r^*).
\end{aligned} \qquad \text{(A8.10)}
$$

From the definition of R_{ij}, we may differentiate logarithmically R_{L1} to obtain

$$R_{L1}^* = \frac{\rho_{L1}C_{L1}^* + \rho_{LM}\rho_{M1}(C_{LM}^* + C_{M1}^*)}{\theta_{L1}}. \qquad \text{(A8.11)}$$

Substituting for C_{L1}^*, C_{LM}^* and C_{M1}^* from (A8.9) and (A8.10) then gives

$$\frac{R_{L1}^*}{(w^* - r^*)} = -\frac{(\alpha + \xi)}{\theta_{L1}} \qquad \text{(A8.12)}$$

where $\quad \alpha = \rho_{L1}\rho_{K1}\sigma_{LK}^1 + \rho_{KM}^2\rho_{L1}\rho_{M1}\sigma_{LM}^1 + \rho_{LM}^2\rho_{K1}\rho_{M1}\sigma_{KM}^1$

and $\quad \xi = \rho_{LM}\rho_{KM}\rho_{M1}\sigma_{LK}^M > 0$.

Similarly, it can be shown that

$$\frac{R_{K1}^*}{(w^* - r^*)} = \frac{(\alpha + \xi)}{\theta_{K1}} \qquad \text{(A8.13)}$$

$$\frac{R_{L2}^*}{(w^* - r^*)} = \frac{-(\beta + \delta)}{\theta_{L2}} \qquad \text{(A8.14)}$$

and

$$\frac{R_{K2}^*}{(w^* - r^*)} = \frac{(\beta + \delta)}{\theta_{K2}} \qquad \text{(A8.15)}$$

where $\quad \beta = \rho_{L2}\rho_{K2}\sigma_{LK}^2 + \rho_{KM}^2\rho_{L2}\rho_{M2}\sigma_{LM}^2 + \rho_{LM}^2\rho_{K2}\rho_{M2}\sigma_{KM}^2$

and $\quad \delta = \rho_{LM}\rho_{KM}\rho_{M2}\sigma_{LK}^M > 0$.

From (A8.12)–(A8.15) it is readily seen that γ_L and γ_K are positive if α and β are positive. We shall now show that $\alpha > 0$. Now, from (A8.4)–(A8.6), it can be ascertained that

$$\sigma_{LL}^1 = \frac{1}{\rho_{L1}^2}(\rho_{K1}^2\sigma_{KK}^1 + 2\rho_{K1}\rho_{M1}\sigma_{KM}^1 + \rho_{M1}^2\sigma_{MM}^1). \quad (A8.16)$$

Since $\sigma_{LL}^1 < 0$, the quadratic form on the R.H.S. of (A8.16) must be negative definite, implying that

$$\sigma_{KK}^1\sigma_{MM}^1 - (\sigma_{KM}^1)^2$$

$$= \frac{\rho_{L1}\sigma_{LK}^1(\rho_{L1}\sigma_{LM}^1 + \rho_{K1}\sigma_{KM}^1) + \rho_{M1}\rho_{L1}\sigma_{LM}^1\sigma_{KM}^1}{\rho_{K1}\rho_{M1}} > 0$$

or

$$\sigma_{LK}^1 > \frac{-\rho_{M1}\sigma_{LM}^1\sigma_{KM}^1}{(\rho_{L1}\sigma_{LM}^1 + \rho_{K1}\sigma_{KM}^1)}.$$

Substituting this in the expression for α, we find that

$$\alpha > \rho_{KM}^2\rho_{L1}\rho_{M1}\sigma_{IM}^1 + \rho_{IM}^2\rho_{K1}\rho_{M1}\sigma_{KM}^1 - \frac{\rho_{L1}\rho_{K1}\rho_{M1}\sigma_{LM}^1\sigma_{KM}^1}{(\rho_{L1}\sigma_{LM}^1 + \rho_{K1}\sigma_{KM}^1)}$$

or

$$\alpha > \frac{\rho_{M1}}{(\rho_{L1}\sigma_{LM}^1 + \rho_{K1}\sigma_{KM}^1)}(\rho_{KM}\rho_{L1}\sigma_{LM}^1 - \rho_{LM}\rho_{K1}\sigma_{KM}^1)^2.$$

Since $(\rho_{L1}\sigma_{LM}^1 + \rho_{K1}\sigma_{KM}^1) = -\rho_{M1}\sigma_{MM}^1 > 0$, it is readily seen that $\alpha > 0$. Similarly, it can be shown that $\beta > 0$.

REFERENCES

[1] Batra, R. N., and Casas, F. R., 'Intermediate Products and the Pure Theory of International Trade: A Neo-Heckscher–Ohlin Framework', *American Economic Review*, LXIII (June 1973).
[2] Casas, F. R., 'Pure Intermediate Products, Factor Intensities and Technical Progress in the Theory of International Trade', *Southern Economic Journal*, XXXIX (July 1972).

SUPPLEMENTARY READINGS

[3] Batra, R. N., and Singh, R., 'The Intermediate Products and the Two-Sector Growth Model', paper presented at the Econometric Society Meetings, Detroit (Dec 1970).
[4] Khang, C., 'A Dynamic Model of Trade between the Final and the Intermediate Products', *Journal of Economic Theory*, I (Dec 1969) 416–37.
[5] Kuo, C., 'A Two-Sector Growth Model with an Intermediate Product in an Open Economy', Ph.D. dissertation, Department of Economics, Univ. of Western Ontario (Apr 1972).

9 The Theory of Effective Protection

Why do countries impose tariffs? The main objective of the tariff-imposing country, apart from curbing imports and possibly capturing the advantage of its natural monopoly power in trade, is to encourage the domestic production of the import-competing industries whose survival is threatened by foreign competition. Until recently, the protective effects of a tariff on the imports of a final good were taken for granted. It was generally believed that a higher rate of tariff or a higher nominal rate of protection would lead to a higher output level for the protected commodity. With the recognition by trade theorists of the importance of trade in intermediate goods, a new measure of protection, widely known as the effective rate of protection (E.R.P.), has been evolved to take into account the implications of the entire tariff structure, rather than tariffs on individual imported commodities, for the pattern of output in the economy. In contrast to the theory of nominal protection, which analyses the impact of tariffs on the total value of final goods, the E.R.P. measures the percentage change in the contribution of the domestic primary factors or, what is the same thing, in the value-added of an industry as the economy moves from a free trade situation to one of protected trade. The ramifications of the new measure of protection are far-reaching. A number of empirical studies have been made concerning the tariff structure of several developed as well as underdeveloped countries,† and the results vary from interesting to unbelievable. Balassa [1], for instance, has discovered that the effective tariff on ingots and steel forms in the U.S. is almost ten times as large as the nominal rate, whereas the corresponding rate on agricultural machinery is actually negative.

† See, for example, Barber [2], Balassa [1], Basevi [3], Grubel and Lloyd [8] and Travis [17] among countless others.

A simple example will illustrate the difference between nominal and effective protection. Suppose a locally produced, import-competing commodity is sold at the fixed world price of $100, and of this the contribution of domestic primary factors is $40 and that of intermediate goods, including the imported inputs, is $60. Suppose further that the prices of all non-primary inputs equal the world prices, and that all factors are used in fixed proportion. If a nominal tariff of 10 per cent is imposed on the importable good alone, its domestic price rises to $110, but since the prices of inter-mediate goods are unchanged, the contribution of the primary factors or the value-added increases by the full amount of $10; the percentage change in the value-added, or the E.R.P., under these conditions is 25 per cent. The E.R.P. in this case exceeds the nominal tariff of 10 per cent. Indeed, the effective rate varies inversely with the proportion of value-added in the total value of the output. For example, if in the free trade equilibrium the value-added equalled $20, the E.R.P. would be 50 per cent. Although this example is based on very simplified conditions, it does suggest that small shifts in nominal tariffs can lead to relatively large changes in effective rates.

Next, suppose that a nominal tariff is also imposed on the im-ported inputs. If this rate also equals 10 per cent, the E.R.P. equals the two nominal rates, because in this case the value-added would increase by $4. Thus if the nominal tariff rates on the imports of final and intermediate goods are the same, the E.R.P. equals the nominal rates. On the other hand, suppose the tariff rate on the imported input equals 5 per cent; then the value-added increases by $7 and the E.R.P. is $17\frac{1}{2}$ per cent. Thus if the nominal tariff on the final products exceeds that on the intermediate product, the E.R.P. is greater than both the nominal rates. By contrast, if the nominal tariff on the final good falls short of the one on the imported inputs, the E.R.P. is less than both nominal rates. For example, suppose the nominal tariff on the material input is 15 per cent. Then the value-added increases by only $1, which means that the E.R.P. equals $2\frac{1}{2}$ per cent. Of greater interest is the case where the E.R.P. may be negative. This would happen if the nominal rate on the imported input was, say, 20 per cent, for this would imply a decline in the value-added of $2 and an E.R.P. of -5 per cent.

In general, the concept of effective protection incorporates two elements that generate conflicting pulls on the output level of the protected commodity: (i) the element of subsidy implicit in the grant of the tariff on the final good tends to raise its output, and (ii) the tax element involved in the tariff on the imported input, by raising the production cost, tends to lower its output. The final result, which is the outcome of these two opposing forces, is that the output of the final good may or may not rise. This suggests that there is a close link between the sign of the E.R.P. and the direction of the change in the output of the import-competing final product. This indeed turns out to be the case in the partial equilibrium analyses which bulked large in the development of the earlier E.R.P. literature. In this sense at least, the prognosis of the 'new' theory of protection constitutes a surprising departure from most other recent developments in trade theory, where the analytical ingredients have been provided by and large by the two-factor, two-good, general equilibrium model. The earlier contributions by Barber [2], Johnson [10], Balassa [1] and Corden [5], among many others, were all cast in the partial equilibrium mould. More recently, however, trade theorists have begun to take stock of the deficiencies in the earlier E.R.P. literature by using general equilibrium models, which, of course, is the only correct approach. For, as suggested above, the interest in the E.R.P. concept was sparked primarily by economists' concern with the resource-allocational implications of a country's tariff structure, and the partial equilibrium models are not adequate for this type of analysis. Yet the partial approach is not without its merits. Apart from being simple, it is perhaps the only way through which the effective tariff rates for various industries and countries can be empirically computed.

In this chapter we begin with a brief account of the partial approach and then turn to the implications of effective protection for resource allocation in a general equilibrium model whose basic framework is one already developed in the previous chapter.

9.1 The E.R.P. Concept and the Partial Equilibrium Approach

The partial analysis of effective protection uses the familiar concepts of demand and supply for an importable commodity; however, since this particular approach ignores the income effects arising from the introduction of tariffs, there is no need to use the demand curve.†

----

† See Leith ([13] p. 74) for this observation. What it really means is that the demand curve does not shift as a result of the imposition of the tariff, implicitly assuming that national income is constant. Hence nothing is lost if the demand curve is ignored.

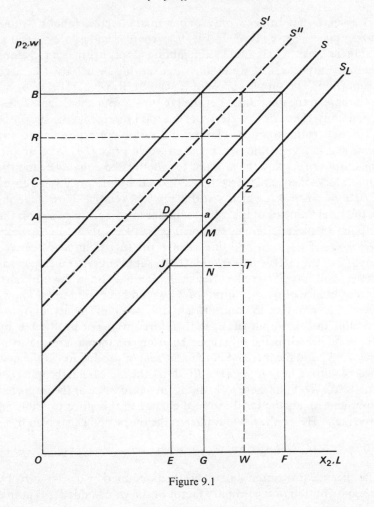

Figure 9.1

Fig. 9.1 accordingly depicts only the supply curve, which is positively inclined like the *S* curve. In order to ensure that the supply curve has the usual positive slope, it is necessary to assume under the partial equilibrium approach that the supply of some inputs is less than perfectly elastic. *Under the small country assumption, the imported inputs are available at constant world prices.* Therefore, if the supply curve is to be less than infinitely elastic, it is necessary to assume that the supply elasticity of at least one of the primary factors falls short of infinity. For the sake of simplicity of diagrammatic construction, we assume that there is only one primary factor, labour, whose supply curve is given by S_L in Fig. 9.1, where w and p_2 are measured along the vertical axis and X_2 and labour supply are measured along the horizontal axis. If we assume that all inputs are used in fixed proportions, the supply curve for X_2 can be drawn parallel to S_L, as is the case in the diagram.† Let the labour–output coefficient, L/X_2, equal unity. Then any point in the diagram represents the supply of X_2 as well as the amount of labour utilisation corresponding to any price and the wage rate. At the given world price OA, for example, the output of X_2 and the amount of labour used equal OE, and the unit value-added under free trade divided by the price is given by $EJ/DE = wL/p_2X_2$, which is nothing but the relative share of labour in the total value of output. If a nominal tariff t_2 is imposed on the imports of the final good, the local price of X_2 rises to OB where $OB = OA(1+t_2)$. In addition, if a tariff (t_Q) is imposed on the imports of the intermediate good, Q, the supply curve shifts upwards to the solid line S' to reflect the consequential rise in the unit cost. In the absence of t_Q, the output of X_2 would have risen to OF; however, in its presence the output rises only to OG. The actual or net stimulus to the output of X_2 is therefore given not by AB but by $AC = ac$, which is the difference between the increase in the local price of X_2 and the increase in the unit cost of production at the new level of output, i.e. $AC = AB - BC$. Now the increase in the unit cost equals $(\Delta p_Q Q/X_2)$, where p_Q is the given world price of the imported input and Δp_Q is the tariff-induced change in this price to the local producers. Hence the net stimulus to the output of X_2 is given by

$$AC = \Delta p_2 - \Delta p_Q C_{Q2}, \quad \text{where} \quad C_{Q2} = Q/X_2.$$

The effective protection rate (e_2) is then obtained by dividing AC by the contribution of the primary factor or the value-added (v_2) in free trade, so that

$$e_2 = \frac{AC}{v_2} = \frac{\Delta p_2 - \Delta p_Q C_{Q2}}{p_2(1 - \theta_{Q2})} = \frac{t_2 - \theta_{Q2} t_Q}{1 - \theta_{Q2}} \tag{9.1}$$

† If all factors were available at constant factor prices, the supply curves for the goods would be infinitely elastic. If one factor has an elasticity of supply less than infinity, the supply curves for goods will have the identical elasticity only if that factor is used in fixed proportions. If it is not, the rise in the unit cost would be less than the rise in the factor price, and the supply curves for goods and the factor would possess different elasticities.

where $\theta_{Q2} = p_Q C_{Q2}/p_2$ is the share of the imported input in the total cost of the imported final good, and

$$t_2 = \frac{p_2(1+t_2)-p_2}{p_2} = \frac{\Delta p_2}{p_2} \quad \text{and} \quad t_Q = \frac{p_Q(1+t_Q)-p_Q}{p_Q} = \frac{\Delta p_Q}{p_Q}.$$

If many imported inputs are used in the production of an importable commodity, then the E.R.P. formula for the jth industry is given by

$$e_j = \frac{t_j - \sum\limits_{i=1}^{n} \theta_{ij} t_i}{1 - \sum\limits_{i=1}^{n} \theta_{ij}}$$

where θ_{ij} is the share of the ith imported input in the total cost of the jth good. It can easily be seen that this formula measures the proportionate change in the value-added that occurs as the economy switches from a free trade situation to one involving tariffs. Let v_2' be the value-added per unit of output in the second industry when tariffs are introduced. Then

$$v_2 = p_2 - p_Q C_{Q2} = p_2(1-\theta_{Q2})$$

and

$$v_2' = p_2(1+t_2) - C_{Q2}p_Q(1+t_Q) = p_2[(1+t_2)-\theta_{Q2}(1+t_Q)]$$

so that

$$e_2 = \frac{v_2'-v_2}{v_2} = \frac{t_2-\theta_{Q2}t_Q}{1-\theta_{Q2}}.$$

It is clear from this formula that

  (i) if $t_2 = t_Q$, $e_2 = t_2 = t_Q$;

  (ii) if $t_2 > t_Q$, $e_2 > t_2 > t_Q$;   and

  (iii) if $t_2 < t_Q$, $e_2 < t_2 < t_Q$.

In terms of Fig. 9.1, the E.R.P. formula implies that

$$e_2 = \frac{AC}{JE} = \frac{ac}{JE} = \frac{MN}{GN}.$$

The derivation of the E.R.P. formula from Fig. 9.1 serves to show that the sign of the formula is linked with the direction of the change in the output. For example, if the input tariff, t_Q, is sufficiently large and raises the supply curve beyond S' to an extent that increased the unit production cost above the increase in p_2, the E.R.P. would be negative. But then the output of X_2 would also decline. *Hence, under the partial approach, there is a one-to-one relationship between the sign of the E.R.P. and the direction of the shift in the output of the protected commodity.* A positive change in the output implies a positive E.R.P., and vice versa.

This conclusion continues to hold even when we allow substitution among inputs, which tends to lower the increase in the unit production cost because the possibility of variablity in production coefficients permits savings in costs by giving the producers the opportunity to economise on the use of inputs with increased prices. Indeed, the higher are the substitution elasticities among inputs, the smaller would be the upward shift in the unit cost. In Fig. 9.1, the supply curve shifts only to the dotted line S'' when substitution among inputs is permitted. The output of X_2 now equals OW and the net stimulus to output is given by $AR > AC$. Hence, other things remaining equal, the substitution among inputs gives rise to a higher E.R.P. Under these conditions

$$v'_2 = p_2(1+t_2) - [C_{Q2}p_Q(1+t_Q) + p_Q\Delta C_{Q2}]$$

so that the E.R.P. formula is given by

$$e'_2 = \frac{t_2 - \theta_{Q2}(t_Q + C^*_{Q2})}{1 - \theta_{Q2}} \tag{9.2}$$

where $C^*_{Q2} = \Delta C_{Q2}/C_{Q2}$ is negative, which simply implies that a rise in p_Q, with all other input prices unchanged, leads to a decline in C_{Q2}. With $C^*_{Q2} < 0$, it is clear that $e'_2 > e_2$. In Fig. 9.1, e'_2 is given by $AR/JE = TZ/WT$. However, in spite of all these changes, the relationship between the E.R.P. and the output of the protected commodity is still positive, as can be seen from Fig. 9.1.

9.2   Negative Value-Added

One result, which has been the cause of some controversy, concerns the appearance of negative value-added in some empirical studies. Several authors have noted that in some cases the free trade value of inputs exceeds the corresponding value of outputs, so that the value-added at world prices for some industries is negative. Considerable debate has been sparked by this discovery, which at first glance appears implausible. Several misgivings have been raised concerning the meaning and the legitimacy of the concept. The issue, however, has recently been resolved by Guisinger [9] who, apart from clarifying the concept, has also shown that the negative value-added is neither the result of the constancy of production coefficients, as contended by some economists,† nor that of the gross inefficiency in the production system, as asserted by others.‡ The reason why negative value-added has occasionally appeared in some empircal studies is attributable to the fact that there is no way of getting actual data on production costs under the free trade situation, because in general few countries follow the policy of universal free trade. Thus most empirical studies have begun with the observed data on the tariff-distorted cost structure in various industries, and worked their way backwards in computing production costs in the free trade situation. The value-added in the absence of the tariffs is then calculated by deducting the value of inputs from the value of outputs at the observed world prices. This procedure is, of course, open to several objections; but even if the procedure yields an accurate approximation, the concept of the negative value-added is not so intractable. The negative value-added at world prices simply implies that the commodity in question cannot be produced in the absence of the tariff and that it is being currently produced only under the umbrella of the protective tariff. Alternatively, the exist-ence of the negative value-added at world prices implies that the industry concerned will have to be granted a production subsidy in the absence of the tariff. That an industry may not exist in the absence of the tariff is hardly surprising. As suggested by Guisinger, it simply implies that at free trade prices the local supply curve of the import-competing industry lies wholly above the world supply curve.

For further exposition of the concept of the negative value-added, consider Fig. 9.2, which is drawn on the same basis as Fig. 9.1; OB is the price of X_2 which can be observed in the protected trade situa-tion and OG is the output of X_2. Now if all tariffs are removed, the local supply curve will shift from S' to S and the local price of X_2 would decline to the free trade price OA. However, at this price nothing will be produced locally because, for the output to be

---

† See, for example, Leith [12].
‡ See Ellsworth [7] for this view.

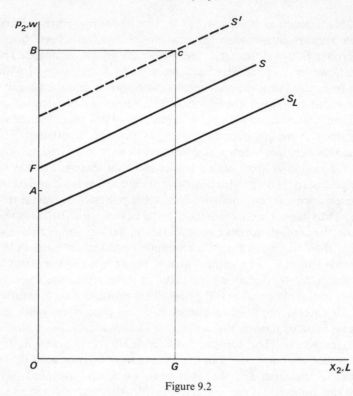

Figure 9.2

positive, the price must be greater than *OF*. Since production is assumed to be taking place under competitive conditions, this implies that the local unit cost or the total value of all inputs per unit of output exceeds the free trade price at all levels of output. All this means that the value-added at free trade prices is negative.

9.3   Effective Protection in General Equilibrium

The formulation of the concept of effective protection in terms of formulae (9.1) and (9.2) derives from the percentage change in the value-added as we move from a *laissez-faire* situation to one of protected trade. It was established that a positive E.R.P. implied a rise in the output of the protected final good above its free trade level, irrespective of whether the production coefficients were fixed or variable. We shall now examine these results in a general equilibrium model where one of the two final goods is produced with the help of two primary factors, K and L, and two intermediate products, one of which is domestically produced but not traded, and the other which is imported but not locally produced. The main difference between this model and the production models used so far is that in the presence of traded inputs the effective factor supplies become variable, for the traded inputs can be imported (or exported) at world prices which are given under our small country assumption that we maintain throughout. This is true in spite of the constancy of the supply of domestic primary factors which is generally assumed in production models without traded inputs. Thus, in the present model, the prices of some inputs are exogenously given but the demand for them is endogenously determined, in direct contrast to the models used up to the previous chapter, where factor supplies were exogenously given but factor prices were dependent variables. This difference is crucial to the existence of paradoxical results that have appeared in some general equilibrium analyses attempting to explore the consequences of the E.R.P. for resource allocation.

Unless otherwise specified, we assume throughout our analysis that there are three domestically produced commodities: X_2, the importable good, X_1, the exportable good, and M, the non-traded intermediate product, which is produced solely to be used as an input in the production of the importable good. A fourth commodity, Q, is imported from abroad and used as an input again in X_2 but not in X_1. The material inputs could also be utilised in X_1, but this would unnecessarily complicate the analysis without adding anything new to the exposition. There is perfect competition in all markets, production functions exhibit constant returns to scale and diminishing marginal rates of substitution, and two primary factors, labour (L) and capital (K), are inelastically supplied and fully employed. World prices of all traded commodities are constant, but domestic prices of the importables as well as the non-traded input may be altered owing to the imposition of tariffs.

Let C_{ij} represent the amount of the ith factor per unit of the jth product $(i = L,K,M,Q; j = 1,2,M)$. With full employment,

$$C_{L1}X_1 + C_{L2}X_2 + C_{LM}M = L \tag{9.3}$$

and

$$C_{K1}X_1 + C_{K2}X_2 + C_{KM}M = K. \tag{9.4}$$

Since $M \equiv C_{M2}X_2$, these two equations can be written as

$$C_{L1}X_1 + (C_{L2} + C_{LM}C_{M2})X_2 = L \qquad (9.3\text{A})$$

$$C_{K1}X_1 + (C_{K2} + C_{KM}C_{M2})X_2 = K. \qquad (9.4\text{A})$$

The price equations are now given by

$$C_{L1}w + C_{K1}r = p_1 \qquad (9.5)$$

$$C_{L2}w + C_{K2}r + C_{M2}p_M + C_{Q2}p_Q = p_2 \qquad (9.6)$$

and

$$C_{LM}w + C_{KM}r = p_M. \qquad (9.7)$$

Substituting (9.7) in (9.6), we obtain

$$(C_{L2} + C_{LM}C_{M2})w + (C_{K2} + C_{KM}C_{M2})r = p_2 - C_{Q2}p_Q. \qquad (9.6\text{A})$$

The production coefficients in turn are determined by the following equations:

$$C_{i2} = C_{i2}(w,r,p_M,p_Q) \qquad (i = L,K,M,Q) \qquad (9.8)$$

$$C_{i1} = C_{i1}(w,r) \qquad (i = L,K) \qquad (9.9)$$

and

$$C_{iM} = C_{iM}(w,r) \qquad (i = L,K) \qquad (9.10)$$

The production side of the model described by the system of equations (9.3)–(9.10) can be solved as follows. First, the three equations (9.5)–(9.7) containing three parameters, p_1, p_2 and p_Q, can be solved to obtain the three unknowns, w, r and p_M, in terms of the international prices of the traded goods and the input–output coefficients. We assume that this solution is unique. With w, r and p_M so determined and with p_Q exogenously given, C_{ij}'s can be solved from (9.8)–(9.10). These values in turn can be substituted in (9.3A) and (9.4A) to derive expressions for X_1 and X_2 in terms of the given supplies of K and L; finally, C_{M2} and X_2 can be used to obtain M. Hence the set of equations (9.3)–(9.10) specifies a completely determinate production side of the model. The demand side will not be presented, since the focus of this chapter is on resource allocation and factor-price changes brought about by changes in the prices of the two importables, X_2 and Q, through the imposition of tariffs.

Factor intensities in the final products are defined by columns of the C matrix which is formed by incorporating the C_{ij}'s appearing in the full-employment equations (9.3A) and (9.4A):

$$C = \begin{bmatrix} C_{L1} & C_{L2} + C_{LM} C_{M2} \\ C_{K1} & C_{K2} + C_{KM} C_{M2} \end{bmatrix}.$$

As regards the price equations (9.5) and (9.6A), the factor intensities are specified by the *rows* of the C matrix, even though it does not contain C_{Q2}; the reason for this asymmetry is attributable to the fact that, although C_{Q2} enters into the determination of p_2, it absorbs no proportion of domestic primary factors, because Q is produced abroad. Since it is the proportion of the domestic primary factors used in the production of each commodity that determines its factor intensity, the use of Q by X_2 causes no modification to the factor intensities.

As in the previous chapter, the presence of the domestically produced intermediate good (M) makes it necessary to introduce a distinction between the net and the gross capital/labour ratio in the second industry. For analytical convenience, we assume that X_2 is capital-intensive relative to X_1 in both the gross and the net sense. This implies that

$$|C| = C_{L1}(C_{K2} + C_{KM} C_{M2}) - C_{K1}(C_{L2} + C_{LM} C_{M2}) > 0$$

because

$$\frac{C_{K2} + C_{KM} C_{M2}}{C_{L2} + C_{LM} C_{M2}} > \frac{C_{K1}}{C_{L1}}.$$

The Structural Relations
The next step in facilitating the exposition is to derive expressions portraying the structural relations in the model. As before, let an asterisk denote the relative rate of change in a variable. Under the procedure that has been used repeatedly in the previous chapter, the following equations can be obtained by differentiating the system of equations presented above:

$$\lambda_{L1} X_1^* + (\lambda_{L2} + \lambda_{LM} \lambda_{M2}) X_2^*$$
$$= -(\lambda_{L1} C_{L1}^* + \lambda_{L2} C_{L2}^* + \lambda_{LM} \lambda_{M2} C_{LM}^* + \lambda_{LM} \lambda_{M2} C_{M2}^*) \quad (9.11)$$

$$\lambda_{K1}X_1^* + (\lambda_{K2} + \lambda_{KM}\lambda_{M2})X_2^*$$
$$= -(\lambda_{K1}C_{K1}^* + \lambda_{K2}C_{K2}^* + \lambda_{KM}\lambda_{M2}C_{KM}^* + \lambda_{KM}\lambda_{M2}C_{M2}^*) \quad (9.12)$$

$$\theta_{L1}w^* + \theta_{K1}r^* = p_1^* \quad (9.13)$$

$$\theta_{L2}w^* + \theta_{K2}r^* + \theta_{M2}p_M^* = p_2^* - \theta_{Q2}p_Q^* \quad (9.14)$$

$$\theta_{LM}w^* + \theta_{KM}r^* = p_M^* \quad (9.15)$$

where in this chapter λ_{ij} equals the proportion of the ith factor used directly in the production of the jth good, and θ_{ij} is the relative share of the ith input in the jth good. Substituting (9.15) in (9.14) yields

$$(\theta_{L2} + \theta_{LM}\theta_{M2})w^* + (\theta_{K2} + \theta_{KM}\theta_{M2})r^* = p_2^* - \theta_{Q2}p_Q^*. \quad (9.16)$$

Let λ and θ, respectively, be the matrices of λ and θ coefficients on the left-hand side of (9.11) and (9.12) and (9.13) and (9.16). Then, since $\lambda_{M2} = 1$,

$$\lambda = \begin{bmatrix} \lambda_{L1} & \lambda_{L2} + \lambda_{LM} \\ \lambda_{K1} & \lambda_{K2} + \lambda_{KM} \end{bmatrix}$$

and

$$\theta = \begin{bmatrix} \theta_{L1} & \theta_{K1} \\ \theta_{L2} + \theta_{LM}\theta_{M2} & \theta_{K2} + \theta_{KM}\theta_{M2} \end{bmatrix}$$

where the determinants of λ and θ are given by

$$|\lambda| = \lambda_{L1}(\lambda_{K2} + \lambda_{KM}) - \lambda_{K1}(\lambda_{L2} + \lambda_{LM})$$
$$= \frac{X_1 X_2}{KL}\left[C_{L1}(C_{K2} + C_{KM}C_{M2}) - C_{K1}(C_{L2} + C_{LM}C_{M2}\right]$$
$$= \frac{X_1 X_2}{KL}|C|$$

and

$$|\theta| = \theta_{L1}(\theta_{K2} + \theta_{KM}\theta_{M2}) - \theta_{K1}(\theta_{L2} + \theta_{LM}\theta_{M2})$$
$$= \frac{wr}{p_1 p_2}\left[C_{L1}(C_{K2} + C_{KM}C_{M2}) - C_{K1}(C_{L2} + C_{LM}C_{M2})\right]$$
$$= \frac{wr}{p_1 p_2}|C|.$$

Evidently, the signs of $|\lambda|$ and $|\theta|$ are the same as the sign of $|C|$, which implies that both $|\lambda|$ and $|\theta|$ are positive if X_2 is capital-intensive relative to X_1 in the gross sense. The determinant of θ can be written in yet another manner which highlights the role played by the imported input. Let $\psi_{L2} = \theta_{L2} + \theta_{LM}\theta_{M2}$ be the gross share of labour and $\psi_{K2} = \theta_{K2} + \theta_{KM}\theta_{M2}$ be the gross share of capital in the second industry. Since factor shares in any industry add up to unity,

$$\psi_{L2} + \psi_{K2} = \theta_{L2} + \theta_{K2} + \theta_{M2}(\theta_{LM} + \theta_{KM}) = 1 - \theta_{Q2}$$

and

$$\theta_{L1} + \theta_{K1} = 1$$

so that

$$|\theta| = \theta_{L1}\psi_{K2} - \theta_{K1}\psi_{L2} = \theta_{L1}\psi_{K2} - (1 - \theta_{L1})(1 - \theta_{Q2} - \psi_{K2})$$
$$= \psi_{K2} - \theta_{K1}(1 - \theta_{Q2}) \tag{9.17}$$

or

$$|\theta| = \theta_{L1}(1 - \theta_{Q2}) - \psi_{L2}. \tag{9.18}$$

If no imported input was being used in X_2, θ_{Q2} would be zero and X_2 would be capital-intensive relative to X_1 in the gross sense if $\psi_{K2} > \theta_{K1}$ from (9.17) or if $\theta_{L1} > \psi_{L2}$ from (9.18). The presence of payments for the use of the imported input, however, gives rise to a decline in the gross share of labour and capital in the second industry. Here X_2 is capital-intensive in the gross sense only if either $\psi_{K2} > \theta_{K1}(1 - \theta_{Q2})$, or $\theta_{L1} > \psi_{L2}/(1 - \theta_{Q2})$. Since $(1 - \theta_{Q2}) < 1$, $|\theta| > 0$ only if $\theta_{L1} > \psi_{L2}$, but ψ_{K2} need not exceed θ_{K1}. These remarks will be fruitful in facilitating the subsequent analysis.

9.4 Effective Protection and Real Wages

Some of the structural relations presented in the preceding section may now be solved to derive the implications of the E.R.P. for real rewards of the primary factors. As noted in Chapter 5, according to the Stolper–Samuelson theorem nominal protection raises the real reward of the factor employed intensively by the importable commodity and lowers the real reward of the factor employed intensively by the exportable good. We now examine the impact of the E.R.P. on real wages and see under what conditions the primary factor employed intensively by the importable good stands to benefit from effective protection. Solving (9.13) and (9.16) yields

$$w^* = -\frac{\theta_{K1}}{|\theta|}(p_2^* - \theta_{Q2}p_Q^*) = -\frac{\theta_{K1}}{|\theta|}e_2(1-\theta_{Q2}) \qquad (9.19)$$

and

$$r^* = \frac{\theta_{L1}}{|\theta|}(p_2^* - \theta_{Q2}p_Q^*) = \frac{\theta_{L1}}{|\theta|}e_2(1-\theta_{Q2}). \qquad (9.20)$$

In obtaining (9.19) and (9.20) we have equated p_1^* to zero in view of the fact that, with given world prices of all tradables, only p_2 and p_Q are subject to change as a result of tariffs. It is clear from these two equations that with $|\theta| > 0$, w is negatively and r positively related to the E.R.P. on X_2. Since

$$\frac{(1-\theta_{Q2})\theta_{L1}}{|\theta|} = \frac{\theta_{L1}(1-\theta_{Q2})}{\theta_{L1}(1-\theta_{Q2})-\psi_{L2}} > 1$$

the proportionate rise in r exceeds e_2. However, it is by no means certain that the proportionate decline in w also exceeds e_2, for

$$\frac{(1-\theta_{Q2})\theta_{K1}}{|\theta|} = \frac{\theta_{K1}(1-\theta_{Q2})}{\psi_{K2}-\theta_{K1}(1-\theta_{Q2})}$$

need not exceed unity. Furthermore, although the grant of effective protection to X_2 causes a rise in r and a decline in w, does it also result in a rise in the real reward of capital and a decline in the real wage rate in terms of the two final commodities? Since p_1 is constant, a decline in w and a rise in r amount to a decline in the real wage rate and a rise in the real reward of capital in terms of the first commodity. Furthermore, since $p_2^* > 0$, the decline in w also implies a decline in the real wage rate in terms of the second commodity. However, the outcome is not so clear for the real reward of capital in terms of the second commodity. Subtracting p_2^* from both sides of (9.20), and using (9.18), we obtain

$$r^* - p_2^* = \frac{p_2^*(\psi_{L2}+\theta_{L1}\theta_{Q2})-\theta_{L1}\theta_{Q2}p_Q^*}{|\theta|}.$$

With $|\theta| > 0$, $r^* > p_2^*$ only if

$$\frac{p_2^*}{p_Q^*} > \frac{\theta_{L1}\theta_{Q2}}{\theta_{L1}\theta_{Q2} + \psi_{L2}}. \tag{9.21}$$

Since the right-hand side of (9.21) is less than unity, a sufficient condition for the real reward of capital to rise is that $p_2^* \geq p_Q^*$. In other words, if the nominal tariff on the final product exceeds or equals that on the intermediate good, Q, the E.R.P. results in a rise in the real reward of capital in terms of both final goods. Even if $p_2^* < p_Q^*$, the real reward of capital may rise unambiguously, provided the share of the non-traded material input, M, is sufficiently large to confer high value on ψ_{L2}.

How does all this fit into the Stolper–Samuelson theorem? Evidently, the theorem continues to hold in terms of the E.R.P. if (9.21) is satisfied. However, if the output tariff is less than the input tariff, the theorem may not be valid even if the E.R.P. itself is positive. An intuitive explanation is not hard to find. According to the E.R.P. formula furnished by (9.1),

$$e_2 \geq t_2 = p_2^* \quad \text{if} \quad t_2 \geq t_Q = p_Q^*.$$

Now r^* always exceeds e_2. Hence if $t_2 \geq t_Q$, r^* will necessarily exceed p_2^*.

Of greater interest is the fact that the E.R.P. always raises the relative reward of capital, as is evident from

$$(r^* - w^*) = (p_2^* - \theta_{Q2}p_Q^*)/|\theta|$$

even though it may not unambiguously raise the real reward of capital. Thus we are back in the pre-Stolper–Samuelson world, for the main contribution of Stolper and Samuelson was to demonstrate that (nominal) protection moves the real and the relative rewards of a factor in the same direction. With effective protection, however, this may no longer be true, and we confront the same 'index number' problem which, prior to the Stolper–Samuelson contribution, is believed to have stood in the way of reaching definite conclusions concerning the effects of protection on income distribution.

9.5 The E.R.P. and Resource Allocation

The results derived in the previous section have direct relevance to the question of the implications of the E.R.P. for the allocation of resources. In the two-factor, two-commodity model without imported inputs, nominal protection always results in the shift of resources away from the unprotected commodity towards the protected commodity, and in the process raises the output of the latter at the expense of the output of the former. Does this result continue to hold when nominal protection gives way to effective protection? The answer depends wholly on how factor prices change in response to the introduction of the E.R.P.

We have shown in the preceding section that the E.R.P. conferred on the capital-intensive commodity, X_2, raises the reward of capital (though not necessarily its real reward) and lowers the wage rate. If the supply of the imported input were fixed, with given supplies of capital and labour, this would ensure a rise in the output of X_2, a decline in the output of X_1 and a rise in the X_2/X_1 ratio. However, when the world prices are given and an intermediate good is imported at these prices, the supply of the imported input is not constant, nor does its demand remain unchanged, especially when substitution between the domestic and imported inputs is permitted. Is it then possible that X_2/X_1 may actually decline even though effective protection was provided to X_2? In this section we first show that such a 'perverse' result is within the realm of possibility, and then derive the conditions that are necessary for the existence of this outcome.

With this purpose in mind, it is natural for us to revert to (9.11) and (9.12). However, the solution of these two equations will not yield any meaningful results unless we obtain the lengthy but indispensable expressions for C_{ij}^*. Differentiating (9.8)–(9.10), we get

$$C_{L1}^* = \theta_{L1}\sigma_{LL}^1 w^* + \theta_{K1}\sigma_{LK}^1 r^*$$

$$C_{K1}^* = \theta_{L1}\sigma_{LK}^1 w^* + \theta_{K1}\sigma_{KK}^1 r^*$$

$$C_{L2}^* = \theta_{L2}\sigma_{LL}^2 w^* + \theta_{K2}\sigma_{LK}^2 r^* + \theta_{M2}\sigma_{LM}^2 p_M^* + \theta_{Q2}\sigma_{LQ}^2 p_Q^*$$

$$C_{K2}^* = \theta_{L2}\sigma_{LK}^2 w^* + \theta_{K2}\sigma_{KK}^2 r^* + \theta_{M2}\sigma_{KM}^2 p_M^* + \theta_{Q2}\sigma_{KQ}^2 p_Q^*$$

$$C_{M2}^* = \theta_{L2}\sigma_{LM}^2 w^* + \theta_{K2}\sigma_{KM}^2 r^* + \theta_{M2}\sigma_{MM}^2 p_M^* + \theta_{Q2}\sigma_{MQ}^2 p_Q^*$$

$$C_{LM}^* = \theta_{LM}\sigma_{LL}^M w^* + \theta_{KM}\sigma_{LK}^M r^*$$

$$C_{KM}^* = \theta_{LM}\sigma_{LK}^M w^* + \theta_{KM}\sigma_{KK}^M r^*$$

where the θ's are as defined and σ_{ik}^j as usual is the partial elasticity of substitution between factors i and k in the jth industry. Substituting these in (9.11), we obtain†

$$\lambda_{L1}X_1^* + (\lambda_{L2} + \lambda_{LM})X_2^*$$
$$= \beta_L(w^* - r^*) + \beta_{Q1}(w^* - p_Q^*) + \beta_{Q2}(r^* - p_Q^*) \qquad (9.22)$$

where

$$\beta_L = \lambda_{L1}\theta_{K1}\sigma_{LK}^1 + \lambda_{L2}\theta_{K2}\sigma_{LK}^2 + \lambda_{LM}\theta_{KM}\sigma_{LK}^M$$
$$+ \lambda_{L2}\theta_{M2}\theta_{KM}^2\sigma_{LM}^2 + \lambda_{LM}\theta_{K2}\theta_{LM}\sigma_{KM}^2$$

$$\beta_{Q1} = \lambda_{L2}\theta_{Q2}\sigma_{LQ}^2 + \lambda_{LM}\theta_{LM}\theta_{Q2}\sigma_{MQ}^2$$

and

$$\beta_{Q2} = \lambda_{LM}\theta_{KM}\theta_{Q2}\sigma_{MQ}^2.$$

Performing analogous substitutions in (9.12) yields

$$\lambda_{K1}X_1^* + (\lambda_{K2} + \lambda_{KM})X_2^*$$
$$= -\beta_K(w^* - r^*) + \beta_{Q3}(w^* - p_Q^*) + \beta_{Q4}(r^* - p_Q^*) \qquad (9.23)$$

where

$$\beta_K = \lambda_{K1}\theta_{L1}\sigma_{LK}^1 + \lambda_{K2}\theta_{L2}\sigma_{LM}^2 + \lambda_{KM}\theta_{LM}\sigma_{LK}^M$$
$$+ \lambda_{KM}\theta_{KM}\theta_{L2}\sigma_{LM}^2 + \lambda_{K2}\theta_{M2}\theta_{LM}^2\sigma_{KM}^2$$

$$\beta_{Q3} = \lambda_{KM}\theta_{LM}\theta_{Q2}\sigma_{MQ}^2$$

and

$$\beta_{Q4} = \lambda_{K2}\theta_{Q2}\sigma_{KQ}^2 + \lambda_{KM}\theta_{KM}\theta_{Q2}\sigma_{MQ}^2.$$

Subtracting (9.23) from (9.22) and performing some manipulations, we derive

$$|\lambda|(X_1^* - X_2^*) = (\beta_L + \beta_K)(w^* - r^*) + \lambda_{L2}\theta_{Q2}\sigma_{LQ}^2(w^* - p_Q^*)$$
$$+ \lambda_{K2}\theta_{Q2}\sigma_{KQ}^2(p_Q^* - r^*) + \theta_{Q2}(\lambda_{LM} - \lambda_{KM})\sigma_{MQ}^2(p_M^* - p_Q^*). \qquad (9.24)$$

From (9.19) and (9.20) we get

$$w^* - r^* = -\frac{e_2(1 - \theta_{Q2})}{|\theta|} \qquad \left[e_2 = \frac{p_2^* - \theta_{Q2}p_Q^*}{1 - \theta_{Q2}} \right] \qquad (9.25)$$

---

† As in the last two chapters, the expressions for C_{ij}^* can be simplified by noting that, if all input-price ratios were constant, $C_{ij}^* = 0$. This is what has been done in obtaining the following equations.

$$w^* - p_Q^* = \frac{-\theta_{K1}p_2^* + (\theta_{K1} - \psi_{K2})p_Q^*}{|\theta|} \tag{9.26}$$

$$p_Q^* - r^* = \frac{-\theta_{L1}p_2^* + (\theta_{L1} - \psi_{L2})p_Q^*}{|\theta|}. \tag{9.27}$$

Subtracting p_Q^* from both sides of (9.15) and using (9.26) and (9.27), we obtain

$$p_M^* - p_Q^* = \frac{(\theta_{KM}\theta_{L1} - \theta_{LM}\theta_{K1})p_2^*}{|\theta|}$$

$$+ \frac{[(\theta_{LM}\theta_{K1} - \theta_{KM}\theta_{L1}) - (\theta_{LM}\theta_{K2} - \theta_{KM}\theta_{L2})]p_Q^*}{|\theta|}. \tag{9.28}$$

With this last equation we have collected all the ingredients necessary to examine the implications of effective protection for the relative outputs of the two final commodities. One of the basic differences between the effective protection and the nominal protection model is that, unlike the latter, there are several ways of conferring protection on a final commodity when tariffs on imported inputs are permitted; for example, X_2 can be protected either by imposing an output tariff, or by lowering the input tariff (or by subsidising the imports of the input), or by any combination of the two such that $(p_2^* - \theta_{Q2}p_Q^*) > 0$. To begin with, we consider the two polar cases which involve the imposition of the output or the input tariff. In a model where only imported intermediate goods are allowed to exist, Jones [11] has demonstrated that when protection is conferred purely through output tariffs, the relative output of the protected commodity must rise even when substitution is allowed between primary factors and imported intermediate inputs; if protection is provided through the other extreme way of lowering the input tariff, the relative output of the protected good may or may not rise, depending on whether or not the imported input is a better substitute of one primary factor than of the other. We shall now examine these results in the context of our model which allows for the existence of two intermediate inputs, one non-traded and the other imported from abroad.

Consider first the case where p_Q^* is zero but $p_2^* > 0$, so that protection is provided by the simplest way of the output tariff. Actually, this case is no different from the conventional model of nominal protection where intermediate inputs are ignored. First, we have to determine the signs of β_L and β_K appearing in (9.24). Following Jones, we assume that all factors are substitutes so that the cross-elasticities are positive, that is, $\sigma_{ik}^j > 0 \ (i \neq k)$.† It follows then that β_L and β_K are both positive. Let us now examine (9.24) and the signs of the four terms that make up the equation to determine the sign of $(X_1^* - X_2^*)$. For analytical convenience, we continue to assume that X_1 is labour-intensive relative to X_2 in the gross sense, so that $|\lambda|$ and $|\theta|$ are positive. With $p_Q^* = 0$, we know that $(w^* - r^*) < 0$, $w^* < 0$ and $r^* > 0$. All this follows from the discussion in the previous section. This means that the first three terms on the right-hand side of (9.24) are all negative, whereas the fourth term may be positive or negative, depending on the signs of $(\lambda_{LM} - \lambda_{KM})$ and p_M^*. From (9.28), $p_M^* \gtrless 0$ if $k_M \lessgtr k_1$; on the other hand,

$$\lambda_{LM} - \lambda_{KM} = \frac{L_M}{K} (k - k_M) \gtrless 0 \quad \text{if} \quad k \gtrless k_M$$

where $k = K/L$ is the overall capital/labour ratio in the economy. It can easily be seen that if both k_1 and k are either greater or less than k_M, p_M^* and $(\lambda_{LM} - \lambda_{KM})$ have opposite signs and the fourth term is negative, in which case $(X_1^* - X_2^*) < 0$, so that the output tariff alone leads unambiguously to a rise in the relative output of X_2. However, if k_M lies between k_1 and k, the fourth term in (9.24) is positive, in which case it is no longer clear that $(X_1^* - X_2^*) < 0$. *The imposition of the output tariff alone may then lead to the paradox of a decline in the relative output of the protected commodity.* Note that this possibility cannot arise if (i) there is no non-traded intermediate input, (ii) there is no substitution possibility between the non-traded and the traded inputs, so that $\sigma_{MQ}^2 = 0$, or (iii) the capital/labour ratio in the domestically produced input equals the overall capital/labour ratio. These are sufficient conditions, and obviously none of them is necessary to avoid the perverse possibility of a decline in the relative output of the protected commodity as a result of the introduction of the nominal (output) tariff. The necessary and sufficient conditions for the paradoxical result can be derived by substituting (9.25)–(9.28) in the general equation (9.24)

---

† There are two reasons why we make this assumption. First, it contributes to simplicity, and second, we want to make sure that some paradoxical results derived below do not depend on the special case where some factors are complementary to each other.

to obtain

$$|\lambda|(X_1^* - X_2^*)$$

$$= -[(\beta_L + \beta_K) + (\lambda_{L2}\theta_{K1}\sigma_{LQ}^2 + \lambda_{K2}\theta_{L1}\sigma_{KQ}^2)\theta_{Q2}]\frac{e_2(1-\theta_{Q2})}{|\theta|}$$

$$- [\theta_{Q2}(\lambda_{LM} - \lambda_{KM})(\theta_{K1} - \theta_{KM})\sigma_{MQ}^2]\frac{e_2(1-\theta_{Q2})}{|\theta|}$$

$$- \theta_{Q2}[(\lambda_{L2}\sigma_{LQ}^2 - \lambda_{K2}\sigma_{KQ}^2) + (\lambda_{LM} - \lambda_{KM})\sigma_{MQ}^2]p_Q^*. \qquad (9.24\text{A})$$

It can be seen that introducing t_2 alone can lead to the lowering of the relative output of X_2 if

$$\frac{(\beta_L + \beta_K)}{\theta_{Q2}} + \lambda_{L2}\theta_{K1}\sigma_{LQ}^2 + \lambda_{K2}\theta_{L1}\sigma_{KQ}^2 < (\lambda_{KM} - \lambda_{LM})(\theta_{K1} - \theta_{KM})\sigma_{MQ}^2.$$
$$(9.29)$$

Since the left-hand side of inequality (9.29) is positive, it is clear that the necessary condition for this inequality to be satisfied and the paradox to occur is that the two terms within the parentheses of the right-hand side of (9.29) have the same sign, which in turn implies that k_M lies between k_1 and k.† The likelihood of this paradox increases if, *ceteris paribus*, σ_{LQ}^2 and σ_{KQ}^2 are close to zero and σ_{MQ}^2 is sufficiently large, that is to say, if the imported input is more substitutive with the domestically produced input than it is with the primary factors. All this discussion gives rise to the following general theorem:

Theorem 9.1. When protection is provided by means of an output tariff alone, the necessary condition for the relative output of the protected commodity to decline is that the capital/labour ratio of the non-traded intermediate product lie between the capital/labour of the unprotected commodity and the overall capital/labour ratio in the economy.

---

† If $\lambda_{KM} > \lambda_{LM}$, then $k > k_M$. If $\theta_{K1} > \theta_{KM}$, the share of capital in the first industry exceeds that in the second industry, which implies that $k_1 > k_M$, as can be seen from the fact that

$$\theta_{K1} = \frac{k_1}{k_1 + \omega} = \frac{1}{1 + (\omega/k_1)}$$

and

$$\theta_{KM} = \frac{k_M}{k_M + \omega} = \frac{1}{1 + (\omega/k_M)}$$

where $\omega = w/r$.
Thus, if $k > k_M > k_1$, both expressions in the parentheses on the right-hand side of (9.29) are positive. The same result holds if $k < k_1 < k_M$.

Next, consider the other polar case where protection is granted to the second commodity by subsidising imports of the intermediate input Q, so that $p_2^* = 0$ and $p_Q^* < 0$. The first and third terms in (9.24) are again negative, but the second and fourth terms may not be.† With $p_Q^* < 0$, the second term is negative if $(w^* - p_Q^*) < 0$, which from (9.26) requires that $\theta_{K1} > \psi_{K2}$; however, from (9.17) we know that θ_{K1} may be less than or greater than ψ_{K2} for $|\theta| > 0$, which introduces the possibility that $(w^* - p_Q^*)$ may be positive, that is, the proportionate decline in w may fall short of the corresponding decline in p_Q as a result of the provision of subsidy to the imports of the input Q. Thus even if the fourth term is zero or even negative, $(X_1^* - X_2^*)$ may be positive. This is the result derived by Jones and, as we have shown, the existence of the non-traded intermediate good may attenuate or reinforce this result. The necessary condition for Jones's result can be obtained as a special case by equating p_2^* and σ_{MQ}^2 to zero in (9.24A) and using the definition of $|\theta|$, so that $(X_1^* - X_2^*) > 0$ only if

$$\theta_{Q2} p_Q^* [(\beta_L + \beta_K) + \lambda_{L2}\sigma_{LQ}^2(\theta_{K1} - \psi_{K2}) + \lambda_{K2}\sigma_{KQ}^2(\theta_{L1} - \psi_{L2})] > 0$$

which, with $p_Q^* < 0$ and $\theta_{L1} > \psi_{L2}$ for $|\theta| > 0$, requires that $\theta_{K1} < \psi_{K2}$. If the non-traded good does not exist, ψ_{K2} reduces to θ_{K2}. Hence the necessary condition for the 'perverse' possibility to arise is that the relative share of capital in the first industry be less than that in the second industry, which is, of course, within the realm of possibility, because it does not, as we have shown above, conflict with the positive sign of $|\theta|$.‡ When a non-traded material input is introduced, but $\sigma_{MQ}^2 = 0$, then the necessary condition involves the comparison between the gross share of capital ψ_{K2} in the second industry using the intermediate goods with the share of capital in the first industry which does not utilise any intermediate good. This discussion leads to the following generalised theorem which applies to Jones's result as well as ours:

Theorem 9.2. Given that $\sigma_{MQ}^2 = 0$, the necessary condition for the relative output of the protected final good to decline, when effective protection is granted by subsidising imports of the

---

† It is perhaps necessary to remind ourselves here that with $p_2^* = 0$, $e_2(1 - \theta_{Q2})$ reduces to $-\theta_{Q2}p_Q^*$.

‡ See the remarks made at the end of section 9.3.

intermediate input, is that the (gross) relative share of the primary factor employed intensively by the protected commodity exceed the relative share of the same factor in the other commodity.

When $\sigma_{MQ}^2 > 0$, this theorem continues to be valid if $k = k_M$ so that the fourth term in (9.24) falls to zero; if the fourth term there is non-zero, evidently $\theta_{K1} < \psi_{K2}$ may no longer be a necessary condition for (X_1/X_2) to rise.

The results derived in this section can be illustrated in terms of what is well known as activity-analysis diagrams. Purely for the sake of analytical convenience, we analyse the case where the non-traded input does not exist, so that the output of M falls to zero. The full-employment equations (9.3) and (9.4) are diagrammatically depicted in Fig. 9.3, where X_2 is measured along the vertical axis and X_1 along the horizontal axis. The given supplies of capital and labour together

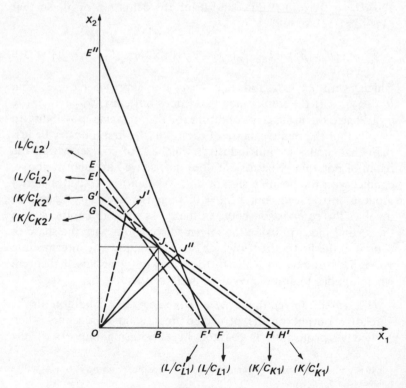

Figure 9.3

with the input coefficients furnish the lines EF and GH which are drawn by joining the points that determine the maximum output of one commodity, with zero output of the other. For example, $OE = L/C_{L2}$ is the maximum output of X_2 (with zero output of X_1)† and is obtained by employing the entire supply of labour in X_2. Along EF labour would be fully employed, along GH capital would be, and at their intersection at J there would be full employment of both factors. The diagram is drawn in such a way as to reflect our assumption that X_2 is capital-intensive relative to X_1. This can be verified by comparing the slopes of EF and GH, which are, respectively, given by C_{L1}/C_{L2} and C_{K1}/C_{K2}, so that $C_{K2}/C_{L2} > C_{K1}/C_{L1}$. At the production point given by J, the output of X_1 equals OB and that of X_2 equals JB, and the ratio between the two outputs, X_2/X_1, is given by the slope of OJ.

If there were no imported inputs, then C_{ij} would be related only to w and r and a rise in r and a decline in w consequent upon the grant of protection to X_2 would lead to a rise in C_{L1} and C_{L2} and a decline in C_{K1} and C_{K2}. This follows from the assumption of linearly homogeneous production functions. Let the prime on an input coefficient denote its magnitude in the new situation involving tariffs. Then

$$C'_{Lj} > C_{Lj} \quad \text{and} \quad C'_{Kj} < C_{Kj} \ (j = 1,2).$$

With given supplies of K and L, all the four points E, F, G and H in Fig. 9.3 would move along the axes either up or down. For example, with $C'_{L2} > C_{L2}$, point E would move down to, say, E'. Similarly, G would shift to G', F to F' and H to H', and the new full-employment equilibrium would be established at J' where the dotted lines $E'F'$ and $G'H'$, representing, respectively, the labour- and capital-constraint lines in the new situation, intersect. It may be observed that X_2 and the (X_2/X_1) ratio have risen and X_1 declined in the new situation. This is how nominal protection in the usual two-good, two-factor model raises the output of the protected commodity at the expense of the output of the unprotected commodity.

Let us now suppose that an intermediate good (Q) is also imported in addition to X_2. If the effective protection is granted only by introducing a nominal tariff on X_2, the conditions of the model do not

---

† Assuming for the time being that each good could be produced with the help of only one factor.

undergo a substantial change; p_Q remains constant and the only factor prices to change are w and r, so that the results are qualitatively similar to those derived above from Fig. 9.3. Consider the other extreme case where effective protection is granted to X_2 by subsidising the import of the intermediate good, so that p_Q declines and $(p_2^* - \theta_{Q2} p_Q^*) > 0$ because $p_2^* = 0$ and $p_Q^* < 0$. This type of effective protection also results in a rise in r and a decline in w. Since the first industry does not use the intermediate product, C_{L1} would rise and C_{K1} would decline as before, so that F in Fig. 9.3 would shift backwards, say again to F', and H would shift outwards, say to H'. The outcome is not so clear in the second industry, where input coefficients now depend on three factor prices, w, r and p_Q. Here the change in C_{L2} and C_{K2} is determined by the changes in w and r relative to the change in p_Q. Since $r^* > 0$, $w^* < 0$ and $p_Q^* < 0$, both (r/w) and (r/p_Q) rise, so that substitution must occur against the amount of capital employed in the second commodity and in favour of labour and Q. In other words, C_{K2} must decline. In addition, if $p_Q^* > w^*$, that is, if the proportionate decline in the wage rate exceeds the corresponding decline in p_Q so that both (p_Q/w) and (r/w) rise, substitution takes place against the imported input and in favour of labour, so that C_{L2} must rise. Thus if

$$r^* > p_Q^* > w^* \tag{9.30}$$

C_{K2} declines and C_{L2} rises, which in turn ensures the outward shift of G to, say, G' and a backward shift of E to, say, E'. In other words, the direction of shifts in the input–output coefficients is the same as was the case when effective protection involved the imposition of a tariff on the imports of X_2 alone. Thus if condition (9.30) is satisfied, the E.R.P. granted to X_2 by subsidising the imports of Q leads to a rise in X_2 relative to X_1. However, if $p_Q^* < w^* < r^*$, that is, if the decline in w falls short of the decline in p_Q so that (w/p_Q) rises, substitution in the second industry may take place against labour and in favour of the imported input, and if this effect is sufficiently large, C_{L2} may actually decline. Thus if

$$r^* > w^* > p_Q^* \tag{9.31}$$

C_{K2} declines as before, but C_{L2} may also decline which means that point E shifts outwards along the vertical axis, and if this shift is sufficiently pronounced, (X_2/X_1) may actually decline.† This possibility has been depicted in Fig. 9.3, where E shifts to E'' and the solid line $E''F'$, which now represents the labour-constraint line, intersects the capital-constraint line $G'H'$ at J'' to show that the (X_2/X_1) ratio has declined from the slope of OJ to that of OJ''.

There are two conditions, supplementing Theorem 9.2, which are necessary for the existence of the perverse output response to effective protection. First, condition (9.31), which provides the basis for C_{L2} to move in the 'wrong' direction, must be satisfied. Second, the intermediate product must be a better substitute of labour than it is of capital. This is because the change in C_{L2} is governed by the sign not only of $(w^* - p_Q^*)$ which is required to be positive, but also of $(w^* - r^*)$ which is negative. The latter tends to raise C_{L2} whereas the former tends to lower it. Therefore, if C_{L2} is to decline on balance, *the imported intermediate product must be a better substitute of labour than it is of capital*. In the diagram, point J'', when compared to J, shows that not only the relative output of X_2 but also its absolute output has declined. However, this is by no means necessary. An interesting property of this model is that both X_2 and X_1 may rise as a result of the effective protection and yet the (X_2/X_1) ratio may decline. This would, for example, be the case if $E''F$ were to intersect $G'H'$ slightly to the left of J'', but to the right of J. This result can be easily verified by solving (9.22) and (9.23) to obtain the expressions for individual outputs.

Until now we have considered two polar cases, one where effective protection involves only the imposition of the tariff on the imports of the final product, and the other where effective protection is provided by subsidising the imports of the intermediate input. The output response is normal in the former case simply because no change in p_Q occurs, whereas with the latter case the output response may be perverse precisely because of the change in p_Q. For the same reason, if the imported input is used in fixed proportions, the perverse output response is ruled out.

In the general case, where effective protection is conferred by means of both the input and the output tariff such that p_2^*, p_Q^* and $(p_2^* - Q_{Q2}p_Q^*)$ are all positive, the output response may again be perverse because of the change in p_Q, provided (i) the imported

† An examination of (9.24) confirms the view that (9.31) is the necessary condition for the validity of this paradoxical result.

input is used in variable proportions, (ii) p_Q^*, though less than p_2^*/θ_{Q2}, is sufficiently large, and (iii) p_Q^* does not lie between r^* and w^*, that is condition (9.30) is not satisfied. The latter alone is of course sufficient to rule out the perverse result. Moreover, the necessary condition for the perverse result when both p_2^* and p_Q^* are positive is not given by condition (9.31), for with $p_Q^* > 0$ and $w^* < 0$ this condition cannot be fulfilled. It is now the following condition, namely,

$$p_Q^* > r^* > w^* \tag{9.32}$$

that is crucial for the existence of the perverse result. As before, C_{K1} declines and C_{L1} rises and as a result H rises to H' and F declines to F' in Fig. 9.4, which is drawn on the same principles as Fig. 9.3. Since both p_Q^* and r^* are greater than w^*, both (r/w) and (p_Q/w) and hence C_{L2} rise, so that E shifts down to E' in Fig. 9.4. However, if $p_Q^* > r^*$, (p_Q/r) also rises and so may C_{K2}; thus it is now C_{K2} (instead of C_{L2}) that may shift in the 'wrong' direction, and if this

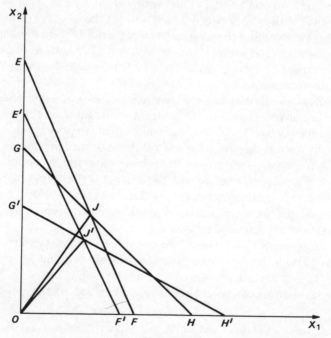

Figure 9.4

shift is sufficiently large, it is possible that the (X_2/X_1) ratio may actually decline. This is depicted in Fig. 9.4, where G moves down to G', $G'H'$ intersects $E'F'$ at J', and, as a consequence, the output ratio (X_2/X_1) declines to the slope of OJ'. It is interesting to note that with this particular type of effective protection the absolute output of both goods may decline.

When a non-traded intermediate product is introduced, the model and the explanatory logic become more complicated. If we allow substitution among all factors of production, we can no longer show that effective protection provided by means of the output tariff alone will necessarily lead to a rise in the output of the protected commodity, as has been demonstrated in the model where the non-traded intermediate product did not exist. The logic behind this result is more or less the same as that given above, where it is the change in p_Q, effected by the input tariff, that is responsible for the perverse output response. If p_Q is unchanged, the latter result cannot occur. In the presence of the domestically produced intermediate product (M), p_M^* from (9.28) may be non-zero as a result of a rise in p_2 irrespective of whether p_Q changed or remained constant. Thus in the model allowing for the existence of traded and non-traded inputs, p_M^* plays the same role as p_Q^* with one difference, namely, the change in p_M, unlike p_Q, is endogenous, so that even when p_Q^* is zero, as is the case in the presence of the output tariff alone, a change in p_M resulting from the rise in p_2 could give rise to the same possibilities as the change in p_Q did in the model without the non-traded input. In the second industry we now have to deal with gross production coefficients in $X_2(R_{i2})$. For normal results we now require a rise in $(C_{L2} + C_{LM}C_{M2})$ and a decline in $(C_{K2} + C_{KM}C_{M2})$ as the (w/r) ratio declines consequent upon the imposition of the output tariff. As usual, C_{K1} declines and C_{L1} rises, because p_M does not influence the input choice in the first industry. For the same reason, C_{LM} rises and C_{KM} declines. Since $r^* > 0$ and $w^* < 0$, and since changes in both w and r affect the change in p_M, it is obvious that

$$r^* > p_M^* > w^*$$

which implies that substitution in the second industry takes place in favour of labour and away from capital, so that C_{L2} rises and C_{K2} declines. These changes serve to raise $(C_{L2} + C_{LM}C_{M2})$ and lower $(C_{K2} + C_{KM}C_{M2})$, as is required for the normal results. However,

C_{M2} may decline or rise because it is influenced by changes in three factor prices, r, p_M and w. Suppose C_{M2} actually declines. This particular change serves to reinforce the decline in the gross capital coefficient in X_2, but tends to raise its gross labour coefficient, and if C_{M2} falls sufficiently, the latter may eventually decline. Such shifts in the production coefficients can be introduced in Fig. 9.3, if we only replace the net production coefficients in X_2 by the gross production coefficients. The interested reader will find that for some level of the decline in C_{M2} the output ratio (X_2/X_1) will also decline, thereby creating the paradox.

Even if C_{M2} was to rise the perverse result could still occur, because this factor tends to raise the gross capital coefficient in X_2, and if the impact is sufficiently pronounced this could actually rise, which would again run into conflict with the conditions sufficient to rule out the paradox.

When effective protection is provided by means of output as well as input tariffs the picture becomes fuzzier, but the explanation advanced above still applies. Specifically, the presence of non-traded material inputs may impair or strengthen the results derived in their absence. However, the source of the paradox always lies in the presence of the imported input which makes the effective factor supply variable, irrespective of the existence or the non-existence of the non-traded material input.† For if there is no imported input in the model, the output of a final good always responds positively to the rise in its relative price, as was established in the previous chapter.

---

† The analysis of this chapter, like most recent general equilibrium studies that have attempted to evaluate the E.R.P. concept in terms of its predictable effect on resource allocation, is far from encouraging to the use of effective tariffs. The villain, as suggested above, is not the non-traded input, not even the concept of the effective tariff, but the imported input whose availability at constant world prices makes the effective factor supply variable when it is substitutable with the domestic inputs. Jones [11], Ramaswami and Srinivasan [14] and Corden [6] have provided some basis for salvaging the E.R.P. concept by demonstrating the necessity of biased substitution effects for the existence of the paradoxical resource-allocational implications. Our analysis, however, destroys even that little hope, for here, even if substitution effects are unbiased, the relative output of the effectively protected commodity may still decline. Witness here the fact that in (9.29) even if

$$\sigma_{LQ}^2 = L_{KQ}^2 = \sigma_{MQ}^2$$

so that there are no biased substitution effects, inequality (9.29) could be satisfied to produce the paradox.

This can also be verified by setting θ_{Q2} to zero, so that (9.24A) reduces to

$$|\lambda| \cdot |\theta|(X_1^* - X_2^*) = -(\beta_L + \beta_K)p_2^* < 0$$

because both β_L and β_K, which include elements of the non-traded material input, are positive.

Up to now in our general equilibrium analysis of effective protection we have used the E.R.P. formula given by (9.1) wherein C_{Q2}^* is taken to be zero. If we use the 'unbiased' E.R.P. formula given by (9.2), the results derived above are unmodified at least qualitatively, if not quantitatively. For this reason alone, the additional complications introduced by the use of the unbiased formula are not worthy of detailed exploration.

9.6 Effective Protection and the Gains from Trade

The perverse resource-allocation implications of effective protection established in the preceding section have interesting and important ramifications for gains from trade. As established above, it is not in general possible to rank the E.R.P. in terms of the relative output of the protected commodity. In this section we shall show that, precisely because of its perverse resource-allocational effects, the E.R.P. cannot be conferred a unique ranking in terms of social welfare as well, in sharp contrast to the nominal tariff rate which, as we demonstrated in Chapter 4, is negatively related to community welfare, barring, of course, the presence of inferior goods.

But first we demonstrate that, for a small country, free trade continues to be the optimal policy even in a world where intermediate products are traded internationally. In order to be able to do this we need an expression for the *MRT* in our model with imported inputs. This can be obtained by differentiating

$$p_1 X_1 + p_2 X_2 - p_Q Q = wL + rK$$

so that, by using (9.3A) and (9.4A),

$$
\begin{aligned}
(p_1 dX_1 + p_2 dX_2 - p_Q dQ) &+ (X_1 dp_1 + X_2 dp_2) \\
&= L dw + K dr + Q dp_Q \\
&= dw[C_{L1} X_1 + R_{L2} X_2] + dr[C_{K1} X_1 + R_{K2} X_2] + X_2 C_{Q2} dp_Q \\
&= X_1[C_{L1} dw + C_{K1} dr] + X_2[R_{L2} dw + R_{K2} dr + C_{Q2} dp_Q] \\
&= X_1 dp_1 + X_2 dp_2
\end{aligned}
$$

whence

$$p_1 dX_1 + p_2 dX_2 - p_Q dQ = 0 \tag{9.33}$$

or

$$\frac{dX_1}{dX_2} = -\frac{(p_2 - p_Q dQ/dX_2)}{p_1} \tag{9.34}$$

which shows that the MRT in the present model equals the ratio between the marginal value-added in each final commodity.† Coming now to the demonstration of the optimality of free trade, let us consider the following system of equations:

$$U = U(D_1, D_2)$$
$$E_1 = (p_2/p_1)E_2 + (p_Q/p_1)Q \quad \text{(under balanced trade)}$$
$$D_1 = X_1 - E_1 = X_1 - [(p_2/p_1)E_2 + (p_Q/p_1)Q]$$

and

$$D_2 = X_2 + E_2.$$

Differentiating the utility function totally with respect to the E.R.P. (e_2), we obtain

$$\frac{dU}{de_2} = U_1\left[\frac{dD_1}{de_2} + \frac{U_2}{U_1}\cdot\frac{dD_2}{de_2}\right] = U_1\left[\frac{dD_1}{de_2} + \frac{p_2(1+t_2)}{p_1}\cdot\frac{dD_2}{de_2}\right]$$

$$= U_1\left[\frac{dX_1}{de_2} - \frac{p_2}{p_1}\cdot\frac{dE_2}{de_2} - \frac{p_Q}{p_1}\cdot\frac{dQ}{de_2} + \frac{p_2(1+t_2)}{p_1}\left\{\frac{dX_2}{de_2} + \frac{dE_2}{de_2}\right\}\right]$$

$$= U_1\left[\left\{\frac{dX_1}{de_2} + \frac{p_2(1+t_2)}{p_1}\cdot\frac{dX_2}{de_2} - \frac{p_Q}{p_1}\cdot\frac{dQ}{de_2}\right\} + \frac{t_2 p_2}{p_1}\cdot\frac{dE_2}{de_2}\right].$$

Now in the presence of the effective tariff, (9.33) can be written as

$$\frac{dX_1}{de_2} + \frac{p_2(1+t_2)}{p_1}\cdot\frac{dX_2}{de_2} - \frac{p_Q(1+t_Q)}{p_1}\cdot\frac{dQ}{de_2} = 0.$$

Using this

$$\frac{dU}{de_2} = U_1\left[t_Q\frac{p_Q}{p_1}\frac{dQ}{de_2} + \frac{t_2 p_2}{p_1}\cdot\frac{dE_2}{de_2}\right]. \tag{9.35}$$

---

† Here R_{L2} and R_{K2} denote the *gross* production coefficients. Furthermore, $C_{Q2} = Q/X_2$, so that Q can be substituted by $X_2 C_{Q2}$.

Since X_1 uses no imported input, the marginal value-added there is the same as its price.

It is clear from (9.35) that if initially there is no tariff, so that $t_2 = t_Q = 0$, $dU/de_2 = 0$. In other words, the initial situation of free trade is the optimal policy.

In order to demonstrate this result geometrically, we follow the geometrical technique developed recently by Ruffin [15], who assumes that C_{Q2} is constant so that the effective tariff necessarily raises the relative output of the import-competing final good. If $C_{Q2} = Q/X_2$ is constant, then $dQ/dX_2 = C_{Q2}$, so that (9.34) reduces to

$$\frac{dX_1}{dX_2} = -\frac{(p_2 - p_Q C_{Q2})}{p_1} = -\frac{v_2}{p_1}.$$

This means that the slope of the transformation curve HH' at any point in Fig. 9.5 reflects not (p_2/p_1) but v_2/p_1. Suppose P is the free trade production point; then AB, whose slope equals v_2/p_1, may be conceived as the budget line facing the producers. The equilibrium on the consumption side, however, is reached when the $MRS = (p_2/p_1) > (v_2/p_1)$. Since X_1 does not use the imported input, the

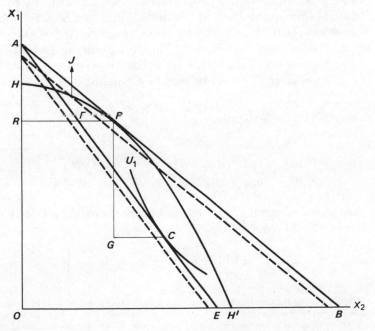

Figure 9.5

value of production and consumption is the same in terms of X_1 ($= OA$), but not in terms of X_2.† Hence the budget line facing the consumers, though steeper than AB, must start from point A. In Fig. 9.5, AE is such a budget line, consumption is at C, and the welfare level under free trade is given by U_1, which is the maximum level of welfare; PG of X_1 is exported and GC of X_2 is imported. The imports of the intermediate good (Q) equal FP in terms of the second good. This can be established by noting that $RP = AR(p_1/v_2)$ and $RF = AR(p_1/p_2)$, so that $FP = RP - RF = ARp_1[(p_2-v_2)/p_2v_2] = RP(p_2-v_2)/p_2$. Since RP is the output of X_2 at the production point P,

$$FP = p_Q Q/p_2.$$

To show that U_1 is the maximum level of welfare, consider any other policy such as the imposition of an input tariff on Q_1 which lowers the output of X_2 and moves the production point, say to J. Since p_2 and p_Q are given, the international price line facing the producers will be parallel to AB but will pass through J, and, as a result, the budget lines facing both producers and consumers will lie below AB and AE respectively (see the dotted lines in Fig. 9.5); social welfare will also then lie below U_1. Thus we see that free trade is the optimal policy even when imported inputs exist in the model.‡

The implications of the E.R.P. for welfare, however, are uncertain if C_{Q2} is not given. This can be seen by expanding (9.35) to get

$$\frac{dU}{de_2} = U_1\left[t_Q\frac{p_Q}{p_1}\frac{dQ}{de_2} + \frac{t_2 p_2}{p_1}\left\{\frac{dD_2}{de_2} - \frac{dX_2}{de_2}\right\}\right]$$

or

$$\frac{1}{U_1}\frac{dU}{de_2} = \frac{p_2}{p_1}\left[t_2\frac{dD_2}{de_2} - \frac{dX_2}{de_2}\left\{t_2 - t_Q\frac{p_Q}{p_2}\cdot\frac{dQ}{dX_2}\right\}\right]. \tag{9.36}$$

If the imported input is used in fixed proportions, $dQ/dX_2 = C_{Q2}$; therefore (9.36) reduces to

$$\frac{1}{U_1}\frac{dU}{de_2} = \frac{p_2}{p_1}\left[t_2\frac{dD_2}{de_2} - e_2(1-\theta_{Q2})\frac{dX_2}{de_2}\right]. \tag{9.37}$$

---

† Since X_2 uses the imported input for which the foreign country must be paid, the value of consumption in terms of X_2 must be less than the value of its production.

‡ This can be seen by drawing a non-intersecting social indifference curve (not drawn) touching the dotted line AE.

Since $D_2 = D_2(p_h, Y)$ where $p_h = p(1+t_2)$, $dD_2/de_2 = (\partial D_2/\partial p_h)$ $(dp_h/de_2)+(m_h/p_h)(dY/de_2)$. Substituting this in (9.37), we obtain

$$\frac{dY}{de_2}\left(1-\frac{m_h t_2}{1+t_2}\right) = pt_2 \frac{\partial D_2}{\partial p_h} \frac{dp_h}{de_2} - pe_2(1-\theta_{Q2})\frac{dX_2}{de_2}.$$

If the effective tariff is increased by a combination of a rise in t_2 and/or t_Q, then $dp_h/de_2 > 0$, and with C_{Q2} constant, $dX_2/de_2 > 0$. Since $\partial D_2/\partial p_h < 0$, all this implies that $dY/de_2 < 0$, given that $0 < m_h < 1$. In other words, if the effective tariff is raised by increasing t_2, then social welfare declines provided C_{Q2} is constant, no matter what happens to t_Q. However, if e_2 is raised by lowering both t_2 and t_Q, then dY/de_2 possesses an ambiguous sign, because then $dp_h/de_2 < 0$, although dX_2/de_2 is still positive. Similarly, if C_{Q2} is not given, the sign of dY/de_2 becomes indeterminate, because now the sign of dX_2/de_2 becomes uncertain.

The analysis of gains from trade in the presence of imported inputs gives rise to some interesting possibilities which do not arise when such inputs are ignored. The credit for opening new directions in this connection goes to Ruffin [15, 16]. He introduces the concept of the optimum effective tariff which maximises the level of welfare in the presence of the nominal tariffs on the inputs and outputs. The principal result derived by Ruffin is that *when the imported input is used only by the importable good, the optimum effective tariff is zero, where the optimal effective tariff is one that maximises the second-best level of welfare.* Since free trade continues to be the optimal policy for a small country even when imported inputs are taken into account, any level of effective tariff, positive or zero or even negative, is bound to cause a decline in social welfare. The problem is to devise that kind of tariff structure which results in the minimum decline in welfare, or, what is the same thing, in the second-best level of welfare.

We shall now derive Ruffin's theorem and then go on to show that his result depends on his special assumption that the initial situation is one involving the tariff on the final good. *If, in the initial situation, the tariff is on the imported input, the optimum effective tariff turns out to be negative.* This latter result has been recently established by Casas [4].

Let us assume that the home and the foreign prices of all importable goods differ because of the home tariffs t_2 and t_Q. Under these conditions, the first differential of the utility function can be shown to equal

$$\frac{dU}{U_1} = dY = t_2 p dE_2 + \frac{t_Q p_Q}{p_1} dQ.$$

This also follows from (9.35). Now from $Q = C_{Q2} X_2$, we have

$$dQ = X_2 dC_{Q2} + C_{Q2} dX_2. \tag{9.38}$$

Using this and the fact that $E_2 = D_2 - X_2$, we obtain

$$dY = t_2 p dD_2 - p dX_2 (t_2 - \theta_{Q2} t_Q) + \frac{t_Q p_Q}{p_1} X_2 dC_{Q2} \tag{9.39}$$

where θ_{Q2}, as before, is the share of the imported input in the total cost of the second good valued at world prices. Now

$$D_2 = D_2[p(1 + t_2), Y]$$

and $$\tag{9.40}$$

$$X_2 = X_2[p(1 + t_2), p_Q(1 + t_Q)/p_1].$$

Suppose we start with an initial situation of the tariff on the final good and keep it fixed at that level. Then

$$dD_2 = \frac{\partial D_2}{\partial Y} \cdot dY = \frac{m_h}{p_h} dY$$

and

$$dX_2 = \frac{\partial X_2(p_Q/p_1)}{\partial [p_Q(1 + t_Q)/p_1]} dt_Q < 0 \quad \text{for} \quad dt_Q > 0$$

where $d[p_Q(1 + t_Q)/p_1]/dt_Q = (p_Q/p_1)$. Substituting these, (9.39) becomes

$$dY = dY(t_2 p m_h/p_h) - p dX_2 (1 - \theta_{Q2}) e_2 + t_Q p_Q X_2 dC_{Q2}/p_1$$

or

$$dY(1 - T_2 m_h) = -p dX_2 (1 - \theta_{Q2}) e_2 + t_Q p_Q X_2 dC_{Q2}/p_1$$

where $T_2 = (t_2/1 + t_2) < 1$. It is clear that $dY = 0$ only if

$$e_2 = \theta_{Q2} C_{Q2}^* p_Q^* / X_2^* (1 - \theta_{Q2}) \quad \text{(where } t_Q = p_Q^*). \tag{9.41}$$

In other words, the second-best level of welfare is maximised when the effective tariff equals the term contained in the right-hand side of (9.41), which in view of the ambiguous sign of p_Q^*/X_2^* may be positive or negative. If the imported input is used in fixed proportions, $C_{Q2}^* = 0$, which means that the optimal effective tariff is zero. This is Ruffin's result. What this really means is that, in the presence of the initial output tariff, an input tariff should be introduced in such a way that (9.41) is satisfied.

However, suppose the initial tariff is on the imported input and is kept unchanged at that level. Then by varying the tariff on the final good we can maximise the tariff-distorted level of welfare. Then, from (9.40),

$$dD_2 = \frac{p\partial D_2}{\partial p(1+t_2)} dt_2 + \frac{\partial D_2}{\partial Y} dY \quad \text{and} \quad dX_2 = \frac{p\partial X_2}{\partial p(1+t_2)} dt_2 > 0$$

because $dp(1+t_2)/dt_2 = p$. Substituting these in (9.39), we get

$$dY(1 - T_2 m_h) = t_2 p^2 \frac{\partial D_2}{\partial p(1+t_2)} dt_2 - p dX_2 (1 - \theta_{Q2}) e_2$$

under the assumption that $C_{Q2}^* = 0$. Maximising welfare in the presence of the initial input tariff then requires that

$$e_2 = \frac{t_2 p}{(1 - \theta_{Q2})} \cdot \frac{\partial D_2}{\partial p(1+t_2)} \frac{dt_2}{dX_2}$$

Since $dX_2/dt_2 > 0$ and $\partial D_2/\partial p(1+t_2) < 0$, the *optimal effective tariff is negative*.

The economic explanation of these results is quite simple. As shown in Chapter 4, the introduction of the output tariff gives rise to a distortion on both the production side and the consumption side and thus to the production and the consumption loss. However, the production loss can be mitigated by introducing an input tariff which tends to lower the output of the importable goods and take it closer to the free trade output level. The production loss is completely eliminated if the tariff on the input is equated to t_2/θ_{Q2}, so that $e_2 = 0$, provided C_{Q2} is constant. The reason lies in the fact that when the imported input is used in fixed proportions, the E.R.P. and the output of X_2 are positively related, so that when $e_2 = 0$, the output of X_2 is the same as what it would have been under free trade, with the result that the production loss resulting from the tariffs disappears. Thus Ruffin's optimal effective tariff is one that leaves the free trade output levels unchanged.

However, this logic does not apply to the case where initially the tariff has been imposed on the input, which by lowering the output of X_2 causes the production loss but not the consumption loss. It is worth noting here that the production loss occurs whenever the actual output pattern differs from the one prevailing under free trade. A tariff on the final good promotes the expansion in its output but also introduces the consumption loss. Therefore, as the production loss is reduced, the consumption loss is introduced, and if t_2 is equated to $\theta_{Q2} t_Q$ so that $e_2 = 0$, the production loss is eliminated, but welfare does not rise to its maximum level because of the introduction of the consumption loss. Hence the optimal effective tariff is one which, apart from minimising the production loss, keeps the consumption loss at its minimum. This inevitably requires that e_2 be negative.

REFERENCES

[1] Balassa, B., 'Tariff Protection in Industrial Countries: An Evaluation', *Journal of Political Economy*, LXXIII (Dec 1965) 572–94.

[2] Barber, C. L., 'Canadian Tariff Policy', *Canadian Journal of Economics and Political Science*, XXI (Nov 1955) 513–30.

[3] Basevi, G., 'The U.S. Tariff Structure: Estimate of Effective Rates of Protection of U.S. Industries and Industrial Labour', *Review of Economics and Statistics*, XLVIII (May 1966) 147–60.

[4] Casas, F. R., 'Optimal Effective Protection in General Equilibrium', *American Economic Review*, LXIII (Sep 1973).

[5] Corden, W. M., 'The Structure of a Tariff System and the Effective Protective Rate', *Journal of Political Economy*, LXXIV (June 1966) 221–37.

[6] ——, 'The Substitution Problem in the Theory of Effective Protection', *Journal of International Economics*,I (Feb 1971) 37–58.

[7] Ellsworth, P. T., 'Import Substitution in Pakistan: Some Comments', *Pakistan Development Review*, VI (autumn 1966) 395–407.

[8] Grubel, H. G., and Lloyd, P. J. 'Factor Substitution and Effective Tariff Rates', *Review of Economic Studies*, XXXVIII (Jan 1971) 95–104.

[9] Guisinger, S. E., 'Negative Value Added and the Theory of Effective Protection', *Quarterly Journal of Economics*, LXXXIII (Aug 1969) 415–33.

[10] Johnson, H. G., 'The Theory of Tariff Structure with Special Reference to World Trade and Development', in *Trade and Development* (Geneva: Institut Universitaire des Hautes Études Internationales, 1965).

[11] Jones, R. W., 'Effective Protection and Substitution', *Journal of International Economics*, I (Feb 1971) 59–82.

[12] Leith, J. C., 'Substitution and Supply Elasticities in Calculating the Effective Protection Rate', *Quarterly Journal of Economics*, LXXXII (Nov 1968) 588–601.

[13] ——, 'The Effects of Tariffs on Production, Consumption and Trade: A Revised Analysis', *American Economic Review*, LXI (Mar 1971) 74–81.

[14] Ramaswami, V. K., and Srinivasan, T. N., 'Tariff Structure and Resource Allocation in the Presence of Factor Substitution', in J. N. Bhagwati *et al.* (eds.), *Trade, Balance of Payments, and Growth* (Amsterdam: North-Holland, 1971),
[15] Ruffin, R. J., 'Tariffs, Intermediate Goods, and Domestic Protection', *American Economic Review*, LIX (June 1969) 261–9.
[16] ——, 'The Welfare Implications of Effective Protection', in H. G. Grubel and H. G. Johnson (eds.), *Effective Tariff Protection* (Geneva: General Agreement on Tariffs and Trade and Graduate Institute of International Studies, 1971) chap. 5.
[17] Travis, W. P., 'The Effective Rate of Protection and the Question of Labour Protection in the United States', *Journal of Political Economy*, LXXVI (May/June 1968) 443–81.

SUPPLEMENTARY READINGS

[18] Anderson, J., and Naya, S., 'Substitution and Two Concepts of Effective Protection', *American Economic Review*, LIX (June 1969) 607–11.
[19] Corden, W. M., *The Theory of Protection* (Oxford: Clarendon Press, 1971).
[20] Ethier, W., 'Input Substitution and the Concept of the Effective Rate of Protection', *Journal of Political Economy*, LXXX (Jan/Feb 1972) 34–47.

10 Factor Market Imperfections

There is a general agreement among economists that perfect competition is a 'myth'. Yet the bulk of the analysis in trade theory – and economic theory in general – has been carried out under this 'mythical' assumption. Perhaps the best case that can be made for a perfect market is that it provides an 'ideal' yardstick to evaluate the efficiency of existing systems which generally fail to satisfy the stringent requirements of competitive conditions. This suggests that the assumption of perfect markets, which up to the previous chapter contributed much to the simplicity of our analysis, stands in need of replacement. Relaxing this assumption in turn permits a wide variety of production systems such as monopoly, oligopoly, imperfect factor markets, etc., all of which, individually or collectively, may characterise the production side of a country. In order to bring the analysis down to manageable proportions, some selectivity in the choice of alternative systems is unavoidable. In this chapter we relax the assumption of perfect factor markets, while product markets continue to be perfect. The discussion of the product market distortions is postponed until the next chapter.

The kind of factor market imperfections analysed here concerns the existence of a stable factor-price differential between the two industries. Such distortions may be the result of taxation, particularly of corporate income taxation which boosts up the cost of capital to the corporate sector over and above its cost to the non-corporate sector (Harberger [7]); they also may arise from the existence of the wage differential between the industrial and the subsistence sector of an underdeveloped economy (Lewis [14]), or from the introduction of unionisation which raises union wages over non-union wages. What is particularly noteworthy is that this type of factor-price differential is compatible with perfect factor mobility which we continue to assume for the better part of this chapter. In order to simplify our analysis we assume that capital continues to earn the same reward in both industries, but that the wage rates differ. The different rates of return in the two industries can be analysed without any difficulty. The crucial factor that prompts this analysis concerns the differential between factor-price ratios, irrespective of whether or not both factor prices differ in the two industries. The rest of the assumptions are the same as those made at the beginning of Chapter 2. Thus product markets are still perfect, production functions exhibit constant returns to scale and diminishing returns to factor proportions, factors are perfectly mobile and factor prices perfectly flexible, and so on.

10.1 The Model with the Wage Differential
The model is now described by the following equations:

$$C_{L1}X_1 + C_{L2}X_2 = L \qquad (10.1)$$

$$C_{K1}X_1 + C_{K2}X_2 = K \qquad (10.2)$$

$$C_{L1}w_1 + C_{K1}r = p_1 \qquad (10.3)$$

$$C_{L2}w_2 + C_{K2}r = p_2 \qquad (10.4)$$

and

$$\alpha w_1 = w_2 \qquad (\alpha \neq 1) \qquad (10.5)$$

where w_j is the wage rate in the jth sector and α is a parameter measuring the extent of the wage differential. By differentiating these equations totally, we obtain

$$\lambda_{L1}X_1^* + \lambda_{L2}X_2^* = L^* - (\lambda_{L1}C_{L1}^* + \lambda_{L2}C_{L2}^*) \qquad (10.6)$$

$$\lambda_{K1}X_1^* + \lambda_{K2}X_2^* = K^* - (\lambda_{K1}C_{K1}^* + \lambda_{K2}C_{K2}^*) \qquad (10.7)$$

$$\theta_{L1}w_1^* + \theta_{K1}r^* = p_1^* \qquad (10.8)$$

$$\theta_{L2}w_1^* + \theta_{K2}r^* = p_2^* - \theta_{L2}\alpha^* \qquad (10.9)$$

and

$$\alpha^* + w_1^* = w_2^* \qquad (10.10)$$

where $\lambda_{Lj} = C_{Lj}X_j/L$ and $\theta_{Lj} = C_{Lj}w_j/p_j$, and so on. As usual, in deriving (10.8) and (10.9) we have made use of the minimum unit cost conditions

$$\theta_{L1}C_{L1}^* + \theta_{K1}C_{K1}^* = 0 \qquad (10.11)$$

and

$$\theta_{L2} C^*_{L2} + \theta_{K2} C^*_{K2} = 0. \tag{10.12}$$

The next step involves the introduction of the elasticity of substitution in each sector, so that

$$\sigma_j = \frac{C^*_{Kj} - C^*_{Lj}}{w^*_j - r^*} \quad (j = 1,2).$$

These, together with (10.10)–(10.12), yield

$$C^*_{L1} = -\theta_{K1}\sigma_1(w^*_1 - r^*)$$
$$C^*_{K1} = \theta_{L1}\sigma_1(w^*_1 - r^*)$$
$$C^*_{L2} = -[\theta_{K2}\sigma_2(w^*_1 - r^*) + \theta_{K2}\sigma_2\alpha^*]$$

and

$$C^*_{K2} = \theta_{L2}\sigma_2(w^*_1 - r^*) + \theta_{L2}\sigma_2\alpha^*.$$

Substituting these in (10.6) and (10.7), we obtain

$$\lambda_{L1} X^*_1 + \lambda_{L2} X^*_2 = L^* + \beta_L(w^*_1 - r^*) + \lambda_{L2}\theta_{K2}\sigma_2\alpha^* \tag{10.13}$$

$$\lambda_{K1} X^*_1 + \lambda_{K2} X^*_2 = K^* - \beta_K(w^*_1 - r^*) - \lambda_{K2}\theta_{L2}\sigma_2\alpha^* \tag{10.14}$$

where

$$\beta_L = \lambda_{L1}\theta_{K1}\sigma_1 + \lambda_{L2}\theta_{K2}\sigma_2 > 0$$

and

$$\beta_K = \lambda_{K1}\theta_{L1}\sigma_1 + \lambda_{K2}\theta_{L2}\sigma_2 > 0.$$

It must be clear by now that we are solving the system of equations presented above in terms of the wage/rental ratio in the first industry. If α is unchanged, the wage/rental ratio in the the second industry is immediately determined. If α is not constant, then the wage/rental ratio in the second industry can be determined with the help of (10.10). Thus once we solve for (w_1/r), we can obtain values for the rest of the variables.

The structural relations presented above can be used to answer a number of interesting problems that were explored in the absence of the wage differential; but first a few remarks on the factor intensities in the present model are in order.

10.2   Factor Intensities and the Wage Differential

As before, let λ be the matrix of coefficients on the left-hand side of (10.13) and (10.14), and let θ be the corresponding matrix in (10.8) and (10.9). Obviously

$$|\lambda| = \frac{X_1 X_2}{KL} \cdot C_{L1} C_{L2}(k_2 - k_1) \tag{10.15}$$

and

$$|\theta| = \frac{w_1 r}{p_1 p_2} \cdot C_{L1} C_{L2}(k_2 - \alpha k_1) \tag{10.16}$$

where $k_j = K_j/L_j$ is the capital/labour ratio in the jth sector. At the same time

$$|\lambda| = \lambda_{L1} - \lambda_{K1} = \lambda_{K2} - \lambda_{L2} \tag{10.17}$$

and

$$|\theta| = \theta_{L1} - \theta_{L2} = \theta_{K2} - \theta_{K1}. \tag{10.18}$$

The main feature of the undistorted two-sector model is that $|\lambda|$ and $|\theta|$ have the same sign, for then $\alpha = 1$. Now the sign of $|\lambda|$ indicates the ranking of industries in terms of the factor intensities in the 'physical' sense, for here the comparison between the employment of the physical units of the factors in the two sectors is involved; the sign of $|\theta|$ on the other hand reflects the ranking of industries in terms of factor intensities in the 'value' sense, for here, as is evident from (10.18), we compare the relative share of any factor in the two sectors in determining whether or not an industry is capital- or labour-intensive relative to the other. This may also be seen directly by using (10.5), so that from (10.16)

$$k_2 - \alpha k_1 = \frac{w_2}{r} \left[\frac{rK_2}{w_2 L_2} - \frac{rK_1}{w_1 L_1} \right].$$

In other words, the sign of $|\theta|$ indicates that, instead of comparing the ratio between physical units of capital and labour employed in the two sectors, which comparison is reflected by the sign of $|\lambda|$, we compare the ratio between the total value of capital and labour employed in the two industries. In the absence of the wage differential, $|\lambda|$ and $|\theta|$ have the same signs. With X_2 capital-intensive relative to X_1, for example, this implies from (10.17) and (10.18) that not only does the proportion of labour exceed the proportion of capital used in the first industry, but also that the relative share of labour in the first industry exceeds that in the second. This, however, may no longer be true in the distorted model. For example, if $\alpha > 1$, the sign of $(k_2 - \alpha k_1)$ and hence of $|\theta|$ may be opposite to the sign of $(k_2 - k_1)$ and $|\lambda|$ when X_2 is capital-intensive relative to X_1 in the physical sense. From (10.5), $\alpha > 1$ implies that $w_1 < w_2$, that is, the differential is paid by the second commodity. With labour being paid a premium in the second industry, it is not difficult to visualise a situation where the relative share of labour in the second industry may exceed that in the first, so that $|\theta| < 0$, even though X_2 employs a greater proportion of capital than labour, i.e. $\lambda_{K2} > \lambda_{L2}$.

What if $\alpha < 1$, that is, $w_1 > w_2$. Here $|\lambda|$ and $|\theta|$ must possess the same sign when $k_2 > k_1$. The premium to labour is now paid by the first industry which is also labour-intensive in the physical sense. From this we conclude that if an industry pays the differential on its intensive factor (in the physical sense), $|\lambda|$ and $|\theta|$ have the same sign, that is, the factor intensities in the physical sense cannot get reversed in the value sense.

The picture is further blurred by the fact that, as first demonstrated by Johnson [10], the physical factor-intensity relationships may also change sign in the presence of the differential, even though in its absence they are non-reversible. This point can be illustrated with the help of the box diagram presented in Fig. 10.1, where X_1 in the absence of distortions is shown to be labour-intensive relative to X_2

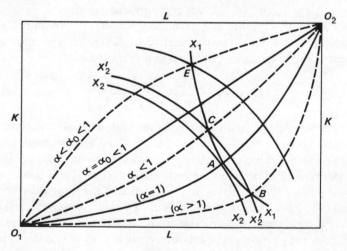

Figure 10.1

in the physical sense. In the undistorted case, the contract curve, O_1AO_2, is defined by the tangency of the isoquants for X_1 and X_2, where the slopes of the two isoquants and hence the wage/rental ratios are the same. In the presence of the factor market distortion, the contract curve will pass through points where the isoquants representing X_1 and X_2 intersect. In Fig. 10.1 the distorted contract curves are given by the dotted curves. If $\alpha > 1$ so that $(w_1/r) < (w_2/r)$, the distorted efficiency locus lies below O_1AO_2 and passes through a point such as B, for only at a point like B are the slope of the X_1 isoquant X_1X_1, and hence (w_1/r), less than the slope of the X_2 isoquant $X'_2X'_2$ and hence (w_2/r). Here the presence of the differential causes an increase in the spread between k_2 and k_1. In the opposite case where $\alpha < 1$, the efficiency locus will lie above O_1AO_2. Three possibilities emerge in this case. The distorted efficiency locus may pass through a point such as C, be identical with the diagonal O_1O_2, or pass through a point such as E which lies not only above O_1AO_2 but also above the diagonal. In the first case $\alpha < 1$ but k_2 is still greater than k_1, although the spread between the two factor intensities has declined; in the second case, for some value of $\alpha = \alpha_0 < 1$, the spread between k_2 and k_1 falls to zero and the contract curve becomes identical with the diagonal; finally, in the third case $\alpha < \alpha_0 < 1$, the relationship between k_2 and k_1 is reversed. Clearly, this result is attributable to the adverse substitution effect that takes place in the first industry against labour when $\alpha < 1$ and $w_1 > w_2$. In the absence of the differential $k_1 < k_2$. However, when the first industry pays the premium to labour, substitution takes place against labour in the first industry and as a result k_1 begins to rise. Therefore, if the premium paid by labour is sufficiently high, k_1 may rise above k_2, in which case the factor intensities in the physical sense will get reversed. From the discussion so far in this section, we may derive the following theorem:

Theorem 10.1. The necessary condition for the factor intensities to get reversed in the physical sense is that an industry pays the wage differential on its intensive factor. On the contrary, the necessary condition for the reversal of factor intensities in the value sense is that an industry pays the differential on its non-intensive factor (in the physical sense).

It follows from this theorem that factor intensities may get reversed in both the physical and the value sense, in which case $|\lambda|$ and

$|\theta|$ will again have the same sign. In the diagram, for example, k_2 becomes less than k_1 for $\alpha < \alpha_0$; then k_2 may also be less than αk_1. Thus factor intensities may get reversed in both the physical and the value sense.

The distinction introduced above between factor intensities in the value and the physical sense is very important. It is clear from (10.6) and (10.7) that the relationship among the physical variables of the system, such as commodity outputs, factor endowments, etc., is influenced by the factor intensities in the physical sense, i.e. by the sign of $|\lambda|$, whereas the relationship among the financial variables, like factor and commodity prices, is regulated by the factor intensities in the value sense, i.e. by the sign of $|\theta|$. If $|\lambda|$ and $|\theta|$ have opposite signs, the usual positive link between financial and physical variables established in the previous chapters will be reversed.

10.3 Factor and Commodity Prices

Let us first consider the relationship between factor and commodity prices at a constant wage differential, so that $\alpha^* = 0$. From (10.8) and (10.9), we can obtain

$$w_1^* - p_j^* = \frac{\theta_{Kj}(p_1^* - p_2^*)}{|\theta|} \tag{10.19}$$

$$r^* - p_j^* = \frac{-\theta_{Lj}(p_1^* - p_2^*)}{|\theta|} \tag{10.20}$$

and

$$w_1^* - r^* = \frac{p_1^* - p_2^*}{|\theta|} \tag{10.21}$$

remembering that, with $\alpha^* = 0$, $w_1^* = w_2^*$.

As expected, $|\theta|$ determines the relationship between commodity and factor prices. If $|\lambda|$ and $|\theta|$ are both positive, then it is clear that a rise in the relative price of the first commodity raises the relative and the real reward of its intensive factor, labour, in both industries (because $w_1^* = w_2^*$) and lowers the relative and the real reward of the other factor, capital. The Stolper–Samuelson theorem continues to hold in the presence of the given wage differential. However, if $|\theta| < 0$ when $|\lambda| > 0$, the Stolper–Samuelson theorem is no longer valid in the presence of the factor market distortion. The reason once again lies in the fact that the sign of $|\lambda|$ has nothing to do with the interrelations among financial variables. Furthermore, $|\theta| < 0$ means that the first industry is capital-intensive in the value sense.

The result may be illustrated in another way. Suppose the wage/rental ratio rises in the economy; then the relative price of that commodity will rise where the relative share of labour is higher; in other words, for $w_1^* - r^* > 0$, $(p_1^* - p_2^*) \gtreqqless 0$ if $\theta_{L1} \gtreqqless \theta_{L2}$, so that $|\theta| \gtreqqless 0$ (see (10.21)).

10.4 The Slope of the Transformation Curve

In the undistorted two-sector model (with or without intermediate goods) we have become accustomed to two facts: (i) the *MRT* reflects the commodity-price ratio, and (ii) the transformation curve is concave towards the origin, a result that derives directly from the positive price–output response. In the distorted model, however, we are in for some jolts. It is no longer true that (i) *MRT* equals the commodity-price ratio, (ii) the transformation curve is necessarily concave towards the origin, (iii) the price–output response is always positive, and (iv) the shape of the transformation curve can be inferred from the price–output response.

All these results can be derived by solving the structural relations presented above *and by setting* α^* *to zero*.

To derive the slope of the transformation curve, we follow a circuitous route which contributes to the relative simplicity of the calculations. Instead of using the procedure employed in the last three chapters, we utilise the one used in Chapter 4. From the production functions for X_1 and X_2 we can get

$$\frac{dX_1}{dX_2} = \frac{v_1 dL_1 + z_1 dK_1}{v_2 dL_2 + z_2 dK_2} \quad (v_j = \partial X_j/\partial L_j \quad \text{and} \quad z_j = \partial X_j/\partial K_j)$$

and since $dL_1 = -dL_2$ and $dK_1 = -dK_2$ from the maintenance of full employment, and since $p_1 z_1 = p_2 z_2$ and, in the presence of the differential, $\alpha p_1 v_1 = p_2 v_2$, we can write

$$\frac{dX_1}{dX_2} = -\frac{p[(v_2 dL_2/\alpha) + z_2 dL_2]}{v_2 dL_2 + z_2 dL_2} = -\beta p \qquad (10.22)$$

where

$$\beta = \frac{(v_2 dL_2/\alpha) + z_2 dK_2}{v_2 dL_2 + z_2 dK_2} > 0 \quad \text{and} \quad p = p_2/p_1.$$

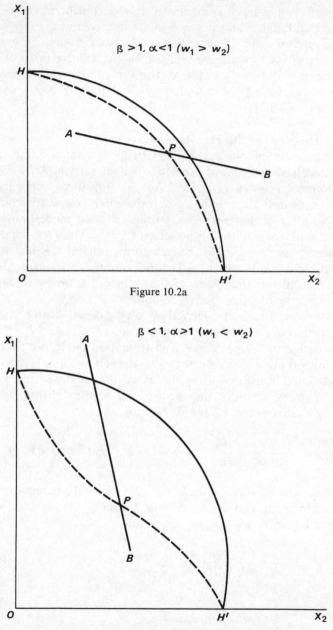

Figure 10.2a

Figure 10.2b

It is clear that $\beta \gtreqless 1$ according as $\alpha \lesseqgtr 1$. A glance at (10.22) suggests that the MRT is no longer equal to $-p$, unless, of course, $\beta = 1$, so that there is no wage differential. Two effects of the wage differential are depicted in Fig. 10.2, where the solid curve HH' is the transformation curve in the undistorted model. The presence of the differential introduces inefficiency in the system, and as a result the transformation curve shrinks towards the origin to the dotted curve HPH' except at the points of complete specialisation, H and H', where the wage differential becomes irrelevant. In Fig. 10.2A the differential is shown to be against the first industry and the price line AB cuts the distorted transformation curve from below to show that the MRT at point P exceeds the relative price of the second commodity. The converse is true in Fig. 10.2B, where the differential is paid by the second industry, the price line cuts the distorted transformation curve from above and the MRT at P falls short of the price ratio. Let us defer for the time being our remarks concerning the shape of the distorted curve.

10.5 The Price–Output Response
Let us now consider the effect of a rise in the relative price of the first commodity on the two outputs at constant factor endowments. From (10.13) and (10.14) and (10.21), we obtain

$$X_1^* = \frac{(\lambda_{K2}\beta_L + \lambda_{L2}\beta_K)(p_1^* - p_2^*)}{|\lambda| \cdot |\theta|} \qquad (10.23)$$

and

$$X_2^* = \frac{-(\lambda_{L1}\beta_K + \lambda_{K1}\dot\beta_L)(p_1^* - p_2^*)}{|\lambda| \cdot |\theta|} \qquad (10.24)$$

Evidently, a rise in the relative price of the first commodity raises the output of X_1 and lowers that of X_2 only if $|\lambda|$ and $|\theta|$ possess identical signs. The rationale behind this result is obvious. A rise in the relative price of the first commodity lowers the wage/rental ratio if the first industry pays a lower share to labour than the second industry (so that $|\theta| < 0$). The decline in the wage/rental ratio in turn tends to lower the physical capital/labour ratio in both industries and thus create an excess demand for labour and an excess supply of capital. In order to restore the full-employment equilibrium, the output of the industry that is capital-intensive in the physical sense rises and that of the other industry falls. With $k_2 > k_1$, and $|\lambda| > 0$, the rise in the output occurs in the second commodity at the expense of the output of the first, even though to begin with it was the relative price of the first commodity that increased. In other words, if $|\lambda|$ and $|\theta|$ have dissimilar signs, the price–output response is negative or 'abnormal', and the *long-run* supply curves are negatively sloped.

10.6   The Shape of the Transformation Curve

We are now analytically equipped to deal with the shape of the transformation curve which has been the subject of analysis in recent articles by Bhagwati and Srinivasan [5], Herberg and Kemp [8] and Jones [13]. The algebra in this case is highly complicated, so we shall rely mainly on the verbal discussion. We have demonstrated above that, in the presence of the given wage differential, the price–output response may be negative. If the *MRT* equalled the commodity-price ratio, this in itself would be sufficient to cause the distorted transformation curve to become globally convex towards the origin. The same would be true if β, the wedge between $-p$ and the *MRT*, were constant. This becomes evident when (10.22) is differentiated with respect to X_2 to obtain

$$\frac{d^2 X_1}{dX_2^2} = - \left[\beta \frac{dp}{dX_2} + p \frac{d\beta}{dX_2} \right]. \tag{10.25}$$

Thus if $d\beta/dX_2 = 0$, the shape of the distorted transformation curve can be inferred directly from the sign of dp/dX_2. In general, $d\beta/dX_2$ may be positive or negative even if α is constant. This factor gives rise to a rich variety of possibilities. First, $(d^2 X_1/dX_2^2)$ may be negative, whatever the sign of (dp/dX_2), in which case the distorted transformation curve will be concave to the origin as in Fig. 10.2A. Second, $(d^2 X_1/dX_2^2)$ may be positive even if $dp/dX_2 > 0$, provided $d\beta/dX_2$ is sufficiently negative, that is, the distorted transformation may be locally (or globally) convex towards the origin as in Fig. 10.2B even if the price–output response is positive. The converse is also true. The distorted transformation curve may be concave to the origin even if the price–output response is negative.

   The crux of this discussion is that, in the presence of the given wage differential, the transformation curve may have any shape irrespective of the nature of the price–output response.

10.7 The Heckscher–Ohlin Theorem

In Chapter 3 we derived sufficient conditions for the validity of the Heckscher–Ohlin theorem, which asserts that a country exports the commodity which is intensive in the use of its relatively abundant factor. Two definitions of relative factor abundance were utilised, namely the price and the physical definition. We shall now show that in terms of the price definition the Heckscher–Ohlin theorem may not be valid in the presence of distorted factor markets even if the degree of distortion, α, is the same in the two countries.

The demonstration of this point in terms of the price definition requires the use of the unpredictable relationship that exists between factor and commodity prices if the factor intensities get reversed in the value sense,† even if in the physical sense, as depicted in Fig. 10.3, they are non-reversible. The wage/rental ratio in the first industry, ω_1, is related to the capital/labour ratio in each industry as well as to the commodity-price ratio, p. In the undistorted case, $k_2 > k_1$ at all ω_1; in the presence of the differential, however,

---

† It is possible to derive precise conditions for the reversal of factor intensities in the value sense for a given α. Since in Fig. 10.3 $k_2 > k_1$, the necessary condition for the factor intensities to get reversed in the value sense is that

$$k_2^* < k_1^*.$$

From the expressions concerning C_{ij}^*,

$$k_1^* = C_{K1}^* - C_{L1}^* = \sigma_1(w_1^* - r^*)$$

and

$$k_2^* = C_{K2}^* - C_{L2}^* = \sigma_2(w_1^* - r^*) + \sigma_2 \alpha^*$$

Therefore, $k_2^* < k_1^*$ for a given α implies that

$$\frac{k_2^* - k_1^*}{w_1^* - r^*} = \sigma_2 - \sigma_1 < 0.$$

If the elasticities of substitution are the same in the two sectors, factor intensities can never get reversed; if they are constant, there can at most be one reversal; if they are variable, there may be more than one reversal points like R; finally, the necessary condition for this reversal is that $\sigma_2 < \sigma_1$. On the other hand, the precise conditions for the reversal with a given ω_1 can be obtained by differentiating $k_2/\alpha k_1$ to obtain

$$k_2^* - \alpha^* - k_1^* = \alpha^*(\sigma_2 - 1).$$

Thus for $k_2/\alpha k_1$ to decline, it is necessary that $\sigma_2 \neq 1$. For further discussion of these points, see Herberg *et al.* [9].

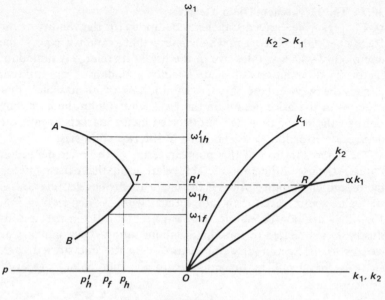

Figure 10.3

$k_2 < \alpha k_1 (\alpha > 1)$ after the factor-intensity reversal point R is reached.† The relationship between ω_1 and p is described by ATB, which appropriately undergoes a change in slope at point T corresponding to the reversal point R. It is easy to realise now that if the autarky ω_1 in each country lies on the different side of R', the pattern of trade may violate the Heckscher–Ohlin dictum.‡ *It is worth pointing out here that the factor-price equalisation will also be disrupted when the unique relationship between commodity and factor prices breaks down.*

If the home country is capital-abundant relative to the foreign country, then from the factor-price definition of factor abundance,

$$\omega_{1h} > \omega_{1f}.$$

† What this really means is that the sign of $|\theta|$ is reversed after point R and so is the relation between ω_1 and p at a given α.

‡ It is worth noting that the discussion of the Heckscher–Ohlin theorem illustrated by Fig. 10.3 is identical with the corresponding discussion in Chapter 3 in terms of Fig. 3.6. The only difference is that the factor-intensity reversal in the earlier chapter was caused by the multiple intersections of the unit isoquants of the two commodities, whereas now it arises from the existence of the differential.

If in Fig. 10.3 each country's ω_1 lies on the same side of R', as is the case given by the pair $O\omega_{1h}$ and $O\omega_{1f}$,

$$p_h < p_f$$

so that the home country will export the capital-intensive commodity X_2 and import the labour-intensive commodity X_1. The Heckscher–Ohlin theorem continues to hold. However, if each country's ω_1 lies on different sides of R', as is described by the pair $O\omega'_{1h}$ and $O\omega_{1f}$,

$$p'_h > p_f$$

so that the home country will export X_1 and import X_2, thereby contradicting the Heckscher–Ohlin theorem. But this result is by no means necessary even if each country's ω_1 lies on different sides of R'. This can be visualised if the home country's ω_1 was to be slightly below $O\omega'_{1h}$ but above R'.

Coming now to the physical definition of relative factor abundance, the Heckscher–Ohlin theorem cannot be disproved if α is the same in the two countries. This is because the Rybczynski theorem, as will be shown later, continues to hold in spite of the differential. Whether or not the factor intensities get reversed in the value sense makes little difference to the discussion of the Heckscher–Ohlin theorem in terms of the physical definition, for, as stated before, the definition of factor intensities in terms of distributive shares does not control the relationship between commodity outputs and factor endowments. Of course, if α is not the same in the two countries, or if one country has no distortions in factor markets, then the factor intensities in the value sense will also play a role in determining the validity of the theorem in question. As we show in the subsequent discussion, the level of output in each commodity at given commodity prices becomes a function not only of the country's factor endowments but also of α, and the effect of the latter on the output levels is determined by the signs of both $|\lambda|$ and $|\theta|$. This is how the factor intensities in the value sense participate in determining whether the theorem under question continues to be valid in the presence of the differential. If α is the same in the two countries, the effect of the distortion on the two outputs is also the same, which means that the sign of $|\theta|$ is of no consequence to the validity of the theorem. Thus we conclude that the Heckscher–Ohlin theorem continues to be valid in terms of the physical definition of relative factor abundance if α is the same internationally. However, if α is not the same then the theorem may not hold, simply because a relatively capital-abundant country may then be producing relatively more of the labour-intensive product at the given commodity prices than the labour-abundant country. The discussion in this section will become transparent when we explore the implications of a change in α on the output levels at constant commodity prices.

10.8 The Implications of the Wage Differential

Up to now we have assumed that the wage differential is constant. In this section we examine the consequences of a change in the wage differential for production, distribution and the terms of trade. Solving for w_j^* and r^* from (10.8)–(10.10), we get

$$w_1^* - p_j^* = \frac{\theta_{Kj}(p_1^* - p_2^*) + \theta_{K1}\theta_{L2}\alpha^*}{|\theta|} \tag{10.26}$$

$$w_2^* - p_j^* = \frac{\theta_{Kj}(p_1^* - p_2^*) + \theta_{K2}\theta_{L1}\alpha^*}{|\theta|} \tag{10.27}$$

$$r^* - p_j^* = -\frac{\theta_{Lj}(p_1^* - p_2^*) + \theta_{L1}\theta_{L2}\alpha^*}{|\theta|} \tag{10.28}$$

$$w_1^* - r^* = \frac{(p_1^* - p_2^*) + \theta_{L2}\alpha^*}{|\theta|}. \tag{10.29}$$

Substituting (10.29) in the expressions for C_{ij}^*, we get

$$k_1^* = C_{K1}^* - C_{L1}^* = \frac{\sigma_1[(p_1^* - p_2^*) + \theta_{L2}\alpha^*]}{|\theta|} \tag{10.30}$$

and

$$k_2^* = C_{K2}^* - C_{L2}^* = \frac{\sigma_2[(p_1^* - p_2^*) + \theta_{L1}\alpha^*]}{|\theta|}. \tag{10.31}$$

Next, we solve for X_1^* and X_2^* from (10.13) and (10.14) to obtain

$$X_1^* = \frac{(\lambda_{K2}\beta_L + \lambda_{L2}\beta_K)(p_1^* - p_2^*) + A\alpha^*}{|\lambda| \cdot |\theta|} \tag{10.32}$$

and

$$X_2^* = -\frac{(\lambda_{L1}\beta_K + \lambda_{K1}\beta_L)(p_1^* - p_2^*) + B\alpha^*}{|\lambda| \cdot |\theta|} \tag{10.33}$$

where

$$A = \theta_{L2}\sigma_1(\lambda_{K2}\lambda_{L1}\theta_{K1} + \lambda_{L2}\lambda_{K1}\theta_{L1}) + \theta_{L1}\lambda_{K2}\lambda_{L2}\sigma_2 > 0$$

and

$$B = \theta_{L1}\sigma_2(\lambda_{K1}\lambda_{L2}\theta_{K2} + \lambda_{L1}\lambda_{K2}\theta_{L2}) + \theta_{L2}\lambda_{L1}\lambda_{K1}\sigma_1 > 0.$$

The conclusions that emerge from (10.26)–(10.33) are categorical for a small country facing given terms of trade, so that $(p_1^* - p_2^*) = 0$. The implications of a rise in α for real factor rewards, capital/labour ratios and the two outputs at constant commodity prices are the same as those of a rise in the relative price of the first commodity at the constant wage differential. The reasoning is straightforward. A rise in p_1/p_2 alone directly serves to benefit the first industry relative to the second. A rise in α alone tends to move the differential against the second industry and thus indirectly benefits the first. In both cases the relative gain accrues to the first industry; hence a rise in α or p_1/p_2 alone generates similar repercussions in the economy.

In our discussion in section 10.2 on factor intensities, we showed that the presence of the differential may cause a reversal in the factor intensities in both the physical as well as the value sense. Following Magee [15], we are now in a position to show that factor intensities in the physical sense can never get reversed if either α or $p(=p_2/p_1)$ alone gets altered. Consider Fig. 10.4, which retains some features of Fig. 10.1. Let us begin with the case where $\alpha = 1$ and the efficiency locus is given by O_1AO_2, A being the actual production point. A decline in α serves to move the efficiency locus towards the diagonal and, for some $\alpha < \alpha_0 < 1$, moves it to the opposite side (see Fig. 10.1). However, from (10.30) and (10.31), a decline in α, with $|\theta| > 0$, leads to a decline in the capital/labour ratio in both industries if the commodity prices are constant. All this implies that a fall in α will move the production point to somewhere above O_1AO_2, below O_1A (so that k_1 declines) and above O_2A (so that k_2 declines). On the contrary, the rise in α will move the production point to somewhere below the undistorted locus O_1AO_2, below O_2A and above O_1A. These considerations suggest that the distorted efficiency locus is bounded from above by the two rays O_1A and O_2A when commodity prices are unaltered. The dashed curve O_1CABO_2 in Fig. 10.4 is one such curve where the new production point is given by either B or C, depending on whether $\alpha^* \gtreqless 0$. It is evident from the

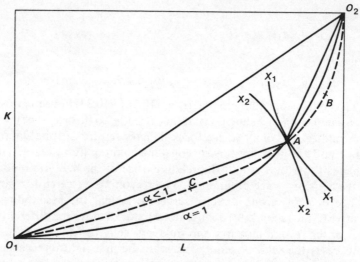

Figure 10.4

diagram that the distorted contract curve cannot cross the diagonal if the terms of trade are constant, whatever the level of α below unity. In the limit there will be complete specialisation in X_2, but factor intensities in the physical sense will never get reversed. This result derives directly from the fact that when commodity prices are fixed, a change in α moves the capital/labour ratios in the same direction. For this reason, the sign of $|\theta|$ is unimportant in this matter. For the same reason alone, if α is given, a change in commodity prices, which also moves the capital/labour ratios in the same direction, can never cause a reversal in the physical factor intensities. However, if commodity prices and α are changing simultaneously, k_1 and k_2 may move in the opposite direction, in which case it is possible for the contract curve to move to the opposite side of the diagonal.[†] It is worth pointing out here that factor intensities may still get reversed in the value sense, even if only one of α and p is altered.

The implications of a shift in α for the real factor rewards have important and interesting policy prescriptions for trade unions. To

† From (10.30) and (10.31) it is clear that k_1 and k_2 move in the opposite direction only if $(\theta_{L2}\alpha^* - p^*)$ and $(\theta_{L1}\alpha^* - p^*)$ possess conflicting signs. Evidently, the necessary condition to ensure this result is that

$$\theta_{L2} \gtrless p^*/\alpha^* \gtrless \theta_{L1}.$$

be specific, assume that the second sector is the unionised sector and $\alpha > 1$ so that $w_1 < w_2$. In other words, suppose that the producers in the unionised sector pay a premium to labour over the labour force employed in the non-union, first sector. Suppose further that the union in the second sector seeks to secure an increase in this premium, thereby increasing the value of α. When the repercussions on the rest of the economy are taken into account, however, the union may end up with a lower real wage rate for its members. As (10.26) and (10.27) suggest, with $(p_1^* - p_2^*) = 0$, the real wage rate will decline in both sectors if $|\theta|$ is negative, that is, if the unionised sector pays a higher share to labour than the non-union sector and hence is labour-intensive in the value sense. The reason should be obvious from (10.30) and (10.31). With $|\theta| < 0$, a rise in α induces substitution of labour for capital in both sectors, resulting in a decline in k_1 and k_2 which in turn leads to a general decline in the wage rate and a rise in the return to capital. The policy prescription is then unmistakable. If the union discovers that the non-union sector pays labour a lower relative share, it should seek a reduction in the inter-industry wage differential. *The union policy could prove self-defeating if it always pressed for higher wages.*

The change in the wage differential affects not only the factor rewards, but has repercussions for the two outputs as well. Here again the identity of the signs of $|\lambda|$ and $|\theta|$ plays the crucial role. Specifically, a rise in α raises the output of X_1 and lowers that of X_2 at constant commodity prices if $|\lambda|$ and $|\theta|$ possess the same sign. The converse is true if $|\lambda|$ and $|\theta|$ have opposite signs.

10.9 The Wage Differential and Welfare

As with other results, the implications of a change in the differential for welfare do not conform to one's intuition. One would expect that a rise in the wage differential would lower national income and welfare. This, however, turns out to be valid only if $|\lambda|$ and $|\theta|$ have the same sign.

Differentiating the utility function $U(D_1, D_2)$ totally with respect to α, and remembering that $D_1 = X_1 - E_1$, $D_2 = X_2 + E_2$ and $pE_2 = E_1$, we obtain

$$\frac{1}{U_1}\frac{dU}{d\alpha} = \frac{dY}{d\alpha} = \frac{dX_1}{d\alpha} + p\frac{dX_2}{d\alpha} - E_2\frac{dp}{d\alpha}.$$

Since $X_j = X_j(p,\alpha)$,

$$\frac{dX_j}{d\alpha} = \frac{\partial X_j}{\partial p} \cdot \frac{dp}{d\alpha} + \frac{\partial X_j}{\partial \alpha}.$$

From (10.22),

$$\frac{\partial X_1}{\partial \alpha} = -\beta p \frac{\partial X_2}{\partial \alpha} \quad \text{and} \quad \frac{\partial X_1}{\partial p} = -\beta p \frac{\partial X_2}{\partial p}.$$

Using these,

$$\frac{dY}{d\alpha} = p \frac{\partial X_2}{\partial \alpha} (1-\beta) + \frac{dp}{d\alpha} \left[p \frac{\partial X_2}{\partial p} (1-\beta) - E_2 \right]. \qquad (10.34)$$

If terms of trade are constant, $dp/d\alpha = 0$, so that the sign of $(dY/d\alpha)$ is determined by the sign of $(\partial X_2/\partial \alpha)$ and the value of β. Let us first consider the case where $|\lambda|$ and $|\theta|$ have the same sign, so that $\partial X_2/\partial \alpha < 0$. Then if $\beta < 1$, $(dY/d\alpha) < 0$. Now $\beta < 1$ implies that $\alpha > 1$ or $w_1 < w_2$. A rise in α here means a rise in the wage differential. In other words, a rise in the wage differential has resulted in a decline in welfare, and vice versa. On the other hand, if $\beta > 1$, $dY/d\alpha > 0$. Here a rise in α implies a decline in the differential. Thus our conclusion remains unchanged, that is, an increase in the distortion level leads to a decline in national income when terms of trade are constant. *It should be clear from this discussion that if $|\lambda|$ and $|\theta|$ have opposite signs so that $(\partial X_2/\partial \alpha) > 0$, an increase in the wage differential will lead to a rise in national income, and conversely.*

A geometrical demonstration contributes much to the comprehension of these results. Consider Fig. 10.5, where for the sake of simplicity the distorted transformation curve is drawn concave to the origin. A rise in the wage differential triggered by a rise in α moves HH' inwards to the dotted curve; if $|\lambda|$ and $|\theta|$ have the same sign, production shifts from P to P', consumption from C to C', and welfare declines from U_2 to U_1 when terms of trade are kept constant at the slope given by FP parallel to FP' and FP''. If $|\lambda|$ and $|\theta|$ have opposite signs, production switches to P'', consumption to C'', and welfare improves to U_3. Thus we see that a rise in the differential may lead to a rise or a decline in welfare, depending on its effect on the output of the two commodities at constant terms of trade.

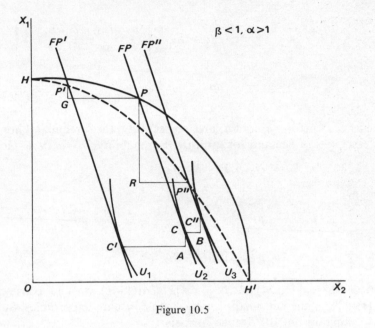

Figure 10.5

10.10 The Wage Differential and the Terms of Trade

The analysis of the preceding two sections has been conducted under the assumption that the country with distorted factor markets is a price-taker and has no influence on world prices. However, if the country possesses monopoly power in trade, p will normally change as a result of the change in α, in which case the results derived above may have to be revised.

Our immediate task, then, is to obtain an expression for the relationship between α and the terms of trade. With this objective in mind, consider the effect of a change in α on the demand for the home country's imports (E_2) at constant terms of trade. The balance-of-trade equilibrium is now described by

$$pE_2(p,\alpha) = E_1$$

so that

$$E_2 \frac{dp}{d\alpha} + p \left[\frac{\partial E_2}{\partial p} \cdot \frac{dp}{d\alpha} + \frac{\partial E_2}{\partial \alpha} \right] = \frac{dE_1}{d\alpha}$$

or

$$p \frac{\partial E_2}{\partial \alpha} = E_2 \frac{dp}{d\alpha} \left[\frac{p}{E_1} \cdot \frac{dE_1}{dp} - \frac{p}{E_2} \frac{\partial E_2}{\partial p} - 1 \right]$$

whence

$$\frac{dp}{d\alpha} = \frac{p \, \partial E_2 / \partial \alpha}{E_2 (a_f + a_{h-1})} \tag{10.35}$$

where, as before, a_f and a_h are, respectively, the foreign and home elasticities of demand for imports. For stability, $a_f + a_h > 1$. Now

$$E_2 = D_2(p, Y) - X_2(p, \alpha)$$

so that

$$p \frac{\partial E_2}{\partial \alpha} = p \frac{\partial D_2}{\partial y} \cdot \frac{\partial Y}{\partial \alpha} - p \frac{\partial X_2}{\partial \alpha} = m_h \frac{\partial Y}{\partial \alpha} - p \frac{\partial X_2}{\partial \alpha}$$

$$= p \frac{\partial X_2}{\partial \alpha} \left[m_h (1 - \beta) - 1 \right]$$

because from (10.34) $dY/d\alpha = (p \partial X_2 / \partial \alpha)(1 - \beta)$ when p is constant. Here m_h is the marginal propensity to consume importables. Substituting this in (10.35) then furnishes

$$\frac{dp}{d\alpha} = \frac{p(\partial X_2 / \partial \alpha) \left[m_h (1 - \beta) - 1 \right]}{E_2 (a_f + a_h - 1)}. \tag{10.36}$$

This expression suggests that the effects of a change in α on the terms of trade depend on three factors, namely, $(\partial X_2 / \partial \alpha)$, m_h and β (or α). In the absence of inferior goods, $0 < m_h < 1$, which means that, whatever the value of β, the square-bracketed term in the numerator of (10.36) is negative. These considerations suggest that the sign of $(dp/d\alpha)$ depends crucially on the sign of $(\partial X_2 / \partial \alpha)$. If initially there is no wage differential, or if $|\lambda|$ and $|\theta|$ possess identical signs, $(\partial X_2 / \partial \alpha) < 0$, which implies that $(dp/d\alpha) > 0$. Now $\alpha > 1$ means that $w_1 < w_2$, so that a rise in α leads to a rise in the differential paid by the import-competing industry; if $\alpha < 1$, $w_1 > w_2$, so that a rise in α causes a decline in the differential paid by the exportable good. *All this leads us to the conclusion that a rise in the differential paid by the import-competing good or a decline in the differential paid by the exportable good gives rise to a deterioration in the terms of trade.* These results are evidently reversed if $|\lambda|$ and $|\theta|$ have opposite signs so that $(\partial X_2 / \partial \alpha) > 0$.

For a graphical illustration of these results, let us revert to Fig. 10.5, where a rise in α shifted the consumption point from C to C' when $|\lambda| \cdot |\theta| > 0$ and to C'' if $|\lambda| \cdot |\theta| < 0$. The home country's demand for imports in the former case rises at the constant terms of trade given by the slope of FP, because the decline in the output of X_2, equal to GP, exceeds the decline in its consumption, equal to AC', whereas in the latter case the demand for imports declines because the rise in output of X_2, given by RP'', exceeds the rise in its consumption, equal to BC. A rise in the demand for imports at constant terms of trade would eventually generate a deterioration in the terms of trade, whereas the decline in the import demand would switch the terms of trade in favour of the home country, provided, of course, that the foreign trade market was stable.

When terms of trade are variable, the conclusions obtained in the last two sections under the assumption of constant commodity prices may have to be modified, for variables in the economy are now regulated not only by a change in α but also by a concomitant movement in p. As established above, $(dp/d\alpha)$ is positive if the factor intensities are identical in the physical as well as the value sense, thereby implying that $(p_1^* - p_2^*)$ and α^* are negatively related. Clearly, then, the implications of a change in α for the capital/labour ratios, factor rewards and output levels are unpredictable from (10.26)–(10.33). *If the magnitude of $(p_1^* - p_2^*)$ is sufficiently large, all the results derived in section 10.8 under the assumption of given terms of trade may actually be reversed.*

Of greater interest is the case where the factor intensities in the physical and the value sense are in conflict, so that $(p_1^* - p_2^*)$ and α^* have similar signs. Here the change in the wage differential not only continues to generate unambiguous repercussions on the variables in the system, but also the results attained in the presence of unaltered terms of trade are reinforced. The reason is not far to seek. As argued before, a rise in α creates the same effects in the economy as a rise in the relative price of the first commodity. Now if the factor intensities in the physical and the value sense are identical, p_1/p_2 moves in the opposite direction to the change in α when terms of trade are variable. All the variables in the system are then subjected to two conflicting pulls so that the final outcome cannot be predicted. In the contrary case where the physical and value factor intensities are dissimilar, both the relative price of the first commodity and α shift in the same direction, and thus each shift strengthens the ramifications of the other.

The implications of a change in the differential for welfare deserve special consideration when terms of trade are variable, for there the inspection of (10.34) makes it clear that even if the factor intensities in the physical and the value sense are divergent, so that $(dp/d\alpha) < 0$, the change in the differential does not give rise to unambiguous shifts in community welfare, because of the ambiguity involved in the sign of $[p(\partial X_2/\partial p)(1-\beta) - E_2]$. This is rather surprising because the latter expression displays the effect of a change in the terms of trade on welfare, which effect was demonstrated to be unambiguous in Chapter 5. However, this premise, a detailed discussion of which is postponed to the next section, turns out to be invalid in the presence of distortions. The full impact of a change in the differential on welfare can be divided into two components: (1) the effect of a change in α at constant terms of trade, plus (2) the effect of a change in p at a given α weighted by the magnitude of $(dp/d\alpha)$. These components may move in the same or the opposite direction, so that the sign of $(dY/d\alpha)$ is uncertain. To obtain a better perspective, let us rewrite (10.34) as

$$\frac{dY}{d\alpha} = p(1-\beta)\left[\frac{\partial X_2}{\partial \alpha} + \frac{\partial X_2}{\partial p}\cdot\frac{dp}{d\alpha}\right] - E_2\frac{dp}{d\alpha}. \qquad (10.34\text{A})$$

It may be observed from (10.33) that $(\partial X_2/\partial \alpha)$ and $(\partial X_2/\partial p)$ are always opposite in sign, which implies that the square-bracketed expression in (10.34A) possesses a categorical sign only if $(dp/d\alpha) < 0$, which in turn requires that $(\partial X_2/\partial \alpha) > 0$ or that the physical and the value factor intensities are divergent. With $(\partial X_2/\partial \alpha) > 0$, $(\partial X_2/\partial p) < 0$ and $(dp/d\alpha) < 0$, the square-bracketed and the last terms in (10.34A) are positive. However, the entire expression will be unambiguously positive only if $\beta < 1$ or if the differential is paid by the import- competing industry, X_2. The conclusion that emerges from this discussion is that $(dY/d\alpha) > (\partial Y/\partial \alpha) > 0$. *In other words, under the conditions cited above, the rise in the real income consequent upon a rise in the differential exceeds the rise in income at constant terms of trade.* Another interesting result is that the real income may rise as a result of the rise in the differential even if the physical and the value factor intensities are identical, provided the terms of trade are variable, because $(dY/d\alpha)$ may be positive even if $|\lambda|\cdot|\theta| > 0$ and hence $(\partial X_2/\partial \alpha)$ is negative and $(\partial X_2/\partial p)$ and $(dp/d\alpha)$ are positive.

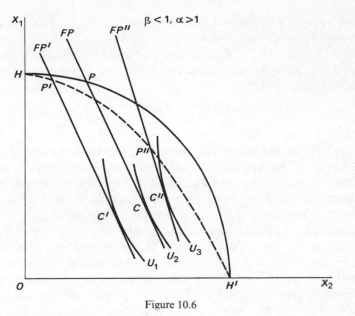

Figure 10.6

This last result is illustrated graphically in Fig. 10.6, where a rise in α at a constant p shifts the production point from P to P' and welfare declines from U_2 to U_1. In the new equilibrium, however, the terms of trade move against the home country because p rises, the production point at the new given level of α moves to P'' and welfare rises to U_3, which lies not only above U_1 but also above U_2. Thus it is clear that welfare may be positively related to α even if $|\lambda| \cdot |\theta| > 0$, provided the terms of trade are variable.

10.11 The Wage Differential and the Gains from Trade
Up to now our analysis has proceeded along the assumption that the country with distorted factor markets follows the policy of *laissez-faire*. A good deal of trade-theory literature in the theory of wage differentials has, however, raised questions as to the optimality of the free trade policy. Several other results in the theory of gains from trade have also been subjected to closer scrutiny. This section is concerned with an examination of these issues under the assumption that the differential is constant.

The most appropriate way to tackle the issues of free trade versus no trade and the optimality of *laissez-faire* is to differentiate the utility function totally with respect to the rate of tariff. The equations involved in this procedure are $U = U(D_1 D_2)$, $D_1 = X_1 - E_1$, $D_2 = X_2 + E_2$, $pE_2 = E_1$, $p_h = p(1 + t_2)$ and $(dX_1/dX_2) = -\beta p(1 + t_2)$. Using these equations and following the procedure used many times before, we obtain

$$\frac{1}{U_1} \frac{dU}{dt_2} = \frac{dY}{dt_2} = pp_h \frac{dX_2}{dp_h} (1 - \beta) + p^2 t_2 \frac{dE_2}{dp_h} \qquad (10.37)$$

remembering that under the assumption of constant terms of trade – an assumption usually made while exploring such issues – $dp_h/dt_2 = p$, where p_h is the price ratio in the home country. In the absence of the differential, this expression reduces to $p^2 t_2 (dE_2/dp_h)$ which is necessarily negative if inferior goods are absent, so that community welfare and the rate of tariff are negatively related; furthermore, free trade turns out to be the optimal policy because if $t_2 = 0$, $(dU/dt_2) = 0$. These results stand in need of drastic revision in the presence of the differential, even if we assume that the price–output response is positive as is the case in the economy without distortions. In this spirit, let $(dX_2/dp_h) > 0$; then $(dE_2/dp_h) < 0$. However, $(dY/dt_2) < 0$ unambiguously only if $\beta > 1$ or $\alpha < 1$, so that $w_1 > w_2$. *In other words, only when the differential is paid by the exportable good can we assert categorically that social welfare is uniquely and negatively related to the rate of tariff, given that the price–output response is positive. If $\beta < 1$, or if the differential is paid by the import-competing industry, X_2, social welfare and the tariff rate are no longer uniquely related.* An increase in the tariff rate may then augment community welfare, and vice versa. It is a simple matter now to deduce that free trade (which is the special case of the tariff policy in that $t_2 = 0$) may be inferior to no trade or to a prohibitive tariff.

Figs. 10.7A and 10.7B resolve this issue geometrically. Fig. 10.7A displays the case where the differential is paid by the exportable good, X_1, the free trade price ratio is given by FP, production is at P, consumption at C and welfare at U_2. A prohibitive tariff shifts the price line from FP to DP, both production and consumption move to S and welfare declines to U_1, indicating that free trade is necessarily superior to no trade. In Fig. 10.7B the outcome is not so definite, because it depends on where the self-sufficiency equilibrium point lies. The diagram depicts the case where the no-trade production and consumption are given by S, so that the autarkic welfare

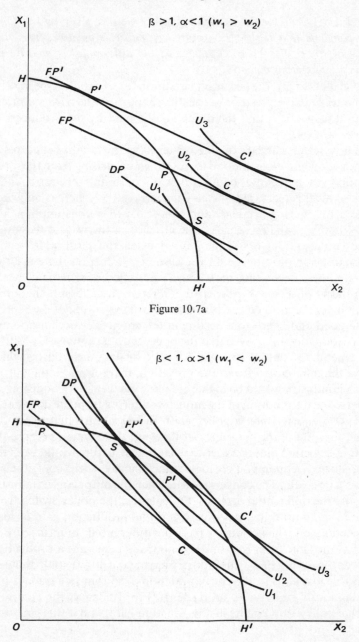

Figure 10.7a

Figure 10.7b

level, U_2, lies above the free trade level of welfare given by U_1. *Thus, we conclude that if the price–output response is positive, free trade may be inferior to no trade, provided the differential is paid by the import-competing industry.*

Needless to say, the necessary condition for free trade to be inferior to no trade in the presence of the differential and the negative price–output response is that the differential is paid by the producers of the exportable good.

These results can be explained in terms of the familiar concepts of production and consumption losses (or gains) arising from the intervention in the free inter-country flow of goods and services.† As the rate of tariff is increased, the consumer has to pay increasingly high prices for the importables, and this leads to a consumption loss irrespective of the presence or the absence of the wage differential. The consumption loss is maximised when the tariff wall is high enough to be prohibitive. In the case of production there are two possibilities, depending on whether the differential is paid by the producers of X_1 or X_2. When the differential is absent, the introduction of the tariff gives rise to a decline in the output of the exportable good and hence to a decline in the country's specialisation or to a production loss, given that the price–output response is positive. In general, the output structure is biased against the industry which pays the differential, for at the prevailing market prices the output of that industry would be higher if factor markets were undistorted. Therefore, if the output of the industry suffering from the differential rises consequent upon a policy shift, the economic inefficiency declines in spite of the constancy of the wage differential, because the output structure moves closer to what that structure would be in the undistorted economy. This loss of inefficiency, then, constitutes a production gain. The converse is true when the output of the industry paying the differential declines. On balance, the policy switch from free trade to no trade may give rise to the production gain or loss, depending on which industry pays the differential. In terms of Fig. 10.7A, the shift from free trade to no trade generates a production loss as the output of X_1, the industry paying the differential, declines, and this loss adds to the consumption loss, so that free trade is unambiguously superior to no trade. In Fig. 10.7B, on the contrary, such a policy shift results in a production gain, and if this gain out-

† These concepts were first introduced in Chapter 4.

weighs the consumption loss, free trade may be inferior to no trade. This is what is pictured by point S in Fig. 10.7B.

What, then, is the optimal policy in the presence of distorted factor markets? Two considerations suggest themselves in this connection, namely (1) the welfare-maximising policy that retains the wage differential, and (2) the policy that eliminates the differential to the producers. The first type of policy will generate a 'second-best' optimum, because the inefficiency caused by the differential in shrinking the undistorted transformation curve still remains, whereas the second type will produce a 'first-best' optimum. The second-best policy follows directly from our discussion concerning the production gain (loss) in the presence of distorted factor markets. Evidently, the production gain rises as the output of the industry paying the differential augments. The welfare in the presence of the differential is then maximised by introducing, in addition to free trade, a policy of production tax-cum-subsidy such that the output of the industry suffering from the differential is at the maximum. Such a policy takes production to P' in Figs. 10.7A and 10.7B, where FP', parallel to FP, is tangential to the distorted transformation curve, consumption is at C' and welfare improves to U_3, which lies above U_1 and U_2. The tax-cum-subsidy policy emerges from a re consideration of (10.37). Suppose the initial situation is one of *laissez-faire* and $t_2 = 0$. It can easily be seen that in this case

$$\frac{dU}{U_1} = dY = pdX_2(1-\beta) \qquad (10.38)$$

which, of course, demonstrates that the initial situation of free trade is not optimal in the presence of the differential, because $\beta \neq 1$, so that $dY \neq 0$. Clearly, then, the second-best policy will be one that makes $dY > 0$ while the differential persists. Such a policy requires that $dX_2 \gtrless 0$ if $\beta \lessgtr 1$, which confirms the fact that the output of the industry paying the differential be raised to its maximum level.

An interesting query may be raised at this stage. Why should this objective be achieved through a tax-cum-subsidy policy and not through any other alternative such as tariffs or import subsidies, etc.? The reason is attributable to the existence of the distortion not in the foreign trade sector but in domestic factor markets, so that there is a divergence between the marginal rate of transformation and the commodity-price ratio. A production tax-cum-subsidy eliminates such divergence, whereas a tariff or import subsidy could do this job but not without generating a divergence between the marginal rate of substitution and the given foreign-price ratio. Hence the production tax-cum-subsidy is superior to taxes or subsidies on imports and to any other policy.

The second-best policy maximises welfare subject to the constraint of the wage differential, and for this reason will not lead to the *optimum optimorum*, which can be achieved only if the value of β to the producers is equated to unity by means of a suitable factor tax-cum-subsidy policy. Thus if β is equated to unity for producers, $dY = 0$ from (10.38). The factor tax-cum-subsidy policy may be administered by any one or all of the following ways which tend to equate (w/r) in both sectors: (1) subsidise the use of labour or tax the use of capital in the industry paying the differential, and/or (2) tax the use of labour or subsidise the use of capital in the other industry.

The operation of the first-best policy is illustrated in Fig. 10.8, where the differential is shown to be paid by the X_2 producers. The grant of the factor subsidy to X_2 in addition to free trade takes production from P to P' on the undistorted transformation curve, consumption moves from C to C', and welfare improves from U_1 to U_2, which under the circumstances is the maximum attainable level of welfare.

Let us now proceed to analyse the effects of a change in the terms of trade on welfare. The expression for the implications of such a change has in fact already been derived in section 10.10, where the consequences of a change in α for welfare were explored. The expression, of course, can be derived via a direct route by totally differentiating the utility function with respect to p to obtain

$$\frac{1}{U_1}\frac{dU}{dp} = \frac{dY}{dp} = p\,\frac{dX_2}{dp}\,(1-\beta) - E_2 \qquad (10.39)$$

where α is assumed to be constant. The economic content contained in (10.39) is clear. In the undistorted case, the expression reduces to $(dY/dp) = -E_2$, confirming the fact that in the absence of distortions the real income rises as a result of the improvement in the terms of trade, and vice versa. However, with (dX_2/dp) and $(1-\beta)$ possessing any sign in the presence of the differential, the terms of trade and real income may no longer have a monotonic relationship, giving rise to the possibility of an increase in real income as a result

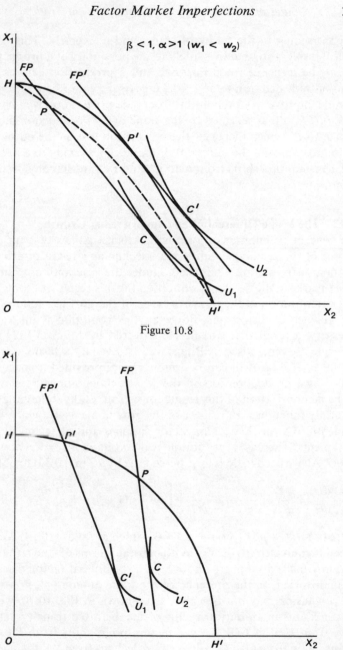

Figure 10.8

Figure 10.9

of a worsening in the terms of trade, and conversely. This paradoxical result is attributable solely to the possibility of a production loss as the terms of trade improve and a production gain as the terms of trade deteriorate. Fig. 10.9 depicts the case where the terms of trade improve from the initial free trade price ratio given by the slope of *FP* to that reflected by the slope of *FP'*, production moves from *P* to *P'*, which increases the production loss as the output of the industry paying the differential, X_2, declines owing to a decline in *p*, consumption shifts from *C* to *C'*, and welfare actually declines from U_2 to U_1.

10.12   The Wage Differential and Immiserising Growth

The concept of immiserising growth, which signifies that the real income of the growing country may decline as a result of growth, was first introduced in Chapter 6. Under the assumption of undistorted markets, the necessary condition for this result was shown to be a deterioration in the terms of trade of the growing country. In the presence of distortions, however, this condition is no longer necessary, a result that was first discovered by Johnson [12] and subsequently generalised by Bhagwati [3]. Even if the terms of trade are unchanged, growth can be immiserising, provided it is accompanied by a production loss in the sense defined above.

The demonstration of this result consists in totally differentiating the utility function with respect to the growth agent, *G*, which may be identified with changes in factor supplies and/or technical improvements. There is a very simple way to obtain an expression for *dY/dG*. All we need to do is to supercede *dα* by *dG* in (10.34) to obtain

$$\frac{1}{U_1}\frac{dU}{dG} = \frac{dY}{dG} = \frac{\partial X_1}{\partial G} + p\frac{\partial X_2}{\partial G} + \left[p\frac{\partial X_2}{\partial p}(1-\beta) - E_2 \right]\frac{dp}{dG} \quad (10.40)$$

where $(\partial X_1/\partial G + p\partial X_2/\partial G) = \partial Y/\partial G$, which as far as (10.34) is concerned is equivalent to $\partial Y/\partial\alpha$. With constant terms of trade, the last term in (10.40) disappears and $\partial Y/\partial G$ is positive if factor markets are undistorted. In the presence of the wage differential, however, this conclusion may not be valid, as is shown in Fig. 10.10, where growth results in an outward shift of the distorted transformation curve from *HH'* to *GG'*, the production point shifts from *P* to *P'*, consumption from *C* to *C'*, and welfare declines from U_2 to U_1, even though the terms of trade are unchanged because *FP* is parallel to

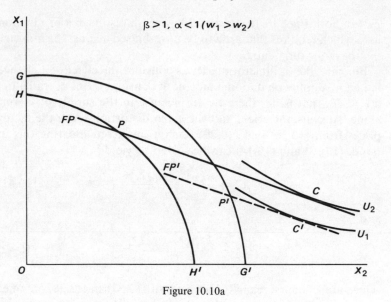

Figure 10.10a

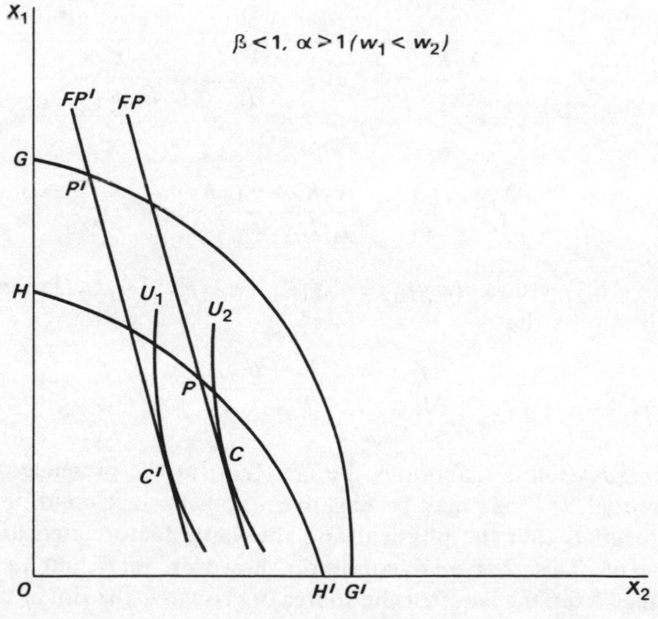

Figure 10.10b

FP'. In both Figs. 10.10A and 10.10B growth results in a production loss, which requires that growth be ultra-biased against the industry that pays the differential.

For the sake of illustration, let us consider the effect of a change in factor supplies on national income at constant terms of trade. Let $dG = dL$, that is, let there be an increase in the supply of labour alone. At constant prices and the given distortion level, the factor prices from (10.28) and (10.29) remain unaltered. Bearing this in mind, (10.13) and (10.14) can be solved to yield

$$X_1^* = \frac{\lambda_{K2}L^* - \lambda_{L2}K^*}{|\lambda|} \tag{10.41}$$

and

$$X_2^* = \frac{\lambda_{L1}K^* - \lambda_{K1}L^*}{|\lambda|} \tag{10.42}$$

which are, of course, exactly identical with (2.37) and (2.38) obtained in Chapter 2, which shows that the Rybczynski theorem continues to be valid in the presence of the wage differential. From these equations,

$$\frac{\partial X_1}{\partial L} = \frac{X_1 K_2}{L_1 L_2 (k_2 - k_1)} \quad \text{and} \quad \frac{\partial X_2}{\partial L} = \frac{-X_2 K_1}{L_1 L_2 (k_2 - k_1)}$$

so that

$$\frac{\partial Y}{\partial L} = \frac{\partial X_1}{\partial L} + p \frac{\partial X_2}{\partial L} = \frac{X_1 K_2 - p X_2 K_1}{L_1 L_2 (k_2 - k_1)}.$$

From (10.3)–(10.5), $(w_1/p_1) = (X_1 K_2 - p X_2 K_1)/[L_1 L_2 (k_2 - \alpha k_1)]$, which implies that

$$\frac{\partial Y}{\partial L} = \frac{w_1}{p_1} \cdot \frac{(k_2 - \alpha k_1)}{(k_2 - k_1)}. \tag{10.43}$$

This expression corroborates the fact that, in the presence of the differential, $(\partial Y/\partial L)$ may be negative; the necessary condition for this result is that the physical and the value factor intensities be divergent. This particular condition, however, turns out to have stemmed from the fact that the source of growth is the rise in supply of the factor that earns a premium in one sector. For example, if growth occurs owing to the rise in the supply of capital alone, then, from (10.41) and (10.42),

$$\frac{\partial X_1}{\partial K} = -\frac{L_2 X_1}{L_1 L_2 (k_2 - k_1)} \quad \text{and} \quad \frac{\partial X_2}{\partial K} = \frac{L_1 X_2}{L_1 L_2 (k_2 - k_1)}$$

so that

$$\frac{\partial Y}{\partial K} = \frac{p L_1 X_2 - L_2 X_1}{L_1 L_2 (k_2 - \alpha k_1)}.$$

Now, from (10.3)–(10.5),

$$\frac{r}{p_1} = \frac{p L_1 X_2 - \alpha L_2 X_1}{L_1 L_2 (k_2 - \alpha k_1)}$$

whence

$$\frac{\partial Y}{\partial K} = \frac{r}{p_1} \cdot \frac{(k_2 - \alpha k_1)}{(k_2 - k_1)} \frac{(p L_1 X_2 - L_2 X_1)}{(p L_1 X_2 - \alpha L_2 X_1)}$$

which makes it clear that $(\partial Y / \partial K)$ will be negative even if the physical and the value factor intensities are identical, provided $(p L_1 X_2 - L_2 X_1)$ and $(p L_1 X_2 - \alpha L_2 X_1)$ have opposite signs. Thus the conclusion is unmistakable. *For growth to be immiserising with unchanged terms of trade, the reversal of the physical and the value factor intensities is necessary only if output expansion occurs because of an increase in the supply of the factor that earns a premium in one sector.*

Having demonstrated that growth may be immiserising in the presence of distorted factor markets, even when terms of trade are constant, a simple inspection of (10.40) reveals that this immiserisation may be reinforced as a result of the growth-induced improvement in the terms of trade, or that if $(\partial Y / \partial G)$ was positive, (dY / dG) may be negative in spite of, or rather because of, the terms of trade improvement fostered by growth and so on.†

The Prebisch Hypothesis

The results derived in this section have a close bearing on the still inconclusive debate initiated by Prebisch [16] over the hypothesis of the secular deterioration in the terms of trade facing the underdeveloped countries producing primary products. The proponents

† For further discussion of this result, see Batra and Scully [2].

of this thesis argue that the cause of poverty in the developing nations lies in the deterioration in their terms of trade which started in the latter part of the nineteenth century and persisted until the beginning of the Second World War. Participants on the other side of the debate have strongly challenged the empirical and analytical soundness of this hypothesis.

We have no intention of getting involved in this still mooted issue. But participants on both sides of the debate have displayed at least tacit consensus on the fact that the deterioration in the terms of trade by itself is a bad thing, that it leads to a decline in the rate of growth of income *per se*. However, we have shown that such a deterioration is no longer directly related to the rate of growth if factor markets are imperfect. To the extent that factor markets in the underdeveloped countries are very likely to be imperfect, it is necessary first to decide whether or not a deterioration in the terms of trade is necessarily harmful before arguing for it or contesting it as a sufficient explanation for ubiquitous poverty in the underdeveloped world.

10.13   Other Types of Factor Market Distortions: Factor Immobility and Factor-Price Rigidity

Distortions in factor markets can arise not only from inter-industry factor-price differentials, but also from imperfect mobility of factors and downward rigidity of factor prices. The implications of the latter type of distortions for gains from trade have been analysed by Haberler [6], Johnson [11] and Batra and Pattanaik [1], and this section is devoted to an examination of their results. Throughout the book so far we have continued to assume that factors are perfectly mobile between the two sectors and that factor prices are perfectly flexible. Both of these are extreme assumptions and it will be useful to see how the relaxation of these assumptions modifies the results. For expository purposes, let us assume that factors are perfectly immobile and factor prices perfectly rigid, notwithstanding the fact that in general there is some degree of factor mobility and factor-price flexibility. The interested reader is referred to Haberler [6] to see that the conclusions derived under the extreme assumptions remain qualitatively unmodified when these assumptions are relaxed. Furthermore, whether or not factor prices differ between sectors turns out to have no bearing on the results under our extreme assumptions.

The method of analysis followed by Haberler as well as Johnson is to start from a position of no trade, introduce free trade, and then compare the level of social welfare attained in these two situations. In actual practice, however, the need for protection arises when the country under consideration, following a policy of free trade, considers it detrimental to its welfare. That Johnson himself is aware of this will be clear from the following passage:

> For the analysis of arguments for protection derived from immobility of factors and downward rigidity of factor prices, it is convenient to pose the problem in terms of whether the opening of the opportunity to trade makes a country worse off when these conditions exist, so that a prohibitive tariff would secure a higher level of welfare than could be attained under free trade, even though in reality the argument for protection usually arises when *trade is already established* and the international price of imports suddenly falls. ([11] p. 14)

Johnson further asserts that 'the difference of assumptions merely simplifies the problem without *altering the conclusions*' (ibid.). One of the objectives of this section is to show that 'the difference of assumptions' does alter the conclusions. Specifically, in contrast to the Haberler–Johnson thesis, it will be shown that free trade is *necessarily* superior to no trade even in the presence of inflexible factor prices, provided we start from a situation of free trade and then introduce a prohibitive tariff.

From No Trade to Free Trade

To begin with, let us see what the transformation curve looks like when factors of production cannot move from one sector to another. Consider Fig. 10.11, where HH' is the transformation curve derived under the assumption that factors are perfectly mobile between the two industries X_1 and X_2, S is the point of self-sufficiency equilibrium, the autarky price ratio is given by the slope of DP, and U_1 reflects the level of welfare. If factors are completely immobile but factor prices continue to be flexible, the transformation curve reduces to the rectangle formed by ASB, reflecting that the output of X_1 and X_2 is fixed as no factor moves from one industry to another; the fact that factor prices are still flexible ensures that factors continue to be fully employed and that the production point remains unaltered, irrespective of the level of relative commodity prices. A

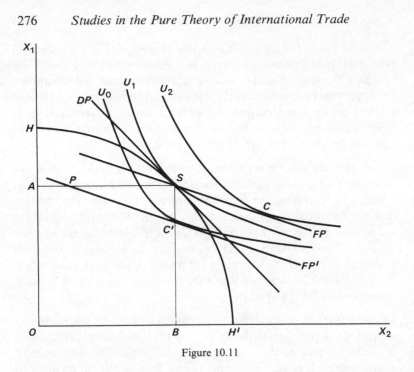

Figure 10.11

switch from no trade to free trade at the given world prices reflected
by the slope of *FP* takes the consumption point to *C*, but under the
postulated conditions leaves the production point unchanged at *S*.
However, the immobility of factors does not interfere with the
superiority of free trade over no trade as U_2 lies above U_1. This
occurs because, although production gain is zero, the consumption
gain remains.

Consider now the case where factor immobility is accompanied
by factor-price rigidity; the switch from no trade to free trade would
cause unemployment of some factors employed in X_2 as a result of
the decline in its relative price from that given by the slope of *DP* to
one furnished by the slope of *FP*. As a consequence the output of X_2
will decline, although that of X_1 will remain unchanged as unutilised
factors cannot move from X_2 to X_1. In other words, the consumption
gain in the presence of factor-price inflexibility will be accompanied
by the production loss, and if the latter is large enough, free trade
may be inferior to no trade. This is the possibility depicted in Fig.
10.11, where free trade takes production to *P*, consumption to *C'*
and welfare to U_0 which lies below the autarky level, U_1. It is this

possibility which was discovered by Haberler and examined further by Johnson.

From Free Trade to No Trade

Let us now reverse the reasoning and consider the case where free trade is already established and the country decides to introduce a prohibitive tariff. Let us go to Fig. 10.12, where the rectangular transformation curve is given by APB, and where P is the free trade production point lying on the transformation curve HH' (not drawn), C is the corresponding consumption point and U_2 is the level of welfare. A prohibitive tariff unaccompanied by factor-price rigidity leads to production and consumption at P and to the welfare level given by U_1; if factor prices are also rigid, the production of X_1 will decline as a result of the switch from FP to DP, whereas the output of X_2 will be unchanged as no factor can move from X_1 to X_2. This case is then just the reverse of the one discussed above. Suppose the new production point is given by S. This will also be the consumption point, so that the welfare level will be given by U_0 which lies below U_2. *Free trade is then necessarily superior to no trade, in spite of rigidity of factor prices.* The reasoning is clear. If the initial situation is one of full employment, any change in relative prices causes

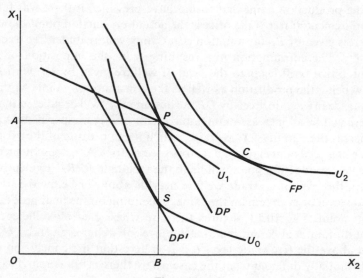

Figure 10.12

a production loss as the output of one industry declines and that of the other remains unchanged. Under this setting, a movement from no trade to free trade gives rise to a consumption gain and a production loss, so that the final outcome for welfare is uncertain, whereas a switch from free trade to no trade causes losses in production as well as consumption, so that free trade is necessarily superior to no trade.

Initial Unemployment

Both Haberler and Johnson assume full employment in the absence of trade in spite of inflexibility of factor prices, and unemployment of a fraction of given factor supplies is caused in their framework only by the introduction of trade. But why should not the rigidity of factor prices result in some unemployment even in the absence of trade, or for that matter in the initial situation of free trade? The analysis of rigid factor prices will not be complete unless this consideration is taken into account.

In the presence of unemployment, the initial production point will lie inside the transformation curve. For the sake of brevity, we consider only the case involving a shift from free trade to no trade, because in the other case of moving from no trade to free trade the results are qualitatively unchanged. Consider Fig. 10.13, where P' is the production point that would have prevailed if there was full employment at free trade prices; the actual production point, however, is given by P, consumption is at C and welfare under free trade at U_2. The consumption loss resulting from the imposition of a prohibitive tariff leads to the level of welfare given by U_1, with P now being the production as well as the consumption point. At the no-trade price ratio given by DP the output of X_1 will decline, so that there will be an increase in unemployment of factors specific to X_1, whereas the output of X_2 will rise, which it can because of the existence of a pool of unemployed factors specific to it. As a consequence, the new production point will lie in the rectangle $BPRT$. Evidently, then, the level of no-trade welfare may lie above or below the free trade level or even remain the same, depending on the final production point. Fig. 10.13 pictures the case where the self-sufficiency equilibrium is at S and the autarky level of welfare, given by U_3, lies above the free trade level U_2. It is here that the conclusion is substantially different from the case where there is full employment initially.

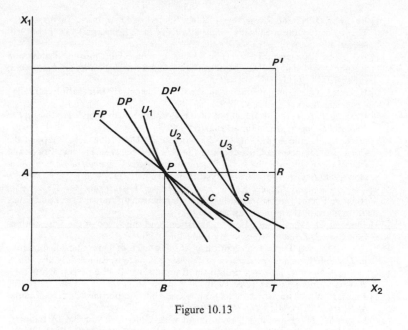

Figure 10.13

10.14 Concluding Remarks

One truth which emerges again and again in the preceding analysis is that virtually all the results derived from undistorted factor markets may be reversed when factor market distortions are taken into account. A Pandora's Box of paradoxes is opened, the moment the assumption of undistorted factor markets is relaxed. However, when we consider the intuitive explanations that are available for all the paradoxical results, the semblances of paradox should disappear. Nevertheless, the novelty of these results catches one's imagination, and perhaps for this reason the recent trade-theory literature abounds in the discussion of factor market distortions.

REFERENCES

[1] Batra, R. N., and Pattanaik, P. K., 'Factor Market Imperfections and Gains from Trade', *Oxford Economic Papers*, XXIII (July 1971) 182–8.
[2] ——, and Scully, G. W., 'The Theory of Wage Differentials: Welfare and Immiserizing Growth', *Journal of International Economics*, I (May 1971) 241–7.
[3] Bhagwati, J. N., 'Distortions and Immiserizing Growth: A Generalization', *Review of Economic Studies*, XXXV (Oct 1968) 481–5.

[4] Bhagwati, J. N., and Ramaswami, V. K., 'Domestic Distortions, Tariffs and the Theory of Optimum Subsidy', *Journal of Political Economy*, LXXI (Feb 1963) 44–50.

[5] ——, and Srinivasan, T. N., 'The Theory of Wage Differentials: Production Response and Factor Price Equalization,' *Journal of International Economics*, I (Feb 1971) 19–35.

[6] Haberler, G., 'Some problems in the Pure Theory of International Trade', *Economic Journal*, LX (June 1950) 223–40.

[7] Harberger, A. C., 'The Incidence of the Corporation Income Tax', *Journal of Political Economy*, LXX (June 1962) 215–40.

[8] Herberg, H., and Kemp, M. C., 'Factor Market Distortions, the Shape of the Locus of Competitive Outputs, and the Relation between Product Prices and Equilibrium Outputs', in J. N. Bhagwati *et al* (eds.), *Trade, Balance of Payments, and Growth* (Amsterdam: North-Holland, 1971).

[9] ——, ——, and Magee, S. P., 'Factor Market Distortions, the Reversal of Relative Factor Intensities, and the Relation between Product Prices and Equilibrium Outputs', mimeographed (1970).

[10] Johnson, H. G., 'Factor Market Distortions and the Shape of the Transformation Curve', *Econometrica*, XXXIV (July 1966) 686–98.

[11] ——, 'Optimal Trade Intervention in the Presence of Domestic Distortions', in *Trade, Growth and the Balance of Payments* (Chicago: Rand McNally, 1965).

[12] ——, 'A Note on Distortions and the Rate of Growth of an Open Economy', *Economic Journal*, LXXX (Dec 1970).

[13] Jones, R. W., 'The Structure of Simple General Equilibrium Models', *Journal of Political Economy*, LXXII (Dec 1965) 557–72.

[14] Lewis, W. A., 'Economic Development with Unlimited Supplies of Labour', *Manchester School of Economics and Social Studies*, XXII (May 1954) 139–91.

[15] Magee, S. P., 'Factor Market Distortions, Production, Distribution and the Pure Theory of International Trade', *Quarterly Journal of Economics*, LXXXV (Nov 1971) 623–43

[16] United Nations, Department of Economic Affairs, *Relative Prices of Exports and Imports of Underdeveloped Countries* (1949).

SUPPLEMENTARY READINGS

[17] Batra, R. N., and Pattanaik, P. K., 'Domestic Distortions and the Gains from Trade', *Economic Journal*, LXXX (Sep 1970) 638–49.

[18] ——, and ——, 'Factor Market Imperfections, the Terms of Trade, and Welfare', *American Economic Review*, LXI (Dec 1971) 946–55.

[19] ——, and Casas, F. R., 'Factor Market Distortions and the Two-Sector Model of Economic Growth', *Canadian Journal of Economics*, IV (Nov 1971) 524–42.

[20] Hagen, E. E., 'An Economic Justification of Protectionism', *Quarterly Journal of Economics*, LXXII (Nov 1958) 496–514.

[21] Magee, S. P., 'Factor Market Distortions, Production and Trade: A Survey', *Oxford Economic Papers* (forthcoming).

[22] Pearce, I. F., 'The Theory of Wage Differentials: The $n \times n$ Case', *Journal of International Economics*, I (May 1971) 205–14.

11 Product Market Imperfections: The Theory of Monopoly in General Equilibrium

The previous chapter was devoted to the analysis of factor market imperfections in the presence of international trade. The quintessence of the chapter was that the existence of distortions in factor markets could cause reversals in nearly all the results derived from the standard undistorted model. Throughout our analysis there, product markets were still assumed to be perfect. In this chapter we turn to the other side of the exercise and assume that different goods are produced by different monopolists, but that factor markets continue to be perfect. It is worth pointing out here that within the theory of market imperfections it is the distortions in factor markets that have borne the brunt of attack from the trade theorist, whereas the existence of distortions in product markets, perhaps because of the intractability of the problem, has by and large been ignored.

The implications of monopoly in general equilibrium constitute the subject of analysis in two recent articles by Melvin and Warne [2] and Batra [1]. Our analysis here runs parallel to theirs. To the delight of those who continue to have undying faith in the existence of competitive markets, the presence of product market distortions alone, in contrast to factor market distortions, leaves virtually all the results derived from the undistorted model unchanged. This is perhaps the major difference between product and factor market distortions. The existence of monopoly does, however, generate a rich variety of new possibilities in terms of the changes in monopoly profits – absent under competitive conditions – that take place consequent upon any change in the system.

11.1 The Model with Pure Monopoly

The assumptions of this chapter are the same as those maintained under the standard model, except that product markets are now characterised by pure monopoly. In order to ensure the continued existence of monopoly, we assume that there is no freedom of entry into the product markets.† All the other assumptions specified at the beginning of Chapter 2 are unaltered. All this implies that the basic modification introduced by monopoly occurs in the price equations, whereas the full-employment equations remain unscathed. In this spirit, we write

$$C_{L1}X_1 + C_{L2}X_2 = L \tag{11.1}$$

$$C_{K1}X_1 + C_{K2}X_2 = K. \tag{11.2}$$

The price equations now include monopoly profits. Let $C_{\pi j}$ stand for monopoly profits per unit of output in the jth sector. Then

$$C_{L1}w + C_{K1}r + C_{\pi 1} = p_1 \tag{11.3}$$

and

$$C_{L2}w + C_{K2}r + C_{\pi 2} = p_2. \tag{11.4}$$

As regards the determination of $C_{\pi j}$, we note that under monopoly the reward of each factor equals the marginal revenue product, which in turn equals the marginal revenue (MR) times the marginal product. Now, as is well known in micro-theory,

$$MR_j = p_j \left(1 - \frac{1}{\varepsilon_j}\right)$$

where ε_j is the price elasticity of demand for the jth product. In other words, under monopoly

$$r = p_j \left(1 - \frac{1}{\varepsilon_j}\right) MPK_j \quad \text{and} \quad w = p_j \left(1 - \frac{1}{\varepsilon_j}\right) MPL_j$$

---

† Freedom of entry may be restricted by assuming that either all production takes place under government franchise, patent laws protect the monopolist, or the monopolist has such an efficient technology that no other producer can possibly compete with him.

where MPK and MPL denote, respectively, the marginal product of capital and labour. Since the excess profit equals total revenue (TR) minus total cost (TC), we may write

$$C_{\pi j} = \frac{TR_j - TC_j}{X_j} = \frac{p_j X_j - (rK_j + wL_j)}{X_j}$$

$$= \frac{p_j X_j - p_j[1 - (1/\varepsilon_j)][MPK_j K_j + MPL_j L_j]}{X_j} = \frac{p_j}{\varepsilon_j} \quad (11.5)$$

because, from Euler's theorem, $MPK_j K_j + MPL_j L_j = X_j$. Under competitive conditions $\varepsilon_j = \infty$, so that the excess profits are zero. With monopoly, however, $C_{\pi j} > 0$, and this brings us directly to the problem of determining ε_j in the context of our general equilibrium system. This indeed is the key to the solution of the system. Perhaps the main reason for the neglect of monopoly in the traditional models has been the difficulties encountered in specifying functional forms for ε_j in the context of general equilibrium. Melvin and Warne have provided an ingenious way out by assuming a homothetic social utility function, one implication of which is that the elasticity of demand for each product becomes a function of the commodity-price ratio and nothing else. In this chapter we assume that the social utility function is of the constant elasticity of substitution (C.E.S.) variety. In a closed economy,

$$U = U(D_1, D_2) = (aX_1^{-\beta} + bX_2^{-\beta})^{-1/\beta} \quad (D_j = X_j)$$

where a, b and β are the parameters such that $a > 0$, $b > 0$, $-1 < \beta < \infty$, $\beta \neq 0$ and $\sigma_D = 1/(1+\beta)$, where σ_D is the elasticity of substitution between the two goods in consumption. Purely for the sake of simplicity of calculation, we assume that $a/b = 1$. For this utility function, the demand functions (derived in the appendix, section 11.7) are

$$X_1 = \frac{Y}{p_1(1 + p^{\beta \sigma_D})} \quad \text{and} \quad X_2 = \frac{Y}{p_2(1 + p^{-\beta \sigma_D})}$$

whence

$$\frac{X_1}{X_2} = \frac{p(1 + p^{-\beta \sigma_D})}{(1 + p^{\beta \sigma_D})} = p^{(1 - \beta \sigma_D)} = p^{\sigma_D} \quad (p = p_2/p_1) \quad (11.6)$$

where Y is national income. From these demand functions, ε_j is given by

$$\varepsilon_1 = \frac{1 + \sigma_D p^{\beta \sigma_D}}{1 + p^{\beta \sigma_D}} \tag{11.7}$$

and

$$\varepsilon_2 = \frac{1 + \sigma_D p^{-\beta \sigma_D}}{1 + p^{-\beta \sigma_D}} \tag{11.8}$$

where

$$\varepsilon_j = -\frac{\partial X_j}{\partial p_j} \cdot \frac{p_j}{X_j} \qquad (j = 1,2).$$

These expressions confirm the fact that, under the homothetic utility function, ε_j is determined solely by p. Furthermore, since the numerator and denominator of (11.7) and (11.8) differ only by σ_D, the magnitude of ε_j is determined only by the magnitude of σ_D. Specifically, $\varepsilon_j \gtreqless 1$, if $\sigma_D \gtreqless 1$.

11.2   The Consumer–Producer Equilibrium

The major problem arising from the introduction of monopolistic product markets into the general equilibrium analysis of a two-sector model stems from the interdependence of supply and demand decisions. In other words, the fundamental difference between perfect competition and monopoly equilibria is that while aggregate demand and supply for products are independent and jointly determine outputs and prices in perfect competition, in monopoly this dichotomy does not exist. The general equilibrium problem under competitive conditions has three aspects. Given a production function and fixed factor and product prices, individual firms attempt to maximise their profits and in the process generate demand for factor services. Their decisions determine demand and supply functions for factor services and outputs, respectively. On the other side, given a utility function and taking the factor and product prices as fixed, the individual households offer factor services and buy goods in such a way as to maximise their flow of satisfaction derived from the consumption of commodities. Their decisions determine supply functions for factor services (which we assume are inelastic) and demand functions for products. Given these demand and supply functions, equilibrium prices are determined in such a way as to clear all product and factor markets.

However, under monopoly conditions in product markets *alone*, although the households make their decisions independent of the production side, the individual monopolists need data about demand for their products in order to make profit-maximising price–output decisions. This is evident from the expressions for factor rewards, which yield

$$p = \frac{p_2}{p_1} = \frac{MPL_1[1-(1/\varepsilon_1)]}{MPL_2[1-(1/\varepsilon_2)]} = \frac{MPK_1[1-(1/\varepsilon_1)]}{MPK_2[1-(1/\varepsilon_2)]}. \quad (11.9)$$

In perfect competition, on the other hand,

$$p = \frac{MPL_1}{MPL_2} = \frac{MPK_1}{MPK_2}$$

and it is clear that the producers' price ratio is determined independent of the consumers' price ratio furnished by (11.6). However, (11.9) shows that, under monopoly, producers' price ratio depends not only on marginal factor productivities but also on the elasticities of demand for the two products. This dependence of monopolist's price on consumer's demand raises an important question about the conditions necessary to ensure the existence of equilibrium. In this section we shall show that, for any given capital/labour ratio, k, all the variables in the model are uniquely related to the wage/rental ratio, ω. It is evident from (11.9) that p is positive if each elasticity of demand is greater than unity. This is, of course, the well-known result in monopoly theory, for the profit-maximising monopolist produces an output where marginal revenue equals positive marginal cost, and the former is positive only if the elasticity of demand exceeds unity. *Thus we may conclude that a necessary condition for the monopoly equilibrium to exist is that both price elasticities of demand are greater than unity, or that $\sigma_D > 1$.*

We have already stated that, under monopoly, producers' price ratio depends, among other things, on the two demand elasticities, which in turn can be shown to depend on the price ratio facing the consumers. Suppose we impose any price ratio on the consumers. From (11.6) we know that the ratio in which commodities may be consumed is uniquely determined by the product-price ratio. Corresponding to this price ratio there also exists a set of elasticities of demand, and given these and the marginal factor productivities from the production functions, the producers' price ratio will be determined uniquely from (11.9). The question is whether or not, and under what conditions, the producers' price ratio will be the same as the price ratio that was initially imposed on the consumers.

We begin by showing that, under the homethetic utility function, the change in the commodity-price ratio facing the consumers (p_c) is uniquely related to the change in the output ratio (X_1/X_2). Differentiating (11.6) totally, we obtain

$$(X_1^* - X_2^*) = \sigma_D p_c^*. \tag{11.10}$$

The next step then is to obtain an expression for ($X_1^* - X_2^*$) in terms of the change in the wage/rental ratio, for the latter can be easily seen to be uniquely related to the price ratio encountered by the producers. This can be accomplished by differentiating the entire system of equations in section 11.1. From (11.1) and (11.2)

$$\lambda_{L1} X_1^* + \lambda_{L2} X_2^* = L^* - (\lambda_{L1} C_{L1}^* + \lambda_{L2} C_{L2}^*) \tag{11.11}$$

$$\lambda_{K1} X_1^* + \lambda_{K2} X_2^* = K^* - (\lambda_{K1} C_{K1}^* + \lambda_{K2} C_{K2}^*) \tag{11.12}$$

where λ_{ij} is as before. Differentiating the price equations (11.3) and (11.4) totally and using the minimum unit cost condition,†

$$\theta_{Lj} C_{Lj}^* + \theta_{Kj} C_{Kj}^* = 0$$

---

† If factor markets are perfect, then the monopolist's profits are maximised when the given factor prices are equated to their marginal revenue productivities, which means that

$$\frac{w}{r} = \frac{MPL_j}{MPK_j}.$$

But this is a condition for unit cost minimisation, which is given by

$$w dC_{Lj} + r dC_{Kj} = 0.$$

The assumption of perfect factor markets, however, needs some justification, for the monopolist is likely to be a monopsonist and therefore aware of the fact that the factor supply curves facing him are not perfectly elastic, in which case the factor prices cannot be considered as given to the producers. This assumption is needed mainly for simplifying the mathematical calculations. Actually, in order to utilise the minimum unit cost condition, what we need to assume is that w and r are considered given by those who hire the factors of production. Suppose the producer is a multi-plant monopolist, and although the price-output decisions are made at the top level of managerial hierarchy, the decisions to hire factors are made at the plant level; if there are numerous plants, each contributing its share of the total output, then for all practical purposes the desiderata for perfect factor markets will be satisfied.

Another solution to the problem could be to assume that factor markets are unionised and the monopolist can hire any amount of inputs at the factor prices which the union agrees to accept. Here again the producer can consider the factor prices as given.

we obtain

$$\theta_{L1}w^* + \theta_{K1}r^* = p_1^*(1-\theta_{\pi1}) + \theta_{\pi1}\varepsilon_1^* \qquad (11.13)$$

and $$\theta_{L2}w^* + \theta_{K2}r^* = p_2^*(1-\theta_{\pi2}) + \theta_{\pi2}\varepsilon_2^* \qquad (11.14)$$

where θ_{ij} is the relative share of the ith factor in the jth good, and where i includes labour, capital and the monopolist. For example, $\theta_{\pi1} = C_{\pi1}/p_1 = 1/\varepsilon_1$. In other words, $\theta_{\pi j}$ is the share that goes to the monopolist's coffers. Clearly, $\theta_{Lj} + \theta_{Kj} + \theta_{\pi j} = 1$. As before, let λ and θ be the matrices of production coefficients in (11.11) and (11.12) and (11.13) and (11.14) respectively. Then

$$|\lambda| = \frac{I_1 L_2(k_2 - k_1)}{L \cdot K} = (\lambda_{L1} - \lambda_{K1}) = (\lambda_{K2} - \lambda_{L2}) \quad (11.15)$$

and

$$|\theta| = \frac{wr(k_2 - k_1)}{p_1 p_2 C_{L1} C_{L2}} = \theta_{K2}(1-\theta_{\pi1}) - \theta_{K1}(1-\theta_{\pi2})$$
$$= \theta_{L1}(1-\theta_{\pi2}) - \theta_{L2}(1-\theta_{\pi1}). \quad (11.16)$$

As expected, the expression for $|\lambda|$ is the same as that obtained in the undistorted model. Furthermore, the signs of $|\lambda|$ and $|\theta|$ are the same. However, when factor intensities are defined in terms of distributive share, i.e. θ's, some interesting possibilities come to light. Suppose $|\lambda|$ and $|\theta|$ are positive, so that $k_2 > k_1$. Under the competitive conditions where $\theta_{\pi j} = 0$, this would imply that $\theta_{L1} > \theta_{L2}$ and $\theta_{K2} > \theta_{K1}$. With monopoly, however, this need not be the case, for $|\theta|$ could be positive even if $\theta_{K2} < \theta_{K1}$, provided $(1-\theta_{\pi1})$ is sufficiently greater than $(1-\theta_{\pi2})$. In other words, even if a commodity is capital-intensive, it may have a lower share of capital than the labour-intensive commodity, provided the former pays a higher share to the monopolist than the latter. Similarly, a labour-intensive commodity may actually pay a lower share to labour than the other.

As usual, the expression for C_{Lj}^* and C_{Kj}^* can be obtained by the interaction of the minimum cost conditions and the definition of the two elasticities of factor substitution σ_j. In the presence of monopoly

$$C_{Lj}^* = -\theta_{Kj}\sigma_j(w^* - r^*)/(1-\theta_{\pi j})$$

and

$$C_{Kj}^* = \theta_{Lj}\sigma_j(w^* - r^*)/(1-\theta_{\pi j}).$$

Substituting these in (11.11) and (11.12) yields

$$\lambda_{L1}X_1^* + \lambda_{L2}X_2^* = L^* + \beta_L(w^* - r^*) \qquad (11.17)$$

and
$$\lambda_{K1}X_1^* + \lambda_{K2}X_2^* = K^* - \beta_K(w^* - r^*) \qquad (11.18)$$

where
$$\beta_L = \frac{\lambda_{L1}\theta_{K1}\sigma_1}{(1 - \theta_{\pi 1})} + \frac{\lambda_{L2}\theta_{K2}\sigma_2}{(1 - \theta_{\pi 2})} > 0$$

and
$$\beta_K = \frac{\lambda_{K1}\theta_{L1}\sigma_1}{(1 - \theta_{\pi 1})} + \frac{\lambda_{K2}\theta_{L2}\sigma_2}{(1 - \theta_{\pi 2})} > 0.$$

Subtracting (11.18) from (11.17) and using the expression for $|\lambda|$ from (11.15), we obtain

$$X_1^* - X_2^* = \frac{L^* - K^*}{|\lambda|} + \frac{(\beta_L + \beta_K)}{|\lambda|}(w^* - r^*). \qquad (11.19)$$

Substituting (11.19) in (11.10), we get

$$\sigma_D p_c^* = \frac{(\beta_L + \beta_K)}{|\lambda|}(w^* - r^*) \qquad (11.20)$$

given that factor endowments are constant, so that $L^* = K^* = 0$. One glance at (11.20) reveals that the price ratio facing the consumers, p_c, is uniquely related to the wage/rental ratio and that this relationship is determined by the sign of $|\lambda|$. It is a relatively simple matter now to observe that a similar relationship also exists between the price ratio facing the producers (call it p_p) and the wage/rental ratio. This can be obtained by solving (11.13) and (11.14) simultaneously to derive

$$|\theta|(w^* - r^*) = -[(1 - \theta_{\pi 1})(1 - \theta_{\pi 2})p_p^* \\ - \theta_{\pi 1}(1 - \theta_{\pi 2})\varepsilon_1^* + \theta_{\pi 2}(1 - \theta_{\pi 1})\varepsilon_2^*].$$

The required expression for ε_j^* in turn can be obtained by totally differentiating (11.7) and (11.8). It turns out that each demand elasticity is an increasing function of its relative price, because†

$$\varepsilon_1^* = \frac{-\beta^2 \sigma_D p_p^{\beta\sigma_D}}{[1 + p_p^{\beta\sigma_D}][1 + \sigma_D p_p^{\beta\sigma_D}]}p_p^* = -A_1 p_p^* \qquad (A_1 > 0) \qquad (11.21)$$

† Equations (11.21) and (11.22) simply show that as the monopolist, facing one of the demand curves derived from the utility function, raises his price, the elasticity of demand for his product rises and vice versa. It is for this reason that ε_j is shown to be related to the producers' price ratio rather than the consumers' price ratio, although on the consumption side ε_j is related to p_c.

$$\varepsilon_2^* = \frac{\beta^2 \sigma_D^2 p_p^{-\beta\sigma_D}}{[1+p_p^{-\beta\sigma_D}][1+\sigma_D p_p^{-\beta\sigma_D}]} p_p^* = A_2 p_p^* \qquad (A_2 > 0). \quad (11.22)$$

Substituting these in $|\theta|(w^*-r^*)$ then yields

$$\omega^* = w^* - r^*$$

$$= -\frac{[(1-\theta_{\pi1})(1-\theta_{\pi2})+\theta_{\pi1}(1-\theta_{\pi2})A_1+\theta_{\pi2}(1-\theta_{\pi1})A_2]}{|\theta|} p_p^*$$

$$= -\frac{E}{|\theta|} p_p^* \qquad (E > 0). \tag{11.23}$$

This expression provides corroboration of the fact that the producers' price ratio is also uniquely related to the wage/rental ratio. With this last expression, we have reached the stage where we can derive conditions necessary to bring about the equality of p_p and p_c in equilibrium. A comparison of (11.20) and (11.23) reveals that the relationships between p_c and ω on the one hand and that between p_p and ω on the other are completely opposite simply because $|\theta|$ and $|\lambda|$ possess the same sign. *This ensures that there is only one wage/ rental ratio at which p_p and p_c are equal.* The result can best be illustrated in terms of Fig. 11.1, which is drawn under the assump-

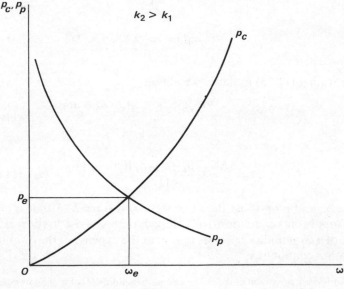

Figure 11.1

tion that $|\lambda|$ and $|\theta|$ are positive, so that p_p is shown to be a decreasing and p_c an increasing function of ω. The equilibrium commodity-price ratio is p_e, and corresponding to it the equilibrium wage/rental ratio is ω_e. It is manifestly clear from the diagram that there is only one wage/rental ratio at which the producers' and consumers' price ratios are identical. It must be remembered, however, that the monopoly equilibrium exists only under the constraint of σ_D exceeding unity, for otherwise p_p will not be positive.†

11.3   The Price–Output Response and the Nature of Autarky Equilibrium

Once the matter of commodity prices facing the consumers and those facing the producers being equal is settled, we can proceed to analyse other questions which until now have been explored under the conditions of perfect competition in product markets. This section is concerned with the change in the two outputs in response to the shift in relative commodity prices. If the factor endowments are kept constant, so that $L^* = K^* = 0$, the solution of (11.17) and (11.18) yields

$$X_1^* = \frac{(\lambda_{K2}\beta_L + \lambda_{L2}\beta_K)(w^* - r^*)}{|\lambda|}$$

and

$$X_2^* = \frac{-(\lambda_{L1}\beta_K + \lambda_{K1}\beta_L)(w^* - r^*)}{|\lambda|}.$$

Substituting (11.23) in these, we obtain

$$X_1^* = \frac{-E(\lambda_{K2}\beta_L + \lambda_{L2}\beta_K)(p_2^* - p_1^*)}{|\lambda|\,|\theta|} \tag{11.24}$$

and

$$X_2^* = \frac{E(\lambda_{L1}\beta_K + \lambda_{K1}\beta_L)(p_2^* - p_1^*)}{|\lambda|\,|\theta|}. \tag{11.25}$$

Since $|\lambda|$ and $|\theta|$ possess the same sign, and since $E > 0$, it is clear that supply curves are positively sloped, that is, a rise in the relative price of a commodity raises its output at the expense of the output of the other commodity.

† For further exposition of the existence and the uniqueness of monopoly equilibrium, see Batra [1] and Melvin and Warne [2].

This discussion leads us directly to the questions of the slope and shape of the transformation curve in the present framework. One point should be clear at once. Since factor markets are still undistorted, the position of the transformation curve remains unaltered. Nevertheless the slope of the transformation curve no longer reflects the commodity-price ratio, for the former is given by the ratio of the marginal costs in the two industries which, under competitive conditions, are equal to the respective prices, but which under monopoly are equal to the respective marginal revenues. In other words, under monopoly

$$-\frac{dX_1}{dX_2} = \frac{MR_2}{MR_1} = \frac{p_2[1-(1/\varepsilon_2)]}{p_1[1-(1/\varepsilon_1)]} = \alpha p \qquad (11.26)$$

where $\alpha = \dfrac{1-(1/\varepsilon_2)}{1-(1/\varepsilon_1)}$. It can be readily seen that $\alpha \gtreqless 1$, according as $\varepsilon_2 \gtreqless \varepsilon_1$. Thus it is only when the elasticities of demand for both goods are the same that the MRT equals the commodity-price ratio.

As already noted, the absence of distortions in factor markets guarantees that the position of the transformation curve itself is not

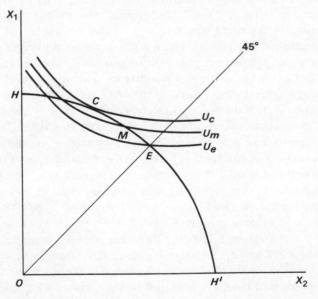

Figure 11.2

affected. At the same time the assumption of full employment ensures that the equilibrium production point will in fact lie on the production locus. Is it then possible to determine uniquely the location of the equilibrium production point under monopoly? The pursuit of a satisfactory answer to this question takes us to Fig. 11.2, where HH' is the transformation curve. If there were no monopoly, the equilibrium production point in autarky would be determined by the tangency of the utility function to the production possibility locus HH'. Such a production point in the diagram is given by C, and corresponding to it the level of welfare is given by U_c. As another point of reference, let us locate the point where $\varepsilon_1 = \varepsilon_2$. This, from (11.7) and (11.8), is possible only if

$$p^{\beta\sigma_D} = p^{-\beta\sigma_D}, \quad \text{or} \quad p = 1.$$

Substituting this value of p in (11.6), we find that

$$\frac{X_1}{X_2} = 1.$$

Thus, when the two elasticities of demand are equal, the output of the two goods is also the same. This rather unusual result is attributable to our particular assumption made for simplifying the calculations, namely, $(a/b) = 1$. In general, the output ratio corresponding to the point where $\varepsilon_1 = \varepsilon_2$ is determined by the value of the parameters a, b and β. Draw a 45° line from the origin which intersects the production possibility locus at E. Then along any point on the ray OE, $\varepsilon_1 = \varepsilon_2$. One characteristic of the production point given by E is that at this point the MRT equals the commodity-price ratio. Thus if the social indifference curve were to touch HH' at E, the autarky equilibrium under monopoly would be identical to that under competitive conditions. However, E is one of an infinity of possible production points and there is no *a priori* reason to believe that community preferences will be such as to lead to the competitive solution, especially when the production and utility functions are independent. Let an indifference curve U_e pass through E. Then it is evident that at E, $MRT = -p_p > MRS = -p_c$. A movement away from E in either direction creates a divergence between the MRT and p_p. As we move along HH' towards H, X_1 rises and X_2 declines, so that the price ratio facing the consumers rises (as can be confirmed from (11.10)) and hence ε_2 rises and ε_1 declines. This in turn leads to a rise in α above unity, and from (11.26) the

MRT comes to exceed p_p. This is true of any point between E and H (excluding E and H); but at C, $MRT = p_c$, which implies that there $p_c > p_p$. Thus we have two points of reference. At E, $p_p > p_c$ and at C, $p_p < p_c$. Hence the production point where $p_p = p_c$ will necessarily lie between E and C. This is how Melvin and Warne have been able to reach the conclusion that the monopoly output ratio is bounded by the competitive output ratio and the one corresponding to the point representing the equality between ε_1 and ε_2. Suppose such a production point is given by M, through which passes another indifference curve U_m. Fig. 11.2 then also indicates that *the monopoly welfare level lies below the competitive level of welfare*.

Until now we have maintained the distinction between p_p and p_c in view of the fact that they are equal only in equilibrium. Since the subsequent sections are concerned with comparative statics where two different equilibrium situations are compared, this distinction will no longer be necessary.

11.4 The Standard Trade Theorems

Up to now our main concern has been with the demonstration that a unique equilibrium under monopoly situation in both sectors does exist, provided $\sigma_D > 1$. The model developed in the previous sections can be easily applied to the standard theorems in international trade.

Let us begin with the Rybczynski theorem, which is concerned with the implications of changes in factor supplies on commodity outputs at constant terms of trade. If commodity prices are constant, then the wage/rental ratio is constant, which implies that the last expression on the right-hand side of (11.17) and (11.18) disappears so that we are left with the usual equations that were encountered in several previous chapters where monopoly was absent. *The interested reader can easily see for himself that the Rybczynski theorem holds in the present model without any qualification.* This can also be confirmed from (11.19) by setting $(w^* - r^*)$ to zero.

The validity of the Rybczynski theorem coupled with the assumption of international identity of consumption patterns ensures the *validity of the Heckscher Ohlin theorem in terms of the physical definition*. Furthermore, since commodity and factor prices continue to be uniquely related, given of course the non-reversal of factor intensities, the *Heckscher–Ohlin theorem also continues to be valid in terms of the factor-price definition* of inter-country relative factor abundance.

Closely related to the Heckscher–Ohlin theorem is the theorem concerning international equalisation of factor prices. In free trade, prices are everywhere the same, which, with similar inter-country utility functions, implies that ε_1 and ε_2 will be the same in the trading partners. Given the unique relationship between commodity and factor prices, the wage/rental ratio will be the same in each country. From the expressions concerning C_{Kj}^* and C_{Lj}^*, one can see that

$$k_j^* = C_{Kj}^* - C_{Lj}^* = \sigma_j(w^* - r^*)$$

which is the same as the one existing in the undistorted markets. Given the international similarity of production functions, the capital/labour ratio in each commodity will be the same in both trading countries; this in turn will ensure the equality of real factor rewards in the two countries, for under linearly homogeneous production functions the marginal product of each factor depends solely on the capital/labour ratio in the *j*th industry. *Since in addition each industry will have the same marginal revenue in both countries, factor rewards will also be the same everywhere.*

An interesting question concerns the profits per unit of output in each country. With so much information at hand, this matter can be resolved by recourse to the definition of $C_{\pi j}$, which from (11.5) is given by

$$C_{\pi j} = \frac{p_j}{\varepsilon_j}$$

With p_j and ε_j identical in the two countries, there is no reason why $C_{\pi j}$ is not also identical. If the rate of monopoly profit is defined as total profits (π_j) per unit of the capital stock (presumably owned by the monopolist), then

$$\frac{\pi_j}{K_j} = \frac{\pi_j}{X_j} \frac{X_j}{L_j} \frac{L_j}{K_j} = \frac{C_{\pi j} \cdot APL_j}{k_j} = \frac{p_j \cdot APL_j}{\varepsilon_j k_j}$$

where APL_j is the average product of labour in the *j*th industry. Since APL_j and MPL_j are interrelated, and since the latter is the same in the two countries, π_j/K_j is also internationally identical. By the same token π_j/L_j will also be similar internationally. *Thus, in whatever way we define them, we find that the rates of monopoly profit in the two sectors will be internationally identical, provided the other conditions usually assumed for the validity of the factor-price equalisation theorem are satisfied.*

Finally, we examine the validity of the Stolper–Samuelson theorem in the presence of monopolised product markets. The two equations (11.13) and (11.14) can be solved to yield

$$w^* - p_1^* = \frac{-[(1-\theta_{\pi 2})\theta_{K1} + \theta_{K2}\theta_{\pi 1}A_1 + \theta_{K1}\theta_{\pi 2}A_2]}{|\theta|}(p_2^* - p_1^*) \quad (11.27)$$

$$w^* - p_2^* = \frac{-[(1-\theta_{\pi 1})\theta_{K2} + \theta_{K2}\theta_{\pi 1}A_1 + \theta_{K1}\theta_{\pi 2}A_2]}{|\theta|}(p_2^* - p_1^*) \quad (11.28)$$

$$r^* - p_1^* = \frac{[(1-\theta_{\pi 2})\theta_{L1} + \theta_{L2}\theta_{\pi 1}A_1 + \theta_{L1}\theta_{\pi 2}A_2]}{|\theta|}(p_2^* - p_1^*) \quad (11.29)$$

$$r^* - p_2^* = \frac{[(1-\theta_{\pi 1})\theta_{L2} + \theta_{L2}\theta_{\pi 1}A_1 + \theta_{L1}\theta_{\pi 2}A_2]}{|\theta|}(p_2^* - p_1^*). \quad (11.30)$$

An inspection of these four equations reveals that real factor rewards are uniquely related to the relative commodity prices. Suppose there occurs a rise in the relative price of the second commodity, so that $(p_2^* - p_1^*) > 0$. If $|\theta| > 0$, that is, if the first industry is labour-intensive relative to the second, the wage rate declines and the return on capital rises in terms of both commodity prices, because $w^* - p_j^* < 0$ and $r^* - p_j^* > 0$. *This is a clear demonstration of the continued validity of the Stolper–Samuelson theorem in spite of the presence of monopoly elements in the product markets.*

A change in commodity prices will also manifest itself through changes in monopoly profits via the change in the outputs and the elasticities of demand. The desired expressions can be obtained by totally differentiating (11.5) and then substituting for X_j^* and ε_j^*. However, we can follow a simpler route by simply analysing the changes in the components that constitute the monopoly profits. From (11.5), we know that $\pi_j = p_j X_j / \varepsilon_j$. Let us first consider the effects of a rise in the relative price of the second commodity on monopoly profits in the same industry. Now

$$\frac{\pi_2}{p_2} = \frac{X_2}{\varepsilon_2} \quad \text{and} \quad \frac{\pi_2}{p_1} = p\frac{X_2}{\varepsilon_2}.$$

A rise in p causes a rise in X_2, but since each demand elasticity is an increasing function of its own relative price, it also causes a rise in ε_2. Since both the numerator and the denominator of the above expressions rise as a result of a rise in p, the outcome on the real rate of profit in the second industry is uncertain in terms of both goods. The same kind of fate awaits the position of the monopolist in the first industry, where

$$\frac{\pi_1}{p_1} = \frac{X_1}{\varepsilon_1} \quad \text{and} \quad \frac{\pi_1}{p_2} = \frac{X_1}{p\varepsilon_1}.$$

Here a rise in p leads to a decline not only in X_1 but also in ε_1, so that once again we cannot predict how the rise in p will affect the real income of the monopolist in the first industry. Thus we arrive at the conclusion that a change in the relative commodity prices exerts a determinate influence on the real incomes of the primary factors but not on those of the monopolists.

The same is true of the relative returns of the monopolists, which are now given by

$$\frac{\pi_2}{\pi_1} = p \frac{X_2}{X_1} \cdot \frac{\varepsilon_1}{\varepsilon_2}$$

because with a rise in p, (X_2/X_1) rises but $(\varepsilon_1/\varepsilon_2)$ declines, so that the final result is indeterminate.

11.5 Monopoly and the Gains from Trade

The theory of gains from trade has kept company with us in almost every chapter. We have demonstrated again and again that in the presence of distortions, whether in the foreign trade sector or in the domestic markets, free trade is not the optimal policy. The presence of monopoly, which comes into the category of a domestic distortion, constitutes no exception to this rule. Yet monopoly in the local product markets gives rise to novel situations which make the discussion of the gains from trade in the present model command more than merely academic interest.

First of all, there is the question of whether domestic monopolies can exist in the face of foreign competition, for if the country in question is relatively small, so that the commodity prices in the free trade equilibrium are fixed, the monopolistic advantages to domestic producers must disappear, for they no longer possess the power to influence prices. Furthermore, since the consumers now face a given set of prices, the elasticities of demand approach infinity and α approaches unity, so that from (11.26) the *MRT* comes to equal the international-price ratio. Under this setting, the introduction of trade serves to eliminate the domestic distortion. Thus three types of gains stem from free trade: the consumption gain, the production gain and the gain from the elimination of the domestic distortion because the *MRT* is no longer different from the commodity-price ratio.

Things get really involved when both trading partners possess monopolistic elements in their local product markets as well as in the foreign trade market, so that the free trade prices can no longer be taken as given. Several conceptual difficulties need to be resolved before any progress can be made towards our objective. With the existence of monopolies in both countries, each commodity is now produced by two producers instead of one. Therefore in the presence of trade we are in effect faced with a situation of duopoly and the multifarious solutions that present themselves under these circumstances, for, as is well known, duopoly, unlike monopoly, has numerous solutions, depending upon the assumptions we make concerning the reactions of one producer to the expected actions of the other. Melvin and Warne have a simple solution for this dilemma. Following them, we assume either that each producer of a commodity behaves as a monopolist and takes its share of the world market as the total demand for his own output, or production is carried out by multinational firms which control the production and distribution of a commodity in both countries. The analysis is the same under any one of these cases.

There still remains the question of the pertinence of the elasticity of demand when each commodity is being sold locally and abroad. If we assume that the utility functions are similar internationally, the elasticities of demand, being functions of commodity prices only, will be the same in both countries under free trade. In autarky equilibrium, the elasticities of demand pertaining to consumption and production are the same. This is no longer tenable in the presence of trade, for the local output of each firm is different from the total consumption of any commodity. Therefore the elasticities of demand relevant to each country's production point on its transformation curve are the ones associated with the local or the world consumption of the two commodities, rather than the elasticities consistent with the local production. This point gains further clarification when we consider the welfare implications of free trade, to which we now turn.

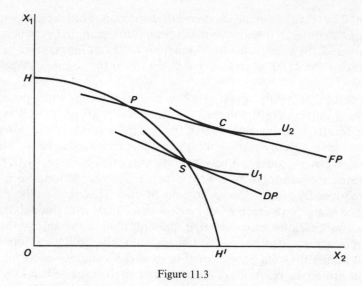

Figure 11.3

Consider Fig. 11.3, where the *MRT* is shown to exceed the relative price of the second good at all production points, reflecting the fact that $\varepsilon_2 > \varepsilon_1$ so that $\alpha > 1$ (see equation (11.26)). The home country, the one under consideration, is assumed to import X_2 and export X_1. The self-sufficiency equilibrium is given by S and the domestic-price ratio by the slope of DP; the free trade price ratio is furnished by the slope of FP, the production point shifts to P, the consumption point to C, and the level of welfare rises from U_1 to U_2. Free trade in this case is superior to no trade. At point S the elasticities of demand facing the consumers and those relevant to production are the same. As trade is introduced, the relative price of the first good rises and so does its output and ε_1; on the other hand the output of X_2 and ε_2 declines, but the new elasticities of demand are the ones consistent with the consumption point C and not with the free trade production point P, simply because in the presence of trade local consumption and production are not identical. Furthermore, in computing the elasticities at P, account must be taken of the elasticities of foreign supply or demand in addition to the elasticities at C. It can be easily seen that the demand elasticities pertaining to P are the weighted average of those associated with C and the elasticities of foreign supply and demand, and there is no reason to suggest that the two sets of elasticities will be the same. This is how the elasticities accompanying the total consumption and local production levels differ when trade is allowed. It may be emphasised here that since the world consumption is equal to world production in equilibrium, the elasticities associated with world output must be the same as those associated with world consumption. This line of reasoning suggests that under our assumptions concerning monopoly behaviour in the two countries and the international similarity of homogeneous utility functions, the existence of the world equilibrium can be established in the same manner as we established the existence of autarky equilibrium.

What we have shown up to now is that free trade is necessarily superior to no trade, provided the country imports the commodity with the higher autarkic elasticity of demand ($\varepsilon_2 > \varepsilon_1$). Let us now proceed to the other case where $\varepsilon_1 > \varepsilon_2$, a case that is depicted in Fig. 11.4, where the MRT is shown to be less than the relative price of the second commodity. In general, the MRT is lower (higher) than the relative price of the commodity with the lower (higher) elasticity. As before, the introduction of free trade, arising from a shift from the autarky price ratio DP to the foreign-price ratio FP, takes production and consumption from S to P and C respectively. As regards welfare, there are two possibilities. If the shift in the

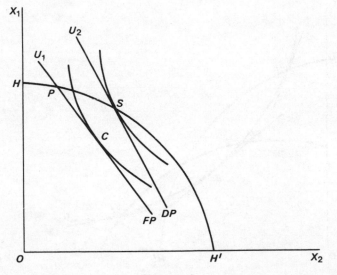

Figure 11.4

production point is not very large, and/or if *FP* is much flatter than
DP, free trade will continue to be superior to no trade. For these
conditions will give rise to high consumption gain and low production loss. In the contrary conditions, however, the production loss
may outweigh the consumption gain, in which case free trade may
be inferior to no trade or a prohibitive tariff. Such a possibility is
illustrated in Fig. 11.4, where welfare declines from U_2 to U_1 after
the introduction of free trade. Thus we conclude that *if a country
exports the commodity with the higher elasticity (in autarky), free
trade may be inferior to no trade.*

One may ask the question: how is *FP* determined? Partly, the
answer has already been given. Fig. 11.5, however, makes it crystal
clear. As stated earlier, demand elasticities are identical in the two
countries under free trade. The converse of this statement is also
true. Free trade prices are those at which demand elasticities are the
same internationally. Fig. 11.5 consists of two transformation curves,
of which *HH'* belongs to the home country and *FF'* to the foreign
country; in view of the international similarity of utility functions,
a common indifference curve U_1 intersects these transformation
curves at S_h and S_f, the former being the autarky equilibrium point

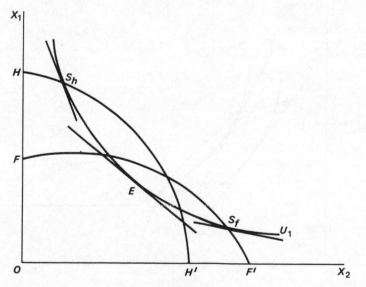

Figure 11.5

in the home country and the latter in the foreign country. It is also evident that p_h, the autarkic relative price of the second good, which is reflected by the slope of U_1 at S_h, exceeds p_f, the corresponding price in the foreign country, indicated of course by the slope of U_1 at S_f. Furthermore, in autarky $\varepsilon_{2h} > \varepsilon_{2f}$ and $\varepsilon_{1h} < \varepsilon_{1f}$, where the subscripts h and f refer as usually to the home and the foreign country. With $p_h > p_f$, the home country will import the second commodity and export the first. Returning now to the original objective for which Fig. 11.5 was introduced, it is easy to see that as p_h and p_f move closer to each other when trade is introduced, $(\varepsilon_2/\varepsilon_1)_h$ and $(\varepsilon_2/\varepsilon_1)_f$ also shift towards each other and at some point are equalised. Such a point is given by E in the diagram, and the slope of U_1 at E furnishes the world-price ratio FP. Indeed, if the world elasticity ratio is known, the free trade price ratio can be computed directly from (11.7) and (11.8), because then

$$\frac{\varepsilon_2}{\varepsilon_1} = \frac{\sigma_D + p^{\beta\sigma_D}}{1 + \sigma_D p^{\beta\sigma_D}}.$$

Let e be the elasticity ratio in the free trade equilibrium. Then

$$e = (\sigma_D + p^{\beta\sigma_D})/(1 + \sigma_D p^{\beta\sigma_D})$$

whence
$$p = \left[\frac{\sigma_D - e}{e\sigma_D - 1}\right]^{1/\beta\sigma_D}$$

which reveals that, once the world elasticity ratio is known, p can be determined immediately because β and σ_D are given parameters. This formula also suggests that σ_D can be equal neither to e nor to $1/e$, for otherwise p will be either zero or infinity. Furthermore, in order to avoid the possibility of a negative p, σ_D is such that it exceeds or falls short of both e and $1/e$.

11.6 Concluding Remarks
The model described in the preceding sections has incorporated the distortions arising from monopoly elements in the product markets, while the distortions occurring in the factor markets, which were explored in the previous chapter, have been ignored. It is heartening to note that, unlike the case with factor market distortions, virtually all the results derived from the undistorted two-sector model continue to hold in the presence of monopoly. Thus the theorems of

Rybczynski, Stolper and Samuelson, and Heckscher and Ohlin all continue to be valid in the present model, which is a very general model in the sense that the competitive system springs from it as a special case where both the elasticities of demand equal infinity. When trade is introduced, free trade still turns out to be the optimal policy if the country with monopolistic product markets in autarky faces a given set of world prices. In the large country case, however, where monopolies exist in both countries, free trade, unlike in the competitive system, may not be superior to no trade. The foregoing results remain unchanged if the monopoly exists in one sector instead of both, except that now the monopoly equilibrium cannot be identical with the competitive equilibrium even by chance, for the two elasticities can never be equal.

11.7   Appendix
Some of the equations presented in the text without proof will now be derived.

Consider a utility function with a constant elasticity of substitution, σ_D, where $\sigma_D = 1/(1+\beta)$, $-1 < \beta < \infty$. With two sectors in the economy producing two goods, X_1 and X_2, the utility function can be represented as

$$U = (aX_1^{-\beta} + bX_2^{-\beta})^{-1/\beta} \tag{A11.1}$$

where a/b is assumed to be unity for the sake of simplicity of calculation. Given the constraint that $Y = p_1 X_1 + p_2 X_2$, we form the Lagrangian function

$$Z = (aX_1^{-\beta} + bX_2^{-\beta})^{-1/\beta} + \gamma(Y - p_1 X_1 - p_2 X_2). \tag{A11.2}$$

Maximising, we obtain

$$\frac{\partial Z}{\partial X_1} = -\frac{1}{\beta}(aX_1^{-\beta} + bX_2^{-\beta})^{-1/\beta\sigma_D}(-a\beta X_1^{-1/\sigma_D}) - p_1\gamma = 0 \tag{A11.3}$$

$$\frac{\partial Z}{\partial X_2} = -\frac{1}{\beta}(aX_1^{-\beta} + bX_2^{-\beta})^{-1/\beta\sigma_D}(-b\beta X_2^{-1/\sigma_D}) - p_2\gamma = 0 \tag{A11.4}$$

$$\frac{\partial Z}{\partial \gamma} = Y - p_1 X_1 - p_2 X_2 = 0. \tag{A11.5}$$

From (A11.3) and (A11.4) we have

$$aX_1^{-1/\sigma_D}(aX_1^{-\beta}+bX_2^{-\beta})^{-1/\beta\sigma_D} = p_1\gamma$$
$$bX_2^{-1/\sigma_D}(aX_1^{-\beta}+bX_2^{-\beta})^{-1/\beta\sigma_D} = p_2\gamma.$$

Dividing, using (A11.5) and solving for X_2, we obtain

$$X_2 = \frac{Y}{p_2(1+p^{-\beta\sigma_D})} \tag{A11.6}$$

$$X_1 = \frac{Y}{p_1(1+p^{\beta\sigma_D})} \tag{A11.7}$$

where, as in the text, $p = p_2/p_1$.

From these demand functions, the 'own' price elasticities are derived as follows:

Differentiating (A11.6) partially with respect to p_2, we have

$$\frac{\partial X_2}{\partial p_2} = \frac{-Y[1+\sigma_D(p_2)^{-\beta\sigma_D}(p_1)^{\beta\sigma_D}]}{[p_2+(p_2)^{\sigma_D}(p_1)^{\beta\sigma_D}]^2} \tag{A11.8}$$

whence

$$-\varepsilon_2 = \frac{\partial X_2}{\partial p_2}\cdot\frac{p_2}{X_2} = -\frac{p_2[1+\sigma_D(p_2)^{-\beta\sigma_D}(p_1)^{\beta\sigma_D}]}{p_2+(p_2)^{\sigma_D}(p_1)^{\beta\sigma_D}}$$

so that

$$\varepsilon_2 = \frac{1+\sigma_D p^{-\beta\sigma_D}}{1+p^{-\beta\sigma_D}}.$$

Similarly,

$$\varepsilon_1 = \frac{1+\sigma_D p^{\beta\sigma_D}}{1+p^{\beta\sigma_D}}$$

It may be observed that, in the derivation of demand elasticities, we have assumed that money national income, Y, is constant at all points on the transformation curve. The validity of this procedure stems from the fact that, for any product-price ratio, individual prices can always be so adjusted as to keep income unchanged. The elasticities will be unaltered, because they depend only on the price ratio.

REFERENCES

[1] Batra, R. N., 'Monopoly Theory in General Equilibrium and the Two-Sector Model of Economic Growth', *Journal of Economic Theory*, IV (June 1972) 355–71.
[2] Melvin, J. R., and Warne, R. D., 'Monopoly and the Theory of International Trade', Research Report No. 7032, Department of Economics, Univ. of Western Ontario, London, Ontario.

12 Non-Traded Goods

Every country produces goods which cannot be traded at all either because of the nature of the goods, like houses, services, etc., or because of political barriers preventing, for example, the export of certain strategic military equipment, or because of artificial trade barriers like prohibitive tariffs. In all the preceding chapters we ignored the presence of such products, much at the expense of economic reality. The objective of this chapter is to examine how and to what extent the results derived from the two-traded-goods model are modified when a non traded final good is incorporated into the framework.

To the two traded goods, X_1 and X_2, assumed so far, we add another, non-traded good, X_n, the demand for which always equals local supply. Thus we now have a three-good, two-factor model; this non-equality of the number of goods and factors introduces some very unexpected problems which must be satisfactorily resolved before we can proceed direct to some of the theorems derived before. The rest of the assumptions continue to be the same as those of the standard two-sector model. That is to say, at least for the time being, we ignore the complications arising from market imperfections which were the subject of analysis in the two previous chapters.

12.1 The Model with Non-Traded Goods

In the presence of an additional good, the full-employment relations are given by

$$C_{L1}X_1 + C_{L2}X_2 + C_{Ln}X_n = L \qquad (12.1)$$

and

$$C_{K1}X_1 + C_{K2}X_2 + C_{Kn}X_n = K \qquad (12.2)$$

where, as before, C_{ij} is the amount of the ith input divided by the jth good ($i = L,K; j = 1,2,n$), for example, $C_{Ln} = (L_n/X_n)$. The price equations, on the other hand, now become

$$C_{L1}w + C_{K1}r = p_1 \qquad (12.3)$$

$$C_{L2}w + C_{K2}r = p_2 \qquad (12.4)$$

and $\qquad C_{Ln}w + C_{Kn}r = p_n \qquad (12.5)$

where p_j is the price of the jth good. As before, the input–output coefficients can be solved from the expressions relating them to factor prices. But we still have one too many unknowns, for there are five equations and six unknowns, X_1, X_2, X_n, w, r and p_n. The system can be given a determinate solution, however, by introducing another equation concerning the demand–supply equality for X_n. Then

$$X_n = X_n(p,q,Y) \qquad (12.6)$$

which shows that the local supply of the non-traded good equals its demand, which in turn depends on p, q and Y, where p and q are, respectively, the relative prices of the second and the non-traded good in terms of the first, and where Y is national income. This gives us a completely determinate system of six equations and six unknowns, given that the production coefficients can be solved from the factor prices.

The solution of the model with the non-traded good proceeds by first solving for w and r from the two price equations (12.3) and (12.4) in terms of the input–output coefficients and p_1 and p_2, which are determined internationally. The values of w and r so obtained can be plugged in (12.5) to solve for p_n in terms of the production coefficients of all three commodities. Since production coefficients themselves are functions of w and r, we get a determinate solution for factor rewards, the price of the non-traded good and capital/labour ratios in all three goods, once the values of the parameters p_1 and p_2 are internationally determined. Note that this solution is obtained independently of demand conditions and factor endowments. If the country in question is a small country and hence faces given prices of traded goods, the demand conditions and factor supplies exert no influence on factor prices and prices of non-traded goods. If in addition we assume that production functions are similar internationally, w and r will also be the same in the two countries. This follows clearly from the solution of (12.3) and

(12.4). Furthermore, if the international identity of production functions extends also to the domestic goods, the prices of these goods will also be the same everywhere in the world in spite of the fact that these goods are not traded. The validity of this result does not depend on the number of domestic goods.

Until now our diagnosis has proceeded on the side of price equations and factor rewards. Let us now explore the system from the side of factor endowments and outputs and see what new features are introduced by the presence of a third, domestic good X_n. It is worth emphasising at this point that many of the new properties of the model stem chiefly from the inequality of the number of goods and factors and not from the fact that one of the goods is purely a domestic good. First of all, when there are three goods and two factors, we should expect indeterminacy in the system if all goods are traded, the reason being that in such a model the production possibility surface becomes a ruled one like *ABC* in Fig. 12.1, for any

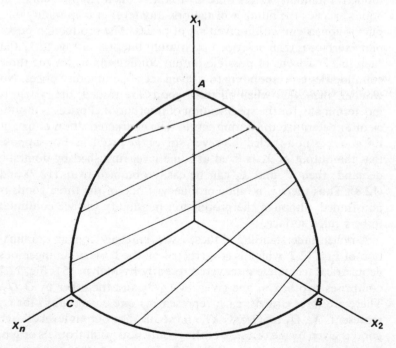

Figure 12.1

amount of output of a commodity is compatible with a given set of prices. This can be seen most readily by solving for X_1 and X_2 in terms of L, K and X_n from (12.1) and (12.2) to obtain

$$X_1 = \frac{C_{L2}L(k_2-k)+C_{L2}C_{Ln}(k_n-k_2)X_n}{|C|} \tag{12.7}$$

$$X_2 = \frac{C_{L1}L(k-k_1)+C_{L1}C_{Ln}(k_1-k_n)X_n}{|C|} \tag{12.8}$$

where, as usual, k_j is the capital/labour ratio in the jth good ($j = 1,2,n$) and $|C|$ is the determinant of the matrix of production coefficients involved in X_1 and X_2, that is, $|C| = C_{K2}C_{L1}-C_{L2}C_{K1}$. If commodity prices are constant, (12.3)–(12.5) show that factor prices and production coefficients will remain unaltered. But this is not sufficient to ensure that X_1 and X_2 will also be unaltered so long as X_n is positive and all capital/labour ratios differ. For then the output of one or both goods will vary with the variation in X_n even though commodity prices were invariant. Thus when the number of goods exceeds the number of factors, any level of commodity outputs is consistent with a given set of prices. The production possibility surface is then described by straight lines (as in Fig. 12.1) and each line is a locus of possible output configurations for the three commodities corresponding to a given set of commodity prices. No wonder, then, that when all three goods are traded, the system is indeterminate, for the specification of international prices is insufficient to determine the output levels. The characterisation of one of the goods as non-traded, however, solves the problem. For suppose that the output of X_n is fixed at some level furnished by domestic demand; then X_1 and X_2 can be easily obtained from (12.7) and (12.8). Thus there is no indeterminacy if one of the three goods is non-traded, although the production possibility surface continues to be a ruled surface.

A richer understanding of these issues emerges from an examination of Fig. 12.2, which is constructed on the basis of an ingenious geometrical technique discovered recently by Melvin [5]. Fig. 12.2 comprises two boxes, one given by O_nO_2 and the other by O_1O_2. There are three origins, each representing one commodity; for O_n represents X_n, O_1 represents X_1, and so on. The output level of each good is given by the distance of the production point from its origin. Suppose the output of X_n is fixed at the level O_1O_n, then the remain-

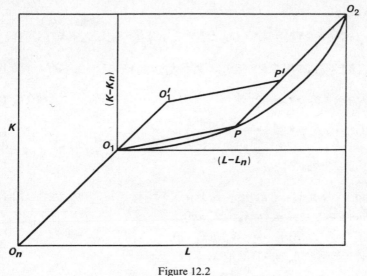

Figure 12.2

ing factor endowments can be allocated between the two traded goods in such a way as to trace a contract curve constrained by factor supplies equal to $(K-K_n)$ and $(L-L_n)$. Such a contract curve between X_1 and X_2 is given by O_1PO_2. Let P be the actual production point, then the output of X_1 equals O_1P and that of X_2 equals O_2P, with their capital/labour ratios given by the slopes of O_1P and O_2P, respectively. Thus once the output of the domestic good is given, the other two outputs are readily determined.

Suppose that, instead of O_nO_1, the output of X_n is fixed at O_nO_1'; draw $O_1'P'$ parallel to O_1P. The diagram makes it clear that even though the capital/labour ratios and hence the commodity prices are constant, the output of X_1 and X_2 has declined when X_n is fixed at a higher level. In other words, there is no unique relationship between commodity outputs and prices when goods exceed factors. We will discover later that, for this reason alone, the output of the traded good may actually decline in response to a rise in its relative price.

12.2 The Price–Output Response of Traded Goods
In order to obtain the expressions for the price–output response of traded goods, the system of equations must be differentiated totally,

to obtain

$$\lambda_{L1}X_1^* + \lambda_{L2}X_2^* = L^* - (\lambda_{L1}C_{L1}^* + \lambda_{L2}C_{L2}^*) - \lambda_{Ln}(C_{Ln}^* + X_n^*) \qquad (12.9)$$

$$\lambda_{K1}X_1^* + \lambda_{K2}X_2^* = K^* - (\lambda_{K1}C_{K1}^* + \lambda_{K2}C_{K2}^*) - \lambda_{Kn}(C_{Kn}^* + X_n^*) \qquad (12.10)$$

$$\theta_{L1}w^* + \theta_{K1}r^* = p_1^* \qquad (12.11)$$

$$\theta_{L2}w^* + \theta_{K2}r^* = p_2^* \qquad (12.12)$$

$$\theta_{Ln}w^* + \theta_{Kn}r^* = p_n^* \qquad (12.13)$$

and $\qquad X_n^* = E_{n2}p^* - E_nq^* + \eta_nY^* \qquad (12.14)$

where $\qquad E_{n2} = (p/X_n)(\partial X_n/\partial p),$

$\qquad\qquad E_n = -(q/X_n)(\partial X_n/\partial q),$

$\qquad\qquad \eta_n = (Y/X_n)(\partial X_n/\partial Y)$

and where, in obtaining (12.11)–(12.13), use has been made of the cost-minimising condition $\theta_{Lj}C_{Lj}^* + \theta_{Kj}C_{Kj}^* = 0$, with θ's as before denoting the relative share of the relevant factor. In (12.14), E_{n2} is the cross-elasticity of demand between the domestic and the second good, E_n is the price elasticity and η_n the income elasticity of demand for the non-traded good. From (12.11) and (12.12)

$$|\theta|(w^* - r^*) = (p_1^* - p_2^*) = -p^*$$

and from (12.11) and (12.13)

$$|\theta_n|(w^* - r^*) = (p_1^* - p_n^*) = -q^*$$

whence $\qquad \dfrac{q^*}{p^*} = \dfrac{|\theta_n|}{|\theta|} \qquad (12.15)$

where $\qquad |\theta| = \begin{vmatrix} \theta_{L1} & \theta_{K1} \\ \theta_{L2} & \theta_{K2} \end{vmatrix}$ and $|\theta_n| = \begin{vmatrix} \theta_{L1} & \theta_{K1} \\ \theta_{Ln} & \theta_{Kn} \end{vmatrix}$

and $|\theta| \gtrless 0$ if $k_2 \gtrless k_1$ and $|\theta_n| \gtrless 0$ if $k_n \gtrless k_1$. From (12.15) it is clear that the effect of a change in the prices of traded goods on the price of the domestic goods depends on the signs of $|\theta|$ and $|\theta_n|$ or on the capital/labour ratios in the three industries. As usual, C_{Lj}^* and C_{Kj}^* can be obtained by solving simultaneously the equations representing the elasticity of factor substitution and cost-minimising condition in each sector.† Thus

$$C_{Lj}^* = -\theta_{Kj}\sigma_j(w^* - r^*)$$

and

$$C_{Kj}^* = \theta_{Lj}\sigma_j(w^* - r^*).$$

Substituting these expressions in (12.9) and (12.10), assuming that $L^* = K^* = 0$, and solving them yields

$$X_1^* = \frac{(\lambda_{K2}\beta_L + \lambda_{L2}\beta_K)(w^* - r^*) + X_n^*(\lambda_{L2}\lambda_{Kn} - \lambda_{K2}\lambda_{Ln})}{|\lambda|}$$

and

$$X_2^* = \frac{-(\lambda_{L1}\beta_K + \lambda_{K1}\beta_L)(w^* - r^*) + X_n^*(\lambda_{K1}\lambda_{Ln} - \lambda_{L1}\lambda_{Kn})}{|\lambda|}$$

where

$$|\lambda| = \begin{vmatrix} \lambda_{L1} & \lambda_{L2} \\ \lambda_{K1} & \lambda_{K2} \end{vmatrix}$$

and

$$\beta_L = \lambda_{L1}\theta_{K1}\sigma_1 + \lambda_{L2}\theta_{K2}\sigma_2 + \lambda_{Ln}\theta_{Kn}\sigma_n > 0$$
$$\beta_K = \lambda_{K1}\theta_{L1}\sigma_1 + \lambda_{K2}\theta_{L2}\sigma_2 + \lambda_{Kn}\theta_{Ln}\sigma_n > 0.$$

Substituting for $(w^* - r^*)$ in these expressions, we get

$$X_1^* = \frac{-(\lambda_{K2}\beta_L + \lambda_{L2}\beta_K)p^*}{|\lambda||\theta|} + \frac{|\lambda_{n2}|}{|\lambda|}\frac{X_n^*}{p^*} \cdot p^* \qquad (12.16)$$

and

$$X_2^* = \frac{(\lambda_{L1}\beta_K + \lambda_{K1}\beta_L)p^*}{|\lambda||\theta|} + \frac{|\lambda_{n1}|}{|\lambda|}\frac{X_n^*}{p^*}p^* \qquad (12.17)$$

where

$$|\lambda_{n2}| = (\lambda_{L2}\lambda_{Kn} - \lambda_{K2}\lambda_{Ln}) \gtreqless 0 \quad \text{if} \quad k_n \gtreqless k_2$$

and

$$|\lambda_{n1}| = (\lambda_{K1}\lambda_{Ln} - \lambda_{L1}\lambda_{Kn}) \gtreqless 0 \quad \text{if} \quad k_1 \gtreqless k_n.$$

These expressions confirm what has already been anticipated, namely, that there may not be a unique relationship between prices of traded goods and their outputs. Consider (12.16), for example. If $X_n^* = 0$, then $X_1^*/p^* < 0$ as usual because $|\lambda||\theta| > 0$. However, if $X_n^* \neq 0$, the last expression may have a sign opposite to that of the first, in which case X_1^*/p^* may not be negative. The change in p affects the demand for the domestic good, which in turn leads to a change in its output and hence in the amount of resources available

---

† This was accomplished in Chapter 2, and the expressions for C_{Lj}^* and C_{Kj}^* derived there remain unchanged in the present model because each good is still produced with the help of two factors.

to the traded goods. Suppose that all goods are *gross* substitutes, so that (X_n^*/p^*) is positive. We still have to reckon with the sign of $|\lambda|$ and $|\lambda_{n2}|$. Suppose $|\lambda| > 0$, so that $k_2 > k_1$; if $|\lambda_{n2}|$ is also positive, so that $k_n > k_2$, then (X_1^*/p^*) may not be unambiguously negative. On the other hand, if the domestic and the second good are complements, so that $(X_n^*/p^*) < 0$, then with both $|\theta|$ and $|\lambda_{n2}| > 0$, (X_1^*/p^*) is unambiguously negative and the price–output response in the first industry is normal. Similar considerations apply to the price–output response in the second industry. *The gist of this discussion is that, in the presence of purely domestic goods, the price–output response of the traded goods is no longer predictable.* The outcome depends not only on the substitution effects on the production side, but also on the nature of the demand for three commodities as well as their relative factor intensities.

This result generates far-reaching ramifications for several results which we derived in the chapter on the theory of nominal tariffs. First, the offer curve may not only be negatively sloped at some volume of trade, but may also bend back towards the origin. In other words, the price elasticity of demand for imports may no longer be negative. This factor tends to create instability in the model. Second, the introduction of the tariff may result in a rise in the import demand at constant terms of trade, and hence eventually cause a deterioration in the terms of trade of the tariff-imposing country.[†]

12.3 The Stolper–Samuelson Theorem

The effect of protection on factor rewards is straightforward in a two-good model. In our three-good model, however, the logic becomes more involved, for a rise in the price of the importable good entails a change in the price of the non-traded good. Is it then possible that factor rewards moving unambiguously in terms of the prices of traded goods may not do so in terms of the prices of purely domestic goods? The answer turns out to be a definite no. This can

---

[†] It is true that, in the presence of the domestic good, the demand for the importable good is also influenced by the price of X_n which may rise or decline as a result of the tariff, and this factor, absent in the usual two-good model, may strengthen or attentuate the resultant decline in the demand for the importable good. Nevertheless, in the absence of the categorical relationship between the output of X_2 and the tariff-induced rise in its local relative price, it is no longer certain that the rate of tariff and the demand for imports are negatively related when world prices are kept constant. For this reason, tariffs may or may not cause an improvement in the terms of trade of the tariff-imposing country. For further discussion, see Komiya [4].

be seen immediately by solving for w^* and r^* from (12.11) and (12.12) to obtain

$$w^* = -\frac{\theta_{K1}}{|\theta|} p_2^* \qquad (12.18)$$

$$r^* = \frac{\theta_{L1}}{|\theta|} p_2^* \qquad (12.19)$$

where we assume that the tariff-imposing country is small, so that its tariff on X_2 leaves p_1 unchanged. Let $|\theta| > 0$, then $w^* < 0$ and $r^* > 0$. Furthermore, $(\theta_{L1}/|\theta|) > 1$, so that $r^* > p_2^*$. In other words, the wage rate declines and the return on capital rises in terms of the second good and also in terms of the first good, because $p_1^* = 0$. Now a decline in w and a rise in r will lead to a change in p_n. However, since from (12.13) the change in p_n is a weighted average of the changes in w and r, the weights being θ_{Ln} and θ_{Kn} which sum up to unity,

$$r^* > p_n^* > w^*.$$

This implies that r rises and w declines in terms of the domestic good also. In other words, factor rewards move unambiguously in terms of all commodities including the non-traded good as a result of the tariff. What is interesting is that since p_n varies with p_2, a rise in p_n will worsen and a decline in p_n will improve the real income position of both factors in comparison to what their positions would be in the absence of the domestic good.

12.4 The Rybczynski Theorem

The implications of a change in factor supplies for output levels have kept recurring in several previous chapters. This one is no exception. In exploring the effects of changes in factor supplies on the two outputs at constant terms of trade, we have to approach the problem in a slightly different manner. A rise in factor supplies culminates in a rise in national income when terms of trade are unchanged. This raises the demand for all products including the domestic good. To match the increase in demand, the output of the domestic good must rise to the same extent. In other words, a part of the additional factor supplies must be absorbed in the domestic good. Thus we conclude that whatever the direction of change in the output of the traded goods, the output of the non-traded good must rise as a result of the increase in factor supplies, when terms of trade are kept constant.

As regards the traded goods, the change in their outputs can be deciphered by solving for X_1^* and X_2^* from (12.9) and (12.10), while remembering that at constant commodity prices $(w^* - r^*) = 0$. Thus

$$X_1^* = \frac{(\lambda_{K2}L^* - \lambda_{L2}K^*) + (\lambda_{L2}\lambda_{Kn} - \lambda_{K2}\lambda_{Ln})X_n^*}{|\lambda|} \quad (12.20)$$

$$X_2^* = \frac{(\lambda_{L1}K^* - \lambda_{K1}L^*) + (\lambda_{K1}\lambda_{Ln} - \lambda_{L1}\lambda_{Kn})X_n^*}{|\lambda|}. \quad (12.21)$$

From (12.6) we know that when terms of trade are unaltered, $X_n^* = \eta_n Y^*$. With $Y = wL + rK$, and with $w^* = r^* = 0$, $Y^* = \theta_L L^* + \theta_K K^*$, where θ_L and θ_K denote respectively the share of labour and capital in national income. This means that

$$X_n^* = \eta_n(\theta_L L^* + \theta_K K^*).$$

Substituting this in (12.20) and (12.21) yields

$$|\lambda|X_1^* = [\lambda_{K2}(1 - \eta_n\theta_L\lambda_{Ln}) + \eta_n\theta_L\lambda_{L2}\lambda_{Kn}]L^*$$
$$- [\lambda_{L2}(1 - \eta_n\theta_K\lambda_{Kn}) + \eta_n\theta_K\lambda_{K2}\lambda_{Ln}]K^*$$

$$|\lambda|X_2^* = [\lambda_{L1}(1 - \eta_n\theta_K\lambda_{Kn}) + \eta_n\theta_K\lambda_{K1}\lambda_{Ln}]K^*$$
$$- [\lambda_{K1}(1 - \eta_n\theta_L\lambda_{Ln}) + \eta_n\theta_L\lambda_{L1}\lambda_{Kn}]L^*$$

Now

$$\eta_n\theta_L\lambda_{Ln} = m_n\theta_{Ln} < 1, \quad \text{and} \quad \eta_n\theta_K\lambda_{Kn} = m_n\theta_{Kn} < 1$$

where m_n is the marginal propensity to consume the domestic good and lies between zero and unity. With so much information at hand, the effects of changes in factor supplies on X_1 and X_2 can be easily derived. Suppose $K^* = 0$. Then with $|\lambda| > 0$, that is, with $k_2 > k_1$, $X_1^*/L^* > 0$ and $X_2^*/L^* < 0$. In other words, an increase in the supply of labour alone raises the output of the labour-intensive traded good and lowers the output of the capital-intensive traded good, when terms of trade are unaltered. The increase in the supply of one factor alone then leads to an ultra-biased growth. This is nothing but a straightforward generalisation of the Rybczynski theorem to the model incorporating the non-traded good. Similarly, for $L^* = 0$, $(X_1^*/K^*) < 0$ and $X_2^*/K^* > 0$ when $|\lambda| > 0$.

12.5 The Gains from Trade Once Again

Most of the results derived in Chapter 4, which was concerned with the analysis of gains from trade, did not ignore the presence of purely domestic goods, except the theorem comparing the welfare implications of higher versus lower tariffs. There we promised a reappraisal of this theorem in the present chapter. The reason must be palpable by now, for, as we have seen above, the relationship between the demand for imports and the rate of tariff is no longer monotonic, that is, (dE_2/dt) may be negative, positive or even zero. Since the sign of the change in welfare is controlled solely by the sign of (dE_2/dt), the effect of an increase in the tariff rate on welfare becomes ambiguous when purely domestic goods are introduced in the model.†

Next, we turn to the question of the optimal policy in the presence of purely domestic goods when factor markets are distorted by the presence of inter-industry wage differentials. The choice of the distortion is of course arbitrary, but the results derived below permit application to any kind of distortion.

In the presence of three goods, the problem may be formulated as one of maximising the social utility function

$$U = U(D_1, D_2, D_n)$$

subject to the constraints

$$D_1 = X_1 - E_1 = X_1 - pE_2 \tag{12.22}$$

$$D_2 = X_2 + E_2 \tag{12.23}$$

and

$$D_n = X_n \tag{12.24}$$

where D_n is the consumption of the non-traded good and $E_1 = pE_2$ from the balance-of-payments constraint. On the production side,

$$X_j = F_j(K_j, L_j) \qquad (j = 1, 2, n) \tag{12.25}$$

$$r = F_{K1} = pF_{K2} = qF_{Kn} \tag{12.26}$$

and

$$\frac{w_1}{\alpha_1} = \frac{w_2}{\alpha_2} = \frac{w_n}{\alpha_n}$$

---

† See the expression for $(1/U_1)(dU/dt)$ in Chapter 4. For a full discussion of gains from trade in the presence of non-traded goods, see Batra [1].

or
$$\frac{F_{L1}}{\alpha_1} = \frac{pF_{L2}}{\alpha_2} = \frac{qF_{Ln}}{\alpha_n} \tag{12.27}$$

where w_j is the wage rate in the jth sector and where $\alpha_j \geq 1$ is a constant. With no wage differential, $\alpha_1 = \alpha_2 = \alpha_3$. In the presence of the differential, however, the following possibilities arise:

1. $\alpha_1 = \alpha_2 < \alpha_n$, and the differential is paid by the non-traded good.
2. $\alpha_1 = \alpha_n < \alpha_2$, and the differential is paid by the import-competing good.
3. $\alpha_2 = \alpha_n < \alpha_1$, and the differential is paid by the exportable good.

In addition to these, there are six more possibilities if the differential exists among all the industries. These are:

$$\alpha_1 \gtrless \alpha_2 \gtrless \alpha_n \quad \text{and} \quad w_1 \gtrless w_2 \gtrless w_n;$$
$$\alpha_1 \gtrless \alpha_n \gtrless \alpha_2 \quad \text{and} \quad w_1 \gtrless w_n \gtrless w_2;$$
$$\alpha_2 \gtrless \alpha_1 \gtrless \alpha_n \quad \text{and} \quad w_2 \gtrless w_1 \gtrless w_n.$$

For expository purposes, we rewrite the full-employment equations as

$$L_1 + L_2 + L_n = L \quad \text{and} \quad K_1 + K_2 + K_n = K.$$

Our first task here is to obtain an expression concerning the relationship between the outputs of all three industries, something similar to the slope of the transformation curve in the two-good case. Totally differentiating (12.25) and dividing through by dX_2, we obtain

$$\frac{dX_1}{dX_2} = \frac{F_{K1}dK_1 + F_{L1}dL_1}{F_{K2}dK_2 + F_{L2}dL_2}. \tag{12.28}$$

From the full-employment equations

$$dL_1 + dL_2 + dL_n = 0 \quad \text{and} \quad dK_1 + dK_2 + dK_n = 0.$$

Using these and (12.26) and (12.27), (12.28) can be written as

$$\frac{dX_1}{dX_2} = -p\left[\frac{F_{K2}(dK_2 + dK_n) + (\alpha_1/\alpha_2)F_{L2}(dL_2 + dL_n)}{F_{K2}dK_2 + F_{L2}dL_2}\right]$$
$$= -p\left[\beta + \frac{F_{K2}dK_n + (\alpha_1/\alpha_2)F_{L2}dL_n}{F_{K2}dK_2 + F_{L2}dL_2}\right] \tag{12.29}$$

where $\beta = \dfrac{F_{K2}dK_2 + (\alpha_1/\alpha_2)F_{L2}dL_2}{F_{K2}dK_2 + F_{L2}dL_2} \gtreqless 1$

according as $(\alpha_1/\alpha_2) \gtreqless 1$. In the analogous manner

$$\frac{dX_n}{dX_2} = \frac{p}{q}\left[\frac{F_{K2}dK_n + (\alpha_n/\alpha_2)F_{L2}dL_n}{(F_{K2}dK_2 + F_{L2}dL_2)}\right]$$

$$= \frac{p}{q}\left[\frac{F_{K2}dK_n + (\alpha_1/\alpha_2)F_{L2}dL_n}{\gamma(F_{K2}dK_2 + F_{L2}dL_2)}\right]$$

where $\dfrac{1}{\gamma} = \dfrac{F_{K2}dK_n + (\alpha_n/\alpha_2)F_{L2}dL_n}{F_{K2}dK_n + (\alpha_1/\alpha_2)F_{L2}dL_n} \gtreqless 1$ if $\dfrac{\alpha_n}{\alpha_2} \gtreqless \dfrac{\alpha_1}{\alpha_2}$

or $\gamma \gtreqless 1$, according as $(\alpha_1/\alpha_n) \gtreqless 1$.

It may now be seen that the second term within the brackets of (12.29) equals $(\gamma q/p)(dX_n/dX_2)$. Hence

$$\frac{dX_1}{dX_2} = -p\left[\beta + \frac{\gamma q}{p} \cdot \frac{dX_n}{dX_2}\right]$$

or $\qquad dX_1 + \beta p\, dX_2 + \gamma q\, dX_n = 0.$ (12.30)

Two special cases deserve further consideration. In the absence of the differentials, $\beta = \gamma = 1$, so that (12.30) reduces to $dX_1 + pdX_2 + qdX_n = 0$. If, in addition, there is no non-traded good, we arrive at the familiar relationship that $(dX_1/dX_2) = -p$.

Reverting to our original objective for deriving (12.30), let us totally differentiate the utility function and the constraints given by (12.22)–(12.24), to obtain $\dfrac{dU}{U_1} = dX_1 + pdX_2 + qdX_n$. Substituting for dX_1 from (12.30) in this expression then yields

$$\frac{dU}{U_1} = pdX_2(1-\beta) + qdX_n(1-\gamma). \qquad (12.31)$$

As usual, we have assumed that the initial situation is one of free trade and that the country in question is a price-taker. This last equation confirms the result that in the absence of the wage differential, so that $\beta = \gamma = 1$, free trade continues to be the *first-best policy*.

Let us now consider the case where factor markets are distorted but the domestic goods do not exist, so that (12.31) becomes

$$\frac{dU}{U_1} = pdX_2(1-\beta).$$

Here β reflects the divergence between the marginal rate of transformation and the international price ratio. As expected, the optimal policy in the presence of the differential requires a change in X_2 such that the divergence between the MRT and the given international price ratio is eliminated, so that the value of β to producers comes to equal unity. The second-best policy in other words requires the imposition of production tax-cum-subsidy on the second and/or the first commodity. The first-best policy of course consists in the elimination of the wage differential to the producers by means of the grant of a factor tax-cum-subsidy, such that (α_1/α_2) and β are equated to one. None of these results is new, but they have been reproduced to present a contrast to the results to be derived below. It is noteworthy here that these results are not modified even if the non-traded good exists, so long as $\gamma = 1$ or $\alpha_1 = \alpha_n$, so that wages are the same in the exportable and the purely domestic-good industries.

Next, consider the case where the non-traded good exists and the wage differential is paid by either X_2 or X_n. In the first case $\alpha_1 = \alpha_n < \alpha_2$, which means that $\gamma = 1$ but $\beta < 1$. Here again the second-best policy calls for a production tax-cum-subsidy to be granted to the traded goods. In the second case where the differential is paid by the non-traded good, $\alpha_1 = \alpha_2 < \alpha_n$ and $\gamma < 1$ but $\beta = 1$, so that the change in welfare reduces to

$$\frac{dU}{U_1} = qdX_n(1-\gamma).$$

Here the second-best policy calls for a *consumption subsidy* to be granted to the domestic good, such that the divergence to the producers between $-(dX_1/dX_2)$ and $p[1 + (q/p)(dX_n/dX_2)]$ is eliminated, that is to say, the effective value of γ to the producers is equalised to unity. Note that this policy does not apply to the traded goods. Since the distortion is in the domestic production sector of the economy, the thrust of the cure should also lie in removing the inequality between $-(dX_1/dX_2)$ and $p[1 + (q/p)(dX_n/dX_2)]$, just as in the two-good model the second-best optimum is achieved by changing the output of X_1 and X_2 in such a way that the difference between

$-(dX_1/dX_2)$ and p is eliminated. If the consumption tax (or subsidy) were to be imposed on one of the traded goods, there will not be any change in outputs, for p, which is exogenously determined, will remain unchanged for the producers. However, in the case of the non-traded good the domestic output of X_n equals its domestic consumption. Therefore, if the wage differential is paid by X_n producers, the second-best optimum will be attained only by increasing its output to such an extent that to its producers γ comes to equal unity. However, in order to raise the output of X_n without creating a discrepancy in its domestic demand and supply, a consumption subsidy to the non-traded good, rather than a production subsidy, is required. It may also be noted from (12.31) that when $\gamma < 1$ and $\beta = 1$, so that the wage differential is paid by the non-traded good, a positive sign of $dD_n = dX_n$ will raise welfare, because (dU/U_1) is then positive.

On the other hand, if a production subsidy was granted to the non-traded-goods industry, the rise in its output will not necessarily be matched by the rise in its demand. Indeed, after the grant of the production subsidy which keeps the prices unchanged to the consumers, the demand–supply equilibrium for the non-traded good will be maintained only through coincidence. There is nothing in the model to guarantee this. The value of production at given world prices will rise as the production loss arising from the wage differential is eliminated through the provision of the requisite amount of the production subsidy to X_n. This by itself would lead to a rise in D_n even if prices to the consumers are constant, but there is nothing to guarantee that the rise in D_n will match the initial rise in X_n. On the other hand, if a consumption subsidy was conferred on the non-traded good, D_n could be raised to the required level of X_n, and the increase in the output of the domestic good would follow automatically, even if prices to the producers were unchanged, for, as demonstrated before, any output configuration is attainable with a given set of prices in our model with three goods and two factors.

Let us now consider the case where the differential is paid by the X_1 producers. Here $\alpha_2 = \alpha_n < \alpha_1$, so that both β and γ exceed unity. An interesting but a *chance* result emerges here. It is possible for (dU/U_1) to be zero, if from (12.31)

$$\frac{q}{p}\frac{(1-\gamma)}{(1-\beta)} = -\frac{dX_2}{dX_n} \tag{12.32}$$

in which case free trade alone is the second-best policy and the imposition of the production tax-cum-subsidy is not needed. Although this result is purely of academic interest, for only by coincidence will γ and β be such as to satisfy (12.32), yet the condition does suggest an interesting possibility. In any case, if the difference between the left- and right-hand sides of (12.32) is small, the gain to be derived from the introduction of the production tax-cum-subsidy may not be more than negligible and may not be worth the administrative headaches and costs. A necessary condition for (12.32) to be satisfied is that (dX_2/dX_n) be negative, because both γ and β exceed unity when the differential is paid by X_1 producers. The chances of (12.32) being satisfied improve if the wage differential exists among all three industries; nor is it necessary any more that (dX_2/dX_n) be negative, because the differentials may be such that $\gamma \gtrless 1$ when $\beta \lessgtr 1$. The essential point is that there exists a certain configuration of wage differentials which will satisfy (12.32). Nevertheless, in all the cases discussed in this section, the first-best policy requires the grant of factor tax-cum-subsidy so that the differential to the producers is eliminated.

An interesting policy device to attain the second-best welfare suggests itself from this discussion. Suppose the level of the inter-industry factor-price differential itself depends on government policy. For example; Johnson [3], referring to Harberger [2], has suggested that the inter-industry factor-price differential will occur if the government imposes a corporation income tax (which is a tax on the use of capital in the corporate sector alone) that drives a wedge between the gross rewards of capital in the corporate and the non-corporate sector. If the government must impose the corporation income tax in order to raise revenue, etc., then our argument suggests that it should be imposed in such a way as to satisfy condition (12.32). Although γ and β represent the wage differentials among the three industries under the assumption of similar reward of capital in all industries, the essential nature of our analysis is unmodified in the case where the rewards of capital differ among industries but the wage rates are similar. Depending on the situation, the level of the tax on the use of capital could be determined in the following manner:

(i)   The entire revenue can be raised from taxing the use of capital alone in the first commodity. If the other two industries constitute the non-corporate sector, this tax can be passed on as the corporation income tax.

(ii) The use of capital can be taxed in the second and the non-traded-good industries, but in order to attain the second-best optimum the tax rate will have to be different in the two industries. This may require taxing the use of capital in the corporate as well as the non-corporate sector. The need for different tax rates arises from the need to keep both β and γ from unity. This enables us to hazard a conjecture that the single corporation income tax rate on all incorporated industries in vogue in some countries (such as the U.S., Canada, etc.) might have had distortionary effects on the second-best level of social welfare.

(iii) Finally, the differential rate of tax on the use of capital can be imposed on all three industries. It may be emphasised again that the tax-rate differential should be such as to select those levels of β and γ that satisfy condition (12.32).

Thus there are several revenue-generating measures at the disposal of the government which will satisfy the dual objective of raising the revenue without lowering the level of welfare below the second-best level.

REFERENCES

[1] Batra, R. N., 'Non-Traded Goods, Factor Market Distortions and the Gains from Trade', *American Economic Review* (Sep 1973).
[2] Harberger, A. C., 'The Incidence of the Corporation Income Tax', *Journal of Political Economy*, LXX (June 1962) 215–40.
[3] Johnson, H. G., 'Factor Market Distortions and the Shape of the Transformation Curve', *Econometrica*, XXXIV (July 1966) 686–98.
[4] Komiya, R., 'Non-Traded Goods and the Pure Theory of International Trade', *International Economic Review*, VIII (June 1967) 132–52.
[5] Melvin, J. R., 'Production and Trade with Two Factors and Three Goods', *American Economic Review*, LVIII (Dec 1968) 1249–68.

13 International Investment

The barter theory of international exchange remains incomplete until the complications arising from the presence of international investment are explored in our standard two-good, two-factor model. This is the task assigned to this chapter. In all, this chapter is concerned with two burning issues. First, it turns out that under certain conditions free international movement of capital is a perfect substitute for free inter-country movement of goods. In other words, the hitherto assumed absence of international immobility of factors turns out to have been made not for convenience but for ensuring that trade will in fact take place among countries. However, the conditions under which capital movement becomes a perfect substitute for goods movement are quite stringent, and it is not at all unlikely to encounter the presence of international movement of both goods and capital. This gives rise to our second question, namely, what are the optimal policies in the presence of trade and international investment? The model described below is a natural extension to the case of international investment of the two-good, two-factor model that we have been using in the past several chapters.

13.1 Capital Mobility as a Substitute for International Trade
Mundell [5] was the first to demonstrate rigorously that under conditions of factor-price equalisation the same international equilibrium can be achieved by either free trade or the unimpeded mobility of capital. In other words, if trade is distorted by tariffs, the uninterrupted international flow of capital will supersede trade and leave unimpaired the efficiency of *laissez-faire*. In this chapter, however, we shall follow the demonstration given by Rakowski [7], who not only derives Mundell's result under less restrictive assumptions, but also points out the serious difficulties that normally stand in the way of capital mobility becoming a perfect substitute of free trade.

Before we proceed to the demonstration, a few remarks concerning the concept of international capital mobility are in order, if only to avoid the possibility of confusion in the subsequent analysis. By international mobility of capital is meant the physical movement of the capital goods in response to different rentals of capital in the two countries. These goods are not subject to any tariffs or transport costs. Furthermore, the owners of capital goods remain in their own country and can consume only the goods that are located there. The consumption of the capital owners depends on the marginal product of capital in any good which, of course, can be exchanged for the equivalent value of the other good. In addition, we assume that labour is still immobile internationally and that the tariffs and taxes are imposed only by the home country.

In a world where capital is mobile, equilibrium is achieved only when the marginal product of capital (MPK) in any commodity is the same in the two countries. For example, consider the case where

$$MPK_{1h} = MPK_{1f}$$

but

$$MPK_{2h} > MPK_{2f}$$

where the subscript f stands for the foreign country and distinguishes the variable from that in the home country. Now since the marginal product of capital in the second good is higher at home than abroad, foreign capital will move to the home country free of cost and will be employed in the production of the second good until MPK_{2h} and MPK_{2f} are equalised. Hence in equilibrium,

$$MPK_{1h} = MPK_{1f}$$

and 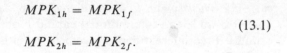 (13.1)

$$MPK_{2h} = MPK_{2f}.$$

Once this is recognised, it is a relatively simple matter to show that goods mobility and capital mobility are perfect substitutes, provided – and this is a crucial point – goods obtained through the repatriation of capital earnings are not subject to any tariffs. In our barter model, where money is absent, the repatriation of capital earnings requires the movement of goods, and if such goods are exempt from tariffs, it is clear that the introduction of any tariff would lead to the absence of all trade in goods that come under the purview of taxation.

For the sake of illustration, let us assume that the home country imposes a tariff (t_h) on the imports of the second good, so that

$$p_h = p(1 + t_h)$$

where, as before, p is the terms of trade and p_h the domestic-price ratio in the home country in terms of the first good. However, in the presence of the tariff the capital market cannot remain in equilibrium. For example, let

$$MPK_{1h} = MPK_{1f} \qquad (13.2)$$

that is, let the return to capital in the first industry be the same in the two countries. However, when exchanged for the equivalent of the second good, $MPK_{1h} = p_h MPK_{2h}$ and $MPK_{1f} = p MPK_{2f}$, so that in view of (13.2)

$$p_h MPK_{2h} = p MPK_{2f}. \qquad (13.3)$$

Since, in the presence of the tariff, $p_h > p$, it follows from (13.3) that

$$MPK_{2h} < MPK_{2f}$$

which evidently violates the equilibrium condition (13.1). For (13.1) to be satisfied, it is clear that p_h must equal p, which is impossible so long as the tariff is positive and operative. The only way in which p_h can be equal to p in the presence of the tariff is that there occurs a complete absence of international trade, so that the tariff is inoperative. *In other words, any impediment to free trade must lead to no trade when capital is internationally mobile.* It is in this sense that free trade and international capital mobility are perfect substitutes. Free international movement of either goods or capital leads to the equality of commodity prices in the trading countries.

It may be noted here that this result does not depend on the conditions necessary to ensure international factor-price equalisation. Thus, for example, even if one or both countries are completely specialised, so that factor-price equalisation is not possible, the result derived above can be established. In this spirit, suppose that the home country is specialised in the first good and the foreign country in the second. A unit of capital invested in the home country earns MPK_{1h} of good 1 or MPK_{1h}/p_h of the second good. Similarly, a unit of capital invested in the foreign country earns MPK_{2f} of the second good or $pMPK_{2f}$ of the first. All this implies that

$$MPK_{1h}/p_h = MPK_{2f}$$

and

$$MPK_{1h} = pMPK_{2f}$$

which can simultaneously hold only if $p = p_h$. Thus even if both countries are completely specialised and factor-price equalisation fails to occur under free trade, any tariff must eventually become a prohibitive tariff if the capital market is to remain in equilibrium. Note further that in arriving at this result we did not have to make the assumption of international identity of production functions, as done by Mundell.

Although Mundell's original proposition can be derived from much weaker conditions, there still remains one restrictive condition which is crucial for capital mobility to be a substitute for goods mobility and which is very unlikely to be satisfied in the real world. The requirement that goods moving across the countries through the repatriation of foreign earnings are not subject to the home country's tariff is really a special one and is unlikely to be satisfied. Thus goods mobility and capital mobility are not perfect substitutes, for capital mobility gives rise to some level of goods mobility. Nevertheless, Mundell's weaker proposition that an increase in trade implements results in increased capital movements is still valid simply because such an increase would normally raise the inter-country differential in the earnings of capital.

13.2 Optimal Tariffs and Taxes
In the preceding section we have seen that, since capital and goods mobility are not perfect substitutes, international trade and foreign investment can coexist in equilibrium. This gives rise to several interesting questions concerning optimal policy facing a large or a small country in a world where movement takes place in both goods and capital across the countries. The presence of foreign investment introduces another variable in the model, and the link between the earnings of capital and the world terms of trade introduces an element of interdependence in trade and investment policies. Fig. 13.1, which depicts the free trade equilibrium in the presence of international investment, highlights the importance of this interdependence between trade and investment. This diagram is a simple

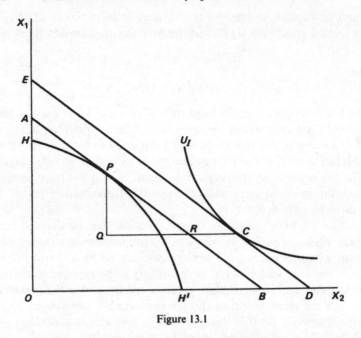

Figure 13.1

extension of the usual free trade diagram drawn in the absence of international investment. In Fig. 13.1, HH' is the home country's transformation curve, the slope of DE (parallel to AB) equals the world terms of trade, P is the production point, C is the consumption point, and the level of welfare is given by U_I. The home country exports PQ of X_1 in exchange for QC of X_2, where RC amount of X_2 represents the home country's foreign earnings in terms of the second commodity. This presentation serves to show the interdependence of trade and investment policies, because any policy change, by changing the world terms of trade, may also alter the foreign rate of return and hence the length RC and the position of the social indifference curve in the diagram. Furthermore, the position of the transformation curve also depends, among other things, on the level of foreign investment.

The link existing between trade and investment policies has been demonstrated by several authors including MacDougall [4], Negishi [6], Kemp [3], Jones [2] and Gehrels [1] among many others. The approach adopted here draws chiefly upon the work of the last three authors.

The setting of the problem is quite simple. We wish to maximise the social utility function

$$U = U(D_1, D_2) \tag{13.4}$$

under the constraints given by

$$D_1 = X_1 - E_1 \tag{13.5}$$

$$D_2 = X_2 + E_2 \tag{13.6}$$

$$\phi(X_1, X_2, I) = 0 \tag{13.7}$$

and

$$E_2 = E_1/p + r_f I \tag{13.8}$$

where (13.5) and (13.6) have been described several times before; (13.7) specifies the production constraint which takes into account the amount of home country's capital (I) invested abroad; and (13.8) describes the balance-of-payments constraint in the presence of the foreign investment, that is, the value of imports equals the value of exports plus the earnings on foreign investment which equal $r_f I$, where r_f is the foreign rate of return on capital expressed in terms of the second commodity. If the home country is a net creditor, I is positive; it is negative if the home country is a net debtor. Using (13.5), (13.6) and (13.8), (13.4) can be written as

$$U = U(X_1 - E_1, X_2 + r_f I + E_1/p). \tag{13.9}$$

The problem now reduces to one of maximising (13.9) subject to the production constraint (13.7). This can be solved by the well-known way of setting up the Lagrangian multiplier to obtain

$$Z = U(X_1 - E_1, X_2 + r_f I + E_1/p) - \gamma \phi(X_1, X_2, I)$$
$$= Z(E_1, I) \tag{13.10}$$

because

$$X_2 = X_2[X_1\{p(E_1, I), I\}I]$$

and

$$r_f = r_f(p, I).$$

If the foreign country is incompletely specialised, r_f depends only on p; otherwise it depends on I and $\partial r_f/\partial I < 0$.

The Optimal Tariff

In the presence of both trade and foreign investment, the function Z is to be maximised with respect to both E_1 and I. A full optimum can be obtained only when the policy-makers are free to vary either E_1 or I without fear of affecting the level of the other, that is, when E_1 and I can be treated independently. Keeping this in mind, let us differentiate (13.10) with respect to E_1 and set the partial derivative to zero. Thus

$$\frac{\partial Z}{\partial E_1} = U_1\left(\frac{\partial X_1}{\partial E_1} - 1\right) + U_2\left(\frac{\partial X_2}{\partial E_1} + \frac{1}{p} + E_1\frac{\partial(1/p)}{\partial E_1} + I\frac{\partial r_f}{\partial E_1}\right)$$

$$-\gamma\left(\phi_1\frac{\partial X_1}{\partial E_1} + \phi_2\frac{\partial X_2}{\partial E_1}\right) = 0 \qquad (13.11)$$

where

$$U_j = \partial U/\partial D_j \quad \text{and} \quad \phi_j = \partial\phi/\partial X_j \qquad (j = 1,2).$$

Since the marginal rates of transformation and substitution reflect the domestic commodity-price ratio under conditions of perfect competition,

$$U_1\frac{\partial X_1}{\partial E_1} + U_2\frac{\partial X_2}{\partial E_1} = 0 \quad \text{and} \quad \frac{U_1}{U_2} = \frac{1}{p_h}.$$

With this (13.11) reduces to

$$\frac{1}{U_2}\frac{\partial Z}{\partial E_1} = \left[\frac{1}{p} - \frac{1}{p_h}\right] + \left[I\frac{\partial r_f}{\partial E_1} + E_1\frac{\partial(1/p)}{\partial E_1}\right]$$

$$-\frac{\gamma}{U_2}\left(\phi_1\frac{\partial X_1}{\partial E_1} + \phi_2\frac{\partial X_2}{\partial E_1}\right). \qquad (13.12)$$

Again, because of the equality between the marginal rate of transformation and the domestic-price ratio, $\phi_1(\partial X_1/\partial E_1) + \phi_2(\partial X_2/\partial E_1) = 0$. Therefore, for $\partial Z/\partial E_1$ to be equal to zero.

$$\frac{p_h - p}{p_h p} = -E_1\frac{\partial(1/p)}{\partial E_1}\left[1 + \frac{I}{E_1}\frac{\partial r_f}{\partial(1/p)}\right]. \qquad (13.13)$$

From (13.13), the policy prescription is clear. If the country in question is a small country, so that $\partial(1/p)/\partial E_1 = 0$, the commercial policy should be such as to equate p_h with p. *In other words, free trade continues to be the optimal policy for a small country even when foreign investment is present.* For a large country, however, where $\partial(1/p)/\partial E_1 \neq 0$, the optimal policy requires the imposition of an optimal tariff, which can be derived from (13.13) by noting that $(p_h - p)/p = t_h$. Thus

$$t_h = \frac{1}{a_f}(1 + \mu_f \gamma_f)(1 + t_h)$$

where $a_f = -[\partial E_1/\partial(1/p)][(1/p)/E_1]$ is the foreign elasticity of demand for imports, μ_f is the ratio of foreign earnings to the value of exports, and $\gamma_f = [\partial r_f/\partial(1/p)][(1/p)/r_f]$ is the elasticity of the foreign rate of return on capital with respect to the world terms of trade. From this expression, the optimum tariff is given by

$$t_h = \frac{1 + \mu_f \gamma_f}{a_f - (1 + \mu_f \gamma_f)}. \tag{13.14}$$

What is interesting in the case of (13.14) is not only that the optimal tariff formula is different in the presence of international investment, but that there also arises the possibility that the optimal tariff may be zero or even negative, for μ_f and γ_f may possess any sign. If the home country is a net creditor, $\mu_f > 0$; γ_f on the other hand depends on whether X_1 is capital- or labour-intensive in the foreign country. If X_1 is capital-intensive abroad, $\gamma_f > 0$, and if it is labour-intensive, $\gamma_f < 0$. This follows from the Stolper–Samuelson theorem, *but only if the foreign country is incompletely specialised. Thus we conclude that in the case of incomplete foreign specialisation the optimal tariff may be of any sign and may even be zero, even if the country in question possesses monopoly power in international trade.* The reason for this surprising result is not far to seek. In the presence of foreign investment two terms of trade are involved, namely, p and r_f, and as a result of the tariff p and r_f may or may not move in the same direction, depending on whether the first good is capital- or labour-intensive abroad. Now the home income rises owing to a decline in p, but declines owing to a decline in r_f. Thus if the two effects cancel out, the optimal tariff is zero. Nevertheless, in the presence of complete foreign specialisation when $\gamma_f = 0$, the optimal tariff reduces to the standard formula derived in Chapter 5.

The Optimal Tax

The optimal rate of taxation on foreign earnings or the earnings of foreign capital can be obtained in an analogous manner. Given that E_1 and I are independent,

$$\frac{\partial Z}{\partial I} = U_1 \frac{\partial X_1}{\partial I} + U_2 \left[\frac{\partial X_2}{\partial I} + E_1 \frac{\partial(1/p)}{\partial I} + r_f + I \frac{\partial r_f}{\partial I} \right]$$
$$- \gamma \left(\phi_1 \frac{\partial X_1}{\partial I} + \phi_2 \frac{\partial X_2}{\partial I} + \phi_f \right) = 0. \quad (13.15)$$

In (13.15), ϕ_f/ϕ_2 is the marginal contribution of a unit of capital to the home country's national product expressed in terms of the second commodity, and equals r_h, the rate of return on capital in the home country, and

$$\frac{\phi_1}{\phi_2} \cdot \frac{\partial X_1}{\partial I} + \frac{\partial X_2}{\partial I} = \frac{U_1}{U_2} \cdot \frac{\partial X_1}{\partial I} + \frac{\partial X_2}{\partial I} = -r_h$$

that is, a unit of capital flowing abroad reduces home income by r_h when commodity prices are kept constant. All this implies that the last term in (13.15) equals zero. Thus (13.15) reduces first to

$$\frac{1}{U_2} \cdot \frac{\partial Z}{\partial I} = -r_h + E_1 \frac{\partial(1/p)}{\partial I} + r_f + I \frac{\partial r_f}{\partial I} = 0$$

and then to

$$r_f - r_h = -E_1 \frac{\partial(1/p)}{\partial I} - I \frac{\partial r_f}{\partial I}. \quad (13.16)$$

Before we derive the optimal rate of taxation on international investment, it is necessary to be clear about the relationship between r_f and r_h in the presence of such taxation. Suppose the home country is a net creditor and she imposes a rate of tax equal to 100τ per cent on her foreign earnings; then the equilibrium condition (13.1) gives way to

$$MPK_{1h} = MPK_{1f}(1 - \tau_h)$$

and

$$MPK_{2h} = MPK_{2f}(1 - \tau_h).$$

But $r_h = MPK_{1h}/p_h$ and $r_f = MPK_{1f}/p$, so that

$$r_h = \frac{MPK_{1f}(1 - \tau_h)}{p_h} = \frac{pr_f(1 - \tau_h)}{p_h}.$$

But if the home country already has a tariff on her imports, $p_h = p(1 + t_h)$. Therefore

$$r_h = r_f \frac{1 - \tau_h}{1 + t_h}. \tag{13.17}$$

On the other hand, if the home country is a net debtor, and imposes a tax τ_f on the earnings of foreign capital, the capital market is in equilibrium if

$$MPK_{1h}(1 - \tau_f) = MPK_{1f}$$

and

$$MPK_{2h}(1 - \tau_f) = MPK_{2f}.$$

Using r_h and r_f, however, this becomes

$$r_h(1 - \tau_f)(1 + t_h) = r_f. \tag{13.18}$$

Substituting for r_h from (13.17) and (13.18) in (13.16), the two optimal rates of taxation are given by

$$1 - \frac{1 - \tau_h}{1 + t_h} = \gamma_I \left[\frac{1}{\mu_f \gamma_f} + 1 \right]$$

and

$$1 - \frac{1}{(1 - \tau_f)(1 + t_h)} = \gamma_I \left[\frac{1}{\mu_f \gamma_f} + 1 \right]$$

where $\gamma_I = -(\partial r_f / \partial I)(I/r_f)$ is the elasticity of the foreign rate of return to capital with respect to international investment and γ_f has been defined as before. Using the expression for the optimum tariff, these formulae become

$$\tau_h = \frac{(1 + \mu_f \gamma_f)(\mu_f \gamma_f - a_f \gamma_I)}{\mu_f \gamma_f [a_f - (1 + \mu_f \gamma_f)]} \tag{13.19}$$

and

$$\tau_f = \frac{(1 + \mu_f \gamma_f)(\mu_f \gamma_f - a_f \gamma_I)}{a_f [\mu_f \gamma_f - \gamma_I (1 + \mu_f \gamma_f)]}. \tag{13.20}$$

As before, the signs of τ_h and τ_f depend on the signs of γ_f and μ_f which in turn depend on the inter-industry factor-intensity relationships in the foreign country and whether $I \gtrless 0$. To begin with, suppose that the optimum tariff is zero, that is, $1 + \mu_f \gamma_f = 0$. This, from (13.19) and (13.20), means that the optimal taxes on foreign investment must also be zero. *In other words, welfare maximisation in the presence of free trade also calls for the absence of intervention in international capital movements. This policy applies to both the small and the large country cases.* For example, suppose that the foreign country is incompletely specialised, so that r_f is influenced only by p and not by I. Then $\gamma_I = 0$, and if the home country is small, $a_f = \infty$; one can see immediately from (13.19) and (13.20) that both τ_h and τ_f then reduce to zero. However, if the optimum tariff is not zero and the home country possesses monopoly power in trade, then it is clear that the optimal taxes on foreign investment may also be non-zero. As an illustration, let us suppose that the home country is a net creditor, so that I and μ_f are positive; if X_1 is the capital-intensive commodity in the foreign country, then in the presence of incomplete foreign specialisation $\gamma_f > 0$ and $\gamma_I = 0$. Furthermore, assume that $a_f > 1 + \mu_f\gamma_f$. Then, under these circumstances, it pays the home country to impose not only an optimum tariff but also an optimal tax (τ_h) on its foreign earnings. However, if γ_f is negative, and μ_f still positive, the optimal tax on foreign earnings is indeterminate. Similar conclusions can be derived for the case where the home country is a net debtor, so that $\mu_f < 0$ and the relevant tax is τ_f. The important point is that, in the presence of international investment, optimal policy may require the imposition of both tariffs on imports and taxes on foreign investment.

Up to now we have assumed that the volume of imports and international investment are independent, so that full optimisation is possible. Quite often, however, policy-makers are not free to vary both imports and foreign investment, in which case E_1 and I no longer remain independent. However, the new constraints need not alter the intrinsic nature of the results derived above, although the optimal tariffs and taxes will be quantitatively altered. The main objective of this chapter was to outline the method of formulating the optimal policy in the presence of foreign investment, and this seems to have been done. The interested reader, however, can easily derive alternative tariff and tax formulae in the case of partial optimisation.

REFERENCES

[1] Gehrels, F., 'Optimal Restrictions on Foreign Trade and Investment', *American Economic Review*, LXI (Mar 1971) 147–59.

[2] Jones, R. W., 'International Capital Movements and the Theory of Tariffs and Trade', *Quarterly Journal of Economics*, LXXVII (Feb 1967) 1–38.

[3] Kemp, M. C., 'The Gain from International Trade and Investment: A Neo-Heckscher–Ohlin Approach', *American Economic Review*, LVI (Sep 1966) 788–809.

[4] MacDougall, G. D. A., 'The Benefits and Costs of Private Investment from Abroad: A Theoretical Approach', *Economic Record*, XXVI (Mar 1960) 13–35.

[5] Mundell, R. A., 'International Trade and Factor Mobility', *American Economic Review*, XLVII (June 1957) 321–37.

[6] Negishi, T., 'Foreign Investment and the Long-Run National Advantage', *Economic Record*, XLI (Dec 1965) 628–32.

[7] Rakowski, J. J., 'Capital Mobility in a Tariff-Ridden International Economy', *American Economic Review*, LX (Sep 1970) 753–60.

14 International Trade in a Dynamic Economy

Recent years have witnessed a steadily growing application of the standard two-factor, two-good model to the solution of questions that arise in a growing economy, questions that were first raised in a seminal contribution by Oniki and Uzawa [5]. Although some insights as to what happens in the economy under conditions of growing factor supplies and technology were gained in Chapter 6, the nature of our analysis there was essentially comparative statics, for we were concerned primarily with the implications of exogenous and once-for-all growth in factor supplies. In the present chapter, however, our concern will be the development of a dynamic model where labour grows exogenously at a certain given rate, but where capital grows endogenously as a result of the savings habits of the factor owners. Oniki and Uzawa and, following them, others† have used a technique which, for want of a better substitute, I call the 'production function' technique. The mathematical calculations under this technique are quite lengthy and oppressive, and a superficial glance is sufficient to discourage the student from getting seriously involved with the problem. Fortunately, the technique suggested by the activity-analysis approach used in the past chapters cuts down the length of the derivations and makes the issues susceptible to better comprehension.

14.1 Assumptions and the Model

In order to transform the standard two-good model into a dynamic model of international trade, it is necessary to assume that one of the traded goods is the capital good whose demand is determined by the quantum of savings generated in the economy. The availability of capital goods in the current period contributes in the next period to the total stock of capital which, if full employment is to

† See, for example, Bardhan [1,2], Kemp [3] and Khang [4].

be maintained, must be fully utilised in conjunction with a labour force that is exogenously growing at a certain rate. The problem is to find that rate of growth of capital which takes the economy to the steady-state equilibrium where both capital and labour grow at the same rate and the capital/labour ratio remains constant over time.

Throughout this chapter it is assumed that the second good is the capital good and the first good is the consumption good. As far as the savings behaviour of the community is concerned, we assume that a certain proportion of income is saved in each time period at a constant rate s. Up to now we have assumed that X_1 is exported and X_2 imported by the home country. However, in a dynamic setting where factor supplies change over time, there is no guarantee that the same pattern of trade will be maintained for ever. Since any commodity can be the import good, we shall assume that $E_j = D_j - X_j$ is the excess demand for the jth good ($j = 1,2$), which is positive if the good is imported and negative if it is exported.† For the sake of simplicity it is assumed that capital is everlasting, so that there is no depreciation factor to worry about. Except for these alterations, the rest of the assumptions are the same as those presented in Chapter 2.

Let us start with the case where the home country imports the capital good, so that its domestic consumption is given by

$$D_2 = E_2 + X_2 \qquad (14.1)$$

but the value of D_2 is constrained by the total amount of savings in the economy, that is,

$$p_2 D_2 = sY = s(rK + wL). \qquad (14.2)$$

Substituting (14.2) in (14.1), we can derive an expression for the import demand for the capital good. Thus

$$E_2 = s\left(\frac{r}{p_2} K + \frac{w}{p_2} L\right) - X_2. \qquad (14.3)$$

---

† Up to this chapter we have assumed that E_1 equals the quantity exported of X_1 and hence equals $X_1 - D_1$, whereas E_2 is the quantity imported of X_2 and equals $D_2 - X_2$. Such specific labelling of the goods was possible in the static model where factor supplies are constant. In a growing world economy, where factor supplies grow over time, this labelling is not possible. That is why both E_1 and E_2 are defined in the same way, remembering that their signs are always opposite.

In addition to (14.3), which specifies the excess demand function for the importable good under conditions of incomplete specialisation, there are two more possibilities, depending upon whether the home country is specialised completely in X_1 or X_2. If the world terms of trade (p) fall below a certain level, the home country will be completely specialised in X_1, and X_2 will decline to zero. Let us call such a p as p_{min}. Then for $p \leq p_{min}$, the excess demand function reduces to

$$E_{2(min)} = s\left(\frac{r}{p_2}K + \frac{w}{p_2}L\right) = s\frac{X_1}{p} \qquad (14.4)$$

because $Y = rK + wL = p_1 X_1$. On the other hand, if p rises above a certain level, the home country will be specialised in X_2. Let us call such a p as p_{max}. Then for $p \geq p_{max}$

$$p_2 X_2 = Y = rK + wL$$

so that the export of the capital good will be given by

$$E_{2(max)} = -\left(\frac{r}{p_2}K + \frac{w}{p_2}L\right)(1 - s) = -(1 - s)X_2. \qquad (14.5)$$

14.2 The Uniqueness of Momentary Equilibrium

At any moment of time, factor supplies in the home and the foreign country are given, so that the excess demand depends solely on the terms of trade. It follows then that if the relationship between p and E_2 is monotonic, the momentary equilibrium will be uniquely determined. In the case of *complete specialisation* in X_1, (14.4) makes it clear that the excess demand curve becomes a *rectangular hyperbola*, for s is given and X_1 remains constant so long as $p \leq p_{min}$. In the case of *complete specialisation* in X_2, however, the excess demand function becomes a *negative constant*, as is evident from (14.5), because X_2 is unchanged so long as $p \geq p_{max}$.

The relationship between E_2 and p is not so straightforward when both goods are being produced. Differentiating (14.3), we have[1]

$$E_2^* = \frac{D_2}{E_2}[\theta_K(r^* - p_2^*) + \theta_L(w^* - p_2^*)] - \frac{X_2}{E_2}X_2^*$$

where θ_K and θ_L are respectively the shares of capital and labour in the economy and $\theta_K + \theta_L = 1$. From equations (2.35) and (2.36) in Chapter 2 we know that

$$w^* - p_2^* = -\frac{\theta_{K2}p^*}{|\theta|} \quad \text{and} \quad r^* - p_2^* = \frac{\theta_{L2}p^*}{|\theta|}.$$

Substituting these, we have

$$E_2^* = \frac{D_2}{E_2}p^*\left[\frac{\theta_K - \theta_{K2}}{|\theta|}\right] - \frac{X_2}{E_2}X_2^*.$$

Now θ_K can be written as

$$\theta_K = \frac{r(K_1 + K_2)}{Y} = \theta_1\theta_{K1} + \theta_2\theta_{K2}$$

where θ_j is the share of the jth good in the economy and $\theta_1 + \theta_2 = 1$. Substituting for θ_K yields

$$\begin{aligned}
E_2^* &= \frac{D_2}{E_2}p^*\left[\frac{\theta_1(\theta_{K1} - \theta_{K2})}{|\theta|}\right] - \frac{X_2}{E_2}X_2^* \\
&= -p^*\left[\frac{D_2}{E_2}\theta_1 + \frac{X_2}{E_2}\cdot\frac{X_2^*}{p^*}\right]
\end{aligned} \quad (14.6)$$

because, from (2.17) in Chapter 2, $|\theta| = \theta_{K2} - \theta_{K1}$. Since X_2^*/p^* is positive, (14.6) shows that E_2 and p are negatively and uniquely related. All this discussion suggests that the excess demand curve would look like the curve AB depicted in Fig. 14.1, where for p between O and p_{min}, AB is a rectangular hyperbola, for $p \geq p_{max}$, AB is a straight line parallel to the horizontal axis, and for p lying between p_{min} and p_{max}, AB reflects a simple negative relationship. For p lying between p_{min} and F the capital good is imported, whereas for the world terms of trade lying above OF the second good becomes too expensive to be imported; instead it becomes an export good of the home country.

In what follows, we assume that the variables without the country subscript refer to the home countries, whereas those with the subscript f pertain to the foreign country. The solution for p can be

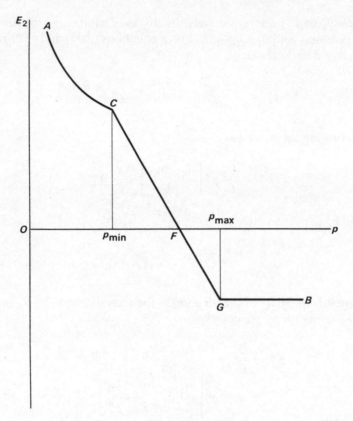

Figure 14.1

obtained from the condition that in equilibrium the world excess demand for any good equals zero, that is,

$$E_2 + E_{2f} = 0. \tag{14.7}$$

Fig. 14.2 makes use of this condition, depicts the excess demand curve for both countrues, HH' for country H and FF' for country F, and shows that equilibrium is achieved when the two curves intersect at Q. The equilibrium terms of trade are given by OA, E_2 equals QA and $E_{2f} = -QA$, so that $E_2 + E_{2f} = 0$.

In order to tackle some more difficult questions in a dynamic economy where labour is growing exogenously at a certain rate, the exposition is simplified if we present the variables in per capita terms. Let the lower-case letters denote the variables in per capita terms.

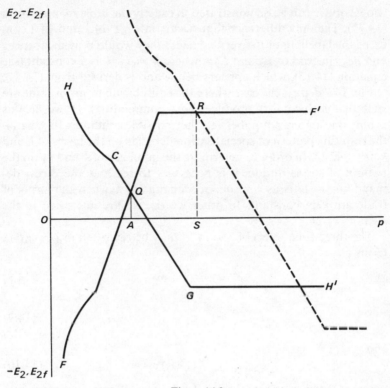

Figure 14.2

Thus $e_j = E_j/L$, $x_j = X_j/L$, $y = Y/L$, and so on. At the outset, it may be noted that the relationship between the excess demand function and the terms of trade remains unchanged even when it is expressed in per capita terms. The reason for this is attributable to the fact that (14.6) has been obtained under the assumption that K and L are given at any moment of time, so that $K^* = L^* = 0$. Using this, (14.6) can be written as

$$e_2^* = -p^* \left[\frac{d_2}{e_2} \theta_1 + \frac{x_2}{e_2} \cdot \frac{x_2^*}{p^*} \right] \qquad (14.7^*)$$

where $e_2^* = E_2^* - L^*$ and $x_2^* = X_2^* - L^*$. Thus the relationship between the excess demand function and the terms of trade changes little when it is stated in per capita terms, provided the factor supplies are constant. The uniqueness of the momentary equilibrium shown above can be demonstrated in exactly the same manner from (14.7*). The only difference that occurs in Figs. 14.1 and 14.2 concerns the labelling of the vertical axes; they would now measure e_2 and ρe_{2f} instead of E_2 and E_{2f}, where $\rho = L_f/L$ is a constant (see equation (14.15), which appears below and is derived from (14.7)).

Fig. 14.2 depicts the case where the equilibrium terms of trade are such that each country produces both commodities. However, this is only one among a number of other possible solutions. In general, the resulting pattern of specialisation depends on the levels of k and $k_f(k = K/L)$. In order to determine the influence of k and k_f on the pattern of specialisation, it is necessary to see how the excess demand curve shifts as a result of a change in k when the terms of trade are kept constant. In other words, we are interested in the sign of $\partial e_2/\partial k$.

The three equations (14.3)–(14.5) may be rewritten in per capita terms as

$$e_2 = \frac{sr}{p_2}(k+\omega) - x_2 \qquad (14.8)$$

$$e_{2(\min)} = \frac{s}{p}x_1 \qquad (14.9)$$

and

$$e_{2(\max)} = -(1-s)x_2 \qquad (14.10)$$

where ω is the wage/rental ratio. In the case of complete specialisation, the sign of $\partial e_2/\partial k$ is apparent from one glance at (14.9) and (14.10). Evidently,

$$\frac{\partial e_{2(\min)}}{\partial k} = \frac{s}{p}\frac{\partial x_1}{\partial k} > 0 \qquad (14.11)$$

and

$$\frac{\partial e_{2(\max)}}{\partial k} = -(1-s)\frac{\partial x_2}{\partial k} < 0 \qquad (14.12)$$

because $(\partial x_j/\partial k) > 0$. The case of incomplete specialisation, however, is not susceptible to such straightforward results. Differentiating (14.8) partially with respect to k and remembering that w and r are constant with a given p, we have

$$\frac{\partial e_2}{\partial k} = \frac{sr}{p_2} - \frac{\partial x_2}{\partial k} \qquad (14.13)$$

Now $p_1(\partial x_1/\partial k) + p_2(\partial x_2/\partial k) = \partial y/\partial k = r$. Substituting this in (14.13) yields

$$\frac{\partial e_2}{\partial k} = \frac{p_1(\partial x_1/\partial k) - (1-s)r}{p_2}. \tag{14.14}$$

The sign of $\partial e_2/\partial k$ depends clearly on the factor-intensity relationship between the consumption good and the capital good. If X_1 is labour-intensive relative to X_2, then from the Rybczynski theorem $\partial x_1/\partial k$ and hence $\partial e_2/\partial k$ are negative. On the other hand, if the consumption good is capital-intensive relative to the capital good, $\partial x_1/\partial k$ is positive and so is $\partial e_2/\partial k$, because with $(\partial x_2/\partial k) < 0$, $p_1\partial x_1/\partial k$ is clearly greater than r and hence $(1-s)r$. This last case is one of special interest. *The hypothesis requiring the capital good to be labour-intensive relative to the consumption good is widely known as the capital-intensity condition, and has been very frequently used in the past in the stability analysis of two-sector growth models.*

We are now in a position to show the influence of k and k_f on the international patterns of specialisation. Suppose there is a once-for-all rise in k, but that k_f is unchanged. Under the capital-intensity condition, $\partial e_2/\partial k > 0$, so that the home country's excess demand curve HH' in Fig. 14.2 shifts upwards to the dotted curve, the equilibrium point shifts to R and the terms of trade rise to OS. The pattern of specialisation at R is such that the home country produces both goods, but the foreign country is completely specialised in its exportable good, X_2. Thus even though k_f was unchanged, a change in k produced a change in the foreign country's level of specialisation. As indicated above, a rise in k also leads to a rise in p. The generalised expression for the sign of $\partial p/\partial k$ can be obtained from the following equilibrium condition:

$$e_2(p,k) + \rho e_{2f}(p,k_f) = 0 \tag{14.15}$$

where $\rho = L_f/L$ is the ratio between the labour force available in the two countries. Hereafter we assume that the labour force in both countries grows at the same rate, so that ρ remains unchanged over time. Differentiating (14.15) partially with respect to k, we obtain

$$\frac{\partial p}{\partial k} = -\frac{\partial e_2/\partial k}{(\partial e_2/\partial p) + \rho(\partial e_{2f}/\partial p)}. \tag{14.16}$$

Similarly,

$$\frac{\partial p}{\partial k_f} = -\frac{\rho(\partial e_{2f}/\partial k_f)}{(\partial e_2/\partial p) + \rho(\partial e_{2f}/\partial p)}. \tag{14.17}$$

Since the denominator in (14.16) and (14.17) is unambiguously negative, the sign of $(\partial p/\partial k)$ or $(\partial p/\partial k_f)$ depends completely on the sign of $(\partial e_2/\partial k)$ or $(\partial e_{2f}/\partial k_f)$. Under the capital-intensity condition, $\partial e_2/\partial k$ and $\partial e_{2f}/\partial k_f$ are positive, and so are $\partial p/\partial k$ and $\partial p/\partial k_f$. However, this need not be the case if the country is completely specialised. If the home country is specialised in the first good and the foreign country in the second, then $\partial p/\partial k > 0$ but $\partial p/\partial k_f < 0$, because from (14.11) and (14.12) one can see that $\partial e_{2(\text{min})}/\partial k > 0$, but $\partial e_{2f(\text{max})}/\partial k_f < 0$. The signs of $\partial p/\partial k$ and $\partial p/\partial k_f$ are reversed when the home country is specialised in the second good and the foreign country in the first.

14.3 The Stability of the Long-Run Equilibrium

The long-run growth path of an economy is determined by the rate of capital accumulation, which equals the domestic production of capital goods plus their imports, and the exogenously given rate of growth of labour, which is assumed to be the same for the two countries. The rate of capital accumulation is then given by

$$K^* = \frac{D_2}{K} = \frac{sr}{p_2} \cdot \frac{(\omega + k)}{k} \tag{14.18}$$

because we have assumed for simplicity that there is no depreciation. Now the long-run equilibrium in each economy is defined by the equality of K^* and L^*, and the capital/labour ratio prevailing at that equilibrium is called the steady-state capital/labour ratio. This steady-state capital/labour ratio is unique if, whenever there is a divergence between K^* and L^*, K^* comes back to the given L^*, such that the steady-state capital/labour ratio remains the same. This means that whenever k rises above the steady-state value of k, the adjustment of the economic system should be such as to lower K^*, and conversely. In other words, the stability of the long-run equilibrium in each country requires that $dK^*/dk < 0$ and $dK_f^*/dk_f < 0$.

The rate of change in the capital/labour ratio in each economy is given by

$$Q = k^* = K^* - L^* = \frac{sr}{p_2}\frac{(\omega + k)}{k} - L^* \qquad (14.19)$$

and

$$Q_f = k_f^* = K_f^* - L^* = \frac{s_f r_f}{p_2} \cdot \frac{(\omega_f + k_f)}{k_f} - L^*. \qquad (14.20)$$

In the steady-state equilibrium, both Q and Q_f are zero. In general, both Q and Q_f depend on k and k_f, but the effects of a change in k or k_f depend on the pattern of specialisation in the two countries. At any moment of time, the pattern of specialisation in any country will conform to any one of the three possible patterns. In the case of the home country, for example, the country may be (a) incompletely specialised, (b) specialised in X_1, or (c) specialised in X_2. As stated before, the reason for these varying patterns lies in the fact that in a dynamic model, where k and k_f are changing over time except when the economies are in the steady state, the patterns of trade and specialisation are themselves subject to changes over time. In the same way, the foreign country may have any of the three possible patterns of specialisation. In the following we shall consider three cases, namely, (a) both countries are incompletely specialised, (b) the home country is incompletely specialised but the foreign country is specialised in the capital goods, and (c) the home country is specialised in the capital goods but the foreign country is incompletely specialised. It turns out that it is sufficient for the stability analysis to consider these three combinations out of a possible seven.

(a) Both Countries Incompletely Specialised
As indicated before, the signs of dK^*/dk and dK_f^*/dk_f determine whether or not the long-run equilibrium in each economy is stable. This evidently calls forth a differentiation of (14.19) and (14.20). Let k_f be constant. Then from (14.19)

$$Q^* = (r^* - p_2^*) + \frac{\omega}{(\omega + k)}(\omega^* - k^*). \qquad (14.21)$$

From equations (2.36) and (2.31) in Chapter 2 we know that with incomplete specialisation

$$r^* - p_2^* = \frac{\theta_{L2} p^*}{|\theta|} \quad \text{and} \quad \omega^* = \frac{-p^*}{|\theta|}.$$

Substituting these in (14.21), we have

$$\frac{Q^*}{K^*} = \left[\theta_{L2} - \frac{\omega}{k+\omega} \right] \frac{p^*}{|\theta|} - \frac{\omega}{k+\omega} k^*.$$

Now

$$\frac{\omega}{k+\omega} = \theta_L = \theta_1 \theta_{L1} + \theta_2 \theta_{L2}.$$

Using this relationship and the fact that

$$|\theta| = \theta_{L1} - \theta_{L2}$$

it is readily seen that

$$\frac{Q^*}{k^*} = - \left[\theta_1 \frac{p^*}{k^*} + \theta_L \right] \frac{K^*}{Q}. \tag{14.22}$$

For the attainment of the steady-state equilibrium in the home country, we require that $Q^*/k^* < 0$. If the capital-intensity condition is satisfied, then from (14.16) $p^*/k^* > 0$, which means that $Q^*/k^* < 0$. However, if the capital-intensity condition is not satisfied, $p^*/k^* < 0$, so that the sign of Q^*/k^* becomes uncertain.

Proceeding in exactly the same manner, keeping k constant, we can show that

$$\frac{Q^*}{k_f^*} = - \theta_1 \frac{p^*}{k_f^*} \frac{K^*}{Q}. \tag{14.23}$$

Similarly, from (14.20),

$$\frac{Q_f^*}{k^*} = - \theta_{1f} \frac{p^*}{k^*} \frac{K_f^*}{Q_f}. \tag{14.24}$$

and

$$\frac{Q_f^*}{k_f^*} = - \left[\theta_{1f} \frac{p^*}{k_f^*} + \theta_{Lf} \right] \frac{K_f^*}{Q_f}. \tag{14.25}$$

These three equations confirm the fact that Q^*/k_f^*, Q_f^*/k^* and Q_f^*/k_f^* are all negative under the capital-intensity condition.

The discussion up to this point suggests that under the capital-intensity condition the long-run equilibrium in each economy is stable. Starting from any arbitrary level, the capital/labour ratio in each country tends to approach the steady state, where both Q and Q_f are equal to zero. However, there still remains the question of what happens to the steady-state capital/labour ratio in one country when there is a change in the capital/labour ratio of the other country. This question is motivated by our interest not only in the conditions ensuring the attainment of the steady-state equilibrium in each country, but also in the simultaneous attainment of the steady state in both countries. Furthermore, how do we determine the pattern of specialisation in each country when the world economy rests in the steady-state equilibrium?

The answer to these questions is hidden in the behaviour of the $Q = 0$ curve as k_f changes and the $Q_f = 0$ curve as k changes. When both countries are incompletely specialised,

$$Q = Q(k,k_f)$$

and

$$Q_f = Q_f(k,k_f).$$

By differentiating the $Q = 0$ curve totally with respect to k, we obtain

$$\frac{Q^*}{k^*}\frac{dk}{k} + \frac{Q^*}{k_f^*}\frac{dk_f}{k_f} = 0.$$

Using (14.22) and (14.23) then gives us

$$\left(\frac{k}{k_f}\frac{dk_f}{dk}\right)_{Q=0} = -\frac{Q^*/k^*}{Q^*/k_f^*} = -\frac{(\theta_1 p^*/k^*)+\theta_L}{\theta_1 p^*/k_f^*}$$

$$= -\frac{(p^*/k^*)+(\theta_L/\theta_1)}{(p^*/k_f^*)}. \tag{14.26}$$

Similarly, we can derive

$$\left(\frac{k}{k_f}\frac{dk_f}{dk}\right)_{Q_f=0} = -\frac{p^*/k^*}{(p^*/k_f^*)+(\theta_{Lf}/\theta_{1f})}. \tag{14.27}$$

It is clear from these two equations that

$$\left(\frac{dk_f}{dk}\right)_{Q=0} < \left(\frac{dk_f}{dk}\right)_{Q_f=0} < 0. \tag{14.28}$$

This last equation will be used in the subsequent analysis.

(b) The Home Country Specialised in the Capital Good, but the Foreign Country Incompletely Specialised

If the home country is specialised in the production of capital goods, then $p_2 D_2 = sp_2 X_2$, so that

$$K^* = \frac{D_2}{K} = \frac{sX_2}{K} = \frac{sx_2}{k}.$$

Moreover, $x_2 = 1/C_{L2}$ and $k = C_{K2}/C_{L2}$. Therefore

$$K^* = \frac{s}{C_{K2}}$$

whence

$$Q = K^* - L^* = \frac{s}{C_{K2}} - L^*. \tag{14.29}$$

However, since the foreign country continues to be incompletely specialised,

$$Q_f = \frac{s_f r_f}{p_2} \left(\frac{\omega_f + k_f}{k_f} \right) - L^*. \tag{14.20}$$

From (14.29), we derive

$$\frac{Q^*}{K^*} = -\frac{C_{K2}^*}{k^*}, \quad \text{but} \quad \frac{Q^*}{k_f^*} = 0$$

because C_{K2} does not change with a change in k_f alone. From the analysis in Chapter 2 we know that

$$C_{K2}^* = \theta_{L2} \sigma_2 \omega^* \quad \text{and} \quad C_{K2}^* - C_{L2}^* = k^* = \sigma_2 \omega^*$$

so that†

$$\frac{Q^*}{k^*} = -\theta_{L2} < 0. \tag{14.30}$$

Evidently in this case‡

$$\left(\frac{k}{k_f} \cdot \frac{dk_f}{dk} \right)_{Q=0} = \infty. \tag{14.31}$$

---

† The reader may be reminded here that in the absence of technical progress C_{Kj}^* is the same as A_{Kj}^*, the notation used in Chapter 2 for a change in the input–output coefficient.

‡ It can easily be seen that the foreign pattern of specialisation plays no role in determining the sign of $(dk_f/dk)_{Q=0}$ when the home country is specialised in the capital good.

(c) *The Home Country Incompletely Specialised, but the Foreign Country Specialised in the Capital Good*

In this case

$$Q_f = -\frac{s}{C_{K2f}}$$

but Q is given by (14.19), so that $Q^*/k^* < 0$ as before, but Q^*/k_f^* is positive because, with the foreign country specialised in the capital good, $p^*/k_f^* < 0$. Clearly, then,

$$\left(\frac{k}{k_f} \cdot \frac{dk_f}{dk}\right)_{Q=0} > 0. \tag{14.32}$$

From our discussion so far,† we can draw the $Q = 0$ curve in the k_f and k space as shown in Fig. 14.3, where the $Q = 0$ curve is

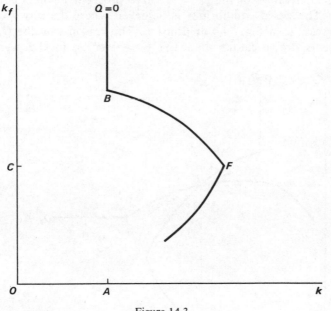

Figure 14.3

† Here again, one can see that the pattern of home specialisation plays no role in determining the sign of $(dk_f/dk)_{Q=0}$, when the foreign country is specialised in the capital good. Thus we see that whenever a country is specialised in the capital good, the level of specialisation in the other country is immaterial in determining the shape of the $Q = 0$ and $Q_f = 0$ curves.

composed of three segments, namely, (i) the negatively sloped segment corresponding to the case of incomplete specialisation and the capital-intensity condition, (ii) a vertical line parallel to the k_f axis corresponding to the case of complete home specialisation in the capital good (see equation (14.31)), and (iii) a positively sloped segment corresponding to the foreign specialisation in the capital good (see equation (14.32)). Now for a country to be specialised in the production of the labour-intensive capital good, its capital/labour ratio ought to be relatively low. For this reason, the maximum level of the capital/labour ratio, below which there will be complete specialisation in the capital good, is relatively low for each country; for the home country it is given by $k \le OA$ where A corresponds to point B, and for the foreign country it is given by $k_f \le OC$ where C corresponds to point F.

The derivation of the $Q_f = 0$ curve proceeds in the analogous way. The world equilibrium is achieved where these two curves intersect, as in Fig. 14.4 at point E. The reason why the $Q_f = 0$ curve is drawn flatter than the $Q = 0$ curve in the segments

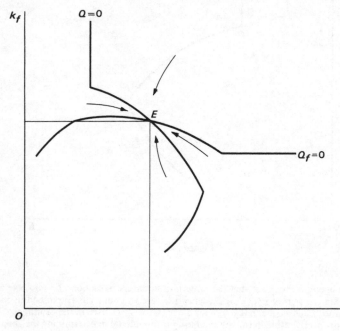

Figure 14.4

relevant to incomplete specialisation is given by (14.28). The steady-state capital/labour ratios in each country corresponding to point E are such that both countries are incompletely specialised. This is how the pattern of specialisation is determined when each country is simultaneously in the steady-state equilibrium. Needless to say, the steady-state world equilibrium depicted in Fig. 14.4 could have occurred at any pattern of specialisation for either country, depending, of course, upon the position and elasticities of the $Q = 0$ and $Q_f = 0$ curves.

The arrows determined by (14.22)–(14.25), (14.30), etc., indicate the direction of capital accumulation in each country wherever the initial capital/labour ratios of the countries are. If the countries are incompletely specialised, then it is easily seen that under the capital-intensity condition any initial capital/labour ratio in the two countries will converge to those corresponding to point E as time approaches infinity. Of greater interest is the case where both countries are completely specialised in their respective exportable goods, for then, as is evident from equations like (14.30), the long-

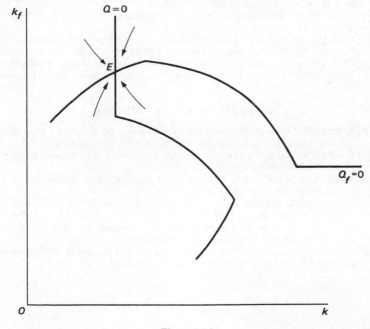

Figure 14.5

run equilibrium in the world economy is stable regardless of whether or not the capital-intensity condition is satisfied. Such an equilibrium is depicted in Fig. 14.5, and k and k_f corresponding to point E are such that the home country is specialised in the capital good whereas the foreign country is specialised in the consumption good.

Up to now we have assumed the capital-intensity condition and shown that the world economy is globally stable. However, if the consumption good is the labour-intensive sector, then, short of complete specialisation in the two countries, our growth model may not be stable, or there may be multiple equilibria in the world economy. From the analysis presented above, the interested reader can easily derive the conditions sufficient to preclude these results.

REFERENCES

[1] Bardhan, P. K., 'On Factor Accumulation and the Pattern of International Specialisation', *Review of Economic Studies*, XXXIII (Jan 1966) 39–44.
[2] ——, 'Equilibrium Growth in the International Economy', *Quarterly Journal of Economics*, LXXXIX (Aug 1965) 455–64.
[3] Kemp, M. C., 'International Trade and Investment in a Context of Growth', *Economic Record*, XLIV (June 1968) 211–23.
[4] Khang, C., 'A Dynamic Model of Trade between the Final and the Intermediate Products', *Journal of Economic Theory*, I (Dec 1969) 416–37.
[5] Oniki, H., and Uzawa, H., 'Patterns of Trade and Investment in a Dynamic Model of International Trade', *Review of Economic Studies*, XXXII (Jan 1965) 15–38.

SUPPLEMENTARY READINGS

[6] Atsumi, H., 'The Long-Run Offer Function and a Dynamic Theory of International Trade', *Journal of International Economics*, I (Aug 1971) 267–99.
[7] Bardhan, P. K., and Lewis, S., 'Models of Growth with Imported Inputs', *Economica*, XXXVII (Nov 1970) 373–85.
[8] Inada, K., 'International Trade, Capital Accumulation, and Factor Price Equalization', *Economic Record*, XLIV (Sept 1968) 322–41.
[9] Johnson, H. G., 'Trade and Growth: A Geometrical Exposition', *Journal of International Economics*, I (Feb 1971) 83–101.
[10] Stiglitz, J. E., 'Factor Price Equalization in a Dynamic Economy', *Journal of Political Economy*, LXXVIII (May–June 1970) 456–88.
[11] Vanek, J., 'Economic Growth and International Trade in Pure Theory', *Quarterly Journal of Economics*, LXXXV (Aug 1971) 377–90.

Author Index

Subject Index